Studies in English Language

A Course Book in English Grammar, 2nd Edition
Dennis Freeborn

From Old English to Standard English
Dennis Freeborn

Style: Text Analysis and Linguistic Criticism
Dennis Freeborn

Varieties of English, 2nd Edition
Dennis Freeborn *with Peter French and David Langford*

Analysing Talk
David Langford

English Language Project Work
Christine McDonald

Series Standing Order

If you would like to receive future titles in this series as they are published, you can make use of our standing order facility. To place a standing order please contact your bookseller or, in case of difficulty, write to us at the address below with your name and address and the name of the series. Please state with which title you wish to begin your standing order. (If you live outside the United Kingdom we may not have the rights for your area, in which case we will forward your order to the publisher concerned.)

Customer Services Department, Macmillan Distribution Ltd
Houndmills, Basingstoke, Hampshire RG21 6XS, England

A COURSE BOOK IN ENGLISH GRAMMAR

STANDARD ENGLISH AND THE DIALECTS
Second Edition

Dennis Freeborn

MACMILLAN

27758
116787

First edition 1987
Reprinted 1987, 1988, 1990, 1991, 1994
Second edition 1995

Published by
MACMILLAN PRESS LTD
Houndmills, Basingstoke, Hampshire RG21 2XS
and London
Companies and representatives
throughout the world

ISBN 0–333–62492–0 hardcover
ISBN 0–333–62493–9 paperback

A catalogue record for this book is available
from the British Library

10   9   8   7   6   5   4   3   2
04   03   02   01   00   99   98   97

Printed in Great Britain by
Antony Rowe Ltd, Chippenham, Wiltshire

Mark Tapley: 'but a Werb is a word as signifies to be, to do, or to suffer (which is all the grammar, and enough too, as ever as I wos taught)'

Charles Dickens, *Martin Chuzzlewit* (1844)

Books are not made to be believed, but to be subjected to inquiry.

A book is made up of signs that speak of other signs, which in their turn speak of things. Without an eye to read them, a book contains signs that produce no concepts; therefore it is dumb.

Umberto Eco, *The Name of the Rose* (1983)

A child speaks his mother tongue properly, though he could never write out its grammar. But the grammarian is not the only one who knows the rules of the language; they are well known, albeit unconsciously, also to the child. The grammarian is merely the one who knows how and why the child knows the language.

Umberto Eco, *Reflections on 'The Name of the Rose'* (1985)

Contents

Symbols

Symbols and abbreviations are useful because they save time and space in describing grammatical features.

Word-classes (parts of speech)

n	noun
v	verb
adj	adjective
adv	adverb
pn	pronoun
p	preposition
cj	conjunction
scj	subordinating conjunction
ccj	coordinating conjunction

Classes of phrase

NP	noun phrase
VP	verb phrase
AdjP	adjective phrase
AdvP	adverb phrase
PrepP	prepositional phrase
PossP	possessive phrase

Classes of clause (form)

NCl	noun clause
PrepCl	prepositional clause
AdvCl	adverbial clause
NonfCl	nonfinite clause

Classes of clause (function)

MCl   main clause
SCl   subordinate clause
RelCl   relative clause

Elements of NP structure

Use lower-case letters:
d   determiner
m   modifier (= pre-modifier)
h   head word
q   qualifier (= post-modifier)

Elements of VP structure

aux   auxiliary verb
op-v   operator-verb
m   modal auxiliary verb
h   have as auxiliary
be-prog   *be* used to form progressive aspect
be-pass   *be* used to form passive voice
s-aux   semi-auxiliary verb
v   main (lexical) verb

Elements of clause structure

Use upper-case letters (capitals):
S   subject
P   predicator
C   complement
A   adverbial

Kinds of complement

O   object (complement) or Co
Od   direct object
Oi   indirect object
Ci   intensive (complement)
Ca   adverbial (complement)
pt   adverb particle (complement)

Bracketing

( )   to mark phrases
[ ]   to mark clauses
⟨ ⟩   to mark coordinated elements (words, phrases or clauses)

Phonetic transcription

Square brackets are also used with symbols of the International Phonetic Alphabet to indicate the pronounciation of spoken words and sounds, e.g. [æ], [ʃ].

Other symbols

An asterisk * is placed before a word or construction which is ungrammatical or unacceptable to make clear that it is not a usable expression.

A question mark ? placed before a word or construction queries its acceptability, which may differ from one person to another.

The sign Ø is used to mark the deletion (or ellipsis) of a word that is 'understood', e.g. *The food Ø I bought yesterday*... from *The food **that** I bought yesterday*. . . .

Acknowledgements

I am very grateful to Tony Fairman, who read and annotated the draft of this enlarged edition with a discerning and critical eye. I was able to revise the whole text in the light of his comments.

The author and publishers wish to thank the following for permission to use copyright material:

The Guardian, for the extracts from the issues of 8 March 1979, 27 August 1983, 19 December 1985, 10 December 1990, 3 May 1993, 1 July 1993 and 19 December 1993;

the Controller of Her Majesty's Stationery Office, for the extract from *English for Ages 5 to 16*, DES, June 1989;

Hodder & Stoughton Publishers, for the table from Hughes & Trudgill, *English Accents and Dialects* (Edward Arnold, 1979);

Newspaper Publishing PLC, for the extract from *The Independent*, 13 September 1990.

Every effort has been made to trace all the copyright-holders, but if any have been inadvertently overlooked, the publishers will be pleased to make the necessary arrangement at the first opportunity.

Introduction to the second edition

The nine chapters of the first edition have been thoroughly revised and enlarged. Chapter 1 is new, and presents what is intended to be an objective linguistic perspective on the perennial arguments over the social concepts of *good English* and *correct English*. Chapters 5 and 6 are new.

Chapter 5 adds a commentary on the vocabulary of English, introducing the concept of *core vocabulary* and describing the relationship of the principal etymological sources of English to our assessments of formal and informal vocabulary. Chapter 6 continues the examination of the texts used in chapter 5 to give a preliminary overview of the types of phrase in English. Chapter 8 in the first edition, 'Complex and Derived Clauses' has now been divided into two separate chapters: chapter 11 'Complex Clauses' and chapter 12 'Derived Clauses' in the course of revision. Similarly, the former final chapter 9 is now chapters 13 and 14, 'Sentences' and 'The grammar of texts and speech'.

Dialectal grammar

The most important additions to this edition are the sections that describe those dialectal features of present-day English which differ from Standard English. If you accept the definition of the English language as 'the sum of all its dialects' (a concept discussed in chapter 1), then any grammar of English should include at least some reference to dialectal grammar. All the dialects of English are, by definition, 'mutually comprehensible' and belong to the same language. The differences between the dialects (and this includes Standard English, the 'prestige dialect') are very few compared with the vocabulary and grammar common to them all, but these differences clearly differentiate them and are especially marked in social attitudes. In England we identify speakers according to where they come from, or their educational attainment or their social class, in relation to how far they speak Standard English in the accent known as Received Pronunciation (RP).

The descriptions of dialectal grammar are general and confined mainly to variants in England. I believe that those forms of the language spoken daily by millions of English speakers in England should be seen as legitimate and fully grammatical in their context of use, not as 'deviations' from the standard. This point of view in no way questions either the status of Standard English as the only acceptable *written* form of the language or the prime responsibility of schools to teach Standard English. To include descriptions of dialectal forms is not to advocate that they should be adopted, only that students of language should be able to recognise and describe them precisely in linguistic terms.

Reference grammars

To use a reference grammar, you have to know what to look up; in other words, you have to know some grammar first. A determined student could sit down and read a reference grammar from beginning to end, but this would be unusual, and is not the best way to learn. *A Course Book in English Grammar* is a different kind of book. It is planned as a textbook, to be read and studied chapter by chapter. Its aim is to describe the grammar of English in relation to its main functions in communication, and to provide enough detailed description to be of practical use in the study of texts in English.

Texts

The word *text* means any piece of writing, or transcription of speech, which is intended to communicate a message and a meaning. A scribbled note left on the table, 'Back at 2.20', is as much a text in this sense as a novel, a hire-purchase agreement or a sermon. It has a definite function, and its grammar is suited to that function.

An important part of the study of English is the reading, understanding and evaluation of texts, and a knowledge of the grammar of English is indispensable if this study is to be full and informed.

Knowing grammar

In one sense of *to know* (*know*$_1$) every speaker of English knows the grammar, because the grammar provides the rules for putting words into the right order so that our meaning is clear, and all speakers of English therefore must know the grammar in order to speak it. But in the sense of *to know about* (*know*$_2$) those who know the grammar are those who have studied it in the way provided in textbooks and reference grammar books, and can talk and write about grammatical structure.

The book has been written with native speakers of English in mind, not students learning English as a foreign language, and so it makes use of a native speaker's knowledge (*know*$_1$) of English or that of an already fluent speaker of English. It does not therefore always provide comprehensive lists of features, and sometimes asks you to apply what you know already (*know₁*) in order to become aware (*know₂*) at a conscious level. In this sense, parts of it are a kind of do-it-yourself manual, although I assume that teachers and lecturers will at all stages be commenting on, developing and criticising what the book has to say.

Neither does the book pretend to 'make grammar easy'. Even the simplest texts (see, for example, the infant reading primer extracts in chapter 2) contain features of grammar which might not appear in a short, over-simplified grammar book. I have had to select, and leave out lots of interesting problems concerned with the best way of describing the language.

Models of language

You would find, if you explored the study of language (linguistics), several different 'models', or theories of language – ways of understanding and describing it: traditional grammar, systemic-functional grammar, transformational-generative grammar, relational grammar, generalized phrase-structure grammar, and so on, all of which are meaningless terms to non-specialists in linguistics.

Nevertheless, you have to choose a model in order to talk about the grammar even at the simplest level. To use the words *sentence, noun* or *word* is to begin to use a theory of language.

The model adopted in this course book is not new or original, but derives mostly from traditional and systemic-functional grammar, making choices between them when there is a difference. Systemic-functional grammar, as its name implies, is concerned to discover the 'network of systems' that relate grammar to the major functions of language. A recent presentation of this model is in Halliday's *An Introduction to Functional Grammar*.

An example of the differences to be found between two descriptive models is in the meaning given to the term *complement*. The dictionary meaning of the word is 'that which completes'. In traditional grammar it means the element in a certain type of clause which refers to the subject (*subject complement*) or the object (*object complement*). In the one-clause sentence,

Meanwhile life was hard.

life would be called the *subject* and *hard* the *subject complement* in the terms of traditional grammar. In the one-clause sentence,

They found life hard.

life would be called the *object* and *hard* the *object complement*.

In this book, however, the meaning of *complement* in a clause is applied to any element which 'completes' the grammar/meaning of the verb. There are therefore three kinds of clause complement, which are introduced in chapter 2, and described in detail in chapter 9.

Traditional and new terms

I have tried to explain clearly what each term means as and when the need for it occurs, and have chosen the more familiar (traditional) terms wherever possible. But new and unfamiliar terms are necessary, for new and unfamiliar concepts, sometimes changing the scope of a familiar word (like *complement*) or introducing non-traditional terms (like *predicators in phase*). There has been a very positive development in our knowledge and understanding of the grammar of English in linguistic studies since the 1940s, which must be integrated with traditional descriptions.

As is said later in the book, no description of the grammar can be the only right one, and there are often alternative ways of describing the same feature. To keep the book to manageable proportions, such alternatives cannot always be described in detail, but they should be discussed rather than avoided wherever possible. In other words, students should be encouraged to think critically, and not to absorb passively.

Using the book

I assume that other descriptive and reference grammars will be used by teachers and lecturers with their students, to supplement and clarify what this course book can only sometimes mention briefly.

I have tried to avoid making up examples to illustrate features of the grammar (though this has not always proved possible), and have drawn upon a variety of texts, literary and non-literary, written and spoken. This is because it is only in the study of 'authentic English' that a knowledge of the grammar can be put to use, and real texts are a challenge, sometimes producing good examples of what you are illustrating, but at the time throwing up interesting problems.

Activities are provided at every stage in each chapter. Teachers will make their own choice, and should modify and add to them according to the needs of their students. For instance, you should look in a variety of other texts for examples of features of the grammar which are being studied.

Fuzzy edges

One important idea to stress is what is called in linguistic study the principle of **indeterminacy**, or 'fuzziness'. This means that we cannot always assign a clear, unambiguous descriptive label to a word, phrase or clause. For example, is *swimming* in *I like swimming* a noun or a verb?

The edges of the boundaries between categories are not necessarily clear, and there are often borderline cases. When this happens, no student should feel a sense of failure or frustration at not knowing the right answer (there may not be one), but should try to see the alternatives, and why there are alternatives – again thinking linguistically and critically.

Concepts

There is, I believe, no short cut or easy way to understanding grammar which you can guarantee for every student. It demands the ability to conceptualise, and students have to make a breakthrough into conceptual thinking at some stage. For some this comes easily and early on; for others it remains a mystery and the penny never drops.

If you consult reference grammars, you will find that they differ from each other in terminology and explanatory description. The same concept may have two or more names. For example, what is called *noun phrase* in this book is also called *nominal group, subordinating conjunctions* are also *binders, coordinating conjunctions* are *listers,* and certain adverbs are *linkers.* The second terms in these pairs are short and clear, but because they are not used in most reference grammars, the traditional and more widely used terms have been used in this book.

Similarly, the same word, used in two descriptive grammars, may be found to have two different meanings, and writers have to define their own particular use of a technical term. An example which has been referred to is the term *complement.*

Another example is the word *complex,* which is used in related but distinct meanings in grammatical description:

- In its everyday meaning of *consisting of several parts, complicated,* with its related noun *complexity* referring to this meaning.
- As a term in the traditional system of classifying sentences – *simple, complex, compound* and *compound-complex.*
- As the head word in the series *word-complex, phrase-complex* and *clause-complex,* terms taken from functional grammar to mean coordinated words, phrases or clauses, used where single words, phrases or clauses also function.

The differences should be clear from the contexts in which *complex* and *complexity* are used. Ambiguity of this sort can be confusing, but to invent new terminology would be, I think, even more confusing, and unsuited to a course book which is based upon existing conventions of descriptive linguistics. I have tried to anticipate some of the learning problems, drawing upon my own experience of teaching grammar, and to chart a way which provides continuity in teaching.

Where do you start? The book begins with a chapter on the meanings of both *grammar* and *English,* and is a contribution to the socio-political argument about *good English* that underlies conflicting attitudes to Standard English and the regional and social dialects of England.

You may prefer to begin with chapter 2. Infants communicate whole meanings in their first 'words', and learn bit by bit to encode their meanings into clauses, which I take to be the basic grammatical unit which conveys whole meanings in the form of 'propositions'. So chapter 2 contains an outline of the function and form of the clause. Successive chapters then look in more detail at words and phrases (constituents of clauses), before once more reaching the clause (chapter 9) and the complex combinations of clause patterns found in speech and writing (chapters 10–14).

Objectives

One practical objective of the book is to provide students with the 'tools of analysis' with which they can study any text in English, and see how far the grammatical structure contributes to its distinctive style and meaning. Chapter 14 is therefore concerned to demonstrate how grammar forms an essential ingredient of style, by using extended extracts of literary and non-literary writing, and transcriptions of spoken English, just as chapter 7 makes extensive use of real newspaper headlines.

Dennis Freeborn

Commentary book

A supplementary book in typescript published by the author is available for teachers and lecturers. The *Commentary Book* contains suggested answers to the questions in the **activities**, with a discussion of problems of analysis where appropriate. For details of the *Commentary Book* write to: Dennis Freeborn, PO Box 82, Easingwold, York YO6 3YY.

1. Standard English and the English language

A course book in English grammar should make clear what is understood by *English* and *grammar* in its title, because we use each of the two words to refer to different ideas about the nature of the English language.

1.1 The meanings of *grammar* and *English*

1.1.1 'Grammar is "correct" English'

One common use of the word *grammar* implies the idea of *correctness* – the study of grammar should teach how we <u>ought</u> to speak and write. This meaning of *grammar* goes back at least to the eighteenth century:

> The principal design of a Grammar of any Language is to teach us to express ourselves with propriety in that Language, and to be able to judge of every phrase and form of construction, whether it be right or not.
>> (Robert Lowth, *A Short Introduction to English Grammar*, 1762)

and was still current in, for instance, 1993 in references to 'grammatically correct Standard English' in one of a series of revisions of the English component of the National Curriculum. The phrase is ambiguous, but a popular interpretation is that Standard English is the only 'grammatically correct' variety of the language, and that by definition the regional dialects are 'grammatically incorrect'.

1.1.2 'Standard English is the English language'

From this point of view **Standard English (StE)** is referred to as *correct English*, *good English* or *the Queen's English*. Nonstandard varieties of English are *incorrect*, or *bad English*. Those who take this point of view have a **model of language** in mind in which StE <u>is</u> the English language, and they will often strongly deplore the use of nonstandard forms. Using nonstandard forms of the language is, however, quite different from writing poorly constructed or ungrammatical English.

Speakers of Standard English can use English just as 'badly' as anyone else: they can write unclear prose, use words ambiguously, and so on.

(*English for Ages 5 to 16*, Department of Education and Science, June 1989)

These two meanings of *grammar* and *English*, in sections 1.1.1 and 1.1.2, are not the meanings which this book is trying to explore.

1.1.3 'The English language consists of all its dialects'

I have written this book in StE because it is the accepted and expected convention to use StE for writing. Whether or not it is written in 'good' StE is for a reader to judge – is it clear, unambiguous and so on?

The book describes the grammar of both standard and dialectal English because the model of language which underlies it defines the English language as 'the sum of all its dialects'. A complete study of the grammar of the English language today would include not only the varieties of the standard language, written and spoken, in England, Scotland, Wales, Ireland, the United States, Australia, and so on (that is, all those countries in which English is either a national or important second language) but also all their regional dialects as well.

By definition, dialects of a language are 'mutually comprehensible' – that is, speakers of one dialect can communicate with speakers of any other. Even if there are difficulties when you first hear a speaker of an unfamiliar dialect, you are able to 'tune in' relatively quickly. You cannot do this with the speaker of an unfamiliar foreign language. Therefore, if we take the view that the English language consists of all its dialects, we have to classify StE also as a dialect in the linguistic sense. This does not affect the importance of StE as the medium for almost all written English:

Standard English is usually analysed by linguists as a *dialect* of English. On purely linguistic grounds, it is not inherently superior to other *nonstandard dialects* of English, but it clearly has social prestige. This is partly because of the purposes it now serves: it is the expected language in the education system and other social institutions (such as the courts and business), in almost all published writing, and it has spread far beyond its historical base in Britain and is used as an *international language* in many parts of the world. Nonstandard dialects of English are *regional dialects*: that is, they are relatively restricted in their geographical spread. Standard English used to be restricted in this way: if we look at Standard English as an *historical dialect*, then we find that 200 years ago it had a much smaller number of speakers in England, and had nothing like the geographical spread it has nowadays. Standard English is also a *social dialect*: its use is a marker of social group membership, and the relationship between standard and nonstandard dialects and social class in Britain is particularly strong.

Although Standard English is not inherently superior to other dialects of English, it is nevertheless true that, because of its long use especially in writing for academic and administrative purposes, the *vocabulary* and to some extent the *sentence syntax* have been greatly elaborated. Nonstandard dialects have the potential to be so developed, but for social and historical reasons they have not been.

(*English for Ages 5 to 16*, DES, June 1989)

So StE is, in linguistic terms, a dialect of the English language, but for practical purposes, when we talk about the 'dialects' we are referring to the regional dialects and excluding StE. This is everyday 'common sense' usage. So StE in England is used as the **reference dialect**, and most of this book sets out to describe the grammar of StE. But an important part of the book consists of those sections which describe the most common differences to be heard in regional (mainly English) dialectal grammars, using authentic examples recorded within the last twenty-five years.

It is because the differences in vocabulary and grammar between StE and the dialects are relatively few that they are 'mutually comprehensible'. These small differences, however, are matters of great concern to those whose beliefs in correct English are prescriptive, and people judge each other in social terms on the evidence of, for example, someone's use of *hisself* rather than *himself*.

In addition, StE as a **social dialect** may be spoken in the **accent** known as **Received Pronunciation (RP)**, popularly called 'BBC English' – or with a pronunciation marked by regional vowels, consonants and intonation. Sometimes RP is mistakenly referred to as 'Standard English', which confuses pronunciation with grammar, and it may be informally described as 'a good accent', but this is, of course, a personal judgement, not a linguistic fact. Remember that in studying language, we use *accent* to refer to pronunciation, and *dialect* to refer to *grammar* and *vocabulary*.

1.1.4 Descriptive and prescriptive grammar

We use StE as a reference dialect to describe nonstandard grammar by **contrastive analysis**. For example, if the StE form is *himself*, then the common dialectal form *hisself* can be objectively described in contrast in this way:

StE and some of the dialects use the **object pronouns** *him* and *them + self/selves*, while other dialects use the **possessive pronouns** *his* and *their + self/selves* to form the **3rd person reflexive pronouns**:

StE	dialectal English
himself/themselves	*hisself/theirselves*

StE is the inconsistent dialect, however, because it requires the **possessive pronouns** in the 1st person *myself* and *ourselves*, and the 2nd person *yourself* and *yourselves*. (The difference between object and possessive pronoun is not marked in *her* when forming *herself*, and is obscured between *it* and *its* when forming *itself*.)

StE	dialectal English
myself/ourselves	*myself/ourselves*
yourself/yourselves	*yourself/yourselves*
himself/themselves	*hisself/theirselves*
herself/themselves	*herself/theirselves*
itself/themselves	*itself/theirselves*

However, no judgement as to which is correct is implied in this **descriptive** method of discussing the grammar of standard and nonstandard English. It differs from the **prescriptive** method implicit in the notion of grammar as correct English, which would assert that *himself* is right and *hisself* wrong.

In practice, prescriptive statements about language use tend to be lists of 'pet hates' – aspects of pronunciation, vocabulary or grammar which people have been brought up or taught to believe are wrong, or else new usages which are unfamiliar and perhaps threatening to their sense of order. They often rationalize their responses as a defence of 'the integrity of the language', as these recent quotations show:

- ...these **assaults** on the English language...   (1984)
- Prince Charles stressed that Britain had produced the worlds most successful language but as its use in the media and theatres showed, it had become **impoverished**, **sloppy** and **limited**.   (1989)
- Perhaps McDonalds would stop **polluting** the usage of the English language by removing the word 'Trash' from its bin notices...   (1990)
- I am writing to report a severe outbreak of a most **contagious disease** which is threatening to **subvert** the English language unless remedial measures are taken as a matter of urgency. I refer to the **misuse** and **over-use** of the phrase 'in terms' of...   (1992)
- It is the English **degradation** of city speech, the **lazy indifference** to what is said that is so **odious**.   (1993)

1.2   Shibboleths

Although the study of grammar is concerned with the form of words and sentences, not pronunciation, the prescriptive attitude criticizes accent as much as grammar, so let us start with a look at some attitudes to accents and their social consequences, beginning with a short historical episode:

> Jephthah then mustered all the men of Gilead and fought Ephraim, and the Gileadites defeated them. The Gileadites seized the fords of the Jordan and held them against Ephraim. When any Ephraimite who had escaped begged leave to cross, the men of Gilead asked him, 'Are you an Ephraimite?', and if he said, 'No', they would retort, 'Say Shibboleth'. He would say 'Sibboleth', and because he could not pronounce the word properly, they seized him and killed him at the fords of Jordan. At that time forty-two thousand men of Ephraim lost their lives.

(New English Bible, 1970)

This short story from Israelite history is recorded in the Old Testament in the Book of Judges, chapter 12. The Gileadites said *Shibboleth* in their dialect and the Ephraimites *Sibboleth* in theirs. Clearly they spoke dialects of the same language, since the same word was pronounced with only a slight variation in the initial consonant – [ʃ] or [s].

Another famous story in which a man's accent gives away his identity is in the New Testament, St Matthew's Gospel, chapter 26, although we are not told which features of his pronunciation marked him out:

Meanwhile Peter was sitting outside in the courtyard when a serving-maid accosted him and said, 'You were there too with Jesus the Galilean.' Peter denied it in face of them all. 'I do not know what you mean', he said. He then went out to the gateway, where another girl, seeing him, said to the people there, 'This fellow was with Jesus of Nazareth.' Once again he denied it, saying with an oath, 'I do not know the man'. Shortly afterwards the bystanders came up and said to Peter, 'Surely you are another of them; **your accent gives you away!**'

(*New English Bible*, 1961)

1.2.1 Shibboleths in pronunciation

The Old Testament story has given the English language the word *shibboleth*, which meant *stream in flood* in the original Hebrew, but which now means in English:

- A word or sound which a person is unable to pronounce correctly; a word used as a test for detecting foreigners, or persons from another district, by their pronunciation.
- A peculiarity of pronunciation or accent indicative of a person's origin.

Examples of the uses of the word are given in the *Oxford English Dictionary*:

- They had a Shibboleth to discover them, he who pronounced *Brot* and *Cawse* for *Bread* and *Cheese* had his head lopt off. (Cleveland, *Rustick Rampant*, 1658)
- *R* was a Shiboleth unto him, which he could not easily pronounce. (Fuller's *Worthies*, 1661)
- The commonalty of Northumberland are remarkably distinguished by a kind of *shibboleth* or *whurle*, being a peculiar way of pronouncing the letter *R*. (*Encyclopedia Britannica*, 1797)
- To that sanctimonious jargon, which was his shibboleth, was opposed another jargon, not less absurd. (Macaulay's *History of England*, 1849)

Activity 1.1

List and discuss features of pronunciation in use today which are shibboleths.

The consequences of pronouncing a word in a way that is unfamiliar to another person, or using certain words or phrases, can be a disadvantage socially, depending upon the speaker's and listener's social status. Think of the relationship between teacher and pupil, employer and employee, parent and child, and so on. Which one in those pairs is likely to comment unfavourably on the other's use of language?

If differences in other people's pronunciation of English are described as 'peculiarities', as in 'a peculiar way of pronouncing the letter *R*' above, this may simply mean that the differences are *exclusive* to those people – they are the only ones who use that pronunciation. But the word *peculiar* has also come to mean *strange*, or *odd*, so that the pronunciation may be thought to be *abnormal*. Regional dialects in a late nineteenth-century grammar book were referred to in this way,

> Distinct and separate errors of pronunciation are peculiar to each dialect, beside which one dialect often contains some of the peculiarities of another.

The word which gives away the underlying attitude of the writer is *errors* rather than *peculiarities*. It asserts that there is a right way to pronounce English. Within this point of view, the belief in 'correct' or 'good' English is created. Varieties of language use not recognised as 'good English' are thought of as corrupted versions of the language, used by people too lazy to learn and use it properly, who give offence by their refusal to conform. Here is Henry Alford, the Dean of Canterbury, writing in 1864:

> There is an offensive vulgarism, most common in the Midland counties, but found more or less everywhere: giving what should be the sound of the *u* in certain words, as if it were *oo*: calling Tuesday, *Toosday*; 'duty', *dooty*. And this is not from incapacity to utter the sound; but it arises from defective education, or from gross carelessness.   (*The Queen's English*, 1864)

Notice the assumptions that underlie this statement:

- That his own pronunciation of *Tuesday* as [tjuzdɛɪ] is implicit in the spelling. He doesn't think it necessary to spell it as he pronounces it, with an interpolated [j], *Tyoosday*, to contrast it with the dialectal pronunciation.
- That not pronouncing words as he does is *offensive*, so the speaker is guilty of a social misdemeanour.
- That his pronounciation is *correct* – this is shown by his use of *should be*.
- That the pronunciation of the name of the letter ⟨u⟩ as [ju] determines its pronunciation in certain words.
- That those who say [tuzdɛɪ] are either uneducated or careless.

Activity 1.2

Are the Dean's assumptions acceptable?

It is interesting to examine the language of those who make confident assertions about 'good English' and the ways in which they refer to 'bad English' and to the people who use it. Here are some examples from the past and present:
- The **depraved Language of common People**, and **the noble refin'd expressions** of the Gentry . . .   (1708)
- There are some **Abuses** among us of great Consequence . . .
  The great **Depravity** of our Taste . . .
  The continual **Corruption** of our English Tongue . . .
  Words and Phrases that are **offensive** to good Sense . . .
  Barbarous Mutilations of Vowels and Syllables . . .   (Jonathan Swift, 1710)
- The powerful influence of **evil habits of speech** contracted in the home and street . . .   (*The Teaching of English in England*, 1919)

- I have been forced to **endure** the following **abominations** on BBC TV...**sloppiness** in BBC spoken English ...
- The increasing **debasement** of our language by those too **ignorant** or **slovenly** to care about it...
- Is he content to leave the language to the **depredation** of those who have no desire to discriminate or who, worse, deliberately promote linguistic **degradation**... (letters to newspapers, 1984)

An expression of personal opinion, 'I don't like this pronunciation', is inflated into a general statement in terms of moral condemnation and indignation – 'How dare they say it like that!'

1.2.2   Shibboleths in vocabulary and grammar

Activity 1.3

Read the following short texts and discuss your response to the attitudes to language use which they demonstrate.

1

(*A daughter wants to be allowed to read some of the books in her father's collection*)

'Now can I read your books?'
'Have you not learned yet,' he crossly replied, 'the distinction between *can* and *may*? I dare say you *can* read my books, just about. But I've told you before and I'm telling you now, You...*may*...not.' And that was that. I never did read his books.
(Jill Tweedie's autobiography *Eating Children*, Viking, 1993)

2

(*A journalist is writing about the retirement of the football manager Brian Clough*)

Yes, he would be returning to the City ground. 'I've got to come back to get me Inkspots tapes.'   (David Lacey, *Guardian*, 3 May 1993)

3

(*Jeremy Paxman, a television presenter, is replying to critical remarks about himself made by Dave Beck – 'That principle makes him unfit to sweep the gutter he obviously lives in.'*)

'So Mr Beck made two basic mistakes – he got his facts wrong and he ended a sentence with a preposition.
(Stephen Goodwin, *Independent*, 13 October 1990)

4

(*From the examiners' report on a GCSE examination, on 'standards of written expression'*)

Many candidates used forms such as 'would of', and 'could of', instead of 'would have', and 'could have'.

Commentary on activity 1.3

1 The father assumes that *can* and *may* each have a single, fixed meaning, *to have the ability to* (*can*) and *to have permission to* (*may*). This is not so. Both words are verbs which belong to the set called **modals**, most of which have more than one meaning. The meanings of *can* and *may* 'overlap', and they are used to mean both *to have permission*, and *to be possible*. For more on modal verbs, see section 8.5.

2 The journalist wanted to reproduce Brian Clough's dialectal accent in writing *me Inkspots tapes*. Written as ⟨me⟩, the pronunciation [mɪ] for [maɪ] looks like a grammatical error, but it is a normal **reduction** of the vowel of *my* when the word is unstressed. Everyone does it, but the effect of manipulating the spelling is to draw attention to Brian Clough's accent. It is an example of how features of pronunciation and grammar can overlap.

3 'You must not end a sentence with a preposition' is one of a small number of artificial 'rules' which have no basis in language use, but which were at one time imposed as rules of good writing. This one dates back to the end of the seventeenth century, and is derived from the literal meaning of the word *preposition*. It was taken from the Latin, in which *pre-* meant *before* – therefore a word which should come before another one cannot come at the end of a sentence. We can rewrite the relevant part of Dave Beck's statement as:

>...the gutter **in which** he obviously lives.

which has connotations of **formal** language. To make it less formal, we can say:

>...the gutter **which** he obviously lives **in**

In this construction we call *in* a **deferred preposition**. It conforms to conventions of grammar based upon what people actually say, and simply marks a difference of style. We have to use a deferred preposition if we choose *that* as the relative pronoun:

>...the gutter **that** he obviously lives **in**

because we don't say:

>*...the gutter **in that** he obviously lives

4 The spellings *could of* and *would of* are very common and need to be corrected to *could have* and *would have*. There is no argument over this. But it is worth asking why such spellings regularly occur. To show their origin in speech, we would write *could've* and *would've*, but in formal writing such abbreviations are usually not acceptable. Children who write *could of* are in fact demonstrating the accuracy of their hearing and applying good principles of phonics to their spelling. It is one more example of confusion between pronunciation, spelling and grammar.

1.3 Rules of grammar

1.3.1 Rules in descriptive grammar

A *rule* in descriptive grammar is not invented and imposed by linguists in the cause of good English, but 'an observed regularity' in the language. For example, it is a rule of StE and many dialects that verbs in the present tense take the suffix *-s* to agree with a 3rd person singular subject: *I, you, we, they* **take**, but *he, she, it* **takes**. In East Anglia, dialect speakers say *he, she, it* **take**. In other dialects, the *-s* inflection is applied to all forms of the present tense – *I, you, he, she, it, we, they* **takes**.

This meaning of *rule* as *an observed regularity* is a technical term in language study. When it is used to describe the grammar of a language or dialect it does not imply that any authority has invented those rules. This kind of linguistic rule differs from those referred to in the commentary on activity 1.3 as 'artificial'. There are only a few of these artificial rules and people use them as criteria for 'good English'. Some of the best-known are described in the next section. We can call this a **proscriptive** attitude to language use.

1.3.2 Proscriptive rules – 'what you may not do'

A typical example of the proscriptive approach to language use can be found in a nineteenth-century textbook called *A Manual of our Mother Tongue* in a section called 'A Collection of Examples of Bad Grammar':

All, or nearly all, the principal points in regard to which it is possible to go wrong are exemplified in this collection.

Then follow 173 sentences, each of which is said to contain an example of 'bad grammar'.

Activity 1.4

The 'Collection of Examples of Bad Grammar' appears to claim that you can learn to write 'good English' by avoiding 173 ways of going wrong. What do you think?

Activity 1.5

Some examples from the collection can be found in D. Freeborn, P. French and D. Langford, *Varieties of English*, 2nd edn, 1993, pp. 9–10. Here are some more:

(i)   Identify and describe the 'bad grammar' in each sentence.

(ii) Discuss whether you think each example is in fact ungrammatical.

(iii) Read the versions corrected by the author of the textbook, and discuss whether his corrections are correct or necessary.

The 'right answers' are printed at the end of this chapter

1   He is stronger than me.
2   Pour the water in the bucket.
3   That was the most unkindest cut of all.   (*Shakespeare*)
4   I have heard those sort of arguments fifty times over.
5   A man may see a metaphor or an allegory in a picture as well as read them in a description.
6   Whether he be the man or no, I cannot tell.
7   This is the man whom I saw was to blame.
8   Neither of these writers can be called true poets.
9   Between you and I, this is not right.
10 Who can this letter be from?
11 Going into the garden, the grass wetted my feet.
12 They were both fond of one another.

This method of teaching students how to write is no longer in fashion, but a few of the proscriptive rules are still being taught and used as markers of good writing. For example:

1.3.2.1 'YOU MAY NOT SPLIT THE INFINITIVE'

In the old days our rulers were educated men, like the present Lord Stockton, who knew a split infinitive when they saw one...

(Gavin Ewart, *Guardian*, 19 December 1985)

The 'split infinitive' is described and discussed in section 3.5.4.

1.3.2.2 'YOU MAY NOT BEGIN A SENTENCE WITH *HOPEFULLY*'

Hundreds of creeping misuses of the English language – including 'hopefully' as a synonym for 'it is to be hoped'...are outlawed or discouraged in a new Oxford dictionary.

(John Ezard, *Guardian*, 8 March 1979)

This use of *hopefully* as a **sentence adverb** is discussed in section 3.5.3.

1.3.2.3 'YOU MAY NOT BEGIN A SENTENCE WITH *AND* OR *BUT*'

...I noticed that a lot of the sentences and even paragraphs began with And or But. My English teacher would hit the roof if I started a sentence that way, and it would be at least one thousand lines and a skipped playtime if I started a paragraph with those two words...

(Jennifer P, aged 11, *Guardian*, 20 December 1990)

This is discussed in section 4.3.1 on **coordinating conjunctions**.

1.3.2.4 'YOU MUST USE *UNTIL*, NOT *TILL*'
This proscription is perhaps not very common, but it is known that some teachers quite wrongly think that *till* is an abbreviation of *until* and say it should not be used. Historically, *till* is the older and original form, coming from Old Norse *til* into northern Old English. The form *until* is a later compound of Old Norse *und* (meaning *as far as*) + *till*, and originated in northern Middle English. (This information is in the *Oxford English Dictionary*.)

1.4 Teaching spoken Standard English

It is generally accepted that all pupils and students should learn to write StE, but the question whether they should also be required to speak StE in school or college is more controversial. The debate over this cannot be solved by a knowledge of linguistics, because it involves social and political issues. However, it should be useful to examine transcripts of some 'class conversation' in a Yorkshire primary school recorded in the 1970s. The teacher was very successful in getting a large proportion of her fourth-year class through the '11-plus', as the selective examination was then called. One of her teaching methods was to spend a whole lesson period in which every child in the class was expected to say something to the whole class. They were encouraged to ask questions of each other and to correct what they heard as well as comment on it. This 'conversation' went on while they were busy with their other tasks – writing or drawing, and so on.

In the course of two or three hours of recording only a dozen examples of 'class correction' in fact occurred, but they throw an interesting light on the kinds of features of speech, vocabulary and grammar that the teacher thought needed correction. It is clear from the recording that all the children spoke in the local accent, and used dialectal lexical and grammatical forms.

Activity 1.6

Read the transcripts and discuss those items that were corrected either by the teacher or by other pupils.

P = pupil; T = teacher.

The sign = in the transcripts marks 'latched' utterances, the second of which follows immediately after the first with no pause. The sign (.) marks a very short break in the speech, a micropause. Figures in brackets, e.g. (2.0), mark pauses in seconds.

1

P	well I an't* really bothered = *pronounced [æːnt]*
T	= I am not
P	I am not really bothered ...

2

P	I think that the mountaineer that was climbing the cove =
T	= the mountaineer (.) ?
P	<u>who</u> was climbing the cove must have had a marvellous view ...

3

P1	Philip did you manage to take a photograph?
P2	yes I did but I don't think it will come out David because I imagine it was going that fast =
P3 and P4	<u>so</u> fast =
P2	= <u>so</u> fast but it might come out

4

P1	...to think that after such a short time the calf was stood there drinking
Chorus	standing
P1	standing there drinking ...

5

P1	when I had a cat it went hunting last night
T	did you say when I had a cat? ...
P1	yes
T	well that's a funny beginning to that sentence
P2	do you have it now?
P1	no
P3	well it couldn't have gone hunting last night could it Irene?
P1	I meant it <u>used</u> to go hunting
T	yes

6

P1	where did the priest used to stand?
	(5.0)
P2	don't know [mɪˈsɛlf]
P3	perhaps it was on top of the steps
T	yes
P4	you shouldn't say [mɪˈsɛlf] you should say [ˈmaɪsɛlf]
T	yes you should

7

P1	Diane tell us what you are painting
P2	I am painting a piece of cupressus
P1	describe it to us

P2	at the bottom =
Chorus	= at the <u>base</u>
P2	at the base some of the twigs are rotted . . .

8

P1	quite early this morning I noticed that it was quite dark (.) and as it got =
Chorus	= as it became
P1	as it became lighter (.) I then felt tired . . .

9

P1	it's like if [ən aʊs]* is =	* an 'ouse
T	= pardon?	
P1	it's like if [ə haʊs] is left because there might be mice and rats crawling around . . .	

10

P1	. . . the hen and the other baby they were the dead same (2.0)
P2	you could say they are very similar
T	yes I think that's better than dead same (.) I know this is what we say in the area but it's a funny expression really (.) dead same

11

P1	they do it on a purpose =
T	= <u>on</u> purpose we say not on a purpose

12

P1	. . . I noticed a silvery trail (.) I followed the trail and there was a slug at the end all shrivelled up (.) and it was hard (1.0) I think this has happened over the night it has been =
T	= through the night
P1	through the night (.) it has been frozen
T	yes probably

Commentary on activity 1.6

1 The teacher corrects the child's **contracted negative** to its full grammatical form *I am not*. There are two issues here.

Firstly, the 'correctness' of using **contractions** like *I don't, she isn't, they shouldn't* in speech. The teacher assumed that encouraging the children to use the full forms helped them in their writing and also made their speech more like StE.

Secondly, the 'correctness' of the pronunciation [æːnt]. It is not a contraction of *I are not*, but of *I am not*, and rhymes with *can't* and *shan't*, from *cannot* and *shall not*, which are both fully accepted. Other dialectal pronunciations include *I ain't* [ɛɪnt] and the Scots *I amn't* [æmənt]. RP speakers do not use any form of this contraction, but only the alternative *I'm not*, although they say both *aren't* and *isn't*. This is most probably because the dialectal pronunciations like *an't* and *ain't* were and still are stigmatized as 'incorrect' because they are associated with a particular social class. But RP speakers are quite happy to use the **tag question** *an't I?* (usually spelt *aren't I?*), so this point of view seems unreasonable. *I an't* tends to be stigmatized as 'bad grammar' rather than as 'poor speech'. (See sections 3.3.4 and 3.3.5 for a description of the forms of the verb *be*.)

2 The teacher has told her class that the **relative pronoun** in a **restrictive relative clause**, when referring to a human person, should be *who*. She believes that *that* should be used for non-human referents only. But both common usage and reference grammar books show that *that* is normally used for both human and non-human referents, as in *The mountaineer **that** was climbing the cove ... and The mountain **that** he climbed* ... (See section 4.2.11 on relative pronouns.)

3 Another use of *that*, this time as an **intensifier**. It is said to be grammatical in StE in a sentence like, *It's not that unusual for men to wash up nowadays*, but dialectal or nonstandard in *It was going that fast*, or *I was that angry* ... The teacher takes this point of view and tries to eliminate this and other local dialectal features from the speech of her pupils.

4 The form of the verb *stand* in a sentence like *The calf was stood there* is widespread, certainly in the north of England, and possibly in other regions. StE grammar requires the **progressive aspect** to be used, *The calf was standing there*, and it will be argued that *was stood* is the **passive** form of *X stood the calf there*. But in this dialectal usage *stood* is functioning as an adjective, like *happy* in *I was happy*. The verb *sit* is also used in this way in dialects in the north and west of England, as in this example from Bradford:

You know, you **were sat** on the chair and she'd kick her knee into your back.

5 This is the only example of clearly ungrammatical English in the data, which the pupil soon recognizes as such and puts right. It is not good English, because it does not convey the intended meaning. *When I had a cat* implies that the girl no longer has a cat; the verb is in the **simple past tense**. In *it went hunting last night* the adjective *last* implies that she had the cat a few hours ago and we assume that she still has it. She corrects herself to *it used to go hunting*, a **habitual** action which matches meaningfully with *When I had a cat* in the past. The other essential correction of *last night* to *at night* was not brought up by the teacher.

6 This is similar to the writing of *me* for *my* referred to in section 1.2.2. The word *my* by itself and in the compound *myself* is reduced from [maɪ] to [mɪ] when unstressed. It is not bad grammar in which a speaker is substituting the word *me* for *my*, but a normal feature of pronunciation.

7 A question of accuracy in vocabulary, and perhaps to do with connotations of the word *bottom* which the teacher wishes to avoid.

8 A long-lasting shibboleth – '*got* isn't a word!', which is refuted by its frequent use, particularly in informal speech. It is not ungrammatical, but is corrected in the interests of teaching formal vocabulary.

9 If *an 'ouse* is the normal pronunciation in the local dialectal accent, it might be said to compare favourably with the common RP pronunciation of *an 'otel*. Adverse judgement on 'dropping h's' is a social comment, not linguistic. The pronunciation of words beginning with letter ⟨h⟩ varies across the dialects. Some dialects have dropped initial [h], others pronounce it in some words and not in others.

10 A use of *dead* as an **intensifier** (compare *that* in *that fast*). It occurs in a significant number of phrases listed in dictionaries, e.g. *dead level, dead loss, dead faint, dead reckoning, dead shot,* so there can be no reasonable objection to its use in *dead same.* Nevertheless, *dead same* is marked as colloquial dialectal usage, like *dead good,* and is therefore proscribed. It is a matter of style, not grammar. The correction, 'are very similar', is not an accurate synonym.

11 The correction is justified if *on a purpose* is not a known usage, and a slip on the child's part. The *OED* does, however, record the following forms: *a purpose, o' purpose, in purpose, of purpose.*

12 The variable use of **prepositions** is a feature of the differences between the dialects (section 4.1.1), but *over the night* is surely acceptable in StE and other dialects?

No doubt other features of the pupils' pronunciation, vocabulary and grammar were 'corrected'. None of these authentic recorded examples of corrections to children's language use in class, except *When I had a cat it went hunting last night,* failed to convey their meaning. The argument is whether spoken English that uses informal dialectal vocabulary and grammar should be discouraged, and formal StE forms substituted.

'Correct answers' to activity 1.5 _____

1 He is stronger than *I* (am).
2 Pour the water *into* the bucket.
3 That was *unkindest* cut of all.
4 I have heard *that* sort of arguments fifty times over.
5 A man may see a metaphor or an allegory in a picture as well as read *it* in a description.
6 Whether he be the man or *not,* I cannot tell.
7 This is the man *who,* I saw, was to blame.
8 Neither of these writers can be called a *true poet.*
9 Between you and *me,* this is not right.
10 *Whom* can this letter be from? or, *From whom can this letter be?*
11 *As I was* going into the garden, the grass wetted my feet.
12 They were fond of *each other.*

2. Encoding experience in language

2.1 Some properties of language

2.1.1 Language, speech and writing

Speech consists of sounds, and **writing** of visible marks on a surface, and so both are **concrete** and exist in the material world. But the sounds of speech and the marks of writing are not language itself. Language is **abstract** or immaterial, something we learned even as small children by listening to other people using it, not by being taught.

Speech and writing, therefore, are said to **realize** language – that is, 'to make it real'. Speech is a **medium** for using language, usually when a speaker and a listener are in close contact, and is impermanent unless recorded. Writing is relatively permanent and is a medium for language use when a listener or reader is not present. The same language, English, is used for both media, and the same message can be communicated, though we tend to use English in different ways, or **styles**, when we talk or write.

2.1.2 Language as a game

In some ways the rules of a *game* can be compared with the rules for using language – what we call the **grammar**. In one sense, every game played – hockey, football, chess and so on – is new and different, but in another sense we can speak of the *same game* being played each time. Similarly, in one sense – that of **language use** – everything we speak or write is different, but in the other sense we are using the *same language* – English. The rules of a game are abstract, and correspond, to some extent, to the abstract rules of a language which we use to construct our sentences in speech and writing. The difference between a standard language and its nonstandard dialects lies in a few minor differences in the rules.

2.1.3 Language as a system

It is also helpful to think of language as a **system** – a set of connected parts making up a whole – which we have learned and which we use to create sentences, in order to communicate to others what we want to mean. As soon as we begin to examine this system which allows us to make sentences, we are in the world of abstraction, because the system itself only exists in the mind. Both *word* and *sentence* are abstract concepts about language. You may find it difficult at first to understand this, since they seem to exist so obviously in the real world of speech and writing.

2.2 Words

2.2.1 *Words and strings*

Speech and writing may be described as **strings** of words, one after the other in succession, either in time (in spoken language), or in space (in written language). The word *string*, like *system* and *structure*, is used as a kind of **metaphor** – words as we speak or write them are in some ways like beads on a thread, one following another. But the meaning of a string of words cannot be properly understood like a sum in arithmetic:

> word 1 + word 2 + word 3 etc. = meaning

and the 'string' metaphor is not a very useful one in explaining how language works.

If language in use has structure, this presents a metaphor of a construction with scaffolding, or perhaps a network, or a complex machine, each of which is very different from a string of beads. In fact, words go together in groups or bundles of different sizes and functions, like *phrases* and *sentences*. In speech and writing we always mark groups of words which hang together, by **intonation** in speech and by **punctuation** in writing. In writing we also mark the boundaries of words. We all learned to put spaces between words as an essential part of written punctuation.

It may surprise you to know, however, that in speech there are no breaks between words. Breaks and pauses in speech are used for a number of different purposes, but we only separate words in very emphatic, slow speech. (You could test this by listening to a recording of an unknown foreign language, making a rough phonetic transcription, and then trying to list the words. You have to know the language to be successful.)

The spaces between words in written English are therefore an adopted convention, not natural and inevitable, but an extremely useful and sensible convention. In some earlier forms of writing, before printing and the invention of paper, parchment was so expensive that it was not wasted on blank spaces between words, and presumably we would soon get used to this convention if we had to.

2.2.2 *When is a word not a word?*

We do not always agree on what constitutes a written word. *Into* has been written as one word for centuries, though it derives from two words, *in* and *to*. But *onto* is probably still marked wrong by many teachers and lecturers, although it appears in print, and the convention of writing two words is changing. *Instead of* is two written words, and not three, *in stead of*. Some students write *inspite of* as two words, which is as reasonable as *instead of*. We write *nevertheless* and *notwithstanding* as one word, not three.

The reason for these conventions comes from general agreement that some phrases of two or three words are single **lexical units** of meaning, and also the fact that we never vary them, or split them with other words. But the adoption of a convention is seldom consistent, and we sometimes disagree over the **orthography** of a word – that is, how it is written and spelt. The phrase **lexical item** is a useful neutral term for one or more words which function as a single unit of meaning.

Creative writers are in a privileged position and make their own conventions of language use, unlike students and journalists, for example, who have to learn and obey the linguistic rules and conventions of their teachers and editors.

Activity 2.1

(i) Discuss which of the following alternative forms of lexical items you prefer, or consider to be correct – written as one word, with or without a hyphen, or as two or more words. If you think there are insufficient grounds for preferring one to another, say so.

(ii) The lexical items in column I of set B are taken from James Joyce's novel *Ulysses*. Comment on the convention that Joyce adopted.

A

noone	no-one	no one
nobody	no-body	no body
cannot	can-not	can not
willnot	will-not	will not
telephonebox	telephone-box	telephone box
matchbox	match-box	match box
tearoom	tea-room	tea room
mushroom	mush-room	mush room
headteacher	head-teacher	head teacher
viceprincipal	vice-principal	vice principal
frontdoor	front-door	front door
greengrocer	green-grocer	green grocer
blackbird	black-bird	black bird
inkbottle	ink-bottle	ink bottle
glassbottle	glass-bottle	glass bottle
rattlesnake	rattle-snake	rattle snake
handkerchief	hand-kerchief	hand kerchief

B

weedgrown rocks	weed-grown rocks	weed grown rocks
curlyheaded boys	curly-headed boys	curly headed boys
whitesmocked men	white-smocked men	white smocked men
inkeraser	ink-eraser	ink eraser
mantailored	man-tailored	man tailored
bathwater	bath-water	bath water
newbaked jampuffs	new-baked jam-puffs	new baked jam puffs
foodheated faces	food-heated faces	food heated faces
halffed	half-fed	half fed
hoofthuds	hoof-thuds	hoof thuds
saucestained	sauce-stained	sauce stained
spoonfed	spoon-fed	spoon fed

2.3   Morphemes and syllables

2.3.1   *Morphemes*

A word, however, is not in fact the smallest unit of the grammar of English:

> The traditional term for the most elemental unit of grammatical form is
> morpheme. A single word may be composed of one or more morphemes.
>   (from V. Fromkin and R. Rodman, *An Introduction to Language*, 1974)

Morphemes could be shown in writing, for instance by using hyphens:

> The tradition-al term for the most element-al unit of gramma-tic-al form is
> morph-cme. A single word may be compos-ed of one or more morph-eme-s.

but it is not conventional to do so. The smallest grammatical unit which has
meaning and which is marked in writing is the word. Also, everyone would agree
in identifying the words of the language (with very few exceptions, like *inspite of*
and *onto*, already mentioned), whereas there is not universal agreement about the
morphemes of English.

   Some morphemes are **inflectional**, and show a grammatical function, like the
past tense *-ed* in *composed*, and the plural *-s* in *morphemes*. Others are **derivational**,
and change the grammatical category of a word, so that by adding *-al*, for
example, the nouns *tradition* and *element* become the adjectives *traditional* and
elemental. A morpheme at the end of words is called a **suffix**.

   By substituting *con-* for *tra-*, *traditional* becomes *conditional*, but there is no
meaning in present-day English for *-dition*, so it can hardly be called a
'grammatical unit of meaning', and is therefore not an English morpheme. The
explanation for the similarity between *tradition* and *condition* is historical. Both
were borrowed from Latin into English as whole words, although in Latin the
source of *-dition* was itself a whole word (*dicere*, meaning *say*).

A morpheme like *un-*, which has the meaning *not* placed at the front of a word to make *untraditional* and *unconditional*, is called a **prefix**. A general term which includes both suffixes and prefixes is **affix**.

2.3.2   Syllables

Spoken words consist of one or more **syllables** as in *then*, *now* (1 syllable), *a/lert*, *to/day* (2), *pa/ssen/ger*, *de/scen/ded* (3), *he/si/ta/ted* (4), *un/in/hi/bi/ted* (5), and so on. Central to a syllable is a **vowel** sound, either on its own – e.g. *I* [aɪ] – or opened and/or closed with a **consonant** – e.g. *tle* [taɪ], *ice* [aɪs], *tight* [taɪt].

Do not confuse the *syllable*, a unit of **sound**, with the *morpheme*, a unit of grammar which has meaning. For example, the word *singer* consists of two syllables, [sɪŋ] + [ə], which at the same time are also morphemes, ⟨sing⟩ + ⟨er⟩ (caret brackets ⟨ ⟩ are used to mark written **letters**). The syllable *sing* is a **free morpheme**, because it can stand alone as a verb, and is therefore also a **word**. We say that the word *sing* 'consists of' one morpheme (grammar), which happens by chance to be one syllable (sound). The morpheme *-er* is a **bound morpheme**, because it is always a suffix, never a word, and its 'meaning' is to create a noun from a verb, to signify a person who performs the action of the verb – *singer* is one who *sings*.

But the word *blather*, apparently similar in structure to *singer*, and having two syllables, [blæ] + [ðə], consists of one morpheme. The ⟨er⟩ in *blather* does not function like the ⟨er⟩ in *singer*. The whole word *blather* is a verb. There is no word *blath*, and the fact that *blather* ends in *-er* is a coincidence, and we must add another *-er* to make *blatherer*, meaning *someone who blathers*. The word *blathering* in,

She told him to stop blathering and talking nonsense

consists of two morphemes, ⟨blather⟩ + ⟨ing⟩, but three syllables, [blæ] + [ðə] + [rɪŋ].

Activity 2.2   Syllables and morphemes

(i)   Mark the syllables in the following words, using the International Phonetic Alphabet if you know it, e.g. the word *pitifully* – [pɪ/tɪ/fʊ/lɪ], or using normal spelling – *pi/ti/fu/lly* = 4 syllables.

(ii)   Mark the morphemes in the same words, eg *piti/ful/ly* = 3 morphemes.

restless	*assert*
familiar	*departure*
exactly	*appearances*
reddening	*undiminished*
premonitions	*chorus*
casual	*performer*

Activity 2.3

(i) Divide the words in bold type in the following text into their constituent morphemes. (The word *constituent* refers to an item which is a part of, or *constitutes*, something larger.)

You should discover some interesting problems to discuss. For example, if ⟨s⟩ is a morpheme meaning *plural*, (one *cup*, two *cups*), where is the plural morpheme in *women*? Or if the suffix ⟨ed⟩ makes the past tense of a verb, (*rub*, *rubbed*), where is the past tense morpheme in *sang*?

NB: Whenever you come across difficulties like these in trying to work out a grammatical problem, do not expect a 'right answer' to be forthcoming every time. There may be several possible answers, and none of them may be completely satisfactory.

(ii) Compare the number of morphemes in the words with the number of syllables, and note any differences.

It was a still, moist night. Just before dawn he was **assisted** in **waking** by the **abnormal reverberation** of familiar music. To the **shepherd**, the note of the sheep-bell, like the ticking of the clock to other people, is a **chronic** sound that only **makes itself** noticed by ceasing or altering in some **unusual manner** from the well-known idle **tinkle** which signifies to the **accustomed** ear, **however** distant, that all is well in the fold. The experienced ear of Oak **knew** the sound he now **heard** to be caused by the running of the **sheep** with great **velocity**.

(Thomas Hardy, *Far from the Madding Crowd*)

2.4   Sentences and phrases

So, the smallest <u>meaningful</u> unit of grammar in language is a morpheme, and in English, one or more morphemes make up a word. We show the boundaries of words in writing by leaving a space between them, although in speech we do not separate words from each other. As listeners, and speaking English ourselves, we know where the word boundaries would be.

But we neither read nor listen to one word at a time in normal circumstances. So there must be other grammatical units which convey meaning, and the one which we have all been taught to observe in writing is the **sentence**.

Words, then, make up sentences, and within sentences words are grouped together to make other meaningful units, for which the word *phrase* has already been used. Let us say that words are grouped into phrases, and phrases are grouped into sentences. The structure of different kinds of phrase is the subject of chapters 6–8.

2.5   Meaning

But when we talk or write, we do not think specifically in terms of words, phrases and sentences (units of the grammar), but of *meanings*. The grammar of English is there because it makes meaning possible when we wish to refer to the world around us, or to the world inside our minds – what we see, hear, touch, think and feel.

One fundamental use of language is to make statements or observations about life to another person, typically in talking about what we have done or seen. For example, if I look out of the window at eight in the morning, and out of a number of things which my eye can see, I observe something which is important, because the milk hasn't been delivered and the family wants its tea at breakfast, I say:

1   I can see the milkman across the road.

This spoken statement contains what is called a **proposition** about seeing, which relates *me*, *the milkman*, and *the road*. The statement uses language by obeying the rules of the grammar of English. It puts the words in a certain order. **Word order** is as much a part of grammar as space is part of punctuation (section 2.13). Other orders are possible:

2   Across the road I can see the milkman.

In (2) the phrase *across the road* has been moved to the front of the sentence.

3   The milkman I can see across the road.

Construction (3) is just about possible in speech if I stress *milkman*. The phrase *the milkman* has been moved to the front. What I cannot do is move other groups or individual words about:

4   *The road I can see the milkman across.
5   *Across I can see the milkman the road.
6   *Can see the milkman I across the road.
7   ?See the milkman across the road I can.

Construction (4) could be a response to the question *Which road do you mean?*, but it is not itself a complete grammatical sentence.

2.6   Phrases as constituents of sentences

So the grammatical **constituents** of a sentence – those units that I can move about to some extent – are not words, but **phrases**. We can now begin to make a **hypothesis** (an intelligent guess based on evidence) about the structure of English:

Sentences consist of phrases

Phrases consist of words

Words consist of morphemes

But in sentence (1), the word *I* stands alone, because *can* and *see* certainly form a phrase, *can see*. And if the family had only just mentioned the milkman, I might have said,

8   I can see him across the road.

The pronoun *him*, a word, does the same job as the phrase *the milkman*. So if this principle applies to each **rank** of the grammar, we can amend our hypothesis to:

Sentences consist of one or more phrases

Phrases consist of one or more words

Words consist of one of more morphemes

We know this applies to phrases and words, so we shall have to verify the hypothesis – that is, establish its correctness – in its application to the sentence, or else modify it later.

2.7   Processes, participants and circumstances

What is this statement *I can see the milkman across the road* about? How am I turning my experience of seeing him into speech, or **encoding** my experience into language?

The phrase *can see* means (i) that I am able to do something at that moment (*can*), and (ii) that I am using my sense of sight (*see*). The word **process** is used as a general term to represent (i) 'events', whether they are physical actions like *walk* and *hit*, or mental like *think*, and *see*; and (ii) 'states' like *be* and *seem*. So to *see* is a **mental process of perception**.

But *process* is an abstraction from reality. Someone or something has to *do* the process. You cannot have a dance without a dancer. The persons or things involved in the process are called **participants**.

In sentence (1), there are two participants, *I* and *the milkman*. Of course, the milkman is not himself participating knowingly in this case, and is not affected by my seeing him. But he is the 'objective' of my seeing, and so in that sense he is a participant in my personal act of seeing.

It is easy to make up a sentence in which the milkman is an active participant, either doing something to a second participant, or being himself affected by the other participant, or simply doing something which does not involve a second participant:

9   The milkman **delivered** three pints yesterday.
10   Next door's dog **has bitten** the milkman in the leg.
11   The milkman **was singing** cheerfully.
12   This morning the milkman **said**, 'Three pints as usual?'

The verbs *delivered* and *has bitten* represent **actional processes**, things which people *do*; the verbs *was singing* and *said* represent **verbal processes**.

There are therefore one or more participants in the process. But (9)–(12) also include further information – about time (when?), *yesterday, this morning*; place (where?), *in the leg, across the road*; manner (how?), *cheerfully*. These are the **circumstances** in which the participant(s) took part in the process, and often they give additional information which could be left out without affecting the grammaticality of the sentence – that is, the sentence remains an acceptable grammatical English sentence without the information about the circumstances in which the process took place:

13   The milkman delivered three pints.
14   Next door's dog has bitten the milkman.
15   The milkman was singing.
16   The milkman said, 'Three pints as usual?'

But what you often cannot do is omit a participant without leaving an ungrammatical sentence or changing the meaning:

17   *The milkman delivered.
18   *Delivered three pints.
19   *Next door's dog has bitten.
20   *Has bitten the milkman.
21   *Was singing.
22   *Said, 'Three pints as usual?'

(This does not always work, as there are many words representing processes which can operate both with and without a second participant. For example, *sing*:

23   Jill sang a group of folk-songs at the concert.
24   Jill sang at the concert.

Construction (23) is a **transitive clause**, because the verb *sang* is followed by a grammatical direct object *a group of folk-songs*; (24) is **intransitive** because the clause contains no direct object (see section 9.1 on *transitivity*.)

The following text is taken from a set of reading primers for infants and used here because it is a very simple text in its grammar. Notice, however, that although simple, it immediately throws up one or two problems of classification. Our hypothesis about processes, participants and circumstances is being tested on a simple text to see if it works.

Activity 2.4

(A commentary on this activity follows, so work out the answers first before looking at the commentary.)

(i)   For each sentence, identify the word or phrase representing the process, the participant(s), and the circumstances of time, place, or manner. Distinguish 'participant I', who acts or performs the process, from 'participant 2' (if any) who is affected by, or is the objective of, the process. A participant need not be a person, e.g. *three pints* in (9) above, and *next door's dog* in (10). The normal unmarked order in a statement is,

1	2	3	4
Participant I	Process	Participant 2	Circumstances

(*Unmarked* means *normal* or *usual*, what we find most often. The word *marked* is used to refer to a feature which is less common, or more noticeable, though it must still be grammatically acceptable.)

Make a four-column page with these headings, 1–4, and put the words or phrases of each sentence in the appropriate column.

(ii)   Then list the processes separately under two headings:

   (a)   those which have one associated participant; and
   (b)   those which have two participants.

(iii) List any process that must have its attendant circumstance in the sentence.

(iv)   List any processes that represent *actional processes* performed by a participant.

(v)   List any processes that represent *mental processes* of feeling, understanding, perceiving and so on, or *verbal processes* of saying.

(vi)   What problem of analysis arises when the 'process' is represented by the words *are* and *is?*

The sentences are numbered for easy reference.

Shopping

1 I go to the shops with my mum. 2 We walk down the street. 3 We go to the supermarket. 4 I carry the basket. 5 We take things from the shelves. 6 We get sugar and tea. 7 I put cornflakes in my basket. 8 We get butter and cheese and sausages. 9 Mum puts frozen peas in the basket. 10 They are hard and cold. 11 My basket is very heavy now. 12 We take tins off the shelf. 13 We take tins of baked beans, fruit and soup. 14 We fill the basket up to the top. 15 We pay for all the things and we buy some sweets. 16 We have to take the shopping home. 17 I like shopping with my mum.
(D. Mackay, B. Thompson and P. Schaub, *Breakthrough to Literacy*)

Commentary on activity 2.4

(i)   The distribution of phrases is as follows:

	Participant 1	*Process*	*Participant 2*	*Circumstances*
1	I	go		to the shops with my mum
2	We	walk		down the street
3	We	go		to the supermarket
4	I	carry	the basket	
5	We	take	things	from the shelves
6	We	get	sugar & tea	
7	I	put	cornflakes	in my basket

	Participant 1	*Process*	*Participant 2*	*Circumstances*
8	We	get	butter & cheese & sausages	
9	Mum	puts	frozen peas	in the basket
10	They	are	?hard & cold	
11	My basket	is	?very heavy	now
12	We	take	tins	off the shelf
13	We	take	tins of baked beans, fruit & soup	
14	We	fill	the basket	up to the top
15	We	pay		for all the things
and	we	buy	some sweets	
16	We	have to take	the shopping	home
17	I	like	X	
	X=	shopping		with my mum

(iia)   Processes with **one** participant: *go, walk, ?pay.*

The word *pay* is, however, not limited to one participant. The sum that was paid, say '£3.50', and the person to whom the money was paid do not have to be included to make a grammatical sentence. But if they are included, they are *participants 2* and *3* in the process of paying. The sentence therefore has several possible grammatical forms, including,

(a)   We pay £3.50 for all the things.
(b)   We pay the shopkeeper £3.50.
(c)   We pay the shopkeeper for all the things.
(d)   We pay the shopkeeper £3.50 for all the things.

(iib)   Processes with **two** participants: *carry, take (4), get, put(s), fill, buy, like.*

(iii)   The process *put* must be completed by a phrase denoting place:

I put cornflakes in my basket.
not   *I put cornflakes.

The processes *go* and *walk* also sound odd without a completing phrase. They are still grammatical but have a rather different meaning:

I go to the shops.
I go with my mum.
?I go.
We walk down the street.
?We walk.

(iv) The following processes represent physical actions, and so are examples of **actional processes**:

go   walk   carry   take   get   put   help   carry   fill   pay   buy

(v) The only **mental process** is *like*.

(vi) The process represented by *are* and *is* is neither an actional nor a mental process. The words link or **relate** the participant 1 – *they* (= *the peas*) and *basket* – to a word or phrase which describes an **attribute** or quality of the participant – *hard, cold, very heavy*. An attribute is not a participant in a process.

The words *are* and *is*, which are different forms of the word *be*, represent **relational processes**. So we must amend our hypothesis to include the concept of an attribute in a statement:

Participant 1	*Process* actional, mental or relational	*Participant 2* or *Attribute*	*Circumstances*

The term **mental process** is used as a label to cover a range of non-actional kinds of process, for example, *admiring* someone (a **behavioural** process), *looking at* something (a **perceptive** process) or *thinking* (a **cognitive** process) and so on. It could also include *saying* or *whispering* something (a **verbal** process). These categories of meaning are quite complex, and will not be developed any further in this introductory book. But the division of processes into the three main types labelled *actional*, *mental* and *relational* is a useful starting-point, provided that you do not take the labels too literally.

Labelling the participants simply as 1 and 2 does not, however, descriptively differentiate the **roles** they play in relation to the processes. All the first participants in the sentences of activity 2.4 who perform actional or mental processes are *acting* by doing something, so they can be called **actors**.

The participants in relational processes, however, are not actually *doing* anything, so their role cannot be that of actor. In fact, the process itself is little more than a link between the participant and the attribute.

The second participants are the people or things that are **affected** by the action of the actor, or they are the **objective** of a mental process. Our hypothesis about the relationships of meaning in a proposition therefore now reads:

Actor	*Process* actional, or mental or relational	*Affected* or *Objective* or *Attribute*	*Circumstances*

More information on the **semantic roles of clause constituents** can be found in reference grammars.

2.8 Clauses

Now look once more at sentence 15 in *Shopping*:

We pay for all the things and we buy some sweets.

The word *and* links what could equally well be written as two sentences:

We pay for all the things. We buy some sweets.

Similarly, sentences 2 and 3 could have been written as a single sentence:

We walk down the street and we go to the supermarket.

So propositions can be written and spoken as single sentences, or linked by *and* to form longer sentences. In fact, the text of *Shopping* seems rather artificial, because we don't usually talk in a series of **simple sentences**.

The problem is that if a single proposition is processed in the grammar as a simple sentence, and yet it is possible to link a whole series of them together in a long complex sentence, we have to talk about sentences within sentences. It is helpful, therefore, to find another word to stand for the concept of a single proposition, or simple sentence. The word commonly used is **clause**.

Our hypothesis about the ranks of grammatical structure in English (section 2.6) can now be amended to:

A sentence consists of one or more clauses.

A clause consists of one or more phrases.

A phrase consists of one or more words.

A word consists of one or more morphemes.

Here is an authentic example of a five-year-old girl talking, written out clause by clause to show how she is linking a series of short 'sentences' in speech. She is trying to explain something she has been told about the working of her electric blanket. The text separates the linking words from the clauses.

linking word	*clause*
if	I switch my blankct off
	there's got a switch
and	you switch it up
and	the light comes on
	an orange light comes on
and	
if	you switch it off
	the light goes off

but		
if		it broke
		we could take it back
and		then he'll mend it
and		
if		it's coming near night
		he'll give me a new one

Activity 2.5

(i) Turn the text from a transcription of speech into punctuated written English of your own. Make any changes that you think necessary to make the meaning clearer. For example, the girl refers to *he* without ever saying who 'he' is, that is, she doesn't name the **referent**, the person she refers to.

(ii) Describe what you have done in order to produce written sentences.

Activity 2.6

Write out the following narrative *A Rainy Day* (another reading primer text) clause by clause in columns. Write out each clause on its own line, with any linking words in a separate column at the front:

link – Actor – Process – Affected/Objective/Attribute – Circumstances

Note or discuss words and phrases that don't seem to fit in with one of the categories of meaning (if any).

A Rainy Day
1 It was raining. 2 It rained all night. 3 I heard it when I was in bed. 4 My mum said put on your raincoat. 5 I went to school in the rain. 6 At school some children were playing in the rain. 7 They were wet. 8 Their shoes were wet. 9 Their hair was wet too. 10 I took off my raincoat. 11 My dress was a bit wet. 12 My teacher said sit here and dry your dress. 13 The children looked out at the rain. 14 It ran down the windows. 15 There were puddles in the playground. 16 We had to stay in school all day. 17 We had no playtime.

2.9   The rank scale

We have discovered that the system of English grammar, which provides a means of encoding thoughts and ideas into speech and writing, can be described in terms of a **rank scale**, from the largest to the smallest unit:

sentence

clause

phrase

word

morpheme

A simple sentence consists of one clause. There is no upper limit in the grammar to the number of clauses that can make up a larger sentence, but in practice the style of speech or writing will determine this. The deliberately simple style of infant reading primers illustrates one extreme, and it is very difficult to find other examples of authentic English like it.

2.10 How clauses make sense

The clause is the central structure in the language, because it represents a complete **proposition**, something that is stated or questioned or requested and so on. Its meaning is complete because it relates processes and participants together.

Evidence for the importance of the clause as a proposition, a self-contained unit of meaning, can be demonstrated from infant speech. Babies communicate to their parents with noises and gestures from a few days old, but their first recognisable 'words', months later, are in fact more like simple sentences than single words in their meaning. A 'one-word' utterance can only be understood in its context. 'Milk' could mean 'I want some milk' or 'I've knocked my milk over' or 'I can see some milk' and so on. These are all clauses.

A most important part of the development of a child's language is its use of grammar, learning to add inflections to words or to change their form, and combining words into phrases and clauses, and clauses into complex sentences.

2.11 How meaning and grammar are related

To sum up so far: one participant actor – someone or something that acts – is essential for a process to take place, in circumstances of time, place or manner, as in the following clauses. The processes of *living, jumping, going, whistling, singing* and *running* involve only one participant, who is involved as the **actor**:

	Actor	*Process*	*Circumstances*
Once upon a time	a little tailor	lived	in a little town
	a great big dog	jumped	out
and on	they	go	
	he	was whistling	
and		singing	
with	the great big dog	running	at his heels

(These and the following sentences are from *Folk and Fairy Tales*, Ruth Manning-Saunders, 1978.)

But in other processes an actor does something to, or **affects**, another person or thing, the **affected**.

Actor	Process	Affected	Circumstances
the tailor	found	little work	
he	put	a clean shirt	in his knapsack
he	slung	the knapsack	over his shoulder
the great big dog	wagged	his tail	
I	have eaten	every scrap of bread	
I	can find	food	

The terms *actor*, *affected* and *process* are **semantic** terms, that is, they refer to **meaning**. *Actor* and *affected* are 'roles' played by people and things. In the grammar of the clause, the actor is the SUBJECT (S), the process is the PREDICATOR (P), the affected person or thing is one kind of COMPLEMENT (C), called the OBJECT COMPLEMENT (Co), or simply the OBJECT (O), and the circumstance is the ADVERBIAL (A). Complements are so called because they *make complete* the meaning of the predicator.

Clauses with grammatical OBJECTS (the affected person or thing) are **transitive** (SPO). For example

Actor as SUBJECT	Process as PREDICATOR	Affected as OBJECT	Circumstance as ADVERBIAL
he	swung	his yardstick	round his head
he	banged	the table	with his fist
the tailor	ordered	a meal	
he	threw	his knapsack	on a bench
he	stood	his yardstick	in a corner
he	seated	himself	in an armchair

Clauses without a grammatical OBJECT are **intransitive** (SP). For example

Actor as SUBJECT	Process as PREDICATOR	Circumstance as ADVERBIAL
he	marched	into the tavern
the host	came running	quickly
he	was whistling	loudly

When the clause is studied in more detail in later chapters you will see that this 'one-to-one relationship', actor = subject and affected = object, does not always occur. SUBJECT (S), PREDICATOR (P), OBJECT (O) and ADVERBIAL (A) are **grammatical** terms, not semantic, that is, they are labels for **relationships** between words and phrases, and their position in a clause.

In an unmarked clause that makes a statement, like those above, the order of the constituents is SPOA. Each phrase has a different job to do in the structure of the clause, and helps to convey the meaning of the proposition which the clause contains. The predicators that do not represent actional or mental processes, but relational processes, function as links between a participant and an attribute of the participant, as in *The host **was** astonished, the stick **looked** short, the ogre seemed very fierce*.

The word *astonished* describes an attribute of the host, *short* of the stick and *very fierce* of the ogre, and they are another form of complement to the predicator. To distinguish their function from objects in a clause, they are called **INTENSIVE COMPLEMENTS (Ci)**.

S	P	Ci = INTENSIVE COMPLEMENT
the host	was	astonished
the stick	looked	short
the ogre	seemed	very fierce

They could have been used as **MODIFIERS** of the nouns – *Astonished, short* and *fierce* are all **adjectives** (section 3.4), but the INTENSIVE COMPLEMENT need not be an adjective:

S	P	Ci
Marzi	was	a young soldier
He	became	a king's son

In these two clauses, the INTENSIVE COMPLEMENTS *a young soldier* and *a king's son* identify or equate with the SUBJECT, saying who or what he is. *Soldier* and *son* are **nouns** (form-class). In the clauses above, both are parts of phrases which do the grammatical job (function) of an INTENSIVE COMPLEMENT. This is taken up also in section 9.4.3.

In the following clauses:

S	P	?
the food	was	on the table
a cord	was	in the knapsack

the relationship is of a different kind. The phrases *on the table* and *in the knapsack* tell us where the food and cord were, not what they are like, and so they are not attributes. They are also essential to complete the meaning of their clauses. They therefore function as COMPLEMENTS as well as ADVERBIALS, because the clauses would not be grammatically complete without them. In other clauses they would function as optional 'circumstance' ADVERBIALS:

S	P	O	A
the tailor	saw	a stick	on the table
he	was carrying	his goods	in the knapsack

So adverbial kinds of phrase functioning as complements can be called **ADVERBIAL COMPLEMENTS (Ca)**, to show that they have a double function.

2.12 Form and function

In this section we have seen that it is necessary to distinguish between what a word or phrase *is* and what it *does*, and the corresponding linguistic terms **form** and **function** have been introduced. The forms and functions of the words and phrases of the last quoted sentences in section 2.11 are:

	form	FUNCTION
the	*definite article*	DETERMINER
tailor	*noun*	HEAD word of noun phrase (NP)
the tailor	*NP*	SUBJECT (clause constituent)
saw	*verb and verb phrase (VP)*	PREDICATOR
a	*indefinite article*	DETERMINER
stick	*noun*	HEAD word of NP
a stick	*NP*	OBJECT (clause constituent)
on	*preposition*	HEAD of prepositional phrase (PrepP)
the	*definite article*	DETERMINER
table	*noun*	HEAD word of NP
the table	*NP*	COMPLEMENT of prepositionon
the table	*PrepP*	ADVERBIAL (clause constituent)

The tailor, *a stick* and *the table* have the same form as NPs, but they each have a different function in the clauses or phrases of which they are constituents. VPs, however, always function as the **PREDICATOR** of a clause.

Note for teachers and lecturers

1. The term *predicator* is used to distinguish the *function* of this constituent, although it is always performed by a verb phrase (VP), in a clause. Traditional and some contemporary grammar books use the word *verb* for both form and function. But the distinction between the form-class of an item and its function is a useful one to keep. Using the functional term *predicator* avoids the anomalous statement 'that the function of *verb* in a clause is performed by a *verb phrase* which consists of one or more verbs'.

2. The term *predicator* must not be confused with the traditional category of *predicate*, which includes predicator, complement(s) and adverbial(s) – all that part of a clause which is not the subject.

3. Similarly, a choice has to be made between the functional terms *adverbial* and *adjunct*, which are virtually interchangeable in grammatical description.

4. The functional term *complement* (*C*) is also used somewhat differently from traditional grammar. It is a superordinate term which includes *direct* and *indirect objects* (*Od, Oi*), and *intensive* and *adverbial complements* (*Ci, Ca*). These are explained below and again in chapter 9.

2.13   Word order

The importance of word order in a clause has already been mentioned. It is an essential part of the grammar of English, and is commonly illustrated by the difference of meaning between *Dog bites man* and *Man bites dog*. Another simple sentence† will demonstrate the way in which words and phrases change their form, function and sometimes meaning, if written in a different order:

NP & subject	*VP & predicator*	*NP & object*
The ducks	crowd	the stone
The crowd	stone	the ducks
The crowd	ducks	the stone

The words *ducks*, *crowd* and *stone* are either **nouns** or **verbs**, functioning as SUBJECT, OBJECT or PREDICATOR, according to their position in the clause. Other grammatical changes then have to take place, such as inflection with *-s* for a 3rd person singular present tense verb, and the addition of the **definite article** *the* as DETERMINER in a NP.

2.14 Summary

The clause states a single proposition, in which at least one participant is involved in a process. In an unmarked clause which makes a statement, the actor is the grammatical SUBJECT (S), the affected person or thing is the grammatical OBJECT (O) – strictly speaking the OBJECT COMPLEMENT, Co. The process is the grammatical PREDICATOR (P). Circumstances of time, place, manner and so on are represented in the ADVERBIAL (A), which is grammatically optional, unless the predicator is the kind that requires an adverbial as COMPLEMENT. If the predicator links an attribute to the subject, then the attribute is the INTENSIVE COMPLEMENT (Ci) of the clause.

meaning:	actor	process	affected/attribute	circumstance
grammar:	SUBJECT (S)	PREDICATOR (P)	COMPLEMENT (C)	ADVERBIAL (A)
			= OBJECT (O), or	
			= INTENSIVE COMPLEMENT (Ci), or	
			= ADVERBIAL COMPLEMENT (Ca)	

In fact, we seldom talk or write in a series or string of unmarked clauses or simple sentences. The texts in this chapter are unusual. We shall return to the clause in chapter 9, after taking a closer look at words and phrases.

Activity 2.7 _____

The following text was written for learners of English, and most of its sentences are simple, and most of its clauses unmarked in the order of their constituents. So it is a useful text at this stage of our exploration of the grammar. Write out the text clause by clause in columns,

Subject Predicator Complement Adverbial

assigning the words or phrases to their proper function in the clause. Note any clauses which cause problems. (You are sure to find some problems, because even though it is a simple text, it contains features of the grammar of English which have not been described yet.)

---

† I am indebted to Tony Fairman, who 'dreamed up' the sentence.

Daily Telegraph News Magazine, no. 2, 1978–9

BRITAIN'S BIGGEST OILFIELD

(Simon Low went to the North Sea. He went to see Britain's biggest oilfield. He was very cold; but he wrote to News and Views.)

Britain's biggest oilfield is called Brent. It is a fantastic place. The oil platforms are enormous. They have to be strong, because the sea and wind are very strong indeed. I saw enormous waves in the sea. Some of the waves were 100 feet high. And the wind was very strong. I nearly fell into the sea. The wind was also as cold as ice.

The oil platforms are in the sea. Men live and work on the platforms. They drill into the sea bed. The oil is in the sea bed, which is 450 feet below the platforms.

It's a difficult life.

The work is noisy and difficult. The men have to lift very heavy things. The men work all day for seven days. Then they go home for seven days. They live in the Shetland Islands. They come back to the platform by helicopter.

Oil is very important. Lots of things need oil. I say 'thank you' to the men who work at Brent.

3. Lexical words and meaning

3.1 Word-classes

Words can be grouped into two sets: (i) those that have meanings which refer to the world and our experience of it; and (ii) those whose job it is to link or hold together the structure that makes sentences from words, phrases and clauses. We call the first set **lexical words** (the subject of this chapter) and the second set **function words** (the subject of chapter 4). The two categories are not altogether separate, but this general distinction is a useful one.

The set of lexical words is continuously being changed, as words drop out of use and new ones are coined. It is therefore called an **open class** of tens of thousands of words. Function words, on the other hand, are much fewer in number, change much more slowly and so make up a small **closed class**.

Here is the opening paragraph of a story, printed firstly with only the open class lexical words, and secondly with only the closed class function words.

Activity 3.1

(i) Read both versions of the story. Does either version make any sense? Does one version make more sense than the other?

(ii) Do any of the function words have some lexical meaning, that is, have they some reference to our experience of the world?

(iii) Combine the two versions to reconstruct the original. (The words are arranged in the order in which they occur in the story.)

1

Michael marched off chapel sister, rapping Sunday shoes down pavement fetch brisk, stinging echo housewalls, wearing detestable blue blazer meaningless badge uniform loaded honours privilege. chapel sat erect, arms folded, curling down spine prawn sinking chin collar-bones steady pressure great hand, usual attitude worship. sang hymns prayers thought exultantly Top Wharf Pub, trying remember time places opened.

2

to beside his, his on to the to the off, the with its as a with and. In he , instead of on to his like a and his between his as under the of a , which was his of. He the and during the of, to what those.

(adapted from 'Sunday', in *Wodwo*, Ted Hughes, 1967)

Commentary on activity 3.1

It would not be difficult to re-create a text from the lexical words, even if we weren't able to be sure of discovering the exact original. Our rewritten texts would probably be very similar. It would be more difficult to write a text with the function words, and no two rewritten texts would be alike, because our choices of lexical words would vary widely. Nevertheless, we can see how necessary the function words are in 'articulating' the sentences. (The original text is printed at the end of the chapter.)

Both sets of words contain a number of different **word-classes**, according to the different jobs that words do in referring to experience, or in relating words, phrases and clauses. The same word can belong to more than one word-class. For example the word *off* appears in each set of words above, and its uses can be illustrated in:

1　Michael got on his bike and rode **off**.
2　He got **off** his bike and padlocked it.

In (1) *off* is an adverb (section 3.5). In (2) it is a preposition (section 4.1).

The traditional term for word-classes is *parts of speech*, and the names for most of them are also traditional. Attempts have been made to change the names, but most linguists stick to the old terms, which is why you need to learn and use them. You can then read or refer to other books on language, and understand the same terms.

3.2　Nouns

In the following extract, the opening of James Joyce's short story 'Eveline', nouns are printed in bold type:

Eveline 1
She sat at the **window** watching the **evening** invade the **avenue**. Her **head** was leaned against the **window curtains**, and in her **nostrils** was the **odour** of dusty **cretonne**.

Nouns have been called *'naming' words*. This definition is based upon meaning (a **semantic** definition) and says nothing about the jobs that nouns do in phrases and clauses – their function.

Activity 3.2

Look back to the texts and numbered sentences in chapter 2, and the nouns in some of the phrases which represented 'participants' or 'circumstances' — words like *milkman*, *road*, *pints*, *door's*, *dog*, *leg*, *shops*, *mum*, *street* and so on. Examine the phrases in which they occur, and see if you find any similarities between them and group them into sets. Some examples follow in alphabetical order.

a king's *son*	off the *shelf*
across the *road*	on a *bench*
cornflakes	some *sweets*
down the *windows*	the *basket*
frozen **peas**	the *milkman*
in an *armchair*	the *shopping*
in the *rain*	three *pints*
next door's *dog*	*tins*
no *playtime*	your *raincoat*

Activity 3.3

Without any further explanation at this stage, but using your discoveries as a guide, see if you can identify the nouns in the next extract

Eveline 2
Few people passed. The man out of the last house passed on his way home; she heard his footsteps clacking along the concrete pavement and afterwards crunching on the cinder path before the new red houses. One time there used to be a field there in which they used to play every evening with other people's children.

3.2.1   Number

3.2.1.1   SINGULAR AND PLURAL, COUNT NOUNS

In *Eveline 1*, the words *curtains* and *nostrils* have an *-s* suffix. It is a morpheme showing that the grammatical **number** of the noun is **plural**, indicating more than one. The grammatical number of the other nouns is **singular**, indicating a single one. Nouns like these that refer to people and things that can be counted are called **count nouns**.

Activity 3.4

The *-s* suffix is pronounced as either [s], [z] or [ɪz].
    Which pronunciation is used in the following plural nouns? Why is there a difference? Are there any other changes in the pronunciation of any of the nouns, when compared with the singular form?

asses	churches	hares	moths
badges	cocks	hens	paths
boxes	colleges	horses	rabbits
calves	dishes	houses	skies
cats	dogs	knives	wolves
chicks	ewes	lambs	youths

3.2.1.2 MASS (NON-COUNT) NOUNS

Some nouns do not change their number, and are either always singular, or always plural. Those that are always singular are **mass nouns** like *tea* or *homework* in:

> Would you like some **tea** with your meal?

> We have to do this for **homework**.

Mass nouns are sometimes referred to as **non-count nouns**. Notice that *tea*, in a different sense, can be a count noun,

> I've bought a couple of different **teas** to try out, some Darjeeling and some Assam.

The words *Darjeeling* and *Assam* are **proper nouns**, and so must be non-count, because proper nouns are names of one specific person, place or thing. You will have already learned to write them with a capital letter. All other nouns are **common nouns**.

The distinctions between singular and plural, count and non-count, are grammatical, but also relate to meaning to some extent. Generally, we think of a non-count or mass noun as 'bounded'. A large cake, as in,

> Have **a piece of** my birthday cake.

or

> Have **some of this** cake.

is thought of as a complete whole, and so the word *cake* is used as a mass noun, and the word *piece* is a count noun. But small cakes are not thought of in this way, and we would say,

> Have **one of these** cakes.

or

> Have **a** cake.

3.2.1.3 CONCRETE AND ABSTRACT NOUNS

A further distinction between kinds of noun is entirely determined by meaning. It is the distinction presented at the beginning of Chapter 2 between the **concrete**, or material in a physical sense, and the **abstract**, or immaterial. It affects the grammar because concrete nouns tend to be count nouns, and abstract nouns tend to be mass nouns.

Activity 3.5

(i)   List the nouns in *Eveline 2* under the headings *singular* and *plural*.

(ii) What is the plural morpheme of the word *children*? Find out from a dictionary or a reference grammar book why it has this form, and why in some English dialects it is *childer*.

(iii) Find and list other irregular plurals in English (nouns whose plural is not formed by adding the suffix *-s*).

Activity 3.6

(i)   Examine the following list of nouns. For each one, make up one or more short sentences in which it is used firstly in the singular, and secondly in the plural (if possible). Note any changes of meaning that occur in addition (if any).

(ii) Classify each word as,

   (a) either a proper or common noun,
   (b) if common, either a count or mass noun, and
   (c) either concrete or abstract.

(iii) If a noun can be used in more than one way (like *cake*), then write a sentence for each use.

(iv) Make a note of any singular nouns that are **invariable** and cannot normally be used in the plural, and of any invariable plural nouns that have no singular.

aluminum	England	oath	shorts
butter	friend	pain	stadium
cattle	headquarters	paper	tooth
criterion	hoof	path	troop
deer	justice	police	Tuesday
dregs	music	secretary	Wales
Dublin	news	sheep	woman

Nouns operate in **noun phrases** (NPs), and the forms and functions of NPs are described in more detail in chapters 6 and 7.

3.2.1.4   IRREGULAR PLURALS

Most plural nouns in English are marked with the suffix *-s*. This is the **regular** form. There is a small number of other, mostly very familiar, **irregular** plurals, which have kept their form from Old English, such as *mouse/mice, louse/lice, foot/ feet, goose/geese, tooth/teeth, woman/women, man/men*. In these nouns, plural is marked by a **change of vowel**.

-ves *plurals*

Some words that end in *-f* form plurals in which the *-f* and the following *-s* suffix are pronounced [vz], spelt *-ves*, as in *knife/knives, loaf/loaves, wolf/wolves, life/lives*, and so on. This does not apply, however, to *belief, cliff, chief* and a few others.

zero plural

Another small group has what linguists call **zero plural** – they remain unchanged when used as plurals – for example *cod, deer, sheep, grouse, salmon, cattle* and *music*. A few others are used with both regular and zero plurals, such as *duck, fish, herring, shrimp*.

There is a very common zero plural, used with **nouns of measurement** which follow numerals or determiners expressing quantity. Examples recorded in the late 1970s are:

From about five **year** old till I started work we lived in dire poverty.

(*Northumberland*)

He kept coming down for about three **month**.   (*North Shields*)

Girls and boys used to have to walk about a couple or three **mile**.   (*Sussex*)

His father worked for a farmer and he'd six **shilling** a week.   (*West Yorks*)

The origin of this zero plural is probably from OE. Here are the same phrases of measurement in their alternative present-day forms and OE.

(i)	*(ii)*	*OE*	*literal translation*
five years	five year	fif geara	five of-years
three months	three month	þreo monþa	three of-months
three miles	three mile	þreo mila	three of-miles
six shillings	six shilling	syx scillinga	six of-shillings

The nouns in these OE phrases of measurement were inflected with the possessive suffix *-a*. The suffix was reduced in pronunciation, firstly from [a] to [ə], and in time it was not pronounced at all. This evidence suggests that forms like *two pound* come directly from OE, while the form *two pounds* has acquired its *-s* suffix by **analogy** from the regular plural nouns.

-en plurals

Old English had several kinds of plural markers, including the suffix *-an*, once very common, but now surviving only in its reduced form [ən] in *children*, *oxen* and *brethren*, a plural of *brother* now reserved only for monks and members of religious orders.

A few other surviving *-en* plurals have been observed in rural dialects – *een* (*eyes*), *shoon* (*shoes*), and some double plurals like *mens* and *mices*.

child/childer/children

The form *children* is actually a **double plural**. The OE *cild* was *cildru* in the plural. This became *childre*, then *childer* in Middle English. Then the other *-en* plural suffix was added to *childer* in some dialects, making *childeren*, then *children*, which is the StE form. The older original plural of *child* still survives, however:

He's kept your **childer** for so many year.   (*Lancashire*)

3.2.2   Possessive case

In Old English, nouns had a variety of suffixes, or **inflections**, according to their function in a clause or phrase, whether they were the subject or the object of a verb, or the complements of prepositions. These different functions were marked by a grammatical category traditionally called **case**. For example, the OE word *stan* (MnE *stone*) shows three of its possible inflections in these short quotations (with word-for-word translations below):

> berað ða gyrda to wuda and þa **stanas** to sæstrande.
> *bear those rods to (the) woods and the **stones** to (the) seashore*

stanas is plural in number and in the objective case because it is the grammatical object of the verb *berað*.

> curfon hie ðæt of beorhtan **stane**
> *carved they it (out) of bright **stone***

stane is singular and in the dative case because it follows the preposition *of*.

> oþ þæt he færinga fyrgenbeamas
> *until he suddenly mountain-trees*

> ofer harne **stan** hleonian funde
> *over (a) grey **stone** lean found*

stan is singular and in the objective case following the preposition *ofer* (over), with a zero suffix.

But MnE has lost all the inflections on nouns except for **plural number** *-s* and to mark **possession** *-'s*, *-s'*, as in *Jane's, John's, the driver's, all the women's, the dogs'*. These nouns are said to be in the **possessive case**. It is only the pronouns which still change according to objective case as well as possessive (section 4.2.5).

3.3   Verbs

In the next extract from *Eveline*, the verbs are in bold type:

Eveline 3
Then a man from Belfast **bought** the field and **built** houses on it – not like their little brown houses, but bright brick houses with shining roofs. The children of the avenue **used to play** together in that field – the Devines, the Waters, the Dunns, little Keogh the cripple, she and her brothers and sisters. Ernest, however, never **played**; he **was** too grown up. Her father **used** often **to hunt** them in out of the field with his blackthorn stick; but usually little Keogh **used to keep** nix and **call** out when he **saw** her father **coming**.

Verbs are popularly referred to as 'doing' words, another semantic term which is a rough guide to the general meaning. They represent the *process* in meaning, and function as the grammatical *predicator* in clauses.

3.3.1 Tense – past and present

In *Eveline 3*, the verb *played* has the morpheme *-ed* as a suffix to the verb *play*, and *built* has a final syllable *-t* instead of the *-d* of *build*. The verb *bought*, [bɔt], comes from *buy*, [baɪ], and has a different vowel [ɔ] and an additional final consonant [t]. The relationship between the pairs of verbs *played/play*, *built/build* and *bought/buy* is that of **past tense** form to **present tense** form.

The present tense verb form is either the unmarked **base form** of the verb – *play*, *build*, *buy* and so on – or the base form with an *-s* suffix – *plays*, *builds*, *buys* – (see the end of section 3.3.2 following). Most verbs, but not all, are marked for the past tense form, but marked in different ways – *played*, *built*, *bought* and so on. The most common, and so **regular**, past tense form of verbs in English is marked by the morpheme suffix spelt *-ed*, pronounced either [d], [t] or [ɪd].

(NB: The verb *used to* in *Eveline 3* has a special function, and is called a **modal auxiliary verb** and is described in section 8.5.)

Activity 3.7

(i) Write down the present and past tenses of the following regular verbs, using *they* as their subject (e.g. *they applied*).

(ii) State the rule which determines how you pronounce the past tense *-ed* morpheme, [d], [t] or [ɪd].

consent	hand	match	wait
fill	look	treat	weigh
forge	marry	try	work

There are about 250 verbs with an **irregular** past tense form. They are mostly very common ones, and many of them show dialectal variations.

Activity 3.8

(i) Write down the StE present and past tense forms of the following verbs, using *you* as their subject, e.g. *you come / you came*. You may find that some verbs have alternative past tense forms.

(ii) Write down any local dialectal variations that you know.

(iii) Arrange the verbs in sets corresponding to their similarities in forming the past tense.

NB: The present and past tense forms of a verb (sometimes called *simple present* and *simple past*) consist of one word only, e.g. *you write/wrote*, *blush/blushed*.

bite	drink	hang	make	sew	speed
bring	eat	hear	mow	shine	spin
build	feed	hit	read	show	spread
buy	feel	hold	rise	shut	sting
come	find	know	run	sit	teach
cut	forget	lean	say	sleep	tear
do	get	learn	sell	sow	think
dream	go	lose	send	speak	win

3.3.2   Finite (tensed) verbs

The present and past tense forms of verbs in English are the only **tensed** forms. The traditional term is **finite** (meaning *limited, not infinite*). *Present* and *past*, when used as grammatical terms for **tense**, do not always refer to present and past **time**. (The relationship between tense and time is discussed in more detail in section 6.5.1.) For example, in the sentence:

They **go** to the Lake District every summer.

the verb *go* is present tense, but it refers to a habitual action which will go on in the future, and has gone on in the past, and need not be happening in the present.

You would enjoy it if you **went** to the Lake District next summer.

The verb *went* is past tense, but refers to a possible future event. Notice also that you cannot refer to the future simply by altering the form of a verb, adding a suffix or changing the vowel. There is no 'future tense' form. You must use additional **auxiliary verbs**:

We **are going to visit** the Lake District next summer.

We **shall stay** with friends on holiday.

Activity 3.9

(i)   Identify the verbs which are in the simple past tense in the next extract.

(ii)   Group the remaining verbs into sets according to their form or meaning.

Eveline 4
Still they **seemed to have been** rather happy then. Her father **was** not so bad then; and besides, her mother **was** alive. That **was** a long time ago; she and her brothers and sisters **were** all **grown** up; her mother **was** dead. Tizzie Dunn **was** dead, too, and the Waters **had gone** back to England. Everything **changes**. Now she **was going to go** away like the others, **to leave** her home. Home! She **looked** round the room, **reviewing** all its familar objects which she **had dusted** once a week for so many years, **wondering** where on earth all the dust **came** from.

In the simple sentence *Everything changes* there is the only example of a present tense verb in the text. It has an -*s* suffix, which marks the present tense verb whose grammatical subject is **3rd person singular** (section 4.2.3 on pronouns). **1st person**

singular (*I*), **2nd person singular** (*you*) and all **plural** subjects, whether 1st, 2nd or 3rd person, (*we, you, they* and plural nouns), are followed by the unmarked **base form** of the verb in the present tense:

> *I* change, *we* change, *you* change, *they* change, *circumstances* change, *times* change, *She* changes, *he* changes, *it* changes, *the weather* changes, *everything* changes, *nothing* changes and so on.

3.3.3 *Infinitive and participles; nonfinite (nontensed) verbs*

In extracts 1–4 from *Eveline*, you will find the following verbs, which are neither present nor past tense:

Set (a)	(to) be	(to) play	(to) hunt	(to) keep	(to) have	(to) go	(to) leave
						(away)	
Set (b)	invade						
Set (c)	watching	clacking	crunching	shining	coming	going	reviewing	wondering
Set (d)	leaned	tired	been	grown (up)	gone (back)	dusted		

3.3.3.1 THE *to*-INFINITIVE
In set (a) the **particle** to precedes the base form of each verb to form an **infinitive phrase**. This form is called the *to-infinitive*.

3.3.3.2 THE BARE INFINITIVE
Set (b) is a single example of the infinitive without *to*, called the *bare infinitive*. Compare:

I saw them **come**.	I wanted them **to come.**
We watched the team **win**.	We urged the team **to win**.
She let it **go**.	She allowed it **to go**.

Notice that the use of *to* depends upon the preceding verbs *wanted*, *urged* and *allowed*.

3.3.3.3 THE *-ing* OR PRESENT PARTICIPLE
In set (c), all the verbs have the suffix *-ing*. This is one of two forms of the verb called **participles** – the *-ing* participle – and is quite regular in its form. It is traditionally called the **present participle**, though this is a misleading term because the *-ing* participle is not 'tensed', that is, the word *present* in the term *present participle* does not refer to the grammatical category tense, but to present *time*.

3.3.3.4 THE *-en/-ed* OR PAST PARTICIPLE
Set (d) contains verbs which have the suffix *-en* or *-ed*, traditionally called the **past participle**. Like the past tense, the forms of the past participle are varied. The form in regular verbs is the same as the past tense – an *-ed* suffix – as in *leaned*, *tired*, *dusted*. In irregular verbs the past participle can either be *-ed*, or *-en* (sometimes reduced to [n] as in *been*, *grown* and *gone*), or the vowel of the verb can change, as in *sing/sang/sung*. The word *past* in *past participle*, like *present* in *present participle*, does not mark grammatical tense, but refers to time.

The infinitive and the participles are called **nonfinite** forms in contrast to the **finite** present and past tense forms. In terms of meaning, the infinitive tends to refer to something about to happen (future time), the *-ing* participle to something currently going on (present time), and the *-en/-ed* participle to something that has happened (past time). These references to time are in relation to the time of the utterance.

3.3.4   Forms of verbs in StE

3.3.4.1   THE VERB *be*
The most common, and the most irregular verb in English and the only one with eight forms, is *be*. The distribution of these forms in StE is:

1	base form/infinitive			*be*
2	present tense	1st person singular	*I*	*am*
3		3rd person singular	*he/she/it*	*is*
4		2nd person singular and plural	*you*	*are*
5	past tense	1st & 3rd person singular	*I/he/she/it*	*was*
6		2nd person singular and all plurals	*you/we/they*	*were*
7	*-ing* (present) participle			*being*
8	*-en/-ed* participle			*been*

3.3.4.2   FORMS OF REGULAR VERBS
Regular verbs have only four forms:

1	base	present tense and infinitive	*I/you/we/they*	**pass, (to) pass**
2	*-s*	3rd person singular, present tense	*he/she/it*	**passes**
3	*-ing*	*-ing* participle		**passing**
4-	*-ed*	past tense and *-en/-ed* participle		**passed**

3.3.4.3   FORMS OF IRREGULAR VERBS
Irregular verbs can have as few as three forms:

1	base	present tense and infinitive, past tense and *-en/-ed* participle	*I/you/we/they*	**put, (to) put**
2	*-s*	3rd person singular, present tense	*he/she/it*	**puts**
3	*-ing*	*-ing* participle		**putting**

or four:

1	base	present tense and infinitive	*I/you/we/they*	**wring, (to) wring**
2	*-s*	3rd person singular, present tense	*he/she/it*	**wrings**
3	*-ing*	*-ing* participle		**wringing**
4		past tense and *-en/-ed* participle		**wrung**

or five, in which case the past tense form is different from the *-en/-ed* participle:

1	base	present tense and infinitive	*I/you/we/they*	**forsake, (to) forsake**
2	*-s*	3rd person singular, present tense	*he/she/it*	**forsakes**
3	*-ing*	*-ing* participle		**forsaking**
4		past tense		**forsook**
5		*-en/-ed participle*		**forsaken**

Activity 3.10

(i) Write out the StE forms of the following verbs under five column heads:

   (I) base   (2) -s   (3) past tense   (4) -ing   (5) -en/-ed participle

(ii) Say whether the verb is regular or irregular. If irregular, how many different forms does it have?

achieve	fall	lie	squeeze
associate	forget	prevent	stand
beat	hide	shake	swim
choose	include	sleep	talk
consider	lay	sow	write

3.3.5   *Forms of verbs in regional dialects*

3.3.5.1   PRESENT TENSE

In StE the 3rd person singular verb in the present tense has the suffix -*s*, e.g. *It makes me laugh*. Some dialects have made the present tense regular by dropping the -*s* suffix – a common process over time called **regularisation**. Here are some recent recorded examples:

> I like the *Beano*, it's good and **make** me laugh... Minnie the Minx is a girl, she **look** like a boy and she **do** the things like a boy – she **do** all these mad things.... My Mum **read** it as well.   (*Norwich*)

> Never let your left hand know what your right hand **do**.   (*Sussex*)

> She **don't** go to work, she **don't** get paid.   (*London*)

The alternative way of regularising the present tense is to apply the -*s* suffix to all the verbs:

> I **likes** playing defender more than anything else   (*Plymouth*)

> You **knows** where East Mill is, don't 'ee   (*Devon*)

> I **says** to Art – he were levelling the box up – and I **says** 'Come on Art, we're firing'.   (*Derbyshire*)

> They **wants** to know where my glasses **is**, and I **tells** them I don't need glasses.
> (*Cornwall*)

> I **goes** down and I **gets** the soldier by the neck...   (*Belfast*)

> Well then yous **knows** as much about him as I do.   (*Belfast*)

3.3.5.2   PAST TENSE AND -*en/-ed* PARTICIPLE

The distribution of regular and irregular verb forms in StE is not based on any principle. They happen to be the forms which were used in the regional dialect from which StE has largely derived. Different choices were made in other dialects of English, some of which are illustrated here.

Come for StE past tense *came* is very widespread:

> 'Course we didn't get the snow until us **come** back. *(Devon)*

> I was playing pool in the pub when this fellow **come** up and **says**, 'I think you'd make a good actress'. *(North Shields)*

> They've been in the business ever since they **come** to Belfast. *(Belfast)*

> I **come** up into the main gate to guard the shot... *(Derbyshire)*

> Last year when I **come** here there wasn't many jobs about then. *(London)*

Other examples of alternative forms of irregular verbs are:

past tense
He **swum** across the river *(West Lancs)*

> Father took over the business then and he **done** most things and repairs and all the rest of it, but he never **done** anything big. *(Norfolk)*

> They **sung** a song that goes back to Saxon days... *(Sussex)*

-en/-ed *participle*
Its no good **sat** about in there...(-en/-ed *participle used, compare StE* sitting) *(York)*

> Well, I was **give** away at three days old. I was a twin. My grandfather and grandmother brought me up. *(Sussex)*

Some verbs which are irregular in StE have been regularised with the *-ed* inflection:

past tense
We wanted the bread just before we **drawed** the voucher, but he wouldn't leave us the bread. *(Lancs)*

-en/-ed *participle*
and I was **blowed** right up there. *(Devon)*

> It's been badly **swolled** all week you know. *(Liverpool)*

> I mean, when you're going to be **throwed** out of your house...
> *(Leicestershire)*

The *-en/-ed* participle of *got* was formerly *gotten*, a form which has been retained in Standard American English, but is no longer StE in Britain. It is still heard in some dialects, however:

> They've **gotten** up to nearly eleven thousand pounds... *(Staffs)*

It is also common to hear the past perfect of *got* – *I have got / I've got* in StE – reduced to a single verb,

> They'll rush over at one o'clock and I **got** a queue there. *(London)*

though it could be argued that the **elision** of [v] is a feature of pronunciation – [aɪɡɒt] from [aɪvɡɒt] – rather than a change in the grammar involving the **deletion** of the reduced form of *have in I've got*.

3.3.5.3   THE VERB *be* IN THE DIALECTS

We saw in section 3.3.4 that the verb *be* is the most irregular verb, having eight different forms, *be, am, is, are, was, were, being, been*. It is not surprising, therefore, that the forms of *be* are among the most obvious markers of difference between the dialects.

present tense, **is** *with plural subject*
They wants to know where my glasses **is**...   (*Cornwall*)

If you go into the field where the youth clubs **is** it's gangs of children down there.   (*Plymouth*)

The bigger boats **is** getting away but a small boat like this hasn't got much chance.   (*North Shields*)

present tense, **am** *regularised*
The hedges used to be high. Now they**'m** all clipped down short.... I don't think they**'m** geared up to it myself.   (*Devon*)

I said to the ferryman, 'How about that for good timing?' And the ferryman said, 'You**'m** lucky – we**'m** late.'   (*Devon*)

was *regularised*
The roundabouts **was** there and all the lot, you know.   (*London*)

Where I lived, the streets **was** rough compared they are today.

(*Birmingham*)

Some on them **was** selling a few flowers.   (*Leicestershire*)

When I came back in 1947 from the army collieries **was** going full steam ahead...and the streets **was** always full of people.   (*Northumberland*)

were *regularised*
There **were** a district called Old Kilburn...   (*Derbyshire*)

A good boss was a good boss. He **were** paying for the stuff that I **were** supposed to make perfect.   (*Lancashire*)

It **were** always such a struggle to get pumps...   (*Leeds*)

My father **were** born in 1849 across on yon hill. He **were** right delicate.   (*West Yorks*)

He's right, I **were** doing a lot of work.   (*Staffs*)

A *Survey of English Dialects* was carried out in the 1950s and 1960s, in which the following forms of the present tense, 1st person singular were recorded: *I am, I are, I be, I bin* and *I is*.

The corresponding negative forms of *I'm not* naturally derived from these, with a variety of pronunciations, which were written down as:

I am	*I are*	*I be*	*I bin*	*I is*
I'm not	I aren't	I bain't	I binno'	I isn't
I ammet	I're not	I baan't	I bisn't	I's not
I amment		I ben't		I in't
I amn'		I byen't		
I amno'		I byun't		
I'm none				
I ain't				
I yen't				
I en't				
I yun't				

3.3.5.4 A NOTE ON SOCIAL CLASS AND DIALECT

A Norwich boy was quoted in section 3.3.5:

> I like the *Beano*, its good and **make** me laugh... Minnie the Minx is a girl, she **look** like a boy and she **do** the things like a boy – she **do** all these mad things.... My Mum **read** it as well.

In his Norwich dialect there is no *-s* inflection on 3rd person singular verbs in the present tense. Research carried out in Norwich in the 1970s showed that there is a relationship between social class and the use of dialect. Whereas no upper-middle-class speakers failed to use StE forms like *makes*, *looks*, *does*, and so on, other social class speakers varied in the percentage of dialectal to StE forms they used:

Social class	% of verbs without *-s*	% of verbs with *-s*
Upper middle	0	100
Lower middle	29	71
Upper working	75	25
Middle working	81	19
Lower working	97	3

From Hughes and Trudgill, *English Accents and Dialects*, 1979.

3.4 Adjectives

3.4.1 *Adjectives as modifiers and complements*

In chapter 2, some propositions were said to contain 'attributes' (INTENSIVE COMPLEMENTS in the clause) referring back to the first participant (the subject of the clause).

In the following examples, the attributes are adjectives, functioning as INTENSIVE COMPLEMENTS in the clauses.

S	P	Ci
They	are	**hard** and **cold**.
My basket	is	very **heavy**.
The host	was	**astonished**.
The stick	looked	**short**.
The ogre	seemed	very **fierce**.

All these adjectives can also be used immediately before nouns, which they are then said to **modify**:

I picked up (some **hard**, **cold**, **frozen** peas).

I carried (the **heavy** basket).

(The **astonished** host) looked on.

The tailor wielded (a **short** stick).

(A **fierce** ogre) appeared.

These adjectives are being used as MODIFIERS within the bracketed noun phrases (see chapters 6 and 7).

Most adjectives can be used in both ways, either as MODIFIERS of nouns in noun phrases, or as INTENSIVE COMPLEMENTS in a clause. Not all, however, can do so, for example:

Our dog was always **afraid** when there was a storm.

*Our **afraid** dog didnt like storms.

The **principal** singer had a cold.

*The singer with the cold was **principal**

3.4.2   Adjectives and nouns as complements

We found in chapter 2 that both adjectives and nouns occur as attributes of participants, and so both can function as the grammatical INTENSIVE COMPLE-MENT in a clause. How then are they to be distinguished as word-classes?

The fact is that nouns perform other, quite different, grammatical functions. Nouns can form noun phrases (NPs) which function as SUBJECT or OBJECT in a clause; adjectives forming adjective phrases (AdjPs) cannot. They each have a different potential, but they overlap in their functions as COMPLEMENT. For example:

Marzi was *a young **soldier***.	(NP as INTENSIVE COMPLEMENT)
*The young **soldier*** was brave.	(NP as SUBJECT)
The king welcomed *the young **soldier***.	(NP as OBJECT)
Marzi the soldier was **young**.	(AdjP as INTENSIVE COMPLEMENT)
*****Young** was brave	(AdjP cannot be SUBJECT)
*The king welcomed **young**.	(AdjP cannot be OBJECT)

3.4.3 *Nouns as modifiers*

On the other hand, nouns have the potential of functioning as modifiers to other nouns in just the same way that adjectives do:

the **window** curtains   (noun as MODIFIER)
dusty cretonne   (adjective as MODIFIER)
concrete pavement   (noun as MODIFIER)
new red houses   (adjectives as MODIFIERS)

Activity 3.11

In the following sentences, the words in bold type are either adjectives or nouns functioning as modifiers or intensive complements.

(i)   Identify the adjectives and nouns.

(ii)   Distinguish modifiers from complements.

(a) Somewhere a **ponderous tower** clock slowly dropped a dozen strokes into the gloom.
(b) **Storm** clouds rode low along the horizon.
(c) Only a **melancholy** chorus of frogs broke the soundlessness.
(d) Then a **strange** figure appeared out of the **nocturnal** somnolence.
(e) The newcomer was a **seafaring** man, and at the sight of him the taverners were **silent**.
(f) There was a **green** parrot on the mans shoulder, and a **tarred** pigtail hung down his back.
(g) His voice when he spoke was as **deep** as a gong in a tomb.
(h) A **lean, silent** man at a **shadowy** table in a corner, wearing a **black** cape and **black** gloves, beckoned to the newcomer.

         (text adapted from *The Wonderful O*, James Thurber, 1951)

Activity 3.12

Repeat the activity with the following sentences. Identify the adjectives and nouns functioning as modifiers or intensive complements.

(a) The weather was fair, and the voyage was long.
(b) The ship could not be seen from shore, even by the sharpest eye and the strongest glass.
(c) Down the marble stairs the Princess floated like a cloud.
(d) Black and Littlejack went ashore, followed by their surly and sinewy crew.
(e) The black room was bright with flaming torches.
(f) The threatening trees had disappeared except for one, all that was left of a stricken oak.
(g) A stream of lantern light flowed slowly up the hill.

3.4.4 Participles as adjectives

Notice the word-class which the modifiers in these phrases belong to:

shining roofs   the **astonished** host   **frozen** peas

They have the suffixes *-ing*, *-ed* and *-en*, which belong to participles of the verbs *shine*, *astonish* and *freeze*. But other forms of verb cannot usually function as MODIFIERS to nouns in this way,

*****shine** roofs   *the **astonish** host   *****freeze** peas

though you may know the term *freeze frame* from the terminology of film and video, which shows how it is always possible to 'break the rules' of the language.

So there are two categories of word-class, noun and verb, which overlap with adjectives in their functions. Verb participles have the property of functioning like adjectives, to the extent that many eventually are regarded as adjectives, and listed in dictionaries as such:

That was an **exciting** match.

I felt most **offended** at what he said.

Some which look like participles may have no corresponding verbs:

Some of my friends are very **talented**.

There is no verb *****to talent**. This can lead to problems in analysis. If we can call verb participles adjectives when they function like adjectives, should we then call noun modifiers, like **cinder** in **cinder path**, adjectives also?

The fact is that there is no one right answer to questions like this. It is important that you recognise the problem and discuss possible answers, however.

The following text is an extract from Laurie Lee's *Cider with Rosie* (1959), telling of his experiences as a three-year-old child. The modifiers and intensive complements are printed in bold type. Some writers can be recognised by their style, and the way they **foreground** features of the language, and create new forms. Laurie Lee has here made up some of the adjectives.

Radiating from that house, with its **crumbling** walls, its thumps and shadows, its **fancied** foxes under the floor, I moved along paths that lengthened inch by inch with my **mounting** strength of days. From stone to stone in the **trackless** yard I sent forth my **acorn** shell of senses, moving through **unfathomable** oceans like a **South Sea** savage island-hopping across the Pacific. Antennae of eyes and nose and **grubbing** fingers captured a **new** tuft of grass, a fern, a slug, the skull of a bird, a grotto of **bright** snails. Through the **long summer** ages of those **first few** days I enlarged my world and mapped it in my mind, its **secure** havens, its **dust-deserts** and puddles, its peaks of dirt and **flag-flying** bushes. Returning too, **dry-throated**, over and over again, to its **several well-prodded** horrors: the bird's gaping bones in its cage of **old** sticks; the **black** flies in the corner, **slimy dead**; **dry** rags of snakes; and the **crowded**, **rotting**, **silent-roaring** city of a cat's **grub-captured** carcass.

Modifiers

adjectives	-ing participles	-en/-ed participles	nouns
trackless	crumbling	fancied	acorn
unfathomable	mounting	dry-throated	South Sea
new	grubbing	well-prodded	summer
bright	flag-flying	crowded	dust
long	rotting	grub-captured	
first	silent-roaring		
few			
secure			
several			
old			
black			
slimy			
dead			
dry			

All the adjectives except *slimy dead* and *dry-throated* are MODIFIERS of nouns. Some of them are derived from verb participles, either singly, *crumbling, mounting, grubbing, gaping, rotting, fancied,* or made into **compound** words, derived from clauses:

compound modifier	clause
flag-flying bushes	the bushes were *flying flags*
silent-roaring city	the city was *roaring silently*
dry-throated	my *throat* was *dry*
well-prodded horrors	I *prodded* the horrors *well*
grub-captured carcass	*grubs* had *captured* the carcass

The other modifiers are adjectives not derived from verbs: *trackless, unfathomable, new, bright, long, first, few, secure, several, old, black, dry.*

As we have already discovered, some of the modifiers are nouns:

acorn shell   **South Sea** savage   **summer** ages   **dust**-deserts

Remember that the word *modifier* describes the **function** of the word (what it does); the word *noun* describes the **form-class** of the word (what it is). This is an important distinction when describing language, already referred to in chapter 2.

To sum up, the grammatical functions of adjectives are to modify nouns in noun phrases, or to act as intensive complements in clauses. Their semantic function is to specify attributes of the participants.

3.4.5 Comparative and superlative

Most adjectives are **gradable** in terms of **degree**, and used for purposes of comparison. For example, the adjective *curious* in:

'What a **curious** feeling!' said Alice, 'I must be shutting up like a telescope!'

appears a little later on in *Alice in Wonderland* in this form:

> '**Curiouser** and **curiouser!**' cried Alice (she was so much surprised, that for the moment she quite forgot how to speak good English). 'Now I'm opening out like the largest telescope that ever was!'

The adjective *curious* forms the first step in a series, or scale, but the *-er* suffix forming Alice's *curiouser* is not StE – not 'good English' in Lewis Carroll's terms. The suffix is quite acceptable however in,

> 'It was much **pleasanter** at home,' thought poor Alice, 'when one wasn't growing **larger** and **smaller**, and being ordered about by mice and rabbits.'

The adjectives *curious*, *pleasant*, *large* and *small* are the **positive** forms, or base forms, and the *-er* suffix forms the **comparative degree**, but not on *curious*, and many other adjectives. To speak proper StE, Alice should have said:

> '**More** and **more** curious!'

and, to take a further step in the series, the **superlative** degree:

> '**Most** curious!'

and not **curiousest*, though *pleasantest*, *largest* and *smallest* are acceptable, taking an *-est* suffix. Notice also that *more pleasant* and *most pleasant* are equally acceptable, but *more/most large* or *more/most small* are less likely to be used.

So there are two ways of forming the comparative and superlative degrees of comparison of adjectives, by using *-er* and *-est* as morpheme suffixes, or *more* and *most* as pre-modifying words.

Activity 3.13

(i) Divide the following adjectives into three sets:

    (a) those that can be inflected only with *-er* and *-est* to form the comparative and superlative degrees;

    (b) those that must use *more* and *most*; and

    (c) those to which either method can normally apply.

    (d) Discuss any problems that occur.

(ii) List any changes of spelling which you have to make.

(iii) List any irregular comparatives and superlatives.

(iv) Can you state any rules for choosing which form of the comparative and superlative to use? (There may be exceptions to the rules you discover.)

Use a reference grammar to help you.

bad	different	hot	pretty	sweet
beautiful	dry	ill	right	unfortunate
big	early	little	serious	valuable

brave	fascinating	lucky	simple	visible
clever	good	narrow	small	well
controversial	happy	patient	solemn	wrong

3.4.5.1 NONSTANDARD DOUBLE COMPARATIVES AND SUPERLATIVES

Double comparatives and superlatives have *more* and *most* together with *-er* and *-est* suffixes, or else one suffix added to another. They are found in Shakespeare's *Julius Caesar*:

This was the **most vnkindest** cut of all ...

but Shakespeare's example has not been followed in the later establishment of StE. They are still to be found in dialectal speech, however,

There were never a **betterer** mental arithmetic reckoner than my father. *(West Yorks)*

If a woman let the New Year in it was the **worsest** of bad luck. *(Sussex)*

3.4.5.2 *TALLER THAN I?* OR *TALLER THAN ME?*

The 'correct' choice between *She is taller than I* and *She is taller than me* has been the subject of argument by prescriptive grammarians, who have argued that the clause is a shortened version of *She is taller than I am*, and so should be *She is taller than I*. In this construction, *than* is functioning as a conjunction between the two clauses *She is taller* and *I am* (*tall*).

But *She is taller than me* has been common usage for a long time, and there is evidence that it is being used more and more by StE speakers. In this construction, *than* is functioning as a preposition, and is therefore followed by a pronoun in the objective case (section 4.2.5) – *me, you, him, her, it, us, them,* as in *Give it to **me**, Put this blanket **over** him* and so on.

3.5 Adverbs

The fourth category of lexical words is the **adverb**. Like adjectives, adverbs are 'modifying' words.

3.5.1 The functions of adverbs

If the main grammatical function of adjectives is to modify nouns, the word *adverb* would suggest that the function of adverbs was to modify verbs. It is, but *adverb* is also used for words which modify adjectives, other adverbs and whole sentences. Instead of labelling four or more separate word-classes, the traditional term *adverb* labels a single class, so we then identify four or more *sub-classes* of adverb. The examples of different kinds of adverbs which follow are taken from sentences from *Cider with Rosie*:

(a) adverbs modifying verbs

Adverbs as single heads of adverb phrases commonly function as the **adverbial** constituent in a clause, representing the *circumstances* of time, place, manner, and so on (section 2.11). The unmarked position is clause-final, that is, as the last constituent of a clause – SPOA:

                                            S

The old food-terraces still showed on the slopes, along which the cows

P   **A**

walked **sideways**.

     S **P**   **O A**

I felt this was overdoing it **rather**.

 S   **P**   **O**   **pt A**

They picked me up **bodily**, kicking and bawling.

                                SP (A) **P**   **A**

The Infant Room was packed with toys such as I 'd never seen **before**.

But adverbials are much more freely 'moveable' than other constituents, and may be placed in a number of positions in a clause, including immediately before the verb:

I felt this was **rather** overdoing it

The Infant Room was packed with toys such as I'd never **before** seen.

The sides of the valley were rich in pasture and the crests **heavily** covered in beech-woods.

I arrived at the school **fatly** wrapped in my scarves.

So I remained, the fat lord of my nursery life, **voluptuously** idling through the milky days.

But adverbs which are part of phrasal verbs consisting of *verb + adverb particle* always follow the verb they modify, as in:

But my time was slowly running **out**.

The rabble closed **in**.

Set (a) are sometimes called **circumstance adverbs**.

(b) adverbs modifying adjectives

Adverbs modifying adjectives may function as **intensifiers**, either 'amplifying' the meaning:

Angry faces surrounded me, **very** *red*.

My brother Jack, who was with me in the Infants, was **too** *clever* to stay there long.

or scaling it down:

'A little **less** *beastly* now?' she would say.

I began to feel **vaguely** uneasy.

or otherwise adding some descriptive element:

My desk companions were two blonde girls, already **puppyishly** pretty.

Miss B, the Head Teacher, was about as **physically** soothing as a rake.

(c) adverbs modifying other adverbs

Adverbs modifying other adverbs function similarly to those which modify adjectives, as intensifiers:

The summons to the Big Room comes **almost** *always* as a complete surprise.

The place had decayed **even** *further*.

Sets (b) and (c) are **degree adverbs**, and modify adjectives and adverbs 'to a certain degree'. Such adjectives and adverbs are said to be **gradable**, because they can be modified to show grades (degrees) of size and quality.

(d) adverbs modifying sentences or clauses

The fourth common function of adverbs is to modify, not one of the constituents of a clause, but the meaning of the whole clause:

Indeed, he was so bright he made us uncomfortable.

Otherwise he was free to come and go.

Young Tony came last, importing **moreover** a kind of outrageous cheekiness.

Set (d) illustrates **sentence adverbs**. They modify the whole clause or sentence and can express a speaker's attitude to or evaluation of what she or he is saying:

Frankly, I never saw such a mess in my life.

or act as a connecting link between sentences or clauses:

Besides, it was too early to start work.

Here is an example of the stylistic use of sentence adverbs from a press advertisement for a new car:

Incredibly, this reaction happens in just 4/100ths of a second.

Importantly, this system also makes Xantia a very safe car to drive.

Obviously a car this desirable is going to attract a lot of attention.

Particularly when you consider we've moved heaven and earth to build it.

We **certainly** didn't play safe when it came to the styling.

This is in contrast to the use of circumstance and degree adverbs in the same advertisement:

It's **pleasingly** distinctive with a series of elegant, yet dynamic lines.

. . . by reading the road and reacting **automatically** to the signal received.

You will also find Xantia **extremely competitively** priced.

(from Citroën advertisement, *Independent*, 22 May 1993)

Activity 3.14

The following list contains words which are commonly used as sentence adverbs.

(i)   Select some words and construct sentences in which they are used as sentence adverbs.

(ii)   Discuss the kind of comment which is implied in the meaning of each sentence adverb.

actually	confidentially	generally	officially	rightly	understandably
admittedly	curiously	happily	perhaps	seriously	undoubtedly
annoyingly	definitely	honestly	personally	strangely	unfortunately
apparently	essentially	ideally	plainly	superficially	unhappily
basically	evidently	indeed	possibly	supposedly	unluckily
bluntly	foolishly	luckily	preferably	surely	unquestionably
briefly	fortunately	maybe	presumably	surprisingly	wrongly
candidly	frankly	naturally	probably	technically	
certainly	fundamentally	nominally	really	theoretically	
clearly	funnily enough	obviously	reportedly	undeniably	

Comparative and superlative adverbs

Most adverbs, like adjectives, are gradable and form comparative and superlative forms with -*er* and -*est*, or *more* and *most* (section 3.4.5).

Activity 3.15

Classify the adverbs (in bold type) in the following sentences, taken from Lewis Carroll's *Alice in Wonderland*, as either (i) circumstance adverbs, (ii) degree adverbs or (iii) sentence adverbs.

You will find it useful to experiment by trying to move the adverbs to other positions in the sentences. Some are moveable, others are not, and this helps in classifying them.

(a)   It was the White Rabbit, trotting **slowly back again**, and looking **anxiously about** as it went.

(b)   She **very good-naturedly** began hunting **about** for them.

(c)   The great hall had vanished **completely**.

(d)   **Very soon** the Rabbit noticed Alice.

(e)   What are you doing **out here**?

(f)   Come **here directly**!

(g)   There was no label this time with the words DRINK ME but **nevertheless** she uncorked it.

(h)   I do hope it'll make me grow large **again**, for **really** I'm **quite** tired of being such a tiny little thing.

Activity 3.16

First identify the adverbs in the following list, and then classify them.

(a) It did so indeed, and much sooner than expected.
(b) As it is I can't get out at the door.
(c) She went on growing and growing, and very soon had to kneel down on the floor.
(d) She tried the effect of lying down.
(e) Still she went on growing.
(f) Luckily for Alice, the little magic bottle had now had its full effect and she grew no larger.
(g) There seemed to be no sort of chance of her ever getting out of the room again.
(h) Presently the Rabbit came up to the door.
(j) As the door opened inwards and Alice's elbow was pressed hard against it, that attempt proved a failure.

Activity 3.17

Identify the word-class of the lexical words in bold type in this extract from James Thurber's *The Wonderful O*, in which the people have been forbidden to use the letter (o) in their speech and writing.

'We **live** in **peril** and in **danger**,' **Andreus told** the **people**, 'and in a **little time** may have **left few things** that we can say. **Already** there is **little** we can **play**. I **have** a **piece** that I shall **read**. It **indicates** the **quandary** we're in.' And **then** he **read** it:
    They are **swing chas**. What is **slid**? What is **left** that's **slace**? We are **begne** and **webegne**. Life is **bring** and **brish**. **Even schling** is **flish**. **Animals** in the z are **less lacnic** than we. **Vices** are **filled** with **paths** and **scial intercurse** is **baths**. Let us **gird up** ur **lins** like **lins** and **rt** the **hrrr** and **ust** the **afs**.'
    'What nannibickering is this?' cried the blacksmith. 'What is this gibberish?'

3.5.2   The forms of adverbs

All the adverbs in the list following Activity 3.14 and many of the adverbs quoted in this section end with the suffix *-ly*, by which adverbs are created from adjectives – *certain/certainly, happy/happily, sure/surely*, and so on, and from *-en/-ed* and *-ing* participles – *admitted/admittedly, supposed/supposedly, surprising/surprisingly*.
    Another less common adverb-forming suffix is *-wards*. For example:

backwards	back (adverb)	seawards	sea (noun)
downwards	down (adverb)	heavenwards	heaven (noun)

But many adverbs have no marker in their structure by which they can be identified, including some of the most common – *almost, always, down, fast, perhaps, rather, then, too, very, yet*, and so on.
    (Adverbs form a complex part of the grammar of English, and this is not developed in detail here. In following up your studies in larger reference grammars, you may find circumstance adverbs described as **adjuncts**, and sentence

adverbs as either **disjuncts, subjuncts** or **conjuncts**, according to their function in a clause. Degree adverbs may be referred to as **modifiers**.)

3.5.3   *A note on* hopefully *as a sentence adverb*

Some people have proscribed the use of the adverb *hopefully* as a sentence adverb, used commonly to mean *I hope that* . . . , or *It is to be hoped that* . . . In a letter to a newspaper, it was referred to as 'an adverbial aberration', and the writer asserted that:

'Hopefully it is going to be a fine day' . . . is lamentable English.

All the adverbs in the list accompanying Activity 3.14 can begin a sentence, implying the speaker's opinion or attitude. For example:

Clearly, he spoke very distinctly   (= It is **clear** to me that . . .)

in addition to their other grammatical uses in modifying verbs, as in:

He spoke **clearly**.

As sentence adverbs they lie outside the meaning of the main part of the sentence.

The use of *hopefully* to mean *I hope that* as one of this relatively large set of sentence adverbs is therefore fully justified in terms of common usage. It represents the economical use of a single word for a clause. The only reason I can suggest for its proscription is that its use as a sentence adverb has been fairly recent. The first recorded occurrence in the 1991 edition of the *OED* is dated 1932, from the *New York Times Book Review*. If it did originate in the United States, then anti-American prejudice may be the reason for its unpopularity. It has been claimed that it was a literal translation into English from German by German-speaking immigrants to the United States. The *OED* entry does include a reference to the German *hoffentlich*:

OED **2nd edition 1991:**
hopefully
2. It is hoped (that); let us hope (cf. German *hoffentlich* it is to be hoped.) orig. US (Avoided by many writers.)

Finally, here is a comment from *A Comprehensive Grammar of the English Language* (1985, section 8.129, note [b], p. 627), on stylistic objections to *hopefully*:

Since the 'general view' in *hopefully* is usefully distinguished from the purely individual viewpoint in *I hope*, the disjunct has considerable convenience, as can be seen in the following textual example from an administrator's note put before a committee:

My assistant has arranged for the matter to be considered by an ad hoc working party, and ***hopefully*** a proposal will be ready in time for our next meeting. ***I hope*** this approach will be acceptable to members.

The two italicized parts are not identical in force and could not in fact be interchanged

There appears to be no convincing reason for not using *hopefully* as a sentence adverb.

3.5.4 *A note on 'splitting the infinitive' with an adverb*

It is claimed that a *to*-infinitive such as *to go* is indivisible, and may not be 'split' by inserting an adverb between *to* and *go*. The phrase *to quickly go* is therefore called a 'split infinitive'.

It is reckoned to be an error of *style*, and to be avoided. This is questionable. The structure *to go* is a **phrase**, and should therefore be referred to as an **infinitive phrase**. The verb *go* is an infinitive, and *to* is an infinitive particle. It is a defining property of a *word* that it may not be split, and of a *phrase* that it may.

We saw in section 3.3.3 that whether *to* marks the infinitive or not depends upon what precedes it, so although it is sometimes convenient to label verbs with *to* in order to distinguish them from nouns – e.g. *to fight/a fight*, *to deal/a deal* – it seems unjustified to regard the infinitive phrase *to fight* as 'indivisible'. The NP *a fight* is never thought of as indivisible.

The prescriptive rule that the infinitive *to + verb* should be an indivisible unit was probably established as a prescriptive rule of style by grammarians in the nineteenth century, Here is Henry Alford, Dean of Canterbury, writing in a book he published in 1864 called *The Queens English – Stray Notes on Speaking and Spelling*:

> A correspondent states as his own usage and defends, the insertion of an adverb between the sign of the infinitive mood and the verb. He gives as an instance, '*to scientifically illustrate*'. But surely this is a practice entirely unknown to English speakers and writers. It seems to me, that we ever regard the *to* of the infinitive as inseparable from its verb. And when we have a choice between two forms of expression, 'scientifically to illustrate', and 'to illustrate scientifically', there seems no good reason for flying in the face of common usage.

There is evidence in eighteenth-century literature that writers were in practice avoiding the 'split infinitive', but the placing of an adverb before an infinitive is in fact common in speech:

> In a Survey of English Usage text of circa 1980 involving four educated British adults (three women and one man) in a professional psychiatric discussion lasting three-quarters of an hour, there were nineteen 'split infinitives'.
> (*A Comprehensive Grammar of the English Language*, R. Quirk *et al.*, 1985)

We have seen that some adverbs can be moved to different positions in a clause, and for many this includes the position immediately before the main verb. For example:

> *S   P   Od   A*
> He implemented the programme **successfully**.

can equally well be written:

> *S   A   P   Od*
> He **successfully** implemented the programme.

If we apply this movement of an adverb from clause-final to pre-verb position to the following clause:

S P   P   Od   A
He tried to implement the programme **successfully**.

by placing *successfully* before the verb *implement*, we get:

S P   A   P   Od
He tried to **successfully** implement the programme.

which is what most people would normally say, but in writing it would be marked wrong if the marker accepted the 'split infinitive' thesis.

Nobody would question, I think, the acceptability of placing the adverb *effectively* in this quotation from a published letter:

Teachers are now faced with the prospect of seeing the work they have done **on effectively delivering** the programmes for study rendered irrelevant.

in which the preposition *on* and verb *delivering* in the phrase *on delivering* are split. However, if the writer had said:

Teachers are now faced with the prospect of seeing the work they had to do **to effectively deliver** the programmes for study rendered irrelevant.

he would have been guilty of 'splitting the infinitive'. There are two problems arising from this.

Firstly, 'not splitting the infinitive' has become an **emblem** of educated usage, and a **shibboleth** (section 1.3) for those of us who do split it. In a letter to a newspaper, a writer said that he had been 'forced to endure the following abominations on BBC TV':

to really mean / to totally deny / to comprehensively rebut...

He asked whether he was 'alone in resenting these assaults on the English language'. It is clear, therefore, that strong feelings are aroused when 'split infinitive' spotters get to work, and you must take this into account in your own writing.

The second problem is linguistic. Not 'splitting the infinitive' can lead to ambiguity of meaning, and unintentional ambiguity is, I believe, an example of bad English. Ambiguity may arise in the construction known as **predicators in phase** (section 8.1.7), if an adverb is placed between two main verbs which are linked together in one complex verb phrase. For example:

Promises to restrain taxes will prevent the revenue being **used seriously to reduce** the level of public spending

Is *the revenue being used seriously* (adverb in final position *SPA*) the intended meaning, or *being seriously reduced* (adverb preceding the verb *APOd*)? You have to guess at the more likely of the two meanings. The order of the words gives an ambiguous meaning

Activity 3.18

Discuss the meanings of the following sentences, all containing examples of the predicators in phase construction, in some of which writers are trying to avoid the 'split infinitive'. Identify the word in each sentence which is qualified by the adverb. Are any of the sentences ambiguous?

(a) Five years ago relatively few may have **wanted voluntarily to leave** agriculture...

(b) Alarms connected to his body had **failed mysteriously to alert** staff to his deterioration.

(c) For about 24 hours senior British ministers **seemed wholeheartedly to adopt** the tabloid style.

(d) In January 1994 the next phase begins, with ERM members **due simultaneously to start wrestling** with the economic convergence terms.

(e) Mr Smith is also **expected finally to silence** any further talk of traditional nationalisation.

(f) Mrs Thatcher **set out deliberately to dismantle** pillars of the old power structure.

(g) Lloyds **plans eventually to introduce** a new type of account for more prosperous customers.

(h) John Major was **forced yesterday angrily to denounce** allegations that British security forces are guilty of human rights abuses.

(i) The Government's new legal advice should not be **allowed artificially to foreclose** parliamentary discussion.

(j) The teaching of literature will be largely self-defeating unless it **helps young readers privately to discover** their own unique tastes and preferences.

(k) The Prime Minister is hardly **going meekly to overturn** his policy.

(l) The City will be **invited regularly to publish** their economic forecasts.

(m) John Major **failed publicly to dispute** Neil Kinnock's claim yesterday that Britain is now suffering the longest recession since the 1930s.

(n) In Florida, state legislators **are trying to introduce laws chemically to castrate** rapists.

3.6 Summary

Lexical words (nouns, verbs, adjectives and adverbs) are our means of referring to the participants in the actions we observe in the world. The four word-classes name people and things, both concrete and abstract (nouns), identify actional, mental and relational processes (verbs) or describe attributes (adjectives and adverbs).

Function words belonging to the other word-classes do not lack meaning entirely, but their primary purpose is grammatical, that is, to refer to, link, or mark other words, phrases and clauses within sentences. Lexical words refer to meanings; function words relate lexical words.

Here is the original text of Activity 3.1:

Michael marched off to church beside his sister, rapping his Sunday shoes down on to the pavement to fetch the brisk, stinging echo off housewalls, wearing the detestable blue blazer with its meaningless badge as a uniform loaded with honours and privilege. In chapel he sat erect, arms folded, instead of curling down on to his spine like a prawn and sinking his chin between his collar-bones as under the steady pressure of a great hand, which was his usual attitude of worship. He sang the hymns and during the prayers thought exultantly of Top Wharf Pub, trying to remember what time those places opened.

4. Function words

4.1 Prepositions

In section 3.1 of chapter 3, two sentences were given to illustrate the fact that words can belong to more than one word-class:

1   Michael got on his bike and rode **off**.

2   He got **off** his bike and padlocked it.

In (1), the word *off* is an adverb. Other adverbs showing direction or place could be substituted, such as *away, across, ahead, homewards, there, past*. But in (2), *off* is immediately followed by the noun phrase *his bike* to form a **constituent**, *off his bike*, of the clause *He got off his bike*.

```
S    P    Ca
He   got  off his bike
```

When words like *off* form part of a phrase like *off his bike*, they are said to belong to the word-class **preposition**. Prepositions can be **simple** (single words), or **complex** (more than one word). Examples of complex prepositions are: *out of, because of, instead of, in common with, by means of, on behalf of, with regard to, in spite of*. They are phrases which have become so common that they function as a **lexical unit**, like a simple preposition.

A preposition (p) is followed by a noun phrase (NP) to form a **prepositional phrase** (PrepP): p + NP = PrepP. The NP is the **complement** of the preposition in the PrepP – it *completes* the phrase. There is therefore a *relational* function between the preposition and its NP complement, which is why prepositions are called function words, even though a preposition also has meaning, like verbs, in its reference to place, direction, time, cause, purpose, manner, and so on.

If the same word can be either a preposition or an adverb, the class of the word can only be defined from its function in a particular sentence. If it has an NP complement, then it is a preposition, and forms a PrepP.

Activity 4.1

What meanings do the prepositions of the following bracketed PrepPs have? (cf. the 'Eveline' text in chapter 3). The prepositions are in bold type.

(a) (**at** the window)
(b) (**against** the window curtains)
(c) (**in** her nostrils)
(d) the odour (**of** dusty cretonne)
(e) (**out of** the last house)
(f) (**along** the concrete pavement)
(g) (**on** the cinder path)
(h) (**before** the new red houses)
(i) (**with** other people's children)
(j) a man (**from** Belfast)
(k) (**like** their little brown houses)
(l) bright brick houses (**with** shining roofs)

Activity 4.2

Bracket the PrepPs and identify the prepositions in the following phrases:

(a) round the room
(b) for so many years
(c) during all those years
(d) the name of the priest
(e) on the wall
(f) above the broken harmonium
(g) beside the coloured print
(h) a school friend of her father

Activity 4.3

Bracket the PrepPs and identify the prepositions in the following clauses:

(a) She had those whom she had known all her life about her.
(b) She had to work hard, both in the house and at business.
(c) What would they say of her in the Stores?
(d) Her place would be filled up by advertisement.
(e) But in her new home it would not be like that.
(f) People would treat her with respect then.
(g) She sometimes felt herself in danger of her father's violence.
(h) The invariable squabble for money on Saturday nights had begun to weary her unspeakably.

(from 'Eveline')

Activity 4.4

Identify the words in bold type as either adverbs or prepositions.

(a) The electricity was **off** yesterday.
(b) Chris fell **off** his bike.
(c) The shops put prices **up** at Christmas.
(d) Prices then come **down** in the January sales.
(e) Sarah came **down** the road with her friend.
(f) Money for famine relief keeps coming **in**.
(g) The teacher got angry and blew **up** the whole class.
(h) Alice blew **up** the tyres on her moped.
(i) Grandad put his pipe in his mouth and blew **up** the stem to clear it.
(j) Please call **round at** my house later.

Prepositions form a convenient link between open, lexical word-classes and the closed, grammatical word-classes. They have a considerable overlap with adverbs in meaning, but their function – relating with NPs to form PrepPs – is clearly different. They are classified as a closed class because the number of simple and complex prepositions is very small when compared with the thousands of nouns and verbs in English.

4.1.1 Prepositions in the regional dialects

StE and the dialects use prepositions in different ways, briefly described below with examples. (Whether or not the use of a particular preposition is standard, dialectal or both is debatable – you may sometimes disagree with the analysis of these examples.)

NB: Vocabulary, word-form and grammar are transcribed as spoken, so the quotations will contain nonstandard grammar.

(a) The same prepositions are used to express different meanings:

	StE	*source*
We was coming **up** the airport.	*to/up to*	(*W Midlands*)
She goes to church **of** a Sunday.	*on*	(*London*)
Some **on** them was selling a few flowers.	*of*	(*Leicestershire*)
There were big sheds **out** the back.	*in/at*	(*London*)
Us went up **round** Peterborough	*to*	(*Devon*)
But you see, that girl **over** the top road ...	*in*	(*Norwich*)
I worked **while** half past five of a night – half past six at morning till half past five **at** night	*until/till* *in (the)*	(*Blackburn*)
We've all got bikes, and **on** the night we have a ride round	*at*	(*Walsall*)
The water drips **out** the overflow	*out of*	(*Bristol*)

(b)   Different complex prepositions are used:

I took it **off of** thc stall.	*off*	(*London*)
Her's **up to** Brent	*in/at*	(*Devon*)

(c)   *Till/intill* are used instead of *to/into*. *Till* is also used instead of the infinitive marker *to*. The quotations were recorded in Belfast. (For a further comment on *for to* and *for till*, section 11.1.7.)

Belfast was the centre for all railway lines for sending **till** all the different parts of the country.

They wanted him in the shipyard at that time for to go as their timber expert **till** America for **till** select timber for them.

They wanted him for to go for **till** select the timber to be sent **till** Harland and Wolff's.

Drumming is something that gets **intill** you and you go **till** a drumming competition.

(d)   Different prepositions are used:

They were standing **outwith** the shop.	*outside*	(*Scots*)

(e)   Prepositions are absent where they might be expected in StE and other dialects:

He comes Ø Saturday or Sunday.	*on*	
We're going Ø pictures.	*to (the)*	
I was offered a job down Ø the waterworks.	*at*	
My head hit the wall and I went Ø Asda and washed it.	*to*	(*Wigan*)
Oh I would move Ø the morn if I got a new job.	*in*	(*Northumberland*)

(f)   Addition *of* or *on*

putting **of** it in its place	Ø
I'm a-doin' **on** it.	Ø
you wanted what she was getting **of**	Ø

4.2   Pronouns

4.2.1   *Pronouns and referents*

The term **pro-word** means a word which stands for (*pro-*) another word, so a pronoun should be a word whose function is to stand for a noun. This definition works sometimes. The following text is the opening of a story written for children:

Sarai sat alone on a big rock. Sarai was sad. Sarai watched as the tents were taken down and rolled up. Sarai watched as the animals were tied together with long ropes: goats, sheep, and cattle.

(from R. Schindler, A Miracle for Sarah,
trans. R. A. Lass-Potter, 1984)

The word *Sarai*, a proper noun, is repeated at the beginning of each sentence, and this reads a little oddly. The author could have written:

Sarai sat alone on a big rock. **She** was sad. **She** watched as the tents were taken down and rolled up. **She** watched as the animals were tied together...

The pronoun *she* seems more natural, and obviously stands for *Sarai*. It refers us back to the noun *Sarai*, which is called its **referent**. The pronoun stands for the noun (pro-noun), and avoids the need for continual repetition of *Sarai*.

The form *she* is used, not *he* or *they*, because the pronoun *he* refers to males, and the name *Sarai* is a girl's name, and the pronoun *they* would refer to more than one person, or else to a person whose sex was not known (section 4.2.4):

I don't recognise the writing on this envelope. I wonder what **they** want?

Activity 4.5

Read the following extract from *Alice in Wonderland* and relate the pronouns (in bold type) to their referents before reading the commentary which follows. Are the referents all nouns?

It was the White Rabbit, trotting slowly back again, and looking anxiously about as **it** went, as if **it** had lost **something**; and **she** heard **it** muttering to **itself**, 'The Duchess! The Duchess! Oh **my** dear paws! Oh **my** fur and whiskers! **She**'ll get **me** executed, as sure as ferrets are ferrets! Where can **I** have dropped **them**, **I** wonder? Alice guessed in a moment that **it** was looking for the fan and the pair of white kid gloves, and **she** very good-naturedly began hunting about for **them**, but **they** were nowhere to be seen – **everything** seemed to have changed since **her** swim in the pool.

Very soon the Rabbit noticed Alice, as **she** went hunting about, and called out to **her**, in an angry tone, 'Why, Mary Ann, **what** *are* **you** doing out here?'

'**He** took **me** for **his** housemaid,' **she** said to **herself** as **she** ran. 'How surprised **he**'ll be when **he** finds out who **I** am!'... 'How queer **it** seems,' Alice said to **herself**, 'to be going messages for a rabbit!'

Commentary on Activity 4.5

The pronouns and their referents are listed below, first in the order in which they occur, and then grouped to show how the same pronouns may have different referents:

pronouns in order of occurrence in the text	*referent*
it	the White Rabbit
something	?
she	Alice
itself	the White Rabbit
my	the White Rabbit's
she	the Duchess
me	the White Rabbit
I	the White Rabbit
them	the fan and the pair of white kid gloves
it	the White Rabbit
she	Alice
them, they	the fan and the pair of white kid gloves
everything	?
her	Alice's
she	Alice
what	?
you	Alice
he	the White Rabbit
me	Alice
his	the White Rabbit's
she	Alice
herself	Alice
I	Alice
it	?

pronoun	*different referents in the text*
everything	*general reference*
he	the White Rabbit
her	Alice's
herself	Alice
his	the White Rabbit's
I	Alice *or* he White Rabbit
it	*general reference or* the White Rabbit
itself	the White Rabbit
me	Alice *or* the White Rabbit
my	the White Rabbit's
she	Alice *or* the Duchess
something	*indefinite*
them	the fan and the pair of white kid gloves
they	the fan and the pair of white kid gloves
what	*indefinite, question*
you	Alice

4.2.2 Pronouns and NPs

Notice firstly that the referents, other than *Alice*, are not words but phrases. A grammatical phrase consists of **one or more words** (section 2.6), so the definition of a pronoun is, more accurately, 'a word that substitutes for a noun phrase (NP)'. Pronouns function like NPs in a clause, and so are one-word NPs themselves.

Secondly, sometimes the referent is not a specific person or thing. In 'How queer it seems', the pronoun *it*, like *something* and *everything*, only refers in a general way.

Thirdly, the same pronouns have different referents according to who is speaking and referring. There are three speakers – the narrator, the White Rabbit and Alice. The pronoun *she* refers to *Alice* when the narrator speaks, and to *the Duchess* when the Rabbit speaks; *I* and *me* to the *White Rabbit* and *Alice* only when they talk about themselves.

4.2.3 Person, number and gender

Like nouns, pronouns are marked for **number**. The narrator refers to the Rabbit as *it*, Alice calls it *he*, and the pronoun for *Alice* is *she*. These three – *he*, *she*, *it* – are the **3rd person singular** pronouns, *singular* because they refer to one person or thing, *3rd person* because they do not refer to either the speaker (**1st person**, *I*) or to the listener (**2nd person**, *you*).

They are marked for **gender** – *she* is **feminine**, *he* is **masculine**, *it* is **neuter**. Gender in present-day English is related to the sex of the referent, and so is called **natural gender**. Old English had, and other modern languages still have **grammatical gender**, in which nouns for things are not necessarily marked as neuter. For example, the moon was masculine in OE, *se mona*, and is feminine in French, *la lune*, but masculine in German, *der Mond*. On the other hand, the OE sun was feminine, *seo sunne*, and is masculine in French, *le soleil*, but feminine in German, *die Sonne*. A German girl is grammatically neuter, *das Mädchen*.

The **plural** pronouns are *we* (1st person), *you* (2nd person) and *they* (3rd person). Notice that the plural 3rd person pronoun is not marked for gender like *he*, *she* and *it*. The 2nd person pronoun *you* has been used for both singular and plural since the singular *thou* dropped out of general use between two and three hundred years ago. When this happened, there is evidence that some people used *you* with *was* when talking to one person, but this is now a regional dialectal form, and not StE, sensible though it seems in distinguishing singular *you was* from plural *you were*.

There is also an **impersonal pronoun**, *one*, which is sometimes used instead of *I*, *we* or *you* to refer to people in general, but it is usually regarded as very formal and is limited in its use:

What can **one** do in such a situation if **one** can't manage by **oneself**?

It sounds less formal if another pronoun is used after the initial *one*:

What can **one** do in such a situation if **you** can't manage by **yourself**?

or:

> What can **one** do in such a situation if **they** can't manage by **themselves**?

In the United States and Canada, the first use of one in writing is followed by *he* or *she*:

> What can **one** do in such a situation if **he** can't manage by **himself**?

> What can **one** do in such a situation if **she** can't manage by **herself**?

4.2.4 *Pronouns, gender and masculine bias*

Because the singular personal pronouns *he*, *she* and *it* are marked for gender according to the sex of the referent (natural gender), problems occur when using words like *visitor*, *leader*, *driver*, *editor*, *doctor*, and so on, which may refer equally to a male or a female. The statement:

> I'm expecting a visitor. Show **her** into the front room when **she** comes.

implies that the speaker is definitely expecting a woman, whereas the statement:

> I'm expecting a visitor. Show **him** into the front room when **he** comes.

could be ambiguous if the identity of the visitor is not known, because the pronoun *him* has traditionally not necessarily implied that the visitor is known to be male. For legal purposes, the pronoun *he* was once formally declared to refer to both sexes. According to an Act of Parliament in 1850, 'Words importing the masculine gender shall be deemed and taken to include females.'

The problem is that with words of **generic** reference (*general*, not specific in reference to sex), and therefore of common gender, the use of the masculine pronoun when referring to visitors, leaders, drivers, editors and doctors in general tends to imply that they are men (male) and not women. Different words have different associations, according to the social roles of men and women, which change and develop. We would all probably think of a train-driver as *he*, because train-drivers are usually men. But a doctor or a teacher is just as likely to be a woman as a man. If you didnt know which sex they were, it was formerly taught that the masculine pronoun *he/him/his* – 'the most customary gender' - should be used.

Ambiguity of the word man
The problem is increased by the ambiguity of the word *man* itself, which has two principal meanings, according to the dictionary:

1   The human race.

2   Adult human male.

The human race consists of human beings, both female and male. In the biblical creation narrative, Genesis, chapter 1, verse 27, we read:

> So God created **man** in his own image; in the image of God he created **him**; male and female he created **them**.

The masculine pronoun has been used to refer to the singular generic use of *man*, meaning *the human race*, because English lacks a singular third-person pronoun which is generic in reference. It is just as reasonable to say:

So God created man in his own image; in the image of God he created **her** . . .

because half the world's population are women, but this will probably sound odd, even if you are in sympathy with the problem.

The problem of the suffix -man

It is argued that in compound words like *chairman*, *postman*, *milkman*, -man has lost its reference to *male* in becoming a suffix, reduced in pronunciation to [mən]. However, this point of view is controversial, and the words *chairperson* or simply *chair* are now widely used as replacements for *chairman*.

But the problem of pronouns still remains, whether you use *chairman*, *chair* or *chairperson*. Here are some alternative ways of writing a sentence – which one do you prefer?

1. If you don't know the sex of the chairman, it's best to use *he* when referring to *him*.
2. If you don't know the sex of the chairman, it's best to use *she* when referring to *her*.
3. If you don't know the sex of the chairman, it's best to use *they* when referring to *them*.

The solution in sentence (3) is very commonly used – that is, to accept the plural pronouns *they/them/their* as having reference to a singular noun when necessary:

I'm expecting a visitor. Show **them** into the front room when **they** come.

If this seems illogical, remember that *you* has been used for centuries to refer to both one (replacing *thou*), or more than one listener. So there is a good precedent.

Activity 4.6

Discuss the following texts in which the problem of gender reference involving nouns or pronouns is illustrated, and suggest alternative ways of expressing their meanings.

(The first four quotations are from Jenny Cheshire, 'A Question of Masculine Bias', in *English Today*, January 1985.)

- The child should be allowed to try to feed himself as soon as he shows any interest in doing so.

- My ambition is to have a show in London with the same sort of reputation that the Crazy Gang had. It would be a glamorous, spicy, but above all a family show. People would bring their wives, mothers and children. (Ken Dodd, in *Woman*)

- The linguist, whatever his persuasion, is single minded in his study of language; but this does not mean he looks at language from one viewpoint only.

- Sharing our compartment were two Norwegians and their wives.

- But this kind of knowing is subordinate to a deeper more encompassing knowing. It is the kind of knowledge implied by the phrase in the Prayer Book Psalm: 'I will lift up mine eyes unto the hills from whence cometh my help'. The place known is distinct and other from the cockney or countryman or sailor or Cornishman who knows it. And yet because the place has helped to make him it has become part of what he is, so that in knowing it he also at the same time knows himself. (H. A. Williams, *True Resurrection*, 1972)

- 'Very well', I said; 'but about this woman question? I saw at the Guest House that the women were waiting on the men: that seems a little like reaction, doesn't it?'
  'Come, now, my friend,' quoth he, 'don't you know that it is a great pleasure to a clever woman to manage a house skilfully, and to do it so that all the house-mates about her look pleased, and are grateful to her? And then, you know, everybody likes to be ordered about by a pretty woman.'
  (William Morris, *News from Nowhere*, 1890)

- (*Two young women are in conversation – Lucille is speaking*)
  'But I am confident, I am even maybe obtuse, where you are too subtle, Fanny. I will go off on the quiet, as you say, and I will, somehow, get educated, and get so that I live with my fellow-men as a fellow-man!'
  (Kate O'Brien, *The Flower of May*, 1953)

The problem in using pronouns does not arise when using the plural, because English has only one 3rd person plural pronoun, *they/them/their*, which is unmarked for gender. So Rebecca West, who was writing brilliant feminist articles as a young woman in the 1910s, can use the plural pronouns, without any ambiguity, to refer to both men and women:

Women know the true damnation of charity because the habit of civilisation has always been to throw **them** cheap alms rather than give **them** good wages. On the way to business **men** give **women their** seats in the tube, and underpay **them** as soon as **they** get there.
(*Clarion*, 13 December 1912,
from *The Young Rebecca*, ed. Jane Marcus, 1982)

but in the same article she uses *fellow-men* as a generic term, referring to *the sane*, women as well as men:

The sane look round on **their fellow-men** and delight to see who will help **them** in **their** work of making the world less madly governed.

And in another article the following sentence occurs:

And second comes in a lingering anti-feminism, banished from the brains of the movement, but occasionally visible when the **ape-man** in **us** stirs **himself**.
(*Clarion*, 24 January 1913)

This evidence, by a feminist writer, suggests that the problem of generic reference and masculine bias in the pronoun system of English was not publicly recognised as early as 1913.

Activity 4.7

Identify and discuss the uses of generic terms and pronouns in the following extract from Rebecca West's journalism.

One gets an impression that the Personal Service Association is doing **the poor** a favour by not taking **their** temperature and giving **them** cod-liver oil during the visit. In this spirit **they** send **their** members to visit families which have come under various charitable societies. 'The ideal **visitor** will enter into every detail of that family with sympathy and interest; **he** will follow up the lives of the **boys and girls**, enter into **their** hopes and fears, **their** work, **their** amusement.' **He** is to do everything except give **them** money, thus proving **himself** the more like the Providence which, we are told, is always watching over us.

(*Clarion*,13 December 1912)

4.2.5 Case in personal pronouns

Those pronouns that refer to persons are called **personal pronouns**. Some of them change their form according to their function in a clause as subject or object, or in an NP when they show possession. This change represents a grammatical category called **case**.

Personal pronouns in standard English			
person	*subjective*	*objective*	*possessive*
singular			
1st person	*I*	*me*	*my*
2nd person	*you*	*you*	*your*
3rd person masculine	*he*	*him*	*his*
3rd person feminine	*she*	*her*	*her*
3rd person neuter	*it*	*it*	*its*
impersonal	*one*	*one*	*one's*
plural			
1st person	*we*	*us*	*our*
2nd person	*you*	*you*	*your*
3rd person	*they*	*them*	*their*

For example, the Lewis Carroll text (activity 4.5) includes *my*, *his* and *her*. If we add *your*, *its*, *our* and *their*, we have the set of pronouns which in NPs show possession, and are said to be in the **possessive case**. The text also has *me* and *them*, two of the forms of the personal pronouns when they function as object (**objective case**), and not subject (**subjective case**). We can add *him*, *her*, and *us*. The 2nd person pronoun *you*, and 3rd person neuter singular *it* remain unmarked for objective case.

Activity 4.8

Describe the StE personal pronouns in the following sentences in terms of: (a) person (1st, 2nd, 3rd), (b) number (singular or plural), (c) gender (masculine, feminine, neuter), (d) case (subjective, objective, possessive).

(a) I felt very encouraged by his support.
(b) She made things rather awkward for me by saying that.
(c) They were put in touch with us by some mutual friends.
(d) Jane puts her foot in it whenever she opens her mouth.
(e) Tell him to be more careful with our car.
(f) We always looked after her when Susan stayed with us.
(g) Ask them where they keep their bank account.
(h) Did you know that my parents knew your parents?
(i) It was only the cat eating its meal.
(j) He said that he saw you last night.

4.2.6 *Pronouns in the regional dialects*

4.2.6.1 HISTORICAL *YE/YOU/YOUR/YOURS* AND *THOU/THEE/THY/THINE*
In Old and Middle English, *ye* and *thou* were **subject**, while *you* and *thee* were **object** pronouns. Chaucer's Host says to the pilgrims:

> **Ye** goon to Caunterbury, god **yow** speed.
> The blisful martir quyte **yow** youre mede.
>
> And wel I woot as **ye** goon by the weye
> **Ye** shapen **yow** to talen and to pleye...

But as well as marking singular and plural, the older forms of the 2nd person pronoun were once used to mark **social relationships** between speakers. Authority of one person over another, or intimacy between two people, was marked by the use of *thou/thee*. A 'superior' would address an 'inferior' as *thou/thee*, but the 'inferior' person would show respect by using *you/ye*. For example, King Lear's daughter Goneril, at the beginning of Shakespeare's play, addresses the king,

> Sir I do loue **you** more than words can weild the matter...

but he replies to her:

> Of all these bounds, euen from this line to this,
> With shady forrests, and wide skirted meades,
> We make **thee** Lady, to **thine** and *Albanies* issue...

In the following lines from *Much Ado about Nothing*, Benedick has come to challenge Claudio, but Claudio is unaware of Benedick's anger at him, and speaks at first as if their close friendship were unchanged:

We haue been vp and downe to seeke **thee** ... What, courage man: what though care kild a catte, **thou** hast mettle enough in **thee** to kill care.

Benedick replies:

Sir, I shall meete **your** wit in the careere, and **you** charge it against me, I pray **you** chuse another subject.

When Claudio is challenged by Benedick, he replies: 'Well I wil meet **you** ...'

Personal pronouns in late sixteenth-century English			
person	*subjective*	*objective*	*possessive*
singular			
1st person	*I*	*me*	*my/mine*
2nd person	*thou*	*thee*	*thy/thine*
3rd person masculine	*he*	*him*	*his*
3rd person feminine	*she*	*her*	*her*
3rd person neuter	*it*	*it*	*its*
plural			
1st person	*we*	*us*	*our*
2nd person	*ye (you)*	*you (ye)*	*your*
3rd person	*they*	*them*	*their*

Thou/thee began to drop out of general use during the seventeenth century, and today they are **archaic** forms in StE, but still in use in some regional dialects.

4.2.6.2 DIALECTAL *YE/YOU/YOUR/YOURS* AND *THOU/THEE/THY/THINE*
tha/thee
Evidence for the survival of forms of *thou/thee* was published in an article written in 1983 about the use of present-day dialectal English in Barnsley, West Yorkshire.

All teachers in Barnsley should be instructed in the conventions of Barnsley dialect so that they can stop children addressing them with the undue familiarity of *thou* and *thee*, says a county councillor, Jack Brown, of Monk Bretton, Barnsley. According to the *Concise Oxford Dictionary*, *thee* and *thou* are archaic or poetical 'except in addressing God, or as used by Quakers'. It should have added 'and in Barnsley'. *Thou* is pronounced *tha*, and is the equivalent of the familiar German *Du* or the French *tu*. *Thee* is the objective case of *tha*, as in 'Tha shurrup or Ah'll thump thee' – and *thissen* and *missen* mean *thyself* and *myself*. For generations the dialect forms of *thee* and *tha* in Barnsley have been governed by a strict unwritten code. They are for use only among familiars – between boys and girls at school, say, or between workmates. A boy would no more say to a teacher 'tha didn't tell me that' than he would could him 'mate'.... The nicety of the usage is illustrated in the relationship between Mr Brown, who is 46, and his father, aged 67. 'He can thee and tha me, but he would be shocked if I did it to him,' he said.

Here is an example recorded recently in Staffordshire:

He used to reside at Cheddleton Asylum, Cheddleton **tha** knows...

you/yous

One useful way of distinguishing singular and plural 2nd person pronouns, following the general loss of *thou/thee*, is shown in these sentences in which *yous* is the plural pronoun:

Well then **yous** knows as much about him as I do. (*Belfast*)

If he has marks on him when he comes back I says it'll not be me **yous**'ll have to contend with. (*Belfast*)

One thing about it, he says, 'I haven't got to stand over **yous**...' (*Liverpool*)

You couldn't stand the winters now...**yous** lot couldn't stand it. (*Newcastle*)

4.2.6.3 DIFFERENT USES OF THE PERSONAL PRONOUNS IN REGIONAL DIALECTS

The forms of pronouns in the subjective and objective cases are widely interchanged. In most dialects one or more of the object forms *me, him, her, us, them* may occur in subject position, though dialects differ as to which of them is used, and where. Here are some examples recorded in Devon, in which *her* is used as the subject feminine singular and *he* as the subject masculine singular pronoun. A reduced form of *thee*, *'ee*, is both subject and object pronoun, and both *we* and *us* are used as the subject plural pronoun.

I was sitting up here writing a letter to dear Willie's mother. **Her**'s up to Brent. **Her** was working but now **her** course has gone...

...and **he** was blowed away.

You knows where East Mill is, don't *'ee*? Oh **us** went up round Peterborough.

Course **we** didn't get the snow until **us** come back.

The fact that both *we* and *us* are used as the subject plural pronoun by the last speaker is evidence that she was drawing upon more than one grammatical system, perhaps influenced by the fact that she was being recorded by someone else.

Her for the feminine subject pronoun is recorded in other dialects also:

I says, are you coming to bed? **Her** says, no, I'm going to finish this.   (*West Midlands*)

Using the plural *us* for the singular *me* is very widespread in colloquial speech:

I thought he was just having **us** on. (*North Shields*)

The *Survey of English Dialects* recorded four forms of the subjective feminine pronoun, *she, shoo, her* and *hoo*, each of which derives from a much wider variety of Middle English forms of the pronoun, beginning with either *h-* or *sh*, including for example,

For þan heom þuhte þat ⟨heo⟩ hadde
●Te houle ouercome... (*Late 12th C*)
*Therefore to-them (it) seemed **she** had*
The owl overcome...

⟨Ho⟩ was þe gladur uor þe rise   (*Late 12th C*)
***She** was the gladder for the branch*

⟨He⟩ song so lude an so scharpe   (*Late 12th C*)
***She** sang so loud and so sharp...*

þo he seghȝ hit nas nowth ⟨ȝhe⟩... (*13th C*)
*When he saw it ne-was not **she**...*

Leiȝande ⟨sche⟩ saide to Blaunchflour... (*13th C*)
*Laughing **she** said to Blaunchflour...*

Fro hir schalt þou or ⟨scho⟩ fro þe... (*c. 1300*)
*From her shalt thou or **she** from thee...*

4.2.7   Reflexive pronouns

In StE the suffix *-self* is added to *my* and *your* to form *myself, yourself,* and to *him, her, it* to form *himself, herself* and *itself*. The plural *-selves* is added to *our, your* and *them* to form *ourselves, yourselves* and *themselves*. The meaning of these pronouns *reflects* back on the person or persons just referred to, and so they are called **reflexive pronouns**. For example:

she heard **it** muttering to **itself**

Alice said to **herself**

Notice that these StE reflexive pronouns use the **possessive case** of the 1st and 2nd person personal pronouns (*my, your, our*), but the **objective case** of the 3rd person pronouns (*him/her/them*) to form the compound with *self/selves*, whereas in an utterance which uses the **emphatic determiner** *own* with *self*, such as *I did it my own self*, the 3rd person possessive pronoun is used – *He did it his own self*, and not **He did it him own self*. It illustrates the **anomalous** StE choice of *himself/themselves*, which many regional dialects have **regularised**.

4.2.7.1 **REFLEXIVE PRONOUNS IN REGIONAL DIALECTS**

Many dialects of English use the possessive case of the 3rd person personal pronouns (*his/their*) to form *hisself* and *theirselves*. (The feminine singular *her* is used for both the objective and possessive, so the difference is not marked in *herself*.) This is another widespread example of regularization in language change. For example:

> He got out **hisself** and swum across the canal. (*Lancashire*)

> I knew eventually if I didn't stop him he would kill **hisself** and I couldn't have stood that. (*Newcastle on Tyne*)

> Drumming was their hobby – they were always drumming **theirselves**. (*Belfast*)

Other dialectal forms are *hissen*, *theirsen*, or *theirsens* (northern England and north Midlands), as quoted in the extract on Barnsley dialect in section 4.2.6.2 above, and in this example:

> These here women at the Women's Fellowship they don't half see **theirsens** right. (*Leicestershire*)

> And if tha does owt for nowt, do it for **thysen**. (*Yorkshire proverb*)

You may also come across personal pronouns used as reflexives without the addition of *-self*, as in:

> She'd probably be sitting up at the fire getting **her** warm. (*Staffordshire*)

4.2.8 *Possessive pronouns as determiners and NPs*

Determiners

The pronouns *my*, *your*, *his*, *her*, *its*, *our* and *their*, which are personal pronouns in the possessive case (section 4.2.5), function as **determiners** when they precede a noun in an NP, *my book*, *your turn* and so on. The commonest determiners in an NP are the two words *the* and *a/an*, traditionally called the **definite article** and the **indefinite article**. Because they are a fixed, closed class, determiners form a small word-class, but except for *the*, *a/an* and possessive nouns used as determiners (d-Poss, as in **Shakespeare's** *plays*), all of them are pronouns.

The use of *us* for *our* is recorded in some regional dialects, as in:

> Let's have **us** dinner.

NPs

Related forms of pronoun are used alone and function like nouns and NPs:

> This one is **mine**, but that's **yours**. These are **his**, those are **hers**. Which is **ours**? What's **theirs**?

There are dialectal forms of these possessives ending with *-n*, as in *hisn*, *hern* and *yourn*. It may be that these forms have developed by analogy with *mine*.

Possessive pronouns as NPs		
	standard	*dialectal*
singular		
1st person	*mine*	*mine*
2nd person	*yours*	*yourn*
3rd person masculine	*his*	*hisn*
3rd person feminine	*her*	*hern*
3rd person neuter	*its*	*its*
plural		
1st person	*our*	*ourn*
2nd person	*your*	*yourn*
3rd person	*their*	*theirn*

4.2.9 Demonstrative pronouns

The determiners in the following short clauses demonstrate, in relation to an action like pointing, what we refer to as being either nearer or further away, like the adverbs *here/there, hither/thither*:

> **This** seat is mine, and **that** one's yours. **These** shoes are his, **those** shoes are hers.

The determiners are called the **demonstrative pronouns**, *this/these, that/those*. They are used as NPs without any change of form:

> **This** is mine, and **that**'s yours. **These** are his, **those** are hers.

4.2.9.1 DEMONSTRATIVE PRONOUNS IN REGIONAL DIALECTS
them or *they* for *those*

In many regional dialects the pronoun *them* is used instead of *those* as a demonstrative pronoun. It is a very widespread difference from StE. For example:

> There was a market in **them** days.   (*Cleveland*)

> In **them** days it was the Tunbridge Wells Corporation did it.   (*Kent*)

> And remember, **them** children had to go four and a half miles every day to school.   (*Newcastle on Tyne*)

> How do you know they'll understand **them** sort of things?   (*Stoke on Trent*)

> I says, 'Do you want to lift **them** boards?'   (*Belfast*)

Here may be added to *this/these*, and *there* to *that/those/them*:

> **These here** women at the Women's Fellowship they don't half see theirsens right. (*Leicestershire*)

Some dialects use *they* for *those*:

> I like **they** big ones best of all . . .

yon

An 'extra dimension' is available in the pronoun *yon*, which is now **archaic** in StE. You find it in older literature, for example John Milton's sonnet:

> O Nightingale, that on **yon** bloomy Spray
> Warbl'st at eeve . . .

but it is still commonly used in present-day dialects. It means something further away than *that/those*, and it is difficult to understand why it should have dropped out of use in the standard dialect.

> My father were born in 1849 across on **yon** hill. He were right delicate. (*West Yorks*)

The English system of demonstrative pronouns for StE and some dialects is therefore a **two-term** system:

singular	this	that
plural	these	those

with corresponding adverbs of place:

> here   there

but for other dialects it is a **three-term** system:

singular	this	that	yon
plural	these	those	yon

with corresponding adverbs of place:

> here   there   yonder

4.2.10 *Pronouns meaning* all *or* some *or* none

Other often-used pronouns are *each, all, both, every, some* and *any*, the last three of which take the suffixes *-one, -body* or *-thing* to form related words, *everyone, everybody, everything* and so on.

The pronouns *no one* (still written as two words), *nobody* and *nothing* are the **negative** forms, with *no, none* and *neither*.

Notice that *each, all, both, some* and *any* function as NPs in clause structure when used as head words of NPs, as in:

> Do you want **some**? I don't want **any**.

but as determiners when they modify another head word in a NP (section 4.4):

> Some people never learn, do they?

4.2.10.1 DIALECTAL FORMS OF *SOMETHING* AND *NOTHING*
owt/nowt/summat
The spelling of *owt* and *nowt* reproduces the dialectal pronunciation [aʊt], [naʊt] of *aught/ought* and *nought*, [ɔːt], [nɔːt] The word *nought* here is the numeral (zero). The word *ought* in this sense probably derived from the phrase *an ought*, meaning *a nought*, in the same way that *a nadder* became *an adder*, and *a napron* became *an apron*.

Similarly, the spelling *summat* reproduces the dialectal pronunciation of *somewhat*, used to mean *something* in the dialects, though in StE *somewhat* implies a lesser degree of *something*.

I didn't give **owt** for it in the end.   (*North Yorks*)

Men were going down the pit for a mere pittance or for **nowt** man – nothing.   (*Northumberland*)

We'll have to get **summat** done about these part-timers else there isn't going to be living for nobody.   (*North Yorks*)

4.2.11   Relative pronouns in StE

These can be seen in the sentences:

wh-S P
He beckoned to the newcomer, **who**   sat down by him.

wh-S P
She knew this chap **who**   'd bought a second-hand car.

wh-S P
We saw a horror movie, **which** was pretty frightening.

(*wh-S* means 'wh-word as Subject of the clause'.)
In each of these, the pronoun *who* or *which* is the **subject** of the verb in the relative clause. We use *who* if the referent is human, and *which* if it is not.

In the following examples, however, the pronouns are the **objects** of the verbs. In informal English, *who* and *which* are again used, but the form *whom* is still used in formal StE as the objective case of *who*, though it seems to be disappearing from general use:

wh-O   S P
He beckoned to the newcomer, **who/whom** he had seen coming into the room.

wh-O   S   P
She recognised the man **who/whom** her friend pointed out.

wh-O S   P
We saw a horror movie which someone had recommended to us.

Often you can substitute *that* for either *who, whom* or *which*:

                     S   P

Did you see the programme about polar bears **that** was on TV last night?

            O   S   *P*

I remember a story **that** an old friend told me once.

but this does not always work. For example, you can say:

> That's the programme **in which** polar bears have been filmed in their natural habitat.

but not:

> *That's the programme **in that** polar bears have been filmed.

These pronouns *relate* a clause to a preceding noun in an NP, and so are called **relative pronouns.** They are part of the grammar of **relative clauses** (sections 10.2.1.4 and 11.2.3). The forms of relative pronoun used in some regional dialects are described in section 10.2.1.6.

4.2.12   *Pronouns in fiction*

Although the grammatical functions of a pronoun are generally to refer to and to substitute for an NP (which may be a proper noun), it is not uncommon in novels and short stories for writers to use pronouns without explicit reference. Here is the opening of a short story. Notice the pronouns, and consider the effect of the author's not naming the characters.

> When **she** opened the door and saw **him** standing there **she** was more pleased than ever before, and **he**, too, as **he** followed **her** into the studio, seemed very very happy to have come ... **he** laid aside his coat and hat gently, lingeringly, as though **he** had time and to spare for everything, or as though **he** were taking leave of them for ever, and came over to the fire and held out **his** hands to the quick, leaping flame.
>
>   ('Psychology', from *Bliss and Other Stories*, Katherine Mansfield, 1947)

Neither character is named in the story, and they remain *he* and *she*.

4.3   Conjunctions

The texts from infant reading primers in chapter 2 were chosen because the chapter was introducing the clause as a basic unit of grammar and meaning, and the texts consisted almost entirely of simple one-clause sentences. They made sense, because the events described followed one another in time, corresponding to the successive clauses. But they did not read like most other kinds of writing, because they lacked the kinds of function word that link and relate words within phrases, phrases within clauses, clauses within sentences, and sentences with other sentences.

4.3.1 *Coordinating conjunctions* and, but, or

One way of linking words, phrases, clauses or sentences together is to use *and*. For example, here is a five-year-old child talking about the Wendy-house in her classroom at school. Some of her language is nonstandard, because she speaks the York dialect. As this is spoken English, it is not transcribed with written punctuation. A momentary break is marked (.).

Activity 4.9

(i)   Note the occurrences of the word *and*, and say whether each occurrence of the word is linking words, phrases or clauses.

(ii) The word *but* also has a linking function. How does it differ in meaning from *and*? Can *but* link words and phrases and clauses?

I play in the Wendy-house (.) we've got a cooker **and** only four people can go in (.) there's only two chairs **and** a table (.) **and** the Wendy-house isn't very big **and** it hasn't got a roof on (.) but we've got a teapot **and** cups **and** saucers (.) **and** we've got a window **and** door **and** a letterbox (.) **and** we've got some little plates **and** a table **and** stools **and** chairs (.) **and** we've got a tablecloth on **and** a telephone (.) but we've lost the thingy what you put on your ears **and** your mouth but we've got the thingy what you press down

Another function word which helps to form lists of items is *or*. It occurs in the following extract from the same child's talk. She is saying what she could do if the class rocking-horse were a real one.

Activity 4.10

(i)   How does *or* differ in meaning from *and* and *but*?

(ii) The word *then* often follows *and* in story-telling. Which word-class does it belong to? Clue: is it possible to move *then* to another part of the clause? Is it possible to move *and*, *but* and *or*?

we could chain it up **and** then leave it there all night **and** then come back to school **and** see if it's all right (.) **or** if you live a long way from school you could go home on it **and** then your Daddy could fetch it back **and** then come back in the car

These three 'listing' words *and*, *but* and *or* are sometimes called *listers*, but the traditional label for this word-class is **co-ordinating conjunction (ccj)**, because they *conjoin* items which are *co-ordinate*, or equal in rank.

You will have discovered that *and* conjoins all types of constituents – words, phrases and clauses. Because the child's language was spoken, it is not possible to mark the sentences as distinct from the clauses, but in written English, it is not unusual to conjoin two sentences by starting the second one with *And*.

The *Authorised Version of the Bible*, published in 1611, is full of examples, especially in its narrative books. See, for example, the Book of Joshua, chapter 8. Each verse from verse 10 to verse 25 inclusive is punctuated as a sentence and begins with *And*, which also occurs frequently within the sentences, joining clauses, phrases and words. The reason is that the story derives from, and retains the style of, *spoken narrative*. Here is a part of it:

And Joshua rose up early in the morning, **and** numbered the people, **and** went up, he **and** the elders of Israel, before the people to Ai.

And all the people, even the people of war that were with him, went up, **and** drew nigh, **and** came before the city, **and** pitched on the north side of Ai: now there was a valley between them **and** Ai. **And** he took about five thousand men, **and** set them to lie in ambush between Beth-el **and** Ai, on the west side of the city.

And when they had set the people, even all the host that was on the north of the city, **and** their liers in wait on the west of the city, Joshua went that night into the midst of the valley.

And it came to pass, when the king of Ai saw it, that they hasted **and** rose up early, **and** the men of the city went out against Israel to battle, he **and** all his people, at a time appointed, before the plain; but he wist not that there were liers in ambush against him behind the city.

The conjunction *or* is like *and* in some ways. You can repeat it in a list:

Would you like tea, **or** coffee, **or** cocoa, **or** a cold drink?

I bought some cornflakes **and** some bread **and** a cake.

In writing you would probably omit all the conjunctions in these lists except the last:

Would you like tea, coffee, cocoa **or** a cold drink?

I bought some cornflakes, some bread **and** a cake.

You cannot use *but* in a list like this, because you cannot use it as a conjunction between more than two items. Try using it like *and* and *or* to test this statement. The conjunction *but* has the meaning, 'on the other hand', and expresses a reservation. The conjunction *or* expresses an alternative, and can be preceded by *either*. If **negative**, we use *neither* and *nor*.

4.3.1.1 *BUT* IN NORTHERN DIALECTS

The inflexible rule of StE and most dialects is that the coordinating conjunctions cannot be moved, but there is evidence that *but* appears at the end of a sentence, used in the same sense as StE *though*. It is recorded in contemporary fiction as a feature of a Yorkshire character's speech,

'I could mebbe manage a Scotch, but.'
'Close enough for him to borrow money, but?'
(Reginald Hill, *Recalled to Life*, Harper Collins, 1992, pp. 182, 185)

and of a Scottish character in Glasgow:

'Ma bones're stapped wae ice, so they are. Plenty of kinneling to be got but.'
(Jeff Torrington, *Swing Hammer Swing*, Secker & Warburg, 1992 p. 70)

4.3.2   *Subordinating conjunctions*

The coordinating conjunctions are, however, contrasted with another set of conjunctions which have a different function. They are also discussed in chapter 11, but here is one example, and a very short explanation. Read the following sentences:

(i)   I'll see you **later**.
(ii)   I'll see you **this evening**.
(iii) I'll see you **in the evening**.
(iv)   I'll see you **when I've finished my tea**.

Sentences (i)–(iii) are simple, one-clause sentences with the same structure: Subject *I*, Predicator *'ll see*, Object *you*, Adverbial *later/this evening /in the evening*. Notice that the Adverbial is an adverb in (i), a noun phrase in (ii) and a prepositional phrase in (iii) – three different *forms* of constituent, but with the same *function*. The meaning of all three is to specify the time of seeing.

Sentence (iv) is very similar. The only difference is that the adverbial function of specifying time is carried out by a clause, not a word or phrase, so it is called an **adverbial clause (AdvCl)**. The important fact for this chapter on function words is this – it is the conjunction *when* which tells us that the clause *when I've finished my tea* is **embedded** as a constituent in the other clause, *I'll see you*.... The traditional term for this kind of embedding is **subordination** – the adverbial clause (AdvCl) is **subordinate** to *I'll see you*, which is called the **main clause (MCl)** of the sentence.

We can show this more clearly by using brackets to mark off the constituents, with round brackets ( ) for phrases, and square brackets [ ] for clauses. The four sentences can then be bracketed and labelled. This is much more economical of space than writing out in full, 'This sentence consists of...which consists of...etc.'

```
        S      P        O      A
(i)    [(I)   ('ll see) (you)  (later)]

        S      P        O      A
(ii)   [(I)   ('ll see) (you)  (this evening)]

        S      P        O      A
(iii)  [(I)   ('ll see) (you)  (in the evening)]

        S      P        O      A = AdvCl
                                scj    S    P        O
(iv)   [(I)   ('ll see) (you)  [when  (I)  ('ve had) (my tea)]]
```

Because the function of the conjunction *when* is to mark its clause as subordinate, it is called a **subordinating conjunction (scj)**. (Some linguists say that it *binds* the AdvCl to the MCl, so they call *when* a *binder*.) There are other subordinating conjunctions and different kinds of subordinate clause to be looked at later, in Chapter 11, where complex clauses are discussed.

4.4 Other function words

The names *prepositions* (section 4.1), *pronouns* (section 4.2) and *conjuctions* (section 4.3) belong to traditional grammar. With nouns, verbs, adjectives and adverbs they form the **parts of speech**. But because one defining feature of function words is that they belong to a *closed class* – few and virtually fixed in number – three other kinds of function word are recognised by some grammarians, even though they already belong to one of the existing word-classes.

4.4.1 Determiners

In sections 4.2.8 and 4.2.9, possessive and demonstrative pronouns have already been classed as **determiners** when they are used to perform a specific function in a noun phrase, that is, as the first pre-modifiers of the head noun – **my** *turn*, **your** *tickets*, **this** *time*, **those** *people*, and so on.

4.4.2 Auxiliary verbs

Although the lexical class *verb* is very large, there is a small group of verbs with a limited and specific function. They come before the **main verb** in a verb phrase and are called **auxiliary verbs**. For example, the main verb in the following verb phrases is *write*, in one form or another. The verbs which precede it are therefore all auxiliary verbs:

> **was** *writing*   **has been** *writing*   **can** *write*   **should have** *written*
> **might be** *writing*   **ought to** *write*   **has to** *write*   **was being** *written*.

There are two classes of auxiliary verb, modals and primary verbs, which are classified as function words.

4.4.2.1 MODAL VERBS
These include *can, could, may, might, will, would, shall, should, ought to*, and are described in section 8.1.5. Modal verbs cannot be used as main verbs.

4.4.2.2 PRIMARY VERBS
These auxiliaries are *be, have* and *do*. They are the most commonly used verbs, and of prime importance, so they are called the **primary verbs**. Unlike other auxiliary verbs, they can be used as **main verbs**:

> She **is** my best friend.   I **had** a bad cold last week.   He **did** the shopping.

as well as auxiliaries, either singly:

> **was** *writing*   **have** *written*   **did**n't *write*

or with *have* and *be* in combination:

> **has been** *writing*   **was being** *written*

Be is described in section 8.2, *have* in 8.3 and *do* in 8.4.

4.5 Summary

The function (grammatical) words in English are therefore:

> **prepositions**
>
> **pronouns**
>
> **conjunctions**

to which we add certain pronouns and verbs according to their use as:

> **determiners**
>
> **modal auxiliary verbs**

and the three common verbs *be*, *have*, *do* when they are used as auxiliaries in a VP:

> **primary auxiliary verbs**

5. Vocabulary

In this chapter we shall examine words in a different way and look at the choices available to us – the **vocabulary** of English – and how different choices affect the meaning and style of what we read.

5.1 Core vocabulary

Activity 5.1

Read the following paragraphs from a story (text 1) and examine the vocabulary:

(i) List the words of one, two, three and four syllables. What is the proportion of each kind of word in the text?

(ii) Are all the words familiar and easy to understand?

(iii) List the function words under the headings: *prepositions, pronouns, conjunctions, determiners, modal verbs, primary verbs.*

(iv) List the lexical words under the headings: *nouns, verbs, adjectives, adverbs.*

Text 1
They had another good day outside. But on the second evening Mole and Rat made Toad help them. He didn't like helping very much.
    The next day they were walking along a quiet road. Mole was leading the horse while Rat and Toad walked behind the caravan.
5   Toad was talking a lot. Suddenly, in front of them there was a cloud of dust. It was coming towards them very fast. There was a lot of noise, too. 'Poop, poop!' The next minute the cloud and the noise were on top of the animals. They couldn't see in the dust and they couldn't think because of the noise. They tried to jump out of the way, but they
10 couldn't. In a minute the thing had passed them. Slowly the dust went away and the three animals could see each other again. The poor old horse was very frightened, and Mole had great difficulty holding him. The caravan was on its side in the road. The windows and two of the wheels were broken. What a sad sight it made! (*179 words*)

Commentary on activity 5.I

The extract is easy to read and understand: 79% of the lexical words are of one-syllable, 17% have two syllables, 3.5% three syllables and 0.5% four syllables.

The text is from the classic story *The Wind in the Willows* by Kenneth Grahame, but not in its original version. It has been simplified for young children learning to read. Its vocabulary is limited to short, familiar words and, as we shall see later, simple grammar.

We can assume that generally speaking, the fewer the syllables, the easier the word – provided that it is already known to the reader in its spoken form. There are only four different words of three syllables – *animals* (2), *another, caravan* (2), *suddenly*, and one of four syllables – *difficulty*.

There are 87 function words altogether (counting the phrases *a lot of, because of, in front of, on top of, out of* and *each other* as single items or **tokens**), but there are only 30 different **types** of word or item. As we have seen in chapter 4, function words are a small closed class, so the same words will occur many times.

Types and tokens

If the same word occurs in a text several times, we describe the occurrences of the same word by referring to **tokens of the same type**. For example in Text 1, there are three tokens each of the words (types) *dust* and *noise*. In this way we we can distinguish between the **range** of vocabulary in a text – the number of different types – from the repetitions (tokens) of the same words.

In Text 1 as a whole we find the proportion of types of lexical words to tokens to be:

nouns	22:39
verbs	14:18
adjectives	12:13
adverbs	9:11.

More than half the nouns occur two or three times each. Much of the repetition is deliberate, because the text was specially written for learners, though in any story some key lexical words in the narrative must occur often.

5.2   The sources of the core vocabulary of English

Familiar everyday words which everyone can understand are said to be part of the **core vocabulary** of English. They are simple, basic words that are used more frequently than other words, and generally have been in the language for a longer time than words which do not belong to the core vocabulary.

The English language was brought to Britain (then a Roman province) by the Angles, Saxons and Jutes who invaded and settled from the fifth century onwards. We call their language **Old English** (OE for short). They in turn were invaded by the Vikings (Danes and Norwegians) from the eigth to the tenth centuries, many of whom settled in the north and east of England. We call their language **Old Norse** (ON). It was similar to OE, and many words from ON have remained in the language.

In 1066 England was conquered by William of Normandy and was governed by speakers of a dialect of **Old French** (OF). Over the next four centuries hundreds of French words were adopted into the English language. French words which came into English at this time came to be spelt and pronounced like English words, that is, they were fully **assimilated** into English.

So the **core vocabulary** of English consists mainly of words derived from Old English, Old Norse and Old French. Modern English contains words from dozens of different languages, but the most important other source is **Latin**, because for many centuries Latin was the international language of the Church and of scholarship. Educated writers introduced hundreds of new words from Latin or Greek in writing, especially from the sixteenth to the eighteenth century, to make up for what they felt to be the lack of English words. Although some of these words have become familiar, they tend to be learned in style and often contain four or more syllables. Academic, medical and scientific vocabularies are full of words taken from Latin or Greek.

It is therefore sometimes possible to have a choice of several words for one meaning, as for example *kingly* (from OE), *royal* (from OF) and *regal* (from Latin). We choose one of the three to suit the style of what we are saying.

Function words are part of the core vocabulary, and nearly all of them derive from Old English. The only exception in text 1 is *because of*, which came from a combination of OE *bi-* , OF *cause* and OE *of*, and is a translation of the French *par cause de*.

Activity 5.2

Divide the lexical words used in text 1 into two sets, those belonging to the core vocabulary and those which do not. Make a guess as to whether the word comes from Old English or Old Norse, French or Latin. Then check your guess with the lists printed at the end of the chapter.

Commentary on activity 5.2

79% of the lexical words of text 1 derive from Old English or Old Norse, 15% from French, 3% from Latin and another 3% from other sources. All the lexical words seem to belong to the core vocabulary of English, including *difficulty* (from Latin, but already in use in the fourteenth century) and *animals*, which was first recorded in English writing in 1541, but is now more often used than the older word *beast*, from OF, which itself replaced the OE word *neat*, now obsolete.

We can now begin to relate our first impression of reading text 1 (simple vocabulary and style) to the sources of the vocabulary. Simple vocabulary tends to belong to the core vocabulary of English, which tends to be derived from OE and ON, and French words which came into the language before the fifteenth century. This is not, of course, an infallible rule.

5.3 The sources of non-core vocabulary

Text 1 was specially written in a simple style, and it is interesting to compare it with what Kenneth Grahame actually wrote. Text 2 consists of that part of the original which was included in the simplified text, and omits what was not used.

Activity 5.3

(i)   Read text 2 and discuss the differences in choice of vocabulary between the two versions. List any words in text 2 which seem to you to be less familiar, and not to belong to the core vocabulary of English. Try to give reasons for your choice.

(ii) Do you have a preference for either version as part of a story?

Text 2
They had a pleasant ramble that day over grassy downs and along narrow by-lanes, only this time the two guests took care that Toad should do his fair share of work. Toad was by no means so rapturous about the simplicity of the primitive life. They were strolling along the
5   high road easily, the Mole by the horse's head, the Toad and the Water Rat walking behind the cart talking together – at least Toad was talking. Glancing back, they saw a small cloud of dust, advancing on them at incredible speed, while from out the dust a faint 'Poop-poop!' wailed like an uneasy animal in pain. In an instant, with a blast of wind and a whirl
10 of sound that made them jump for the nearest ditch, it was on them! (It) flung an enveloping cloud of dust that blinded and enwrapped them utterly, and then dwindled to a speck in the far distance. The old grey horse simply abandoned himself to his natural emotions, in spite of all the Mole's efforts at his head. The canary-coloured cart lay on its side in
15 the ditch, an irredeemable wreck.   (*188 words*)

Activity 5.4

(i)   Use your list of words from text 2 which you have judged to be less familiar, or not to be from the core vocabulary, and look up their derivation. (A dictionary like the *Oxford English Dictionary* provides quotations from the earliest known sources of each word. This information could be useful, because it gives you the words earliest recorded date in manuscript or print.)

(ii) Does this activity support your assessment of the vocabulary of text 2?

Commentary on activity 5.4

(A list of the vocabulary of text 2 is printed at the end of the chapter.)

The vocabulary of the original, text 2, is radically changed in the simplified edition. Only twenty lexical words occur in both texts:

animal	Mole	there
cloud	old	Toad
day	'Poop-poop'	towards
dust	Rat	two
horse	road	walked/walking
jump (*v*)	side	
made	talking	

and if we box those words in text 2 which were taken from Latin or from French, it is likely that they will be the words which you have judged not to belong to the core vocabulary of English, or to be less 'everyday' in their use. Those taken into English from the sixteenth and seventeenth centuries onwards tend to be among the least familiar.

Text 2 – words derived from French or Latin (words borrowed in the sixteenth & seventeenth centuries are printed in **bold type**)

They had a pleasant ramble that day over grassy downs and along narrow by-lanes, only this time the two guests took care that Toad should do his fair share of work . Toad was by no means so **rapturous** about the simplicity of the primitive life. They were strolling along the high road easily , the Mole by the horses head, the Toad and the Water Rat walking behind the cart talking together – at least Toad was talking. Glancing back, they saw a small cloud of dust, advancing on them at **incredible** speed, while from out the dust a faint 'Poop-poop!' wailed like an uneasy **animal** in pain . In an instant , with a blast of wind and a whirl of sound that made them jump for the nearest ditch, it was on them! (It) flung an enveloping cloud of dust that blinded and enwrapped them utterly, and then dwindled to a speck in the far distance. The old grey horse simply abandoned himself to his natural **emotions** , in spite of all the Moles efforts at his head. The **canary**-coloured cart lay on its side in the ditch, an **irredeemable** wreck .

Commentary on Text 2 vocabulary

70% of the lexical words in text 2 derive from Old English or Old Norse, 26% from French and 4% from Latin. This compares with 79%, 15% and 3% in text 1, which has more words of OE origin, and fewer from French and Latin. This suggests that there is some relationship between the style of a text, its choice of words in terms of core vocabulary, simplicity and familiarity, and the derivation of the words. As we are dealing with samples of only 188 and 179 words each, we cannot say that this is always true, but we can use it as a hypothesis in studying the style of literary and other texts (see section 2.6 for a simple definition of *hypothesis*).

Text 2 contained the original wording which was simplified in text 1. But the full original, printed below as text 3, is more than twice as long (488 words), because a lot of the text was omitted in the simplified version.

Activity 5.5

(i)   Read Text 3 and compare its content and style with texts 1 and 2.

(ii) Look up the derivation of the lexical words, under the headings OE, ON, OF, French, Latin, in the lists at the end of the chapter.

(iii) Use the analysis of the vocabulary to discuss the hypothesis about the relationship between style and the derivation of words.

Text 3

They had a pleasant ramble that day over grassy downs and along narrow by-lanes, and camped, as before, on a common, only this time the two guests took care that Toad should do his fair share of work. In consequence, when the time came for starting next morning, Toad was
5   by no means so rapturous about the simplicity of the primitive life, and indeed attempted to resume his place in his bunk, whence he was hauled by force. Their way lay, as before, across country by narrow lanes, and it was not till the afternoon that they came out on the high road, their first high road; and there disaster, fleet and unforeseen,
10 sprang out on them – disaster momentous indeed to their expedition, but simply overwhelming in its effect on the after-career of Toad.

     They were strolling along the high road easily, the Mole by the horse's head, talking to him, since the horse had complained that he was being frightfully left out of it, and nobody considered him in the
15 least; the Toad and the Water Rat walking behind the cart talking together – at least Toad was talking, and Rat was saying at intervals, 'Yes, precisely; and what did you say to him?' – and thinking all the time of something very different, when far behind them they heard a faint warning hum, like the drone of a distant bee. Glancing back, they
20 saw a small cloud of dust, with a dark centre of energy, advancing on them at incredible speed, while from out the dust a faint 'Poop-poop!' wailed like an uneasy animal in pain. Hardly regarding it, they turned to resume their conversation, when in an instant (as it seemed) the peaceful scene was changed, and with a blast of wind and a whirl of
25 sound that made them jump for the nearest ditch, it was on them! The 'poop-poop' rang with a brazen shout in their ears, they had a moment's glimpse of an interior of glittering plate-glass and rich morocco, and the magnificent motor-car, immense, breath-snatching, passionate, with its pilot tense and hugging his wheel, possessed all
30 earth and air for the fraction of a second, flung an enveloping cloud of dust that blinded and enwrapped them utterly, and then dwindled to a speck in the far distance, changed back into a droning bee once more.

     The old grey horse, dreaming, as he plodded along, of his quiet paddock, in a new raw situation such as this simply abandoned himself
35 to his natural emotions. Rearing, plunging, backing steadily, in spite of all the Mole's efforts at his head, and all the Mole's lively language

directed at his better feelings, he drove the cart backwards towards the
deep ditch at the side of the road. It wavered an instant – then there
was a heart-rending crash – and the canary-coloured cart, their pride
40   and their joy, lay on its side in the ditch, an irredeemable wreck. (*488 words*)

The original text is here printed in two columns, which will help you to see more clearly how it was divided into two parts. The left-hand column was simplified, and the right was omitted.

The parts of the original text used and adapted in the simplified version

They had a pleasant ramble that day over grassy downs and along narrow by-lanes, ➡

only this time the two guests took care that Toad should do his fair share of work. ➡

Toad was by no means so rapturous about the simplicity of the primitive life, ➡

They were strolling along the high road easily, the Mole by the horse's head, ➡

the Toad and the Water Rat walking behind the cart talking together – at least Toad was talking, ➡

The parts of the original text not used or adapted in the simplified version:

and camped, as before, on a common,

In consequence, when the time came for starting next morning

and indeed attempted to resume his place in his bunk, whence he was hauled by force. Their way lay, as before, across country by narrow lanes, and it was not till the afternoon that they came out on the high road, their first high road; and there disaster, fleet and unforeseen, sprang out on them – disaster momentous indeed to their expedition, but simply overwhelming in its effect on the after-career of Toad.

talking to him, since the horse had complained that he was being frightfully left out of it, and nobody considered him in the least;

and Rat was saying at intervals, 'Yes, precisely; and what did you say to him?' – and thinking all the time of something very different, when far behind them they heard a faint warning hum, like the drone of a distant bee.

The parts of the original text used and adapted in the simplified version

The parts of the original text not used or adapted in the simplified version:

Glancing back, they saw a small cloud of dust, ➡

with a dark centre of energy,

advancing on them at incredible speed, while from out the dust a faint 'Poop-poop!' wailed like an uneasy animal in pain. ➡

Hardly regarding it, they turned to resume their conversation, when
(as it seemed) the peaceful scene was changed, and

in an instant ➡

with a blast of wind and a whirl of sound that made them jump for the nearest ditch, it was on them! ➡

The 'poop-poop' rang with a brazen shout in their ears, they had a moment's glimpse of an interior of glittering plate-glass and rich morocco, and the magnificent motor-car, immense, breath-snatching, passionate, with its pilot tense and hugging his wheel, possessed all earth and air for the fraction of a second,

flung an enveloping cloud of dust that blinded and enwrapped them utterly, and then dwindled to a speck in the far distance, ➡

changed back into a droning bee once more.
dreaming, as he plodded along, of his quiet paddock, in a new raw situation such as this

The old grey horse, ➡

simply abandoned himself to his natural emotions. ➡

Rearing, plunging, backing steadily,

in spite of all the Mole's efforts at his head, ➡

and all the Mole's lively language directed at his better feelings, he drove the cart backwards towards the deep ditch at the side of the road. It wavered an instant – then there was a heart-rending crash –

and the canary-coloured cart, ➡
lay on its side in the ditch, an irredeemable wreck.

their pride and their joy,

5.4   Informal vocabulary - dialectal, colloquial and slang

A large number of words are spoken and written which are not generally included in the vocabulary of StE, that is, they would not be acceptable in formal speech or writing. Both formal and informal vocabulary are restricted in their use, depending upon the relationship of speaker/writer to listener/reader, the topic and other features of the **context of situation**.

Dialectal vocabulary should not be identified with the **colloquial**, that is, the informal, spoken language of ordinary conversation, which may include **slang**. Slang words are at first spoken within a small group, and sometimes spread into the colloquial vocabulary of the majority. There are many words which we all use in speech which we tend to avoid in writing. At the start of the previous sentence I could have written:

> There are **umpteen** words which we all use in speech,

but didn't, because *umpteen* is marked, for me, as used in colloquial speech only. The general term to include dialectal, colloquial and slang vocabulary is *informal*, in contrast to the *formal* vocabulary of certain kinds of written and spoken English.

You cannot, however, make a precise distinction between dialectal, colloquial and slang vocabulary, or even between formal and informal, because judgement is subjective – we each have different opinions and experiences – and it also changes over time. In the early eighteenth century, Jonathan Swift could not tolerate the word *mob* because it derived from slang usage.

Some people seek an authority by asking the question 'Is the word in the dictionary?'. The word *umpteen* now appears in the 1991 second edition of the *Oxford English Dictionary*, but it is marked as 'colloquial'. Here are a few other examples of recently recorded vocabulary which might cause argument over their classification as formal or informal, dialectal or colloquial:

to spruce

> I'm not **sprucing** you ... (*deceiving*)   (*Sussex*)

The verb *to spruce* is recorded in the *OED* as slang and of 'military' origin, meaning *to lie, deceive*. Its earliest recorded written source is dated 1917.

to thirl

> They'd **thirled** in the clay ... (*excavated*)   (*Derbyshire*)

This is an example of an OE word, *þyrlian*, meaning *pierce*, and later *excavate*, which has survived in dialectal vocabulary, but it is now **obsolete** in StE. Chaucer used it in his *Knight's Tale*,

> ... namely oon
> That with a speer was **thirled** his brest boon.

jigger

The word *jigger* has a wide variety of meanings recorded in the *OED*, and includes that used in:

> ...and he's necking in the **jigger** (*back entry, alley*)   (*Liverpool*)

It is listed under *Various slang uses*, and marked as specific to Merseyside, which is confirmed by the authentic recent spoken example just quoted. Its origin is uncertain. However, *jigger* is no more a slang word to a Liverpudlian than are its equivalents *snicket, ginnel* or *alley* in other areas.

nosh

> They used to **nosh** 'em there.   (*London Cockney*)

Nosh is derived from Yiddish, the 'language used by Jews in Europe and America, consisting mainly of German... with admixture of Balto-Slavic or Hebrew words' (*OED*). Its German source is the verb *naschen*, meaning *nibble*, and the earliest recorded written example in the dictionary is dated 1957. So, however common it has now become in colloquial speech, it is clearly not an English dialectal word, unlike the next example,

canny

> Well, youve got a **canny** bunch of **marrers** working with you... it's a **canny** place to work.   (*Northumberland*)

Canny in Scots has several related meanings, but the main one is *cautious, careful, prudent*. This is not its meaning, however, in the Northumberland speech quoted above, where it describes something *very good, first class, excellent* – in formal StE terms 'a general epithet of approbation or satisfaction'. The word is not recorded in print before the seventeenth century, and is presumed to derive ultimately from *can*, in the sense of *to know how, be able*.

The word *marrers* is not recorded in the *OED*, and is a colloquial word in the dialect meaning *friends, pals, mates*. It is pronounced [mærəz].

to learn

The verb *learn* in StE means exclusively to *acquire knowledge*, but it is also widely used in regional dialects to mean *to teach*. It is important to recognise that the latter meaning is justified from the historical evidence of its use. StE has restricted its meaning to its original *learn* (from OE *leornian*), while the dialects continue with both its meanings of to *impart* and *to acquire knowledge*. Those who use *learn* in the sense of *teach* are not confusing two meanings but continuing a traditional use.

Here is some contemporary evidence of its wide distribution:

> ...probably catch other people, **learn** them how to do things like read and write.   (*Stoke on Trent*)

> No, I **learned** bell-ringing in 1929. I **learned** my grand-daughter to ring and that set my son going... and then I've had my daughter's two children – we've **learned** them too...   (*Oxfordshire*)

> We **learned** her to just write her name.   (*West Yorks*)

And here is some historical evidence of its development of the meaning *teach*:

> 1450 A man aught to **lerne** his doughters with good ensaumples. (*'The Book of the Knight of La Tour-Landry'*)

> 1480 Gentilmens children ben **lerned** and taught from their yongth to speke frenssh. (*William Caxton*)

> 1792 We should **learn** them, above all things, to lay a due restraint on themselves. (*Mary Wollstonecraft*)

lay

StE usage today distinguishes between *lie* (*down*), an intransitive verb, and *lay*, a transitive verb as in *I'm going to **lay** the table* and *Hens **lay** eggs*. The StE past tense of *lie* is *lay*, and of *lay* is *laid*, so it is not surprising that the forms of the two verbs are confused. Nonstandard dialectal forms of *lay* for StE *lie* are very common:

> They let me **lay** there. (*Norwich*)

> I was just **laying** on the bed. (*London Cockney*)

gan

> You've got to **gan** up to Faroe, Iceland to get a nice piece of tasty fish. (*North Shields*)

A final example of an interesting survival of the unchanged OE word *gan*, meaning *go*. The development elsewhere from *gan* through *gon* to its StE form *go* did not happen in the north-east of England. Compare Scots *gae/gang*.

Appendix – Data from the three texts

Text 1 – Lexical words by derivation

Old English and Old Norse

OE	again	OE	old
OE	away	OE	other
OE	broken	OE	outside
OE	cloud	OE	Rat
OE	coming	OE	road
OE	day	OE	sad
OE	dust	OE	see
OE	each	OE	side
OE	evening	OE	sight
OE	fast	OE	slowly
OE	frightened	OE	there
OE	good	OE	thing
OE	great	OE	think
OE	had	OE	three
OE	help(ing)	OE	Toad
OE	holding	OE	too
OE	horse	OE	top
OE	leading	OE	towards
OE	like	OE	two
OE	lot	OE	walk(ing)
OE	made	OE	way
OE	much	OE	went
OE	next	OE	wheels

ON	windows
ME *fr* OE	talking
ME *fr* ?	Mole
ME *fr* ?	poop-poop

French

ME *fr* Fr	minute
ME *fr* Fr	noise
ME *fr* Fr	passed
ME *fr* Fr	second (*n*)
OF	front
OF	poor
OF	quiet
OF	suddenly
OF	tried
OF	very

Latin

ME *fr* Lat	difficulty
Lat 1541	animals

Other

fr Persian	caravan
fr ? 1511	jump (*v*)

TEXT 2 – Lexical words by derivation

Old English and Old Norse

OE	by-lanes	OE	side	
OE	back (*adv*)	OE	small	
OE	blast	OE	speck	
OE	blinded	OE	speed	
OE	care	OE	steadily	
OE	cloud	OE	then	
OE	day	OE	there	
OE	ditch	OE	time	
OE	downs	OE	Toad	
OE	dust	OE	together	
OE	dwindled	OE	took	
OE	far	OE	towards	
OE	grassy	OE	two	
OE	grey	OE	utterly	
OE	guests	OE	walking	
OE	head	OE	wind (*n*)	
OE	high	OE	work	
OE	horse	ME *fr* OE	talking	
OE	lay (*past v*)	ME *fr* OE	whence	
OE	least	ME *fr* ?	enwrapped	
OE	life	ME *fr* ?	Mole	
OE	made	ME *fr* ?	Poop-poop	
OE	narrow	*fr* ? 1511	jump (*v*)	
OE	nearest	*fr* ? 1603	strolling	
OE	no	*fr* ? 1620	ramble	
OE	old	ON	cart	
OE	only	ON	flung	
OE	Rat	ON	wailed	
OE	road	ON	whirl	
OE	saw	ON	wreck	
OE	share (*n*)			

Vocabulary derived from French

OF	abandoned
OF	advancing
OF	coloured
OF	distance
OF	easily
OF	enveloping
OF	faint
OF	fair
OF	means
OF	natural
OF	pain
ME *fr* OF	pleasant
ME *fr* OF	simplicity
ME *fr* OF	simply
ME *fr* OF	sound
ME *fr* OF	spite
ME *fr* OF	uneasy
ME *fr* F	primitive
Fr 1450	glancing
Fr 1477	instant
Fr 1489	efforts
Fr 1592	canary
Fr 1609	irredeemable

Vocabulary derived from Latin

ME *fr* Lat	incredible
Lat 1541	animal
Lat 1579	emotions
Lat 1678	rapturous

TEXT 3 – Lexical words in alphabetical order with derivations

Word	Derivation	Word	Derivation	Word	Derivation
abandoned	OF	fleet (*adj*)	ON	pleasant	ME *fr* OF
advancing	OF	flung	ON	plodded	?1562
after	OE	force	ME *fr* Fr	plunging	ME *fr* OF
-career	Fr 1534	fraction	OF	'Poop-poop'	ME *fr* ?
afternoon	ME	frightfully	OF	possessed	OF 1465
air	OF	glancing	Fr 1450	precisely	Fr 1526
animal	Lat 1541	glimpse	OE	pride	OE
attempted	Fr 1513	glittering	ON	primitive	ME *fr* Fr
back (*adv*)	OE	grassy	OE	quiet	ME *fr* OF
backing	OE	grey	OE	ramble	?1620
backwards	ME	guests	OE	rang	OE
bee	OE	hardly	OE	rapturous	Lat 1678
better	OE	hauled	OF	raw	OE
blast	OE	head	OE	rearing	OE
blinded	OE	heard	OE	regarding	ME *fr* Fr
brazen	OE	heart	OE	resume	ME *fr* Fr
breath	OE	-rending	OE	rich	OE
-snatching	ME	high	OE	road	OE
bunk	?1815	horse	OE	saw	OE
by-lanes	OE	hugging	? ON 1567	say/saying	OE
came	OE	hum	ME	scene	Fr 1540
camped	Fr 1543	immense	Fr 1490	second	ME *fr* Fr
canary	Fr 1592	incredible	ME *fr* Lat	seemed	ON
-coloured	OF	indeed	ME *fr* OE	share (*n*)	OE
care	OE	instant	Fr 1477	shout	ME *fr* OE
cart	ON	interior	Lat 1490	side	OE
centre	ME *fr* Fr	intervals	ME *fr* Lat	simplicity	ME *fr* OF
changed	OF	irredeemable	Fr 1609	simply	ME *fi* OF
cloud	OE	joy	OF	situation	Fr 1490
common (*n*)	Fr/Lat	jump (*v*)	*fr* ? 1511	small	OE
complained	ME *fr* Fr	language	ME *fr*Fr	something	OE
consequence	ME *fr* Fr	lay (*past t, v*)	OE	sound	ME *fr* OF
considered	ME *fr* Fr	least	OE	speck	OE
conversation	OF	left	OE	speed	OE
country	OF	life	OE	spite	ME *fr* OF
crash (*n*)	?1549	lively	OE	sprang	OE
dark	OE	made	OE	standing	OE
day	OE	magnificent	OF 1513	steadily	OE
deep	OE	means	OF	strolling	?1603
different	ME *fr* Fr	Mole	ME *fr* ?	talking	ME *fr* OE
directed	ME *fr* Lat	moments	ME *fr* Lat	tense	ME *fr* OF
disaster	Fr 1590	momentous	Lat 1652	then	OE
distance	OF	more	OE	there	OE
distant	OF	morning	ME *fr* OE	thinking	GE
ditch	OE	morocco	1634 *fr* Arabic	time	OE
downs	OE	motor	Lat 1586	Toad	OE
dreaming	OE	-car	OF	together	OE
dron(ing)	OE	narrow	OE	took	OE
drove	OE	natural	OF	turned	OE
dust	OE	nearest	OE	two	OE
dwindled	OE	new	OE	uneasy	ME *fr* OF
ears	OE	next	OE	unforeseen	OE
earth	OE	no	OE	utterly	OE
easily	OF	not	OE	very	ME *fr* OF
effect	OF	old	OE	wailed	ON
efforts	Fr 1489	once	OE	walking	OE
emotions	Lat 1579	only	OE	warning	OE
energy	Lat 1599	overwhelming	ME *fr* OE	Water Rat	OE
enveloping	OF	paddock	OE	wavered	ON
enwrapped	ME *fr* ?	pain	OF	way	OE
expedition	ME *fr* Lat	passionate	Lat 1450	wheel	OE
faint	OF	peaceful	OF	whence	ME *fr* OE
fair	OF	pilot	Fr 1530	whirl	ON
far	OE	place	OF	wind (*n*)	OE
feelings	ME *fr* OE	plate	OF	work	OE
first	OE	-glass	OF	wreck	ON

6. Six kinds of phrase

We have looked at the classification of words in chapters 3–5 and distinguished lexical words – *nouns, verbs, adjectives* and *adverbs* – from function words – *pronouns, conjunctions, prepositions, determiners, modal and primary verbs*, and core vocabulary from formal vocabulary. We shall now begin to look more closely at the larger units of the grammar which were introduced in chapter 2 – the rank scale from phrases, through clauses to sentences – and begin with another look at Text 1 from chapter 5.

6.1 Revision – sentence, clause and phrase in the rank scale

6.1.1 *Sentences*

The first sentence of Text 1, *They had another good day outside*, is an example of what is called a **simple sentence**. It consists of one **clause**. The sentence:

[Mole was leading the horse [while Rat and Toad walked behind the caravan]]

contains two clauses, a **main clause** *Mole was leading the horse* and a **subordinate clause** *while Rat and Toad walked behind the caravan*. This is called a **complex sentence**.

The sentence:

[They couldn't see in the dust] and [they couldn't think because of the noise].

contains two main clauses linked, or coordinated, by the conjunction *and*. It is called a **compound sentence**. The structure of sentences is described in more detail in chapter 13.

6.1.2 *Clauses*

A clause is the unit of language which contains a single **proposition**, and has from two to four basic **constituents**. In most clauses, two constituents are essential, the **subject (S)** and the **predicator (P)**. These terms describe the **function** of these two constituents – what they <u>do</u> in a clause. The other constituents are dependent upon what we want to say, and so a clause may contain one or more **complements (C)** of the verb and one or more **adverbials (A)**. The simple sentence just quoted consists of one clause which contains each of the four constituents:

S	*P*	*C*	*A*
They	had	another good day	outside.

6.1.3 *Noun phrases (NPs)*

If we now turn to the nouns and pronouns in the text, we find that as well as occurring singly, e.g. the pronoun *they*, or the proper noun *Mole*, they are often part of a **phrase** of two or more words, e.g. *another good day*. A pronoun (*pronoun*) in fact replaces a noun phrase (section 4.2.2).

Clauses consist of **one or more phrases**, and in many clauses, there are more **noun phrases (NPs)** than any other kind of phrase, because they can function as three of the four clause constituents.

(a) as **subject**:

S	*P*	*C*
NP		
The poor old horse	was	very frightened

(b) as **complement**:

S	*P*	*O*
		NP
Mole	was leading	**the horse**

(c) as **adverbial**:

A	*S*	*P*	*A*
NP			
The next day	they	were walking	along a quiet road.

and also as complement to a preposition (p) in a prepositional phrase (PrepP):

A	*S*	*P*	*A*	
			p	NP
The next day	they	were walking	**along**	**a quiet road.**

The functions of S, P C and A in clauses will be described in more detail in chapter 9.

A NP must contain a **noun** or a **pronoun**. It can be a single noun, like *Toad* or a pronoun like *he*, *her* or *they*. These single nouns or pronouns are by definition the **head word** or **head** of their one-word NPs. A NP consists of **one or more words**.

The head word of a NP may be **pre-modified** by a **determiner (d)** and/or one or more **modifiers (m)**, and **post-modified** by a **qualifier (q).**

So the formula for a NP is **(d) (m) h (q)**; the brackets mean 'optional' and also 'possibly more than one'. Turning the formula into words: 'a NP consists of an obligatory head word, which may be pre-modified by one or more determiners and modifiers, and post-modified by one or more qualifiers'.

6.1.4 Prepositional phrases (PrepPs)

PrepPs commonly function as adverbials in clauses, or else they post-modify NPs as qualifiers (sections 6.2.5 and 7.2.4). Because a PrepP consists of a **preposition** with a NP as its **complement**, our study of NPs would be very limited if we did not include PrepPs as well.

Here is text 1 reproduced with all the NPs and PrepPs marked in boxes. To make identification easier for you, determiners are printed in *italics*, modifiers in normal type, noun head-words in SMALL CAPITALS and pronoun head words in *ITALIC CAPITALS*. Qualifiers are printed in a ⌐box⌐ after the head word.

NP = *determiner* (d) – modifier (m) – HEAD (h) – ⌐qualifier⌐ (q)   **(d) (m) h (q)**
PrepP = ⌐preposition (p) + NP⌐   **p (d) (m) h (q)**

Text 1 – NPs and PrepPs marked

THEY had *another* good DAY outside. But on *the* second EVENING MOLE and RAT made TOAD help *THEM*. *He* didn't like helping very much.
The next DAY *THEY* were walking along *a* quiet ROAD. MOLE was leading *the* HORSE while RAT and TOAD walked behind *the* CARAVAN. TOAD was talking *a* LOT. Suddenly, in front of *THEM* *THERE* was A CLOUD of DUST. *IT* was coming towards *THEM* very fast. *THERE* was *a* LOT of NOISE, too. 'POOP POOP!' *The* next MINUTE *the* CLOUD and *the* NOISE were on top of *the* ANIMALS. *THEY* couldn't see in *the* DUST and *THEY* couldn't think because of *the* NOISE. *THEY* tried to jump out of *the* WAY, but *THEY* couldn't. In *a* MINUTE *the* THING had passed *THEM*. Slowly *the* DUST went away and *the* three ANIMALS could see *each* OTHER again. *The* poor old HORSE was very frightened, and MOLE had great DIFFICULTY holding *HIM*. *The* CARAVAN was on *its* SIDE in *the* ROAD. *The* WINDOWS and *two* of *the* WHEELS were broken. *What a* sad SIGHT *IT* made!

6.2   NPs and PrepPs in text 1

6.2.1 Head words

The simplest NPs in text 1 consist of a head word only, either pronouns, *he*, *him*, *it* (2), *them* (2), *they* (2) and *there* used as subject, or proper nouns, *Mole* (3), *Rat* (2), *Toad* (3).

6.2.2 Determiners

Determiners are the words which tell us the kind of **reference** which the NP has (sections 4.2.8 and 4.4.1). It may be **definite**, when we use *the*, or **indefinite**, *a/an*, or refer to a part of the noun, like *some*, or to every example, like *all*. When *Toad*, *Mole*, *Rat* are used with capital letters as proper nouns they don't need a determiner, because they are unique and specific names in themselves. The following examples of NPs with the structure **dh** occur in text 1:

a lot	the horse
the caravan	the noise
the cloud	the thing
the dust	the windows

6.2.3 Head words without a determiner

Plural nouns may occur without a determiner, as in **Plums** *are cheap in the market today*. (there are no examples in text 1) and **noncount nouns** which do not normally have a plural form with the same sense, as in *Water freezes at 0°C and becomes ice*. There is only one example of an NP without a determiner in text 1, *great difficulty*.

6.2.4 Modifiers

The function of modifiers is to describe or limit the reference of the head. In text 1 all the modifiers are **adjectives** like *good, old* or **numerals** such as *three, second*. But it is equally possible for nouns to be modifiers, as in *the brick wall, a milk jug*. NPs with the structure **dmh** in text 1 are:

another *good* day	the *poor old* horse (= **dmmh**)
the *next* day	
the *next* minute	
the *three* animals	

6.2.5 Qualifiers

The function of qualifiers in a NP is very similar to that of modifiers, but they follow the head as post-modifiers, because they are almost always phrases of two or more words or clauses, and you cannot precede a head word with a modifying phrase or clause, as in **an of dust cloud*. There are only two examples in text 1, both of them simple PrepPs with *of*:

a cloud *of dust*   a lot *of noise* (= **dhq**)

6.2.6 Pre-determiners

Sometimes we modify the reference of a determiner with a word or phrase which goes before it, for example, ***all** the people*, ***twice** the value*, ***such** a nice time*, so the term **pre-determiner** simply describes its place in the structure. The following example occurs in text 1: *two of* the wheels (= **pre-d d h**).

6.2.7 NPs as complements of PrepPs

The variations in structure of NPs which we have just looked at are also to be found when NPs function as the complement to a preposition in a PrepP.

Activity 6.1

The following PrepPs occur in Text 1. Sort them into sets according to their structure as **ph, pdh** or **pdmh**. (NB: some of the prepositions are complex, and consist of more than one word, like *instead of, owing to, in spite of, in common with.*

along a quiet road	in front of them	on the second evening
because of the noise	in the dust	on top of the animals
behind the caravan	in the road	out of the way
in a minute	on its side	towards them

6.3   NPs and PrepPs in text 2

In chapter 5 we found that some of the vocabulary of Text 2, taken from Kenneth Grahame's original narrative, was a little more complex than the simplified version of Text 1. Complexity is to be found not only in words, but at each level of grammar – in phrases, clauses and sentences – and the structure of the NPs and PrepPs in Text 2 is more complex than those in Text 1, as you can see in a diagram of Text 2 with the NPs and PrepPs in boxes. Boxes that 'nest' within larger ones represent grammatical items which modify or complement others.

Text 2 – NPs and PrepPs

THEY had a pleasant RAMBLE *that* DAY over grassy DOWNS and along narrow BY-LANES, only *this* TIME *the* two GUESTS took CARE that TOAD should do *his* fair SHARE of WORK. TOAD was by *no* MEANS so rapturous about *the* simplicity of *the* primitive LIFE. THEY were strolling along *the* high ROAD easily, *the* MOLE by *the* horse's HEAD, *the* TOAD and *the* WATER RAT walking behind *the* CART talking together – at LEAST TOAD was talking. Glancing back, *THEY* saw a small CLOUD of DUST, advancing on *THEM* at incredible SPEED, while from out *the* DUST a faint 'POOP-POOP!' wailed like *an* uneasy ANIMAL in PAIN. In *an* INSTANT, with a BLAST of WIND and a WHIRL of SOUND

[*THAT* made *THEM* jump for *the* nearest DITCH]

[*IT*] was [on *THEM*] ! [*IT*] flung [an enveloping CLOUD

of DUST [[[*THAT*] blinded and enwrapped [*THEM*] utterly]]] ,

and then dwindled [to *a* SPECK] [in *the* far DISTANCE]. [*The* old grey HORSE]
simply abandoned [*HIMSELF*] [to *his* natural EMOTIONS],
in spite of [*all the Mole's* EFFORTS [at *his* HEAD]]. [*The* canary-coloured CART]
lay [on *its* SIDE] [in *the* DITCH] , [an irredeemable WRECK].

6.3.1 Relative clauses as qualifiers

The most complex structure of NPs or PrepPs in text 2, which do not occur in text
1, are:

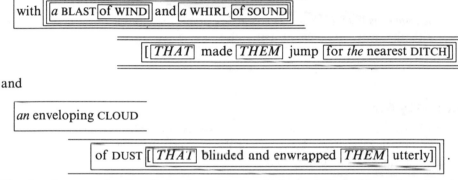

and

The first is a complex PrepP (*with* + NP), in which two NPs, *a blast of wind* and *a
whirl of sound*, are **coordinated** by the conjunction *and*, and qualified by a **relative
clause**, *that made them jump for the nearest ditch*. The relative clause contains a
PrepP, *for the nearest ditch*.

The second is a complex NP. Its PrepP qualifier, *of dust*, is itself qualified by the
relative clause *that blinded and enwrapped them utterly*, in which the two verbs are
coordinated. When a clause, a unit of higher 'rank' than a phrase, is embedded
within a phrase as qualifier, it is an example of **rank-shift** (section 7.4.2 for more
on rank-shifted clauses).

6.3.2 NP and PrepP structures in text 2

Text 2 contains examples of a variety of combinations of the structural
constituents **dmhq** in NPs and **pdmhq** in PrepPs:

NPs		PrepPs	
h	care	**ph**	in pain
dh	that day	**pdh**	at his head
dmh	a pleasant ramble	**pmh**	along narrow by-lanes
dmhq	his fair share of work	**pdmh**	along the high road
		pdhq	about the simplicity of the primitive life
		pdmhq	like an uneasy animal in pain

6.3.3 Possessive phrases

In the PrepPs *by the horse's head* and *in spite of all the Mole's efforts at his head*, the nouns *horse's* and *Mole's* are **inflected** with the suffix -*'s*, a morpheme. The noun is in the **possessive case** (section 4.2.5), and so the phrase in which it occurs is called a **possessive phrase (PossP)**. The PossPs *the horse's* and *all the Mole's* function as determiners (**d-Poss**), while *all* in *all the Mole's* is a pre-determiner. So we can represent the structure of the two phrases as:

```
p    d-Poss      h
by   the horse's  head
```

```
 p            d                h    q
           pre-d  d-Poss
in spite of  all    the Mole's  efforts  at his head
```

(NB: *in spite of* is here analysed as a **complex preposition** and a single grammatical item, although it has its own structure also.)

Activity 6.2

The list below contains the NPs and PrepPs of text 2 in the order in which they occur in the text, omitting those just discussed and also any repetitions of identical phrases.
 Sort them into sets according to their similarity of structure:

NPs   h, dh, dmh, dmhq
PrepPs ph, pdh, pmh, pdmh, pdhq

---

they	the Water Rat	in an instant
over grassy downs	behind the cart	it
this time	at least	to a speck
the two guests	a small cloud of dust	in the far distance
Toad	(of dust)	the canary-coloured cart
by no means	on them	on its side
the Mole	at incredible speed	in the ditch
the Toad	from out the dust	an irredeemable wreck
	a faint 'Poop-poop'	

6.4   NPs and PrepPs in text 3

6.4.1   *Nonfinite clauses as qualifiers*

The complete original text of the extract produces its full share of NPs and PrepPs, some of which include other complex structures. We saw in text 2 that a NP or PrepP may be qualified (post-modified) with a relative clause as well as another PrepP. The following complex NP illustrates another possible qualifier:

all the Mole's lively language [directed [at his better feelings]]

whose qualifier *directed at his better feelings* is a **nonfinite clause**. It is nonfinite because the verb *directed* is the *-en/-ed* participle (sections 3.3.3.4 and 11.1.4). Nonfinite clauses, with *-en/-ed* or *-ing* participles or *to*-infinitives are therefore possible qualifiers of NPs and PrepPs.

6.4.2   *Recursion*

The fact that NPs and PrepPs commonly function as qualifiers to other NPs and PrepPs, as in (*to*) *the people **next door**, (for) the people in the **neighbouring house***, means that any noun head word in a NP or PrepP may be post-modified again and again, or **recursively**. Examples of recursion are not hard to make up, and in the box-diagrams already used they show up as 'nesting' one within the other – the more boxes, the greater the amount of recursion, or **embedding**:

the people in the house

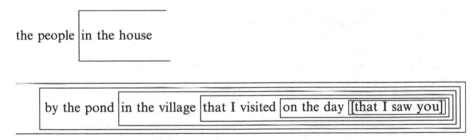

by the pond in the village that I visited on the day [[that I saw you]]

The post-modifying relative clause *that I visited* has a PrepP, *on the day*, as its adverbial, and the occurrence of *day* allows further recursion with another relative clause *that I saw you*. Such complex NPs are uncommon, but they are certainly possible. The NP just constructed could be the complex subject of a clause:

S
The people in the house by the pond in the village

                                              P   *C*
that I visited on the day that I saw you   are called   Jones.

You will find some examples of recursive structures in text 3 which follows.

Activity 6.3

Analyse the NP and PrepP structures in the complete original text 3, as illustrated below. List and describe any recursive structures.

(The two phrases post-modified by relative clauses have already been discussed in section 6.3.1.)

h	they, Rat	**ph**	of wind
dh	this time	**pmh**	over grassy downs
dmh	the peaceful scene	**pdh**	in their ears
dmmh	the old grey horse	**pdmh**	on the high road
dmhq	a small cloud of dust	**pdhq**	like the drone of a distant bee
		pdmhq	with a dark centre of energy

Text 3 – NPs and PrepPs

[They] had [a pleasant ramble] [that day] [over grassy downs] and [along narrow by-lanes], and camped, as before, [on a common], only [this time] [the two guests] took [care] that [Toad] should do [his fair share [of work.]] [In consequence], when [the time] came for starting [next morning], [Toad] was [by no means] so rapturous [about the simplicity [of the primitive life]], and indeed attempted to resume [his place [in his bunk]], whence [he] was hauled [by force]. [Their way] lay, as before, [across country] [by narrow lanes], and [it] was not [till the afternoon] that [they] came out [on the high road], [their first high road]; and there [disaster], fleet and unforeseen, sprang out [on them] – [disaster] momentous indeed [to their expedition], but simply overwhelming [in its effect [on the after-career [of Toad]]]. [They] were strolling [along the high road] easily, [the Mole] [by [the horse's] head], talking [to him,] since [the horse] had complained that [he] was being frightfully left [out of it,] and [nobody] considered [him] [in the least]; [the Toad] and [the Water Rat] walking [behind the cart] talking together – [at least] [Toad] was talking, and [Rat] was saying [at intervals], 'Yes, precisely; and what did [you] say [to him]?' – and thinking [all the time] [of something [very different]], when [far behind them] [they] heard [a faint warning hum], [like the drone [of a distant bee]]. Glancing back, [they] saw [a small cloud [of dust]], [with a dark centre [of energy]], advancing [on them] [at incredible speed], while [from out the dust] [a faint 'Poop-poop!']

wailed ⌈like an uneasy animal ⌈in pain⌉⌉. Hardly regarding ⌈it⌉, ⌈they⌉ turned to resume ⌈their conversation⌉, when ⌈in an instant⌉ (as ⌈it⌉ seemed) ⌈the peaceful scene⌉ was changed, and

with ⌈⌈a BLAST ⌈of WIND⌉⌉ and ⌈a WHIRL ⌈of SOUND⌉⌉⌉

⌈⌈THAT⌉ made ⌈THEM⌉ jump ⌈for the nearest DITCH⌉⌉

⌈it⌉ was ⌈on them⌉! ⌈The 'poop-poop'⌉ rang ⌈with a brazen shout ⌈in their ears⌉⌉, ⌈they⌉ had ⌈a moment's⌉ glimpse ⌈of an interior ⌈of glittering plate-glass and rich morocco⌉⌉, and ⌈the magnificent motor-car⌉, immense, breath-snatching, passionate, with ⌈its pilot⌉ tense and hugging ⌈his wheel,⌉ possessed ⌈all earth and air⌉ for the fraction ⌈of a second⌉, flung

an enveloping cloud ⌈of dust ⌈that blinded and enwrapped ⌈them⌉ utterly⌉⌉, and then dwindled ⌈to a speck ⌈in the far distance⌉⌉, changed back ⌈into a droning bee⌉ once more. The ⌈old grey horse⌉, dreaming, as ⌈he⌉ plodded along, ⌈of his quiet paddock⌉, ⌈in a new raw situation ⌈such as this⌉⌉ simply abandoned ⌈himself⌉ ⌈to his natural emotions⌉. Rearing, plunging, backing steadily, ⌈in spite of all the Mole's efforts ⌈at his head⌉⌉, and

all the Mole's lively language ⌈directed ⌈at his better feelings⌉⌉, ⌈he⌉ drove ⌈the cart⌉ backwards ⌈towards the deep ditch ⌈at the side ⌈of the road⌉⌉⌉.
⌈It⌉ wavered ⌈an instant⌉ – then ⌈there⌉ was ⌈a heart-rending crash⌉ – and ⌈the canary-coloured cart⌉, ⌈their pride⌉ and ⌈their joy⌉, lay ⌈on its side ⌈in the ditch⌉⌉, ⌈an irredeemable wreck⌉.

6.5 Verb phrases (VPs) in text I

So far we have looked at the two commonest kinds of kinds of phrase, NPs and PrepPs, and at PossPs as determiners. But in some ways, the 'centre' of a clause is its predicator – the process or action that is going on and which the subject of an active clause 'does', and to which any complements are related. The function of predicator is always performed by a **verb phrase (VP)**, consisting of one or more verbs.

Text 1 – VPs
They ⌈had⌉ another good day outside. But on the second evening Mole and Rat ⌈made ⌈*Toad*⌉ help⌉ them. He ⌈didn't like helping⌉ very much.

The next day they were walking along a quiet road. Mole was leading the horse while Rat and Toad walked behind the caravan. Toad was talking a lot. Suddenly, in front of them there was a cloud of dust. It was coming towards them very fast. There was a lot of noise, too. 'Poop, poop!' The next minute the cloud and the noise were on top of the animals. They couldn't see in the dust and they couldn't think because of the noise. They tried to jump out of the way, but they couldn't . In a minute the thing had passed them. Slowly the dust went away and the three animals could see each other again. The poor old horse was very frightened, and Mole had great difficulty holding him. The caravan was on its side in the road. The windows and two of the wheels were broken. What a sad sight it made!

VPs in Text 1

simple past **have and be**	*simple past*	*non-finite* -ing	*past progressive*
had (*another good day*)	walked	holding	were walking
had (*great difficulty*)	went (*away*)	*phase*	was leading
was (*a cloud of dust*)	made	made (*Toad*) help	was talking
was (*a lot of noise*)		didn't like helping	was coming
was (*very frightened*)		tried to jump	*past perfect*
was (*on its side*)		*passive*	had passed
were (*on top of...*)		–	*modal*
were (*broken*)			couldn't see
			couldn't think
			couldn't (jump)
			could see

6.5.1 Tense

There are only two tenses in English that are marked by the form of the verb – **simple past** and **simple present**.

6.5.1.1 PRESENT AND PAST TENSE; PRESENT, PAST AND FUTURE TIME
Normally, we use the past tense to refer to past time, but we don't use the present tense in such a direct 'one-to-one' way. Present tense can refer to present time, but much less often than its reference to actions that are habitual, like *I catch the bus every morning at eight o'clock*. Present tense can also be used to refer to the future, as in *When I catch the bus tomorrow morning*. Because of this, some grammarians prefer to call it the **non-past** tense. We usually refer to the future by using one or other of the set of auxiliary verbs called **modal verbs**, *will* and *shall*, as in *I shall catch the bus in the morning*, or else a **semi-auxiliary verb** like *be to, have to, be going to*, e.g. *I am to see her on Friday, I have to be in Newcastle next week, She is going to visit her friends later*. Although we use the term 'future tense' to refer to these ways of talking about the future, it is strictly speaking inaccurate, because it is not marked by a change of form of the main verb.

6.5.1.2 TENSE, ASPECT AND MODAL VERBS IN VPs
(a) Simple present and past tense
A single main verb in a finite clause is marked for present or past tense (section 8.1). In Text 1 there are no examples of the simple present, because it is a story, and written stories are rarely told in the present tense. The examples of **simple past tense** VPs are as follows. Notice that the primary verbs *have* and *be* are here used as main verbs:

had (*a good day*)	was (*a cloud of dust*)	made (*a sad sight*)
had (*difficulty*)	was (*a lot of noise*)	went (*away*)
	was (*on its side*)	walked
	was (*very frightened*)	
	were (*on top of*)	

(b) *be* as an auxiliary verb – progressive aspect and passive voice
In a VP with more than one verb, the **main verb** always comes last, and may be preceded by one or more **auxiliary verbs**. The first verb in a finite VP is always marked for tense. The primary verb *be* is commonly used as an auxiliary verb.

If it is followed by the *-ing* participle, it indicates a **progressive** or **continuous action**. When we describe an action using a verb, we may want to indicate that the action is either completed or still going on in time. The traditional term for the grammatical category which marks this is **aspect** (section 8.8.1). The examples in Text 1 are all marked for past tense, and also say that the actions were *progressing*, so this form of a VP is called the **past progressive** – past tense + progressive aspect:

	past tense	*progressive aspect*		*past tense*	*progressive aspect*
It	was	coming	Toad	was	talking
Mole	was	leading	they	were	walking

If the first verb is in the present tense, *e.g. they **are** walking*, then the VP form is called **present progressive.**

If *be* as an auxiliary verb is followed by the *-en/-ed* participle, it marks the **passive voice**, which means that the subject of the VP did not perform the action, but 'suffered' it – someone or something else actually did it (section 8.10). The only example in Text 1 is *were broken* in *The windows and two of the wheels **were broken***

(c) *have* as an auxiliary verb – perfect aspect
The verb *have* as an auxiliary verb is followed by the *-en/-ed* participle of the main verb, and means that the action of the verb is complete ('perfected' in an older sense). This is traditionally called **perfect aspect** (section 8.8.2). There is one example, marked for past tense, in Text 1 – *In a minute the thing **had passed** them*. We can refer to this form as the **past perfect** (past tense + perfect aspect).

(d) Modal verbs
The set of auxiliary verbs called **modals** enables us to talk about things that are not facts, but about possibility, probability, certainty, uncertainty, permission and

so on. This includes the future, which is unknown. They are described in section 8.5. *Could* is the only example of a modal verb in Text 1

could see	couldn't see
couldn't (jump)	couldn't think

(e) Predicators in phase
We often use two or more main verbs in a kind of 'series', one after the other, and the three examples in Text 1 show some of the different forms that **predicators in phase** can take (section 8.7):

didn't like helping – the main verb *like* is followed by the *-ing* participle *helping*.

tried to jump is an example of a very common form of predicators in phase, *verb 1 + to + verb 2*.

made (Toad) help is also a common construction, *verb 1 + NP + verb 2*, in which the NP functions as the **object** of the first verb, and the **subject** of the second.

6.5.1.3 NONFINITE VERBS
There are therefore three nonfinite forms of verbs:

1. the *-ing* (present) participle
2. the *-en/-ed* (past) participle
3. the infinitive

The infinitive has the unmarked base form of a verb. Here are some examples of the three nonfinite forms of verb in use:

-ing *participle*	Mole was **leading** the horse
	Mole had great difficulty **holding** him
-en/-ed *participle*	Having **eaten** a hearty breakfast, he fell asleep.
	He had **been seen** that morning.
	In a minute the thing had **passed** them
	There was the noise of a bolt **shot** back
infinitive	Mole and Rat made Toad **help** them
	They couldn't **see** in the dust
	They tried to **jump** out of the way

6.6 Text 2 VPs

Activity 6.4

Examine the VPs in Text 2, that part of the original text adapted in the simplified version of Text I. Are they more complex than those of Text I?

Text 2 – VPs

They ⬚had⬚ a pleasant ramble that day over grassy downs and along narrow by-lanes, only this time the two guests ⬚took⬚ care that Toad ⬚should do⬚ his fair share of work. Toad ⬚was⬚ by no means so rapturous about the simplicity of the primitive life. They ⬚were strolling⬚ along the high road easily, the Mole by the horse's head, the Toad and the Water Rat ⬚walking⬚ behind the cart ⬚talking⬚ together – at least Toad ⬚was talking⬚ . ⬚Glancing⬚ back, they ⬚saw⬚ a small cloud of dust, ⬚advancing⬚ on them at incredible speed, while from out the dust a faint 'Poop-poop!' ⬚wailed⬚ like an uneasy animal in pain. In an instant, with a blast of wind and a whirl of sound that ⬚made *them* jump⬚ for the nearest ditch, it ⬚was⬚ on them! (It) ⬚flung⬚ an enveloping cloud of dust that ⬚blinded⬚ and ⬚enwrapped⬚ them utterly, and then ⬚dwindled⬚ to a speck in the far distance. The old grey horse simply ⬚abandoned⬚ himself to his natural emotions, in spite of all the Mole's efforts at his head. The canary-coloured cart ⬚lay⬚ on its side in the ditch, an irredeemable wreck.

6.6.1 *VP structures in text 2*

In fact, the VPs in text 2 are no more complex in structure, but show a different choice of vocabulary which affects the style. Text 1 uses *be* as main verb five times, and text 2 twice only. Text 2 has ten main verbs in the simple past, and uses the *-ing* participle in three nonfinite clauses. You can see other differences in the following tables. Text 1 is more repetitive and less lively in its choice of verbs.

VPs in Text

simple past **have and be**	*simple past*	*nonfinite* -ing	*past progressive*
had (*a pleasant ramble*)	abandoned	advancing	was talking
was (*by no means so rapturous*)	blinded	glancing	were strolling
	dwindled	talking	*past perfect*
was (*on them*)	enwrapped	walking	—
	flung	*phase*	*modal*
	lay	made them jump	should do (*his fair share*)
	saw		
	took (*care*)	*passive*	
	wailed	—	

6.6.2 *Summary of VP forms*

The following formula shows in brief what are the possible structures of a VP used as the predicator of a finite clause to make a statement (declarative mood) in the active voice (not passive). The items in brackets are optional, meaning that a finite VP is grammatical without them. Of course, they are not optional if needed to convey a particular meaning.

VP = *tense* + (*modal*) + (*have* + *-en/-ed*) + (*be* + *-ing*) + *main verb*
Tense = present *or*
    past

In ordinary language, this means that a finite verb phrase must contain:

1. *present* or *past* **tense**, which marks the first verb; and
2. a main verb.

Depending upon the meaning of the VP, it may also contain:

3. a modal verb; and/or
4. auxiliary verb *have*.

If the VP contains auxiliary *have*, the verb which follows must be in the *-en/-ed* participle form. The VP may also contain:

5. auxiliary verb *be*.

If the VP contains auxiliary *be*, then the main verb which follows is in the *-ing* participle form.

Activity 6.5

Put the following short sentences into sets according to the tense and aspect of their VPs: simple present of *be*, simple past of *be*, simple present, simple past, present progressive, past progressive, present perfective, past perfective, present perfective/progressive, past perfective/progressive, modals and semi-auxiliaries.

Badger lives there.
He couldn't bear to disappoint his
   friends.
He has been a complete idiot!
He has got some great qualities, has
   Toad!
I'm going there.
I'm going to get the boat.
I'm in it.
I've got a lot of friends.
I might have lost my way.
I'll teach you to row.
I'm looking at that streak of bubbles
   in the water.
I've given up boating long ago.
It was the Water Rat!
Mole and Rat were both in the
   water.
Mole had fallen in love with the cart.
Mole scraped and scratched and
   scrabbled.

Rat had held him firmly by the leg.
Rat stooped and unfastened a rope.
Rat was carrying a very large basket.
That would be lovely.
The horse had been grazing
   contentedly.
The Mole had been working hard all
   morning.
There are hundreds of animals and
   birds.
They've finished dinner.
This is better than whitewashing!
Toad had never been in a boat
   before.
Toad was splashing badly in the
   boat.
We can take some food.
We needn't decide anything in a
   hurry.
We ought to stick by Toad now.
We were just coming over to see you.

Mole was happy.
Nothing seems to matter in fine
    weather.
Otter saw the food basket.

We've been looking for you all
    morning.
We've called on you unexpectedly.
What a day I'm having!
You never do anything in particular.

6.7   VPs in text 3

Activity 6.6

Examine the VPs in the original, Text 3, and list them in sets:

(i)   if finite, according to tense and aspect;

(ii)   if nonfinite, whether -*ing* or -*en*/-*ed* participles or infinitives.

The text includes one example of a clause in **interrogative mood**, asking a question,
What did (you) say? (section 8.4.1), and three of **passive voice**, *was hauled, was being
frightfully left out* and *was changed* (section 8.10 on voice). Otherwise all the clauses are
declarative and active.

Text 3 – Ps

They |had| a pleasant ramble that day over grassy downs and along narrow
by-lanes, and |camped|, as before, on a common, only this time the two guests
|took| care that Toad |should do| his fair share of work. In consequence, when
the time |came| for |starting| next morning, Toad |was| by no means so
rapturous about the simplicity of the primitive life, and indeed
|attempted to resume| his place in his bunk, whence he |was hauled| by force.
Their way |lay| , as before, across country by narrow lanes, and it |was| not till
the afternoon that they |came| out on the high road, their first high road; and
there disaster, fleet and unforeseen, |sprang| out on them – disaster momentous
indeed to their expedition, but simply over-whelming in its effect on the
after-career of Toad.

   They |were strolling| along the high road easily, the Mole by the horse's head,
|talking| to him, since the horse |had complained| that he
|was being [*frightfully*]| left *out* of it, and nobody |considered| him in the least; the
Toad and the Water Rat |walking| behind the cart |talking| together – at least
Toad |was talking|, and Rat |was saying| at intervals, 'Yes, precisely; and what
|did [*you*] say| to him?' – and |thinking| all the time of something very different,
when far behind them they |heard| a faint warning hum, like the drone of a
distant bee. |Glancing| back, they |saw| a small cloud of dust, with a dark centre
of energy, |advancing| on them at incredible speed, while from out the dust a
faint 'Poop-poop!' |wailed| like an uneasy animal in pain. Hardly |regarding|
it, they |turned to resume| their conversation, when in an instant (as it
|seemed|) the peaceful scene |was changed|, and with a blast of wind and a
whirl of sound that |made [*them*] jump| for the nearest ditch, it |was| on them!

The 'poop-poop' rang with a brazen shout in their ears, they had a moment's glimpse of an interior of glittering plate-glass and rich morocco, and the magnificent motor-car, immense, breath-snatching, passionate, with its pilot tense and hugging his wheel, possessed all earth and air for the fraction of a second, flung an enveloping cloud of dust that blinded and enwrapped them utterly, and then dwindled to a speck in the far distance, changed back into a droning bee once more.

The old grey horse, dreaming, as he plodded along, of his quiet paddock, in a new raw situation such as this simply abandoned himself to his natural emotions. Rearing, plunging, backing steadily, in spite of all the Mole's efforts at his head, and all the Mole's lively language directed at his better feelings, he drove the cart backwards towards the deep ditch at the side of the road. It wavered an instant – then there was a heart-rending crash – and the canary-coloured cart, their pride and their joy, lay on its side in the ditch, an irredeemable wreck.

6.8 Adjective phrases (AdjPs)

Here is text 1 again with the AdjPs marked:

Text 1 – adjectives and adjective phrases
They had another good day outside. But on the second evening Mole and Rat made Toad help them. He didn't like helping very much.

The next day they were walking along a quiet road. Mole was leading the horse while Rat and Toad walked behind the caravan. Toad was talking a lot. Suddenly, in front of them there was a cloud of dust. It was coming towards them very fast. There was a lot of noise, too. 'Poop, poop!' The next minute the cloud and the noise were on top of the animals. They couldn't see in the dust and they couldn't think because of the noise. They tried to jump out of the way, but they couldn't. In a minute the thing had passed them. Slowly the dust went away and the three animals could see each other again. The poor old horse was very frightened, and Mole had great difficulty holding him. The caravan was on its side in the road. The windows and two of the wheels were broken. What a sad sight it made!

6.8.1 *AdjPs in text 1*

There are eleven AdjPs, most of them consisting of single adjectives, but one, *very frightened,* is modified by the adverb *very*. AdjPs can occur either as modifiers in NPs, as in *the **next** day*, or following relational verbs like *be, become, seem,* as in *The poor old horse was **very frightened***. The fact that adjectives can be modified and form phrases suggests that we should call them **adjective phrases (AdjPs)**, consisting of one or more words with an adjective head.

Adjectives are called **attributive** when they pre-modify nouns (what they describe is an **attribute** of the noun), e.g. **grassy** *downs*. Those which follow linking verbs are called **predicative**,[†] because they occur in the **predicate**[†] of a clause, e.g. *Toad was by no means so **rapturous***.

Text 1

attributive adjectives

good	quiet	old
second	three	great
next (2)	poor	sad

predicative adjectives
(very) frightened

In section 6.2.4 it was pointed out that the function of a pre-modifier can also be carried out by another noun, e.g. *the **railway** station*, as against *the **new** station*. You can tell the difference not only by the meaning of the word, but by trying to use a noun like a predicative adjective – you can say *the station is new* but you don't usually say ***the station is railway*.

6.8.2 *AdjPs in text 2*

Activity 6.7

Are there any significant differences between the number and choice of AdjPs in text 2 when compared with text 1?

Text 2 – AdjPs
They had a ⌷pleasant⌷ ramble that day over ⌷grassy⌷ downs and along ⌷narrow⌷ by-lanes, only this time the ⌷two⌷ guests took care that Toad should do his ⌷fair⌷ share of work. Toad was by no means so ⌷rapturous⌷ about the simplicity of the ⌷primitive⌷ life. They were strolling along the ⌷high⌷ road easily, the Mole by the horse's head, the Toad and the Water Rat walking behind the cart talking together – at least Toad was talking. Glancing back, they saw a ⌷small⌷ cloud of dust, advancing on them at ⌷incredible⌷ speed, while from out the dust a faint 'Poop-poop!' wailed like an uneasy animal in pain. In an instant, with a blast of wind and a whirl of sound that made them jump for the

† Note on predicate – To *predicate* something is to assert or declare that it is true. The word is being used as a verb. It is also used in traditional grammar as a noun, *the predicate*, to refer to the rest of a clause apart from the subject, and which is 'asserting' something about the subject:

Subject	*Predicate*
The poor old horse	was very frightened

A *predicative adjective* is therefore an adjective following the verb and part of the predicate of the clause.

The word *predicator*, used in functional grammar and in this book for the VP representing the 'process', is derived from the same word *predicate*, and means *that which predicates*. The same clause is analysed in terms of clause structure, already briefly discussed, as:

Subject	*Predicator*	*Complement*
The poor old horse	was	very frightened

nearest ditch, it was on them! (It) flung an enveloping cloud of dust that blinded and enwrapped them utterly, and then dwindled to a speck in the far distance. The old grey horse simply abandoned himself to his natural emotions, in spite of all the Mole's efforts at his head. The canary-coloured cart lay on its side in the ditch, an irredeemable wreck.

Commentary on activity 6.7

There are nearly twice as many AdjPs in text 2, which include words like *incredible*, *primitive*, *rapturous* and *irredeemable* which were noted in chapter 5 as outside the core vocabulary of English, with formal connotations.

Text 2

attributive adjectives

canary-coloured	grassy	narrow	primitive
enveloping	grey	natural	small
faint	high	nearest	two
fair	incredible	old	uneasy
far	irredeemable	pleasant	

predicative adjectives
rapturous

6.8.3   AdjPs in text 3

Activity 6.8

Examine the AdjPs in the original text 3. Divide them into two sets, *attributive* and *predicative adjectives*, and comment, if there is anything of interest.

Text 3 – AdjPs
They had a pleasant ramble that day over grassy downs and along narrow by-lanes, and camped, as before, on a common, only this time the two guests took care that Toad should do his fair share of work. In consequence, when the time came for starting next morning, Toad was by no means so rapturous about the simplicity of the primitive life, and indeed attempted to resume his place in his bunk, whence he was hauled by force. Their way lay, as before, across country by narrow lanes, and it was not till the afternoon that they came out on the high road, their first high road; and there disaster, fleet and unforeseen, sprang out on them – disaster momentous indeed to their expedition, but simply overwhelming in its effect on the after-career of Toad.

They were strolling along the high road easily, the Mole by the horse's head, talking to him, since the horse had complained that he was being frightfully left out of it, and nobody considered him in the least; the Toad and the Water Rat walking behind the cart talking together – at least Toad was talking, and Rat was saying at intervals, 'Yes, precisely; and what did you say to him?' – and thinking all the time of something very different, when far behind them they heard a ⌐faint¬ ⌐warning¬ hum, like the drone of a ⌐distant¬ bee. Glancing back, they saw a ⌐small¬ cloud of dust, with a ⌐dark¬ centre of energy, advancing on them at ⌐incredible¬ speed, while from out the dust a ⌐faint¬ 'Poop-poop!' wailed like an ⌐uneasy¬ animal in pain. Hardly regarding it, they turned to resume their conversation, when in an instant (as it seemed) the ⌐peaceful¬ scene was changed, and with a blast of wind and a whirl of sound that made them jump for the ⌐nearest¬ ditch, it was on them! The 'poop-poop' rang with a ⌐brazen¬ shout in their ears, they had a moment's glimpse of an interior of ⌐glittering¬ plate-glass and ⌐rich¬ morocco, and the ⌐magnificent¬ motor-car, ⌐immense¬, ⌐breath-snatching¬, ⌐passionate¬, with its pilot ⌐tense¬ and hugging his wheel, possessed all earth and air for the fraction of a second, flung an ⌐enveloping¬ cloud of dust that blinded and enwrapped them utterly, and then dwindled to a speck in the ⌐far¬ distance, changed back into a ⌐droning¬ bee once more.

The ⌐old¬ ⌐grey¬ horse, dreaming, as he plodded along, of his ⌐quiet¬ paddock, in a ⌐new¬ ⌐raw¬ situation such as this simply abandoned himself to his ⌐natural¬ emotions. Rearing, plunging, backing steadily, in spite of all the Mole's efforts at his head, and all the Mole's ⌐lively¬ language directed at his ⌐better¬ feelings, he drove the cart backwards towards the ⌐deep¬ ditch at the side of the road. It wavered an instant – then there was a ⌐heart-rending¬ crash – and the ⌐canary-coloured¬ cart, their pride and their joy, lay on its side in the ditch, an ⌐irredeemable¬ wreck.

6.9   Adverbs and Adverb Phrases (AdvPs)

6.9.1   *AdvPs in text I*

Text 1 – adverbs and adverb phrases
They had another good day ⌐outside¬ . But on the second evening Mole and Rat made Toad help them. He didn't like helping ⌐very¬ much⌐.

The next day they were walking along a quiet road. Mole was leading the horse while Rat and Toad walked behind the caravan. Toad was talking a lot. ⌐Suddenly¬, in front of them there was a cloud of dust. It was coming towards them ⌐very¬ fast⌐. There was a lot of noise, ⌐too¬. 'Poop, poop!' The next minute the cloud and the noise were on top of the animals. They couldn't see in the dust and they couldn't think because of the noise. They tried to jump out of the way, but they couldn't. In a minute the thing had passed them. ⌐Slowly¬ the dust went ⌐away¬ and the three animals could see each other ⌐again¬ . The poor old horse was ⌐very¬ frightened, and Mole had great difficulty holding him. The caravan was on its side in the road. The windows and two of the wheels were broken. What a sad sight it made!

Adverbs were introduced in section 3.5, under the following categories:

Circumstance adverbs
One important **semantic** function of adverbs (that is, what they contribute to meaning) is to represent the 'circumstances' of **time**, **place** or **manner** in a clause,

e.g. in text 1 *again* is an adverb of <u>time</u>, *outside, away,* of <u>place</u>, and *suddenly, very fast, slowly,* of <u>manner</u>. They function as **adverbial** constituents in the structure of a clause (sections 2.11 and 9.5.4), as does *too,* which has a 'reinforcing' function.

Degree adverbs

Very is used three times in text 1, modifying other adverbs in *very much* and *very fast,* and an adjective in *very frightened.* It indicates the **degree** of the adverbs and adjective, which are said to be 'gradable', e.g. *fast, more fast, somewhat fast, very fast, extremely fast* are ways of grading *fast,* as well as using the comparative and superlative degrees of *fast, faster, fastest.*

Sentence adverbs

There are no examples of this category in text 1. They express the attitude of speakers towards what they say and so comment on the sentence as a whole. They often come first, separated from the clause on which they are commenting, marked by intonation in speech and by a comma in writing: ***Obviously***, *she knew about it all the time.*

Since adverbs can themselves be modified, we can talk of adverb phrases (AdvPs) consisting of one or more words with an adverb head, as we have already done with NPs, VPs and AdjPs.

Adverbs and AdvPs in text 1

outside	very fast	away
very much	too	again
suddenly	slowly	very

6.9.2　AdvPs in text 2

Activity 6.9

Are there any significant differences between the number and choice of AdvPs in text 2 when compared with text 1?

Text 2 – Adverbs and AdvPs

They had a pleasant ramble that day over grassy downs and along narrow by-lanes, only this time the two guests took care that Toad should do his fair share of work. Toad was by no means so rapturous about the simplicity of the primitive life. They were strolling along the high road |easily|, the Mole by the horse's head, the Toad and the Water Rat walking behind the cart talking |together| – at least Toad was talking. Glancing |back|, they saw a small cloud of dust, advancing on them at incredible speed, while from out the dust a faint 'Poop-poop!' wailed like an uneasy animal in pain. In an instant, with a blast of wind and a whirl of sound that made them jump for the nearest ditch, it was on them! (It) flung an enveloping cloud of dust that blinded and enwrapped them |utterly| , and |then| dwindled to a speck in the far distance. The old grey horse |simply| abandoned himself to his natural emotions, in spite of all the Mole's efforts at his head. The canary-coloured cart lay on its side in the ditch, an irredeemable wreck.

Adverbs and AdvPs in Text 2

easily	utterly
together	then
back	simply

There are in fact fewer AdvPs (5) in the original Text 2 than in the simplified Text 1 (6), and they are all different. But because the adverbial slot in clauses is not only filled by AdvPs, but also by PrepPs and NPs, it would be misleading to draw any conclusions about the style of the text from the use of AdvPs only. The adverbials in the clause structures of text 2 are marked as follows:

Text 2 – Adverbials

They had a pleasant ramble [that day] [over grassy downs] and [along narrow by-lanes], only [this time] the two guests took care that Toad should do his fair share of work. Toad was [by no means] so rapturous [about the simplicity of the primitive life]. They were strolling [along the high road] [easily], the Mole [by the horse's head], the Toad and the Water Rat walking [behind the cart] talking [together] – [at least] Toad was talking. Glancing [back], they saw a small cloud of dust, advancing on them [at incredible speed], while [from out the dust] a faint 'Poop-poop!' wailed [like an uneasy animal in pain]. [In an instant], [with a blast of wind and a whirl of sound that made them jump for the nearest ditch], it was [on them]! (It) flung an enveloping cloud of dust that blinded and enwrapped them [utterly], and [then] dwindled [to a speck] [in the far distance]. The old grey horse [simply] abandoned himself [to his natural emotions], [in spite of all the Mole's efforts at his head]. The canary-coloured cart lay [on its side] [in the ditch], an irredeemable wreck.

You will see how important in clause structure PrepPs are as adverbials in providing the circumstances of time, place, manner, and so on in a narrative.

Activity 6.10

Examine the AdvPs in the original text 3, and comment, if there is anything of interest.

6.9.3 *AdvPs in text 3*

They had a pleasant ramble that day over grassy downs and along narrow by-lanes, and camped, as [before], on a common, [only] this time the two guests took care that Toad should do his fair share of work. In consequence, when the time came for starting next morning, Toad was by no means [so] rapturous about the simplicity of the primitive life, and [indeed] attempted to resume his place in his bunk, [whence] he was hauled by force. Their way lay, as [before], across country by narrow lanes, and it was [not] till the afternoon that they came out on the high road, their first high road; and [there] disaster, fleet and unforeseen, sprang [out] on them – disaster momentous [indeed] to their expedition, but [simply] overwhelming in its effect on the after-career of Toad.

They were strolling along the high road ⸢easily⸣, the Mole by the horse's head, talking to him, since the horse had complained that he was being ⸢frightfully⸣ left out of it, and nobody considered him in the least; the Toad and the Water Rat walking behind the cart talking ⸢together⸣ – at least Toad was talking, and Rat was saying at intervals, 'Yes, ⸢precisely⸣; and what did you say to him?' – and thinking all the time of something ⸢very⸣ different, when ⸢far⸣ behind them they heard a faint warning hum, like the drone of a distant bee. Glancing ⸢back⸣, they saw a small cloud of dust, with a dark centre of energy, advancing on them at incredible speed, while from out the dust a faint 'Poop-poop!' wailed like an uneasy animal in pain. ⸢Hardly⸣ regarding it, they turned to resume their conversation, when in an instant (as it seemed) the peaceful scene was changed, and with a blast of wind and a whirl of sound that made them jump for the nearest ditch, it was on them! The 'poop-poop' rang with a brazen shout in their ears, they had a moment's glimpse of an interior of glittering plate-glass and rich morocco, and the magnificent motor-car, immense, breath- snatching, passionate, with its pilot tense and hugging his wheel, possessed all earth and air for the fraction of a second, flung an enveloping cloud of dust that blinded and enwrapped them ⸢utterly⸣, and ⸢then⸣ dwindled to a speck in the far distance, changed ⸢back⸣ into a droning bee ⸢once more⸣.

The old grey horse, dreaming, as he plodded along, of his quiet paddock, in a new raw situation such as this ⸢simply⸣ abandoned himself to his natural emotions. Rearing, plunging, backing ⸢steadily⸣, in spite of all the Mole's efforts at his head, and all the Mole's lively language directed at his better feelings, he drove the cart ⸢backwards⸣ towards the deep ditch at the side of the road. It wavered an instant – ⸢then⸣ there was a heart-rending crash – and the canary-coloured cart, their pride and their joy, lay on its side in the ditch, an irredeemable wreck.

Adverbs and AdvPs in text 3

before (2)	simply (2)	hardly
only	easily	utterly
so	frightfully	then (2)
indeed (2)	together	once more
whence	precisely	steadily
not	very	backwards
there	far	
out	back (2)	

In the following chapters we shall study in more detail how phrases are structured, and what their function is in clauses and embedded in other phrases.

7. Noun and prepositional phrases

7.1 Revision – six kinds of phrase

Some kinds of phrase are labelled according to the word-class of their head word. A one word phrase consists of the head word only:

S	*P*	*O*	*A*	
Mary	greeted	Harry	affectionately	= function labels
n	v	n	adv	
NP	VP	NP	AdvP	= form-class labels

Mary and *Harry* are proper nouns, single head words of noun phrases (NPs). *Greeted* is a verb, and so the single head word of a verb phrase (VP). *Affectionately* is an adverb, and the single head word of an adverb phrase (AdvP). The following clause has a similar structure and meaning:

S	*P*	*O*	*A*
My sister	was greeting	her boy friend	with great affection
NP	VP	NP	PrepP

My sister is a NP, because its head word is *sister*, which is a noun. *Her boy friend* is also a NP, since the head word is the noun *friend*. *Was greeting* is a VP, because its head word is the verb *greeting*. The phrase *with great affection* contains the noun *affection*, the head word of the NP *great affection*, but the first word *with* is a preposition, and this is regarded as the head word, and the noun phrase is the complement of the preposition (section 6.1.4). This structure is therefore called a prepositional phrase (PrepP).

The PrepP *with great affection* is functioning like the single-word AdvP *affectionately*, and this is why the function label **Adverbial** is used – a constituent that either is an AdvP or that functions like one. A fifth kind of phrase is contained in the next example:

S	*P*	*Ci*
My sister	is	very affectionate
NP	VP	AdjP

The VP is the single-word linking verb *is*. *Affectionate* is an adjective, and the head word of the adjective phrase (AdjP) *very affectionate*. It is functioning as the intensive complement (Ci) of the clause. In the clause:

S	P	O
I	have	a very affectionate sister
NP	VP	NP

the AdjP *very affectionate* is now a constituent of a larger phrase, modifying the noun *sister* in the NP *a very affectionate sister*, whose head word is *sister* (section 6.8.1).

Finally, a sixth category of phrase, illustrated in this clause:

S	P	Ci
Harry	is	*my sister's* boy friend.
		(*PossP*)
NP	VP	NP

The NP *my sister's boy friend* is the intensive complement of the clause. Its head word is the noun *friend*. It has two modifiers, the noun *boy* and the phrase *my sister's*. This looks like a NP, but the -'s suffix shows that the noun *sister* is in the possessive case, like the pronouns *my*, *your*, *his* and so on. (sections 3.2.2 and 4.2.5).

A NP ending with -'s is therefore called a possessive phrase (PossP), and its function in *my sister's boy friend* is to act as the determiner in the NP, a special kind of modifier (sections 4.4.1 and 6.2.2, and in this chapter, section 7.2.2).

Activity 7.1

Identify the **marked** words and phrases in the following text as either: nouns/pronouns/NPs, verbs/VPs, adjectives/AdjPs, adverbs/AdvPs, PrepPs or PossPs.

Hari had been **so tired** and weak and anxious **that first night** that he had not **really** been aware of the place in which he **found** himself. He only saw it **for the first time** when he woke **next morning.**

The Sri Krishna Eating House was the meanest and **shabbiest** restaurant Hari had **ever** seen: even in Thul and along the Alibagh–Rewas highway there **were** cafés that were pleasanter; **usually** wooden shacks **built** in the shade of a mango or frangipani tree with a handful of marigolds and hibiscus crammed **into an old ink bottle** for a vase, coloured cigarette packets and bottles of **aerated** drinks **attractively** arranged **on the shelves,** and possibly a bright picture of a god or goddess on the wall with a tinsel garland **around the frame** and **heavily scented** joss sticks **burning** before it.

But the Sri Krishna Eating House of Gowalia Tank, Bombay, **did not have** even so much as a **coloured** picture **of Krishna** cut out of a magazine and glued to the wall. Or **perhaps** there had been one and it **had disappeared** under the layers and layers of grime and soot with which the walls were coated. **The**

ceiling was thick with cobwebs that trapped **the soot** and made a kind of furry blanket over **one's** head. The floor and **the wooden tables** were all black, **too**, since they all got an even share of soot from the open stoves in the back room where the lentils were cooked all day in a **huge** aluminium pan and the chapatis were rolled **by hand** and baked.

(Anita Desai, *The Village by the Sea*, 1982, ch. 8)

7.2 NPs and PrepPs in news headlines

Newspaper headlines generally consist either of short clauses like:

S	P	O
EUROPE MPs	LEAD	ATTACK

which contain a predicator, or of phrases like:

m	h
HOTEL	WEAKNESSES

which is a NP, with head noun *weaknesses*. Headlines are a useful variety of English with which to illustrate the different kinds of structure we can choose from to make NPs. Headlines consisting of NPs have been called labels, and those with a predicator VP 'truncated sentences'.

7.2.1 Pre-modifiers (i) – adjective and noun modifiers (m)

Adjectives and nouns in a NP which describe or identify the head noun (that is, which **modify** its meaning) precede it, as in

m	h	m	h
SHIPSHAPE	ENDEAVOUR	RHINE	AXING
adj	n	n	n

m	h
HEALTH	KICK
n	n

The head nouns, *endeavour*, *axing*, and *kick*, each have one **modifier**. The relationship between the modifier and head word is not the same for each NP. *Shipshape* is an adjective modifier, and could be the complement in a clause:

The endeavour is shipshape.

(There is a play on words in the headline, as the report is about a ship.) *Rhine axing* must mean *axing on the Rhine*, journalistic shorthand for cuts in expenditure which are to do with the British Army on the Rhine in Germany. The word *Rhine* is a proper noun. *Health kick* uses a colloquial meaning for the head noun *kick – pleasure* or *thrill –* and the modifier *health* is another noun. Notice that you cannot say:

    *The axing is Rhine   *The kick is health

so that the nouns *Rhine* and *health*, when used as modifiers, resemble determiners rather than adjectives in their relationship to *axing* and *kick*. They identify rather than describe. *Rhine* is not an attribute of axing, but identifies where it takes place.

Notice also that headlines omit many function words – determiners like *the*, and prepositions like *on*.

m	m	h
CHARLES	BOMB	SCARE
n	n	n

m	m	m	h
TV	ASSAULT	CASE	REMAND
n	n	n	n

m	m	h
£100,000	ART	THEFT
n	n	n

In this set the head words still come last, *scare*, *remand*, *theft*, but they are modified by more than one word. They could be expanded into clauses something like,

(There has been a) **scare** (over a) **bomb** (intended for Prince) **Charles**

(There has been a) **remand** (in a) **case** (of) **assault** (on) **TV**

(There has been a) **theft** (of) **art** (worth) **£100,000**

In *Charles bomb scare*, there are two modifiers, *Charles* and *bomb*. The headline, without any function words, is somewhat ambiguous, because it is not clear whether *Charles* first modifies *bomb*, and then *Charles bomb* modifies scare, as in this diagram:

| Charles bomb | scare |

or whether *bomb* first modifies *scare*:

Charles | bomb scare |

In *TV assault case remand*, the constituents are *assault case*, itself a NP (with *case* as head and *assault* as modifier) and TV:

TV | assault case | remand

In *£100,000 art theft*, *art* first modifies *theft*, and then *£100,000* modifies *art theft*,

£100,000 | art theft |

Notice that the order of the key words in the expanded clauses is reversed in the compressed NPs of the headlines, when they become pre-modifiers of a noun:

scare (over a) **bomb** (intended for Prince) **Charles** $\Rightarrow$ **Charles bomb scare**

remand (in a) **case** (of) **assault** (on) **TV** $\Rightarrow$ **TV assault case remand**

theft (of) **art** (worth) **£100,000** $\Rightarrow$ **£100,000 art theft**

The rules of English grammar allow us to pre-modify nouns with adjectives, nouns, AdjPs, NPs, and PossPs, but not usually with PrepPs. It would normally be ungrammatical to write, *an over a bomb scare*, *an of assault case*, *an on TV assault*, *an in an of assault case remand*, and so on, but a NP like *that over-the-moon kind of feeling* is a typical 'exception that proves the rule'.

7.2.2 Pre-modifiers (ii) – determiners (d) and possessive phrases (d-Poss)

7.2.2.1 DETERMINERS

Identification is also made by using determiners. Headlines almost always omit determiners, so it is rarely possible to illustrate their use with examples from newspapers. Determiners have a function which is to 'point' to the reference of a noun, it. This is called **deixis**, from a Greek word, and the determiner is said to have a **deictic** function.

The commonest determiners are *the* and *a/an*, traditionally called the **definite article** and **indefinite article**. How you use them depends upon whether the head noun is singular or plural, and a count or mass (non-count) noun (section 3.2.1):

Definite and indefinite articles

		definite	*indefinite*
singular	*count noun*	**the** sleeve	**a** coat
	mass noun	**the** evidence	Ø evidence
plural	*count noun*	**the** sleeves	Ø sleeves
	mass noun	–	–

You will see that the indefinite article is **zero** for singular mass nouns and plural count nouns – *She gave Ø* **evidence** *before the court, I want a jumper without Ø* **sleeves**.

Other common determiners are illustrated in the following sentences:

possessives

my	*'I had been looking forward to* **my** *retirement,' said Boxer.*
your	*You had to watch* **your** *comrades torn to pieces after confessing...*
his	*Napoleon set out with* **his** *dogs in attendance.*
her	*There was no thought of rebellion in* **her** *mind.*
its	*The poor beast was frightened out of* **its** *wits.*
our	*'That was* **our** *mistake, comrade.'*
their	**Their** *method was to fly up to the rafters and there lay their eggs.*

relatives

| whose | *There were four animals* **whose** *fate was not known.* |
| which | *Squealer emerged, by* **which** *time the fighting was over.* |

interrogative

what	*They thought of* **what** *obstacles they had overcome . . .*
which	*He did not know* **which** *animals had done it.*
whose	*They asked* **whose** *fault it was.*

negative

no	*Hitherto, they had had* **no** *contact with the outside world.*

quantitative

some	**Some** *progress was made in the dry frosty weather*
any	**Any** *animals giving grain to a hen would be punished.*
enough	*There was* **enough** *money left to buy the machinery.*
every	*At* **every** *few steps he stopped and snuffed the ground.*
each	*The house was guarded at* **each** *door by fierce-looking dogs.*
either	*They were unable to work for* **either** *side.*
neither	**Neither** *alternative seemed to be worth trying.*

demonstrative

this	*It was vitally necessary to conceal* **this** *fact*
that	*The rats had been troublesome* **that** *winter.*
these	*In* **these** *days Napoleon rarely appeared in public.*
those	*All* **those** *pigs supervising the work carried whips in their trotters.*

7.2.2.2 POSSESSIVE PHRASES AS DETERMINERS

The category of phrase referred to as the **possessive phrase** (PossP) (sections 6.3.3, 7.1) may function as a determiner just like a possessive pronoun. In the following NPs:

    the plays **of Shakespeare**

    the birthday **of my brother**

    the family **of the Queen of England**

the PrepPs post-modify, or **qualify** the noun head words, with the preposition *of* indicating possession or some kind of relationship. But if the PrepPs are converted into PossPs, with the -*'s* morpheme suffix, *Shakespeare's, my brother's, the Queen of England's*, they pre-modify the head noun as the determiner (d-Poss) of a NP:

    d-Poss   h
    Shakespeare's   plays

    d-Poss   h
    my brother's   birthday

    d-Poss   h
    the Queen of England's   family

otherwise the NPs with PossPs would have been:

d	m	h
*the	*Shakespeare's*	plays
	PossP	

d	m	h
*the	*my brother's*	birthday
	PossP	

d	m		h
*the	*the Queen of England's*		family
	PossP		

which are ungrammatical.

7.2.2.3 PRE-DETERMINERS

Determiners usually come first in the NP, but there is a set of similar words, already mentioned in section 6.2.6, which precede and modify them, and are therefore called pre-determiners:

> **all** the teachers, **all of** the teachers, **each of** the students, **some of** the time, **many of** the books, **twice** the price, **half** the amount, **what** a fine mess!

and so on. These pre-determiners, without *of,* can also function as determiners with a slightly changed meaning:

> **all** teachers, **each** student, **some** time, **many** books

7.2.2.4 NUMERALS

Finally, the set of numerals (num), either the **cardinal** numbers, *one, two, three* and so on, or the **ordinal** numbers, *first, second, third* and so on also function as pre-modifiers to the noun head word:

> For a horse, it was said, the pension would be *five pounds of corn* a day and, in winter, *fifteen pounds of hay* ... Boxer's *twelfth birthday* was due in the late summer of the following year
>
> > (*Animal Farm*, ch. IX)

7.2.3 The order of pre-modifiers

Pre-modifiers cannot appear in any order. We have already seen that determiners precede modifiers, and that pre-determiners precede determiners – (pre-d) (d) (m) – but we divide modifiers into different subcategories, which must be used in a certain order.

For example, the adjective modifier *old* and noun modifier *cart* in the NP *the old cart horse* are in an acceptable, normal order. The order of the modifiers in **the cart old horse* is not acceptable. The word *cart* **classifies** the kind of horse, like, for example, *race* in *a race horse*, whereas *old* is said to define a **quality** of the horse.

You can test the difference between the two kinds of modifier by trying to make them comparative or superlative. You can say *the older horse* and *the oldest horse,* but not *the most cart horse*. This is partly because *cart* is a noun, and many classifying modifiers are in fact nouns. But it also applies to adjectives when they are used as classifying modifiers. For example you can't make the adjective *annual* in *my annual holiday* either comparative, *my more annual holiday*, or superlative, *my most annual holiday*.

Another test, for adjective and noun modifiers, referred to in section 7.2.1, may also be applied. You can say *The horse is old* but not *The horse is cart*.

If we use two modifiers belonging to the same subcategory, the order matters less, and we often separate them with a comma in writing:

a placid, satisfied expression   *or*   a satisfied, placid expression
a glorious, stirring sight!   *or*   a stirring, glorious sight!
the spell-bound, sleep-walking Toad   *or*   a sleep-walking, spell-bound Toad

Here are some NPs containing two or more modifiers. The original NPs are printed in the left-hand column; in the right-hand column the order of the modifiers is changed.

Activity 7.2

(i)   Discuss how far the order of the modifiers in the re-written NPs is acceptable.

(ii)   Try to explain what determines the correct order of the modifiers before the head word.

a faint warning hum	a warning faint hum
a new raw situation	a raw new situation
their cosy river-side parlour	their river-side cosy parlour
he solitary grey Badger	the grey solitary Badger
ther small domestic jobs	other domestic small jobs
pink sunset cloud	a sunset pink cloud
tiny golden shafts of sun	golden tiny shafts of sun
those short winter days	those winter short days

Activity 7.3

(i)   Arrange the following nouns, pronouns, adjectives and prepositions as pre-modifiers to the head noun *dogs* in an acceptable order in a single NP, using *and* and *but* if necessary.

(ii)   Label the words with their function - pre-determiner (pre-d), determiner (d), numeral (num), PossP (d-Poss), modifier (m) or head word (h).

(iii)   What determined the order that you decided on for the modifiers ?

affectionate	long-eared	of
all	my	puppy
bassett	neighbour's	three
black	next-door	white
brown	noisy	+ *dogs*

Here are some more examples of pre-modifiers from headlines:

m	h	m	h	m	h	
LITERARY	CHEF	ELECTION	DATE	VERY	TOUGH	GOING
adj	n	n	n	adv	adj	n
				AdjP		

m	m	h	d-Poss		h
NUCLEAR	SAFETY	APPROVAL	STRIKING	MINERS'	CLAIMS
adj	n	n	adj	n	n
NP			PossP		

If we change the last two headlines into another form with PrepPs, the PrepPs have to follow the head words which they modify:

approval for *nuclear safety*   claims of *striking miners*

You cannot use them as pre-modifiers in an NP:

*for nuclear safety approval   **of striking miner's* claims

Because the PrepPs have to follow their head nouns, they are **post-head modifiers**, or **post-modifiers**. A useful alternative shorter name is **qualifier** (q), which we shall use.

A note for teachers and lecturers on the terminology

Some linguists distinguish post-head modifiers from pre-head modifiers by saying that a post-head modifier **qualifies** its noun head word, or is a **qualifier**. If we follow this latter convention, it will allow us to use the abbreviation (q) for qualifier as a clear label for a post-head modifier. We have been using the abbreviation (m) for **modifier** in a similar way, to label adjective and noun pre-head modifiers. The constituents of a noun phrase are therefore:

descriptive phrase	shorter version	single term adopted	abbreviation
head word		head	h
pre-head modifier	pre-modifier	(a) modifier	m
		(b) determiner	d
		(c) PossP	d-Poss
		(d) pre-determiner	pre-d
		(e) numeral	num
post-head modifier	post-modifier	qualifier	q

7.2.4 Post-head modifiers, or qualifiers (q) – PrepPs

Here is a group of headlines that contain qualifiers:

h	q	h	q
ONE	UNDER THE EIGHT	MISSION	OF DEATH
n	PrepP	n	PrepP

```
h          q
HELP    FOR STRIKE-HIT BUSINESSES
n          PrepP
```

```
h            q            q
PRESSURE   ON PRESS    OVER CHARLES TAPES
n            PrepP        PrepP
```

In this set, the noun head word comes first, and is qualified by PrepPs which follow, *under the eight, of death, for strike-hit businesses*. The fourth headline has two qualifying PrepPs, *on press* and *over Charles tapes*. As you would expect, the rules of the grammar allow us to use pre- and post-modifiers together:

```
d          h        q
ROME'S   PEACE    OF      MIND
PossP             PrepP
n          n        p       n
```

```
m              h            q
SKILLCENTRE   DILEMMA     OVER    CASH
                           PrepP
n              n            p       n
```

```
m        h          q
IRISH   PROTEST    OVER    ARRESTS
                   PrepP
adj      n          p        n
```

```
m          h          q
£340,000  DAMAGES    FOR    BOY
                     PrepP
n          n          p      n
```

```
d-Poss         m            m          h        q
LIVERPOOL'S   AWAY-DAY    RETURN    TICKET   TO      FINAL
PossP                                        PrepP
n              n            n          n        p      n
```

Headlines are rather a special case in English grammar, but they help to show the structure of NPs very clearly as (**m**)**h**(**q**), where the brackets mean an 'optional choice' and also 'choose as many as you need'. In other words, a NP consists of a noun head, with one or more optional pre-modifiers and one or more optional post-modifiers. A NP may be a single word, which must be the head word.

Activity 7.4

All the following headlines are NPs.

(i) Label the constituent words or phrases (h) for the head noun, (m) for modifiers (pre-head modifiers), and (q) for qualifiers (post-head modifiers).

(ii) Label the constituent words with their word-classes, and phrases with their form labels.

(a) SIEGE AT HOUSE
(b) TOUGH GOING
(c) SMOKE SCREEN
(d) ART BY POST
(e) CAMERAS HAUL
(f) £35 FOR THIEVES
(g) TODDLER PROBE
(h) EXTENSION TO MILL
(i) WORDS OF WISDOM ABOUT MARRIAGE
(j) SOUR NOTE ON RADIO YORK
(k) METHODIST GIFT FOR HOSPITAL
(l) CHURCH BROWSER'S BIBLE

7.2.5 NPs in PrepPs and PrepPs in NPs

The NP which is the complement of the preposition in a PrepP can itself have the same variety of structures as any other NP. For example, the NP *Holiday slides of sunny days* has the structure (mhq); the modifier is *holiday*, the head noun is *slides* and the qualifier is *of sunny days*. We can then go on to break down the PrepP *of sunny days* into its own constituents, so that the complete NP is analysed as:

m	h	q	
HOLIDAY	SLIDES	OF SUNNY DAYS	= NP
n	n	PrepP	

p	m	h	
OF	SUNNY	DAYS	= PrepP
p	adj	n	

Diagramming and labelling is more economical and clearer than a descriptive statement like,

The noun phrase *Holiday slides of sunny days* consists of the head noun *slides*, pre-modified by the noun *holiday* and post-modified by the prepositional phrase *of sunny days*, which consists of the preposition *of* and the noun phrase complement *sunny days*, which consists of the head noun *days* pre-modified by the adjective *sunny*.

Activity 7.5

Make a similar analysis of the following headlines, placing grammatical function labels above, and form or word-class labels below, each word or phrase.

(a) SAFETY PLEA BY PRIEST
(b) FINE OVER ASSAULT AFTER RECEPTION ROW
(c) JEWELLERY HAUL IN HOTEL RAID
(d) CENTURY OF MOTORING MANIA
(e) NATIONAL ART GEMS IN U.S. EXHIBITION

(f)   FIRST SHIFTS IN AFTERNOON AT SELBY PITS
(g)   HOUSING CASH BLOW
(h)   UNEASE OVER POLICEMAN'S PAINFUL ORDEAL
(i)   BUS CUTS DELAY
(j)   THOSE CASH BENEFITS FOR SINGLE PARENTS

7.2.6   *PrepPs embedded in PrepPs*

In section 4.3.2, the grammatical **embedding** of one clause within another was first
mentioned, in which one clause is **subordinate** to a **main** clause. The same process
of embedding applied to NPs and PrepPs was described in sections 6.2, 6.3 and
6.4. In the following NP:

DPP DENIAL OVER VETTING OF JURY

the PrepP *of jury* qualifies *vetting*, so that it is the NP *vetting of jury* that is the
complement in the PrepP *over vetting of jury*. This process of embedding one
constituent within another is extremely common, and forms what is called a
hierarchy of constituents, that is, a structure organised in classes one above the
other. Another simple analogy or image for this kind of embedding is that of
wooden Russian dolls, carved to fit one within the other, or Chinese boxes
illustrated in one kind of diagram already used:

| DPP DENIAL | OVER | VETTING | OF JURY |

Although we are dealing with abstract ideas about structure (see the beginning
of chapter 2 again), we need to use mental images of concrete things to help us
understand how language works. So the structure of the same headline can be
represented as:

These diagrams are not suitable for ordinary writing or typing, so it is quite usual
to use brackets with labels to show the embedding of constituents.

```
m       h           q
            p           h           q
                                    p       h
(DPP   DENIAL   (OVER   VETTING   (BY JURY)))
```

Notice that in the headline *Pressure on Press over Charles tapes* there are two
separate PrepPs of equal status. You can reverse them, *Pressure over Charles tapes
on Press*. A bracketed description would be:

```
h               q               q
        p       h       p       m           h
(PRESSURE   (ON   PRESS)   (OVER   CHARLES   TAPES))
```

PRESSURE ON PRESS OVER CHARLES TAPES

But you cannot reverse the two PrepPs of *DPP denial over vetting by jury* without changing the meaning – **DPP denial by jury over vetting*. So you must be careful to distinguish between a phrase which is **subordinated** to another one (embedded in it), and one which is **coordinated** with another one.

Activity 7.6

The following headlines have two or more PrepPs at (q). Identify and bracket the constituent PrepPs to show whether one is embedded in the other or not.

(a) COLOUREDS CALL FOR SCRAPPING OF LAWS ON APARTHEID
(b) ROUND-UP OF ANC MEN IN SWAZILAND
(c) FIVE HELD OVER ATTACK ON GRAVE OF DUKE
(d) CREDIT-CARD BONANZA FOR SHOPS IN MANCHESTER
(e) MICHELLE IN LINE-UP FOR BEAUTY FINAL

7.2.7 *Nonfinite clauses embedded in NPs*

So far, the post-modifiers of an NP have been PrepPs. But as we have seen in sections 6.3.1 and 6.4.1, other kinds of constituent may appear at (q) in NP structure:

FAMILY AMONG 16 KILLED IN HOUSE FIRES

AIMS SET FOR ENGLISH COULD BE HARMFUL

In both headlines, the completer grammatical version with normal function words includes the pronouns *who* or *which*.

A complete family was among sixteen people **who** were killed in house fires

The aims **which** have been set for English could be harmful.

In this version, the pronouns are functioning in a **relative clause** which is embedded within a NP (sections 4.2.11 and 6.3.1). The **relative pronoun** (*who/ which*) refers back to a noun head, *sixteen (people) who...*, *the aims which...*, and the relative clause defines the noun more specifically. The word *that* also functions as a relative pronoun. Notice that the verbs *killed* and *set* are the forms of nonfinite verb called *-en/-ed* participle (sections 3.3.3 and 6.5.1.3) and so form the **passive voice** (section 8.10). When the relative pronouns *who, which* or *that*, and the relational verb *be*, are omitted in the shorter versions of the clauses, we can describe the clause as a **reduced relative clause**. Such clauses are common in all varieties of spoken and written English, not just headlines.

The structure of the first headline is:

```
S               P    Ca
[(FAMILY)      (Ø)   (AMONG  16   [KILLED IN HOUSE FIRES])]
                      p             h   q = Clause


p              h    q
(AMONG        16    [KILLED IN HOUSE FIRES])
p              n    Clause


P              Ca
[(KILLED)     (IN HOUSE FIRES)]
v              PrepP


p     m       h
(IN   HOUSE   FIRES)
p     n       n
```

The qualifier of the NP *16* is a non-finite clause, *killed in house fires*.

The second headline *Aims set for English could be harmful* is a clause with the structure SPC.

```
S                            P            Ci
[(AIMS SET FOR ENGLISH)     (COULD BE)   (HARMFUL)]
NP


h        q
(AIMS   SET FOR ENGLISH])
n        Clause


Clause
P       A
[(SET)  (FOR ENGLISH)]
        PrepP
```

The following headline also contains a qualifying structure:

SIT-IN TO SAVE FACTORY

Its structure may be analysed as:

```
NP
h        q
(SIT-IN  [TO SAVE FACTORY])
n        Clause


Clause
P           O
[TO  SAVE  FACTORY]
      v     n
```

The qualifier is again a clause, but its verb is the nonfinite form called **infinitive**.

The third form of verb which can post-modify a head noun is the non-finite *-ing* **participle**:

CHIMNEY-POT FALLING FROM ROOF INJURES TWO

which has the structure:

Clause

S		P	O
[(CHIMNEY-POT [FALLING FROM ROOF])		(INJURES)	(TWO)]
NP			

h	**q**
(CHIMNEY-POT	[FALLING FROM ROOF])
n	clause

Clause

P	A
[(FALLING)	(FROM ROOF)] =
v	PrepP

Activity 7.7

Bracket the clauses [ ] functioning as qualifiers (post-modifiers) of nouns in the following headlines. Some headlines are NPs, others are clauses.

(a)   MAN TRAPPED IN CRASH CAR SLIGHTLY HURT
(b)   THIEVES FOILED BY ALARM REPORT ARRESTED
(c)   THREAT TO DIG UP PLAYING FIELD
(d)   WOMAN CARRYING CHILD COLLAPSES
(e)   SWIMMER SAVED BY LIFEBOAT IN HOSPITAL
(f)   CAMPAIGN TO SAVE FISHING LAKE
(g)   MOVE TO LIMIT PARTIES' POLL SPENDING
(h)   GROUP LEADING DEMO ATTACKED

7.3   NPs and PrepPs as constituents of clauses

Because the principal functions of NPs are as subject, object or intensive complement in clause structure, or as complement in PrepP structure, most English texts contain lots of NPs. This of course includes newspaper headlines. There is a common type of headline already mentioned which looks as if it has no predicator, but which must be clearly distinguished from the NP 'label' type:

THATCHER ADAMANT ON REFUSING CONCESSIONS

CND READY FOR COURT CHALLENGE

In both headlines the main verb *be* has been **deleted**, together with other function words:

>Mrs Thatcher **is** adamant...

>The CND **is** ready...

The verb **be** is also deleted from headlines when it is the first **auxiliary** verb in a VP. The following examples illustrate this:

(a) SAUCE HURLED AT THE QUEEN   Sauce **is** hurled at the Queen
(b) JONES STANDING FOR
     PARLIAMENT   Jones **is** standing for Parliament
(c) MANAGER TO RETIRE   The manager **is** to retire
     MANAGER GOING TO RETIRE   The manager **is** going to retire
     MANAGER ABOUT TO RETIRE   The manager **is** about to retire

(The structure of VPs is described in Chapter 8; example (a) is the **passive voice**, (b) **progressive aspect** and (c) other uses of be as a **semi-auxiliary** in *be to*, *be going to* and *be about to*.) So in looking at the structure of headlines, be careful to notice whether the verb *be* has been deleted from a clause.

Activity 7.8

(i) Supply an appropriate form of the verb *be* to complete these headlines.

(ii) Identify the NPs and PrepPs, and use bracketing to show their structure.

(a) STEEL WORKERS SACKED
(b) TOFFEE APPLE TEENIES GANG LICKED!
(c) MANY ROADS IN COUNTY UNDER WATER
(d) PRISON CLIMBING LESSONS 'CRAZY'
(e) COUNCILLORS TO LET IN FRESH AIR
(f) WORKING MINERS DRIFTING BACK
(g) REFUGEES STARVING
(h) FUMES RISK FIRM FINED

Headlines with main verbs are clauses, and are very common. In the following examples, the clause structure is shown by bracketing and labelling:

S   *P*   *O*
[(EUROPE MPS) (LEAD) (ATTACK)]

S   *P*   *O*   *A*
[(PAISLEY) (CALLS) (A DEMO) (OVER SANDS SERVICE)]

S   *P*   *O*
[(SORTER) (SPOTS) (DANGER PARCEL [ADDRESSED TO PALACE])]

Notice that in the third headline the object is the NP *danger parcel addressed to Palace*, in which *addressed to Palace* is a post-modifying nonfinite clause:

NP
m   *h*   *q*
(DANGER   PARCEL   [ADDRESSED TO PALACE])

Clause
P   *A*
[ADDRESSED   TO PALACE]

Activity 7.9

(i)   Identify the VPs functioning as predicators, including *be* when deleted, in the following headlines.

(ii)   Identify the NPs and PrepPs, and show their structure by bracketing.

(a)   JENKIN DELAYS RATE-CAP ORDERS
(b)   NARROW NEC VOTE UPHOLDS MILITANT EXPULSION
(c)   UNIONS' PENALTIES DEFERRED
(d)   BBC WINS CHINESE DEAL
(e)   GERMANY DISCOVERS SOVIET SPY MANUAL
(f)   HOWE PLANS VISITS TO EASTERN EUROPE

7.4   NPs and PrepPs in texts

7.4.1   Animal Farm – *NPs and PrepPs*

The variety of patterns of NP and PrepP can best be illustrated from texts. Here is a paragraph from George Orwell's *Animal Farm*, chapter IX, with the NPs and PrepPs marked in bold type:

> **Boxer's split hoof** was **a long time in healing**. **They** had started **the rebuilding of the windmill the day after the victory celebrations** were ended. **Boxer** refused to take **even a day off work**, and made **it a point of honour** not to let **it** be seen that **he** was **in pain**. **In the evening he** would admit privately **to Clover** that **the hoof** troubled **him a great deal**. **Clover** treated **the hoof with poultices of herbs which she** prepared by chewing **them**, and both **she** and **Benjamin** urged **Boxer** to work less hard. '**A horse's lungs** do not last **for ever**,' **she** said **to him**. But **Boxer** would not listen. **He** had, **he** said, **only one real ambition left** – to see **the windmill** well **under way** before **he** reached **the age of retirement**.

The NPs and PrepPs in this paragraph can be grouped into small sets showing similarities of structure and choice:

(a) Pronouns **(b) Proper nouns**
he (5)   Benjamin
him   Boxer (3)
it (2)   Clover
she (3)
them
they
which

(c) NPs

d h   **d   h**   d h q   **d   h   q**
             the hoof (2)   q = PrepP   **p   h**
                                                      a day off work

d-Poss h   **d-Poss   h**
             a horse's lungs   d m h q   **d   m   h   q**
                                     q = PrepCl   **p NonfCl**
                                                      a long time in healing

d-Poss m h   **d-Poss   m   h**
             Boxer's split hoof   d m h q   **d   m   h   q**
                                                                          NonfCl
                                     q = NonfCl only one real ambition left

d m h   **d   m   h**
             a great deal

(d) PrepPs

p h   **p   h**   p d m h   **d   h   q**
        in pain   **p   d   m   h**
                                           the day after the victory celebrations

p d h   **p   d   h**
        in the evening   p h q   **p   h   q**
                                 q = PrepP   **p   h**
                                                 with poultices of herbs

7.4.2 Animal Farm - *relative clauses as qualifiers*

NPs and PrepPs with RelCls as qualifiers are marked in these extracts from chapter X:

1

For once Benjamin consented to break his rule, and he read out to Clover what was written on the wall. There was nothing there now except a single commandment. It ran:

ALL ANIMALS ARE EQUAL
BUT SOME ANIMALS ARE MORE
EQUAL THAN OTHERS

After that it did not seem strange when next day **the pigs who were supervising the work of the farm** all carried whips in their trotters....

2

Napoleon himself appeared in a black coat, ratcatcher breeches, and leather leggings, while his favourite sow appeared **in the watered silk dress which Mrs Jones had been used to wear on Sundays.**

3

No one noticed **the wondering faces of the animals that gazed in at the window**.

Each of the marked phrases contains an embedded RelCl, the first marked by the relative pronoun *who*:

```
       d     h    q
                  RelCl
NP    (the  pigs  [who were supervising the work of the farm])
```

although its **referent** is the noun *pigs*, which are usually thought of as non-human (as the use of *which* just made shows). But in the novel they have become familiar characters, and so are referred to with *who*, usually reserved for human referents. The RelCl in the second extract is in a PrepP introduced by *which*:

```
p  d    m             h      q
PrepP                        RelCl
(in the watered silk dress [which Mrs Jones had been used to wear on
                                                            Sundays])
```

In the third extract, the RelCl is marked with *that*, an alternative relative pronoun to either *who* or *which*. It qualifies the PrepP *of the animals*, which is itself the qualifier of the NP *the wondering faces*:

```
d    m        h    q
                   p  d  h     q
NP                 RelCl
(the wondering faces of the animals [that gazed in at the window])
```

A clause embedded in a phrase like these RelCl qualifiers of NPs and PrepPs is an example of **rank-shift** (section 6.3.1), because we normally expect a clause to consist of one or more phrases, rather than a phrase to contain a clause.

Notice that in extract 1 above Orwell uses the usually ungradable adjective *equal* ironically as a **gradable adjective** (section 3.4.5), in the slogan just quoted:

ALL ANIMALS ARE EQUAL
BUT SOME ANIMALS ARE MORE
EQUAL THAN OTHERS

which illustrates how the rules of grammar are creatively broken.

Activity 7.10

Some NPs and PrepPs in the following sentences are printed in bold type. Analyse their structure in terms of p, m, h and q constituents, including any embedded constituents, as demonstrated in the examples in this chapter.

(a) **The cold Duke** gazed **out a window of the castle**, as if **he** were watching **flowers in bloom** or **flying birds**.

(b) **His voice** sounded **like iron dropped on velvet**.

(c) We shall think **of some amusing task for you to do**.

(d) **Her voice** was **faraway music**, and her eyes were **candles burning on a tranquil night**.

(from James Thurber, *The 13 Clocks*, 1951, ch. 3)

(e) **The poorest families in Britain** suffered **a cut of 14 percent in their real income** during the Thatcher years.

(f) **The huge widening of the gulf between rich and poor** means the less well-off half of the population now receive only a quarter of total income.

(from *Guardian*, 1 July 1993)

7.4.3 NPs and PrepPs in academic writing

Formal academic writing tends to use a characteristic style which caters for other academics rather than students and the general public, and so often appears 'difficult'. There tend to be a lot of NPs and PrepPs which are **nominalisations** of verbs, that is, instead of writing:

In this book we **aim** to **study** how to **work out** an empirical method by which we **can analyse** what people **assume** when they **converse** together socially.

in which there are five active VPs, the academic authors actually wrote:

The aim of this study **is to work out** an empirical method of conversational analysis capable of **recovering** the social assumptions that **underlie** the verbal communication process.

(J.Gumperz and E. Herasimchuk,
The Conversational Analysis of Social Meaning, ch. 1)

Five of the active verbs in the rewritten version are nouns or NPs in the original. Actions which could have been represented by verbs ('doing words') have been **nominalised**, expressed as nouns. An action or process becomes a 'thing':

we aim to study (*clause*)   the aim of this study (*NP*)
analyse (*verb*)   analysis (*noun*)
assume (*verb*)   assumption (*noun*)
converse (*verb*)   conversation (*noun*)

In this style of writing, NPs and PrepPs tend to predominate.

Activity 7.11

Identify the NPs and PrepPs in the following text (the first paragraph of the book cited above), and rewrite the extract using verbs instead of nominalisations representing actions.

The aim of this study is to work out an empirical method of conversational analysis capable of recovering the social assumptions that underlie the verbal communication process by focusing on actors' use of speech to interact, i.e., to create and maintain a particular definition of a social situation. The basic theoretical position that sets this work apart from other work in sociolinguistics is that, in the analysis of face-to-face encounters, the sorts of things that social anthropologists and sociologists refer to by such terms as role, status, social identities, and social relationships will be treated as communicative symbols. They are signaled in the act of speaking and have a function in the communication process akin to that of syntax in the communication of referential meaning.

Activity 7.12

In the following text from George Orwell's *Animal Farm*, identify the NPs and PrepPs. Write out the structure of the NPs and PrepPs, and label the constituents.

One Sunday morning, when the animals assembled to receive their orders, Napoleon announced that he had decided upon a new policy. From now onwards Animal Farm would engage in trade with the neighbouring farms: not, of course, for any commercial purpose, but simply in order to obtain certain materials which were urgently necessary. The needs of the windmill must override everything else, he said. He was therefore making arrangements to sell a stack of hay and part of the current year's wheat crop, and later on, if more money were needed, it would have to be made up by the sale of eggs, for which there was always a market in Willingdon. The hens, said Napoleon, should welcome this sacrifice as their own special contribution towards the building of the windmill.

7.5   Summary

NP function
Noun phrases (NPs) regularly function in clause structure as subject (S), object (O), intensive complement (Ci) and sometimes as adverbial (A), and in prepositional phrase structure as complement - PrepP = (p + NP).

NP form
A NP has a noun head word (h), and may be pre-modified by a determiner (d) or a possessive phrase (PossP) functioning as determiner, a numeral (num), an adjective (adj) or adjective phrase (AdjP), and a noun (n) or noun phrase (NP). A determiner may be preceded by a pre-determiner (pre-d).

NPs are post-modified by qualifiers (q), which are most often PrepPs, NonfCls or RelCls.

PrepP function
PrepPs function as adverbials (Ca or A) in clause structure, and as qualifiers (q), post-modifying the head noun in NP structure.

PrepP form
A PrepP has a preposition head and NP complement. Because PrepPs can post-modify NPs, the structures containing them may have a series of embedded PrepPs or NPs. This is known as a recursive structure, as the same constituents recur, one within the other. NPs and PrepPs can be very complex.

Pronouns
Since the function of pronouns is to substitute for nouns and NPs, it follows that pronouns may occur as head of a NP wherever an NP with a noun head can. Pronouns can, however, only be pre- or post-modified in very limited ways.

8. Verb phrases

In chapter 2 it was said that at the centre of a **proposition**, something stated about experience, was a **process**, and that the process was represented by the grammatical **predicator**. The function of a predicator is always performed by a VP. The VP is the 'head' of the clause, even though there are usually more NPs, because they can potentially function in clauses as either subject, object, intensive complement or adverbial.

The forms of verbs have been briefly described in section 3.3 and the forms of verb phrases in section 6.5. We can now examine VPs in a little more detail. The important difference between **finite** and **nonfinite** verbs is applied equally to verb phrases functioning in a clause, so that we speak of finite and nonfinite clauses. Finite verbs are marked for tense, which is the topic of section 8.1 following. Newspaper headlines will again be used to demonstrate this part of the description of VPs.

8.1 Present and past tense

8.1.1 *Tense in main verbs*

The statement that there are only two tenses in English (section 3.3.1) seems puzzling, because it is quite clear that we can refer to past, present and future time, and that therefore there should be at least three tenses to do this. But if we limit the strict use of *tense* to a grammatical, marked form of a verb, you will see that in English there is no future tense form, because we cannot refer to the future by simply inflecting a verb, that is, by adding a suffix or changing its vowel. The French for *I shall eat* is *je mangerai*, in which the suffix *-erai* on the verb stem *mang-* (*eat*) marks future tense. We cannot do this in English – there was no future tense inflection on verbs in Old English – so we have to use additional **auxiliary** verbs like *shall*.

In practice, the word *tense* is used in a more general way, and there is some inconsistency of reference to tense (a grammatical category) and time (a semantic category).

Typical of headlines which are grammatical clauses are:

S	P	
(i) BISHOPS	*TAKE*	FISH OFF MENU FOR PENANCE
(ii) TEACHERS	*PASS*	COMPUTER TEST
(iii) POUND	*FALLS*	
(iv) INDIANS	*QUESTION*	1,500 IN SPY PROBE
(v) PEACE FORMULA	*GOES*	TO MINERS' EXECUTIVE

The predicators, *take, pass, falls, question* and *goes*, are all **lexical** or **main verbs** in the **present tense**. Most news is about what has happened in the past, but because it is the immediate past, it is thought of as currently going on. So the **present tense** is almost always used in the headlines of newspapers. This is not an inflexible convention, however, and the **past tense** can be found:

(vi) PUBLICAN IN ROW	*BROKE*	DRIVING BAN
(vii) LIGHTNING	*KILLED*	MARINE

The terms **simple past tense** and **simple present tense** are used to refer to those finite VPs which consist of a single main verb, and the main verb itself is marked for present or past tense. In finite VPs with more than one verb, it is the <u>first</u> verb which carries present or past tense. Auxiliary, or 'helping' verbs, always come before the main verb, so it is the first auxiliary verb that is marked for tense (sections 8.2 to 8.6).

The simple present tense is not used a lot in ordinary conversation, but writers sometimes use it in narratives to create a sense of the story actually taking place as you read. In the following extract from a short story, most of the verbs are either finite simple present tense, or nonfinite *-ing* participles which indicate present time (the only exception is *were*, a past tense **subjunctive** form expressing something hypothetical):

A crowd **collects**, **eating** oranges and bananas, **tearing** off the skins, **dividing**, **sharing**. One young girl **has** even a basket of strawberries, but she **does** not eat them.

'Aren't they dear!' She **stares** at the tiny pointed fruits as if she were afraid of them. The Australian soldier **laughs**.

(Katherine Mansfield, 'Bank Holiday',
The Garden Party & Other Stories, 1922)

A familiar variety of English in which the simple present tense occurs (together with a lot of deletion of function words) is unscripted radio and TV commentary:

Becker **serves** to the forehand (.) return down the line **passes** him Becker towards us left-hand court **serves** to the backhand (.) Lendl **returns** half-volley but **nets** it

If the main verb is *be*, headline writers (and commentators) nearly always omit it,

(viii) TORIES Ø JITTERY OVER 3m JOBLESS THREAT
(ix) MISSING WOMAN Ø DEAD IN FIELD
(x) HOMES PLAN Ø OFF
(xi) RAIL PAY RISES Ø AT RISK

Activity 8.1

Identify the main verbs in the following headlines and say whether they are simple present or simple past tense.

   (i)   NEGAS GIVES ASSURANCE ON LEAKS
   (ii)   PLAY GROUPS WIN GRANTS
  (iii) YOUTHS DROVE VAN INTO WALL
  (iv) WIFE WAITS
   (v)   LEAD TAKES BACKSTAGE ROLE
  (vi) RESTORATION HITS SNAG
 (vii) VILLAGERS SEEK BYPASS CROSSING
(viii) RADIO HAMS TUNE-IN TO THE SAME WAVELENGTH
  (ix) PUB CASH GAVE SCHOOL A COMPUTER
   (x)   BOARD NAMES TALKS TERMS

Among the most likely texts in which to find plenty of occurrences of the past tense are newspaper reports and narrative stories. These can be briefly illustrated in the following extracts.

Activity 8.2

Before reading the commentary which follows:

(i)   Identify the verbs marked for past tense in each text.

(ii)   Change the past tense verbs to present tense and notice whether the texts are still grammatical and make good sense.

(iii)   Discuss the reasons why this change is possible with the novel extract but not with the newspaper report, unless other changes are made to the text. What are these changes?

(Remember that in finite VPs of two or more words, the auxiliary verb which comes *first* is marked for present or past tense, not the main verb, which comes last, or other auxiliaries.)

A – extract from a novel

Mrs Jones looked out of the bedroom window, saw what was happening, hurriedly flung a few possessions into a carpet bag, and slipped out of the farm by another way. Moses sprang off his perch and flapped after her, croaking loudly. Meanwhile the animals had chased Jones and his men out on to the road and slammed the five-barred gate behind them. And so, almost before they knew what was happening, the Rebellion had been successfully carried through: Jones was expelled, and the Manor Farm was theirs.

(George Orwell, *Animal Farm*, ch. 2)

B – newspaper report (the personal and place names have been changed)

A teacher who claimed he was sacked because he stuck to the three Rs lost his claim for unfair dismissal yesterday.

John Brown, aged 59, was fired in April last year after 10 years at Woolford Junior School, Barsetshire, for alleged professional incompetence, despite support for him from several parents.

He told an industrial tribunal that he clashed with the new headteacher, Jim White, over 'trendy' teaching methods and homework and claimed that he had been ordered to throw away books including bibles and dictionaries.

But during the three-day hearing Jane Black, the chairwoman of the school governors, had said that there was no alternative to dismissing Mr Brown after the county councils chief education inspector concluded that his performance was well below professional standards.

Commentary on activity 8.2

In the paragraph from *Animal Farm*, all the finite verbs are marked for past tense, and there are no references to other events taking place at a time other than that of the narrative. It would not make sense, for example, to use an adverbial of time like *yesterday afternoon* in a clause such as:

*She arrives home at three o'clock yesterday afternoon.

because the meaning of *arrives* implies 'present' or 'future', and so does not **collocate** with *yesterday*, whose meaning implies 'past'. The adverbials *this afternoon* or *tomorrow afternoon* would collocate quite acceptably with *arrives*. A present tense narrative in the *Animal Farm* paragraph is therefore quite acceptable:

Mrs Jones **looks** out of the bedroom window, **sees** what **is** happening, hurriedly **flings** a few possessions into a carpet bag, and **slips** out of the farm by another way. Moses **springs** off his perch and **flaps** after her, croaking loudly. Meanwhile the animals **have** chased Jones and his men out on to the road and slammed the five-barred gate behind them. And so, almost before they **know** what **is** happening, the Rebellion **has** been successfully carried through: Jones **is** expelled, and the Manor Farm **is** theirs.

Not all the verbs in the newspaper report, however, can be put into the present tense. The adverbials *yesterday* and *in April last year*, the adverbial clause (AdvCl) **after** *the county councils chief education inspector* **concluded** ..., and the reported clause following *claimed, he was sacked*, all refer to events before those being reported, and so cannot be narrated in the present. On the other hand, some verbs describe actions which we can assume are ongoing, or continuous, so that the present tense is acceptable, as in *because he sticks to the three Rs, he clashes with the headmaster* and *his performance is well below professional standards*.

(Verbs changed to the present tense are in bold type, and verbs and phrases which remain unchanged are underlined):

A teacher who **claims** <u>he was sacked</u> because he **sticks** to the three Rs <u>lost</u> his claim for unfair dismissal <u>yesterday</u>.

John Brown, aged 59, <u>was fired</u> <u>in April last year</u> after 10 years at Woolford Junior School, Barsetshire, for alleged professional incompetence, despite support for him from several parents.

He **tells** an industrial tribunal that he **clashes** with the new headteacher, Jim White, over 'trendy' teaching methods and homework and **claims** that he **has** been ordered to throw away books including bibles and dictionaries.

But during the three-day hearing Jane Black, the chairwoman of the school governors, **has** said that there **is** no alternative to dismissing Mr Brown <u>after</u> the county councils chief education inspector <u>concluded</u> that his performance **is** well below professional standards.

8.2 Auxiliary verbs – *be*

The verb *be* is usually deleted from headlines when it functions as an **auxiliary verb** as well as when it is the single main verb.

Activity 8.3

Replace the sign Ø with the appropriate form of the auxiliary verb *be*, (a) in the present tense, and (b) in the past tense, in the following headlines.

(a) GEMS THIEF Ø LOST IN CHASE AT MALTON
(b) FOUR Ø SAVED
(c) SURVEYOR Ø GIVING UP POST
(d) NEIGHBOURS Ø CHASING TOP DOG TITLES
(e) COUNCILLORS Ø TO LET IN FRESH AIR
(f) WOMAN Ø TO QUIT

Headlines (a) and (b) are in the **passive voice**, in which *be* is followed by the *-en/-ed* participles of the main verbs *lost* and *saved* (section 8.10). In (c) and (d) *be* followed by the *-ing* participles *giving* and *chasing* represents **progressive aspect** (section 8.8.1). In (e) and (f) *be* is part of the construction *be to* followed by the infinitive of the main verb, and refers to future events, like *be going to* and *be about to*. It is then part of a construction called a **semi-auxiliary verb** (section 8.6).

Activity 8.4

(i) Rewrite these headlines as complete sentences with main verbs, supplying the appropriate form of the deleted verb *be* (a) in the present tense, and (b) in the past tense.

(ii) Say whether the verb *be* is a main or auxiliary verb.

(a) BAG SCANS URGED
(b) SINGERS ASSAULT CLAIM DISMISSED
(c) FALSE CLAIM MAN PUT ON PROBATION
(d) TOP DEGREES DEFENDED
(e) CORONER'S OFFICER TO RETIRE
(f) EGYPT UNLIKELY TO REPATRIATE MEN
(g) COUNCIL STAFF ANGRY AT CUTS
(h) DOCTORS SEEKING CHANGES IN DRUGS LIST SCHEME
(i) UN CHIEF STILL HOPEFUL AFTER COLLAPSE OF TALKS
(j) OPEC NOT CUTTING PRICE OF OIL

8.3 Auxiliary verbs – *have*

Like the verb *be*, *have* is commonly used as both a main verb and an auxiliary. As main verb, it occurs as a single-word VP, as in:

(i)   She **had** very long fair hair.

or following an auxiliary:

(ii) The women would **have** their tea at six oclock.

As an auxiliary, *have* is always followed by the *-en/-ed* participle of the next verb, which may be the main verb:

(iii) The matron **had given** her leave to go out.

or another auxiliary:

(iv) They **had been cut** into long thick even slices.
(i–iv adapted from 'Clay', *Dubliners*, James Joyce)

Auxiliary *have* in (iii) and (iv) is used to express **perfect aspect** (section 8.8.2). If it is followed by the particle *to* in a verb phrase, it means something like *must*, and is called a **semi-auxiliary,** like *be to* and *be going to* (section 8.6):

I **have to** go by eight oclock.

I **must** go by eight oclock.

The verb *must* has no past tense form in StE. It was originally a past tense form in OE, and has since changed its meaning to refer to the present, so you have to use the past tense of *have to* instead:

I **had to** go by eight oclock.

Activity 8.5

(i) Identify the verb *have* in the following sentences as either a main verb, auxiliary *have* or semi-auxiliary *have to*.

(ii) Say whether its tense is present or past.

(a) Her father has come home from work.
(b) Have you change for a pound, please?
(c) I had to throw that broken cup away.
(d) She had her comfortable old things on.
(e) Jane has been waiting for over half an hour.
(f) You didn't tell me whether you had to go early.

You can use *have* or *be* as either auxiliaries (aux), main verbs (v), and semi-auxiliaries (s-aux) in the same VP:

> *aux v*
> Jim **has had** a good time on holiday.

> *aux s-aux v*
> Judy **has had to have** her TV repaired

> *aux aux v*
> The child **has been being** rather naughty.

> *aux v*
> They **were having** a snack in the kitchen.

> *s-aux aux v*
> We **were to have had** time to finish.

8.4 Auxiliary verbs – *do*

A third auxiliary verb that has a number of functions is *do*. Like the other primary verbs *have* and *be* it can be a main verb:

Will you help me **do** the washing-up?

and can also function as a kind of 'general' main verb, substituting for others:

What are you **doing** out there?

That restaurant **does** good meals very cheaply.

Who locked the door? Someone must have **done**.

Apart from this variety of uses as a main verb, it is an important constituent as an auxiliary verb in several constructions.

Activity 8.6

Examine the following sentences, which all contain forms of the verb *do* used as an auxiliary, and identify the several different functions.

Identify the tense as present or past.

(a)   Do you know whether Jane will come with you?
(b)   I **don't** think I can manage it till next week.
(c)   I **do** hope you'll come and see me again.
(d)   When **did** her brother get that job?
(e)   Well, she came last time, **didn't** she?
(f)   Only after several applications **did** he succeed.

We shall now look at these functions of auxiliary *do* in more detail.

8.4.I   Asking questions – interrogative mood

There are two common but contrasting ways of asking question, one where we are asking for specific information and another where we only want a simple *yes* or *no* as an answer.

8.4.1.1   *WH-* INTERROGATIVES

Questions which ask for specific information make use of a set of function words, all of which except *how* begin with *wh-*. The *wh*-word focuses on the item that we want further information about. *Wh*-questions cannot be answered by *yes* or *no*. The common *wh*-words are:

who, whom, whose, which, why, when, where, how ?

and a few which are now old-fashioned and seldom used except in very formal speech:

whence, whither, wherefore?

       wh-S **P**
(i)   Who   has not been / to the pantomime?

       wh-S   **P**
(ii) Which of you two is going / to the match / tomorrow?

In (i) the *wh*-word is the subject of the clause, and in (ii) *which* is the head word of the NP *which of you two*. The order of the auxiliary and main verbs is unchanged from that of declarative clauses like:

       S   **P**
(iii) Claire has not been / to the pantomime.

       S   **P**
(iv) Philip is going / to the match / tomorrow.

But if the *wh*-word is not the subject of the clause, the first auxiliary is moved in front of the subject of its clause, and *operates* as a marker of **interrogative mood**. Such verbs are then called **operator-verbs (op-v)**.

       wh-   **op-v** **S**   **P**
(v)   Why has   Claire   not been / to the pantomime?

       wh-   **op-v** **S**   **P**
(vi) When is   Philip   going / to the match?

8.4.1.2 YES/NO INTERROGATIVES

The following clauses, or simple sentences, make statements. The grammatical term for this statement-making function is **declarative mood,** because we are *declaring* something (section 9.2.1). It is the grammatical equivalent of a *proposition*, the term used in chapter 2 to refer to the meaning of a clause. The subject comes first and the predicator second.

>   *S*   *P*
> (vii) You **are enjoying** / your breakfast.

>   *S P*
> (viii) I **have told** / you / everything.

>   *S*   *P*
> (ix) Michael and Sue **can go** / to the disco / on Friday.

(The auxiliary *can* in (iii) is a **modal** auxiliary verb, and modals are discussed in the next section 8.5)

If these statements are to become questions looking for a yes/no answer, the first auxiliary verb is moved to the front of the clause as the operator-verb:

>   *op-v* *S*   *P*
> (x) **Are** you **enjoying** / your breakfast?

>   *op-v* *S P*
> (xi) **Have** I **told** / you / everything?

>   *op-v* *S*   *P*
> (xii) **Can** Michael and Sue **go** / to the disco / on Friday?

If an operator-verb is required in order to ask yes/no questions and some kinds of *wh*-question, in which the subject and the operator change places, what happens in VPs consisting of a single main verb? Can a main verb also be an operator-verb? In older English it could. For example, in Shakespeare's *The Tragedie of Macbeth*, Banquo asks the witches:

>   *P*   *S*
> **Liue** **you**? or are you aught
> That man may question?

To Macbeth's question *Hath he ask'd for me*?, Lady Macbeth replies:

>   *P*   *S*
> **Know** **you** not, he has?

But although in early seventeenth century English it was possible to reverse the subject and main verb to ask a question, it is no longer so, and the verb 'do' is used as a 'dummy' operator-verb:

>   *op-v* *S*   *P*
> **Do** you live?

>   *op-v* *S*   *P*
> **Do** you not know, he lives?

Only *be* and *have* can still combine the functions of both operator-verb and main verb at the same time in interrogative mood:

Were you aware of that fact?

Have you change for a five pound note, please?

and *have* actually allows both forms of interrogative:

Do you **have** change for a five pound note, please?

Activity 8.7

(i)   Identify the interrogatives in the following quotations from *Macbeth* as yes/no or *wh-* questions

(ii) In which of the questions is the grammar of the interrogative **archaic** — no longer used in MnE? Explain why. (You can ignore the now archaic use of *thou* and verb forms like *hath* and *art*.)

(Texts from the *Original-Spelling Edition* of Shakespeare's works, Oxford University Press, 1986).

(a)	*Lady Macbeth*	He has almost supt: why haue you left the chamber?
(b)	*Lady Macbeth*	Who dares receiue it other,
		As we shall make our griefes and Clamor rore,
		Vpon his Death?
(c)	*Banquo*	How goes the Night, Boy?
(d)	*Macbeth*	Is this a Dagger, which I see before me,
		The handle toward my Hand?
(e)	*Lady Macbeth*	What doe you meane?
(f)	*Lenox*	Goes the King hence to day?
(g)	*Lenox*	Meane you his Maiestie?
(h)	*Rosse*	Is't known who did this more then bloody deed?
(i)	*Rosse*	Will you to Scone?
(j)	*Macbeth*	Sirra, a word with you: Attend those men
		Our pleasure?
(k)	*Macbeth*	Which of you haue done this?
(l)	*Lady Macbeth*	Did you send to him Sir?

8.4.2   *Expressing the negative in StE*

In a very similar way, *do* has to be used as a dummy operator-verb when a single verb VP is made negative. In VPs with two or more verbs, the adverb *not* follows the operator, as in Shakespeare's,

Lady Macbeth   . . . hearke! I layd their Daggers ready,
                He could not misse 'em.

and this is still the rule in modern English. But in Shakespeare's English we also find negative constructions with a single main verb like:

Macbeth   I **haue** thee **not**, and yet I see thee still,

Macbeth   **Heare** it **not**, *Duncan,* for it is a Knell
That summons thee to Heauen, or to Hell.

which are no longer StE, and would have to be *I **do not** have thee*, and ***Do not** hear it*.

8.4.3   *Expressing the negative in the dialects*

8.4.3.1   MULTIPLE NEGATIVES
In most of the dialects of English you will hear sentences like this one from Norwich:

When I heard the knocking I **never** thought **nothing** like that could ever happen.

This use of two negative words where a StE speaker would say:

When I heard the knocking I **never** thought **anything** like that could ever happen.

is one of the *shibboleths* (see section 1.3.2 again) which give away a speaker's use of dialectal forms. It is said that 'two negatives make a positive', and that therefore the sentence implies that speaker <u>did</u> think that *something like that could happen,* but this is a false analogy from mathematics.

Other examples of an extremely common nonstandard form are:

I did**n't** have to do **nothing** to help her.   (*Liverpool*)

Well they **never** spent **no** money.   (*West Midlands*)

which derive in a direct line from Old and Middle English.

The multiple negative in OE and ME
In Old and Middle English, the double and multiple negative construction was regularly used, with second and third negatives acting to <u>reinforce</u> the first, not to reverse it. The **negative particle** was originally *ne*, as in:

Ic **ne** dyde
I ne did = I didnt do (it)

When *ne* preceded some common verbs like *woldon* (would) and *wære* (were), the two words were **assimilated** in pronunciation and were written *noldon* and *nære* instead of *ne woldon* and *ne wære,* (*they*) *wouldn't* and (*he*) *wasn't*.

(*Old English, eighth century*)

Ond þa cuædon hie þæt him **nænig** mæg leofra **nære** þonne hiera hlaford
*And then said they that to-them **none** kinsman dearer **ne**-was than their lord*

ond hie næfre his banan folgian **noldon**.
*and they **never** his murderer follow **ne**-would.*

If we were to translate this literally into MnE, it would read:

> And then they said that **no** kinsman **wasn't** dearer to them than their lord, and they **wouldn't never** follow his murderer.

which is similar in its use of a double negative construction to present-day London Cockney, which clearly derives from the older grammatical tradition:

> I do**n't** suppose you'll **never** stop the tradition of the Pearlies...because there wo**n't** be **no** tradition left in London at all, will there?

Here is more evidence of the continuity of the double or multiple negative in Middle English:

(early 13th C, East Midlands dialect)

He **nis no** fol **ne no** coward   *(nis = ne + is)*
*He **ne**-is **no** fool **nor no** coward*

(*Chaucer*, Miller's Tale, *late fourteenth century*)

In al the town **nas** brewhouse **ne** tauerne   *(nas = ne + was)*
That he **ne** visited with his solas...

                  I **nam no** labbe,   *(nam = ne + am)*
And thogh I seye, I **nam nat** lief to gabbe.

Be wel auysed on that ilke nyght
That we been entred into shippes bord
That **noon** of vs **ne** speke **noght** a word...

In the last two quotations from Chaucer, the negatives *nat, noght* show how MnE *not* originated as a 'reinforcing' negative to *ne*, with *ne...noght* similar in function to French *ne...pas*.

The important point to remember is that the frequency of the double or multiple negative in everyday speech is not evidence of wrongly learned StE, but shows the continuous tradition of a grammatical construction which is widespread both in English and many other languages.

> I says you can stick them, I do**n't** want 'em **no** more. (*Leeds*)

> Well have to get summat done about these part-timers else there is**n't** going to be living for **nobody**. (*North Yorks*)

8.4.3.2 *NEVER* AS A NEGATIVE MARKER

Also common in spoken English is the use of the adverb *never* as a negative particle,

> Father took over the business then and he done most things and repairs and all the rest of it, but he **never** done anything big. (Norfolk)

8.4.3.3 NEGATIVE SUFFIX *-na/-nae*

The negative alternative to *couldn't* in this dialectal form:

> We had no money and I could**na** buy any. (*Staffs*)

is common in Scots, especially with auxiliary verbs like *can* and *do*, as *canna* and *dinna*. The following examples are taken from *The New Testament in Scots* (1983), translated by William Lorimer. He uses an adapted form of spelling to show contemporary Scots pronunciation. A word-for-word version in MnE is printed below each text:

He socht tae get a visie o Jesus an see whatlike he wis, but he **coudna** for the croud... (Luke 19.3)

*He sought to get a glimpse of Jesus and see what he was like, but he **couldnt** for the crowd...*

'Ye kent, did ye, at I'm a dooms siccar man, at uplifts what he **hesna** pitten doun, an shears what he **hesna** sawn? (Luke 19.22)

*'You knew, did you, that I'm a very cautious man, that collects what he **hasn't** put down, and reaps what he **hasn't** sown?'*

This third example shows a main verb with the suffix -*na*:

'We **wantna** this man made King owre us.' (Luke 19.14)

*'We **want not** this man made King over us.'*

This suffix is sometimes spelt -*nae*. Here are some everyday examples from Edinburgh speech, in which either -*nae* as a suffix or *no* as a separate word occur as negative markers, just as -'*nt* as suffix corresponds to *not* as word in English speech :

English speech	**Edinburgh speech**
He **isn't** coming *or* He's **not** coming	He **isnae** coming *or* He's **no** coming
I **don't** know	I **dinnae** ken
Isn't he coming?	Is he **no** coming?
Don't do that! *or* **Don't** you do that!	**Dinnae** do that! *or* **Dinnae** you do that!

8.4.3.4 A NOTE ON *ain't*
The contraction *ain't* is widely spoken for the negative forms of the present tense of the verb *be*, as in *I **ain't** bothered*, *She **ain't** coming*, *We **ain't** worried about that*, but also for the negative form of the present tense of *have* when it is an auxiliary verb, for example *We **ain't** been there for some time*, *I **ain't** got any of them*.
The other functions of *do* as an auxiliary verb can be briefly described.

8.4.4 Emphasis

It is used to make an **emphatic** statement, as in (c) in Activity 8.6, like:

I **do** wish you would hurry up!

No, that's not true. I **do** like rice pudding.

Do be nice to Auntie when she arrives!

8.4.5 Tags

It also appears in **tag-questions**, following a clause in which the VP is a single main verb, as in (e) in Activity 8.6:

Well, she **came** last time, **didn't** she?

Contrast sentences with VPs containing auxiliary as well as main verbs, like:

I **can bring** my dog, **can't** I?

John **won't be** there, **will** he?

in which the same operator-verbs appear in the tag, with:

Jane **came** yesterday, **didn't** she?

The shop **opens** at nine o'clock, **doesn't** it?

You cannot say,

*Jane **came** yesterday, **came** she **not**?

*The shop **opens** at nine o'clock, **opens** it **not**?

so *do* is used as a dummy verb.

8.4.6 After semi-negatives

Sentence (f) in Activity 8.6 shows how *do* has to be used following a phrase containing *only*, *hardly*, *never* and other **semi-negative adverbs**.

Only after several applications **did** she **succeed**.

***Only** after several applications she **succeeded**.

If the phrase containing the semi-negative adverb *follows* the VP, then normal word order is used and *do* is not required if there is no operator-verb:

She **succeeded only** after several applications.

8.4.7 Marking simple present or past tense

Do was formerly used to mark present or past tense without implying any emphasis:

Macduffe   Was it so late, friend, ere you went to Bed,
           That you **doe** lye so late?

Macduffe   He **did** command me to call timely on him,
           I haue almost slipt the houre.

This is now archaic in StE, where we would say *That you lie so late* and *He commanded me*, though still in use in some dialects.

Activity 8.8

(i) Identify the uses of the verb *do* in the following sentences as a main or auxiliary verb.

(ii) If auxiliary, say whether it is functioning as the dummy-operator in a question, negative or tag, or for emphasis.

(iii) If *do* carries tense, identify the tense as present or past.

(a) I am glad I **did** not forget her birthday.
(b) What **do** you **do** in the evenings?
(c) You **did** look pale, **didn't** you!
(d) Never **did** I see such crowds in the sales!
(e) **Don't** you say such things to me!
(f) **Do** you know where the scissors are?
(g) **Do** ask her to come to lunch!
(h) I'll come when I've **done** the potatoes.
(i) **Do** you feel well enough to **do** all that work?
(j) A nice cup of tea **does** you a world of good, **doesn't** it?
(k) Macbeth I am afraid, to thinke what I have **done**:
        Looke on't againe I dare not.
(l) Macduffe I beleeue, Drinke gaue thee the Lye last Night.
        Porter That it **did**, Sir, i'the very Throat on me:

8.5 Auxiliary verbs – modals

The word *modality* represents a very important part of the resources of the language. Roughly speaking, **modality** enables us to refer not to facts, but to the *possibility* or *impossibility* of something happening, its *necessity*, *probability*, or *certainty*, whether an action is *permitted*, and so on. Modality can be expressed through **modal adverbs**, as in:

Possibly I'll manage to finish it by ten o'clock.

The past tense itself has a modal function, because it refers to 'not-now', and can express more doubt than the present tense. Compare the two tenses in:

present tense
(ia) If I **come** tomorrow, I **shall** bring the book with me.
(ib) If I **come** tomorrow, I'**ll** bring the book with me.

past tense
(iia) If I **came** tomorrow, I **should** bring the book with me.
(iib) If I **came** tomorrow, I'**d** bring the book with me.

(*The (b) versions are more likely in ordinary speech.*)

In sentence (ii), the speaker implies that the possibility of coming on the next day is less likely than the speaker's intention in sentence (i), and this is conveyed by the fact that *came* and *should* are both marked for past tense.

Modality in its expression of meaning is a complex part of English grammar, and this section will briefly describe how modality can be expressed in a VP, using a set of auxiliary verbs. In (i) and (ii) above, *shall* and *should* are **modal auxiliary verbs**. The use of *shall* and *should* implies firstly, the speaker's *intention* to bring the book, on the condition in both sentences that she did in fact come, and secondly, refers to *future* time, though *shall* is in the present tense, and *should* is past tense. (Remember that in the short references to tense in previous sections it was stressed that tense is a grammatical category, not semantic.)

Present tense modals are never inflected to agree with the 3rd person singular subject, and in this they differ from all other verbs. To remind you, agreement with the 3rd person singular subject is shown by the suffix *-s* on the verbs in, for example:

When the sun **goes** in a shadow **flies** over; when it **comes** out again it is fiery.

The wind **has** dropped.

He **doesn't** want her to know.

But modals are unmarked. For example, *will*, *must* and *can* are modal auxiliaries, and you would never say:

*I think she **wills** enjoy meeting him.

*He **musts** remember to do it.

*She **cans** not come tomorrow.

This is one way of identifying the modal verbs.

In a finite VP, the first verb always carries the tense. Since modal verbs come first in a finite VP, they are always marked for either present or past tense, although their meaning may not express present or past time. The verb following a modal, whether another auxiliary or the main verb, is always in the base form.

Here is a list of those verbs generally considered to be the modal auxiliaries in English:

present tense	*past tense*
can	could
may	might
shall	should
will	would
must	–
ought to	–
–	used to

Only in a large reference grammar or a book on the English verb is it possible to describe the whole range of meanings of modal verbs in any detail. The grammar of modals is simple. The meanings, however, are often complex, subtle and ambiguous. The following list contains the principal meanings which you may discover in modal verbs, together with the verbs which most commonly represent those meanings:

(i)   stating someone's **ability** to do something
       can (= be able to), *could*

(ii) giving or asking **permission** to do something
       can (= *be allowed to*), *could, may, might*

(iii) suggesting the **possibility** of something happening
       (a) theoretical: *can* (= *be possible for*), *could*
       (b) factual: *could, may, might*

(iv) suggesting the **probability** of something happening
       should, would, ought to

(v)   expressing the **wish** to do something
       may, might

(vi) stating **willingness** to do something
       shall, should, will, would

(vii) expressing the **intention** of doing something
       shall, should, will, would

(viii) to **insist** upon something
       shall, should, will, would

(ix) describing someone's **obligation** to do something
       should, must, ought to

(x)   to express **politeness** or **tentativeness**
       could, should, would

(xi) to **predict** a future event
       will, would, shall, should

(xii) to state that something is logically **necessary**
       should, must, ought to

In general terms, modals express meanings that are *hypothetical* or *tentative*, or that are concerned with the *truth* of the statement being made. They often represent a speaker's attitude. As you can see, the meanings just listed overlap. Modals share similar meanings and each of them has more than one meaning. Because of this, they can be very ambiguous.

For example, *can* is commonly used to express both ability and permission, and people who like to think that words should have precise meanings are inclined to insist that *can* means ability only, and that *may* expresses permission, as illustrated in the first quotation in section 1.2.2 and in this one:

Child: Can I have some more tea, please?
Parent: Yes, you *can*. But do you *want* some?
Child: *May* I have some more tea, please?
Parent: That's better.

In practice, this distinction is not consistently kept, and we all use *can* to ask permission for something to be done. Its style in this sense is more informal than *may*.

Activity 8.9

(i)   Write short sentences containing each of the modal verbs, giving examples of the various meanings suggested in the list (i)–(xii) above.

(ii) Consider whether or not the tense of the modal is directly related to present or past time in meaning.

The following sentences are taken from dialogue in the novel *A Family and a Fortune*, ch. VII, by Ivy Compton-Burnett (1939). They represent some of the possible meanings of the modals *can, could, may, might, shall, should, will* and *would*.

Activity 8.10

(i)   Discuss the modals in the VPs (i)–(viii) printed in bold type. Consider two aspects of each modal:

(a)   whether there is clear reference to present, future or past time in relation to the tense of the modal,

(b)   what meaning or combination of meanings the modal probably conveys (give alternatives if possible).

(ii) Suggest contexts (kinds of speaker and listener, place, topic and so on), wherever possible, in which the modal could have different meanings.

(i)   *can*
        I **cannot ask** you to wish us happiness, but I **can** hardly **believe**, with my knowledge of you, that you will not wish it.

(ii)   *could*
        Mark and I hoped that we **could bridge** the gulf, but we found our mistake.

(iii)   *may*
        think I **may stay** here, dear.

(iv)   *might*
        Our marriage **might not have been** loveless, but I think our new relation may be.

(v)   *shall*
        We **shall be** a wretched household if Uncle goes.

(vi)   *should*
        You **should not be** always listening to grown up talk.

(vii)   *will*
        Well, we **will not anticipate** trouble. It **will be** on us soon enough.

(viii) *would*
   It **would not be** my way, but I must not impose my will on hers.

Other modals are illustrated in the following sentences, again from the same novel:

 (ix) *must*
   People **must have** their private lives and you **must leave** them.

The modal *must* is marked for present tense, but has no past tense form itself. As we saw in section 8.3, *had to* is used, the past tense form of *have to*, in which the verb *have* takes on a modal sense.

  (x) *ought to*
   I **ought to have thought** of this myself.

Historically, *ought* is the past tense of *owe*, but it has long ago lost this meaning, and is used to refer to present or past time. In (x) it works in conjunction with *have* to refer to the past.

 (xi) *used to*
   I **used not to understand** it. But when I had money myself, I understood.

This modal, like *ought*, is always followed by the particle *to*, and has lost its historical relationship with the verb *use*. It always refers to past time, things that we did repeatedly, or that we have stopped doing. Notice that its pronunciation is [juːst tu], which differs from the past tense of the main verb *use*, pronounced [juːzd].

(xii) *need*
   We **need not grasp** more than is there.

Need is also used with *to* as a **catenative** (section 8.6), *You **need to have** your hair cut.*
   The fact that *need* can also be used as a main verb, as in *I **need** a haircut*, makes it a less typical modal verb. You cannot use the modals (i)–(xi) as main verbs. Another 'fuzzy' modal is *dare*:

(xiii) *dare*
   I hardly **dare to look** at the future.

which can also be used without *to*, *I hardly **dare look***. *Dare* can also be a main verb, *I **dared** the bad weather and went out walking.*
   Modals cannot occur in nonfinite VPs, nor can more than one modal auxiliary be used in a VP, except in some dialects. That is, in StE, you cannot say:

   *I **shall must** come to see you tomorrow.

but you would probably say:

   I shall **have to** come to see you tomorrow.

Have to is a **semi-auxiliary** (section 8.6). It is modal in meaning, but its grammatical use is different, and therefore it is given a different grammatical label.

8.5.1   Modals in the dialects

The occurrence and meaning of modal auxiliary verbs varies from StE usage in some dialects. The following differences have been recorded in Edinburgh speech:

- *may* does not occur. For the permissive sense of StE *may*, *can* is used, and for the expression of possibility, *maybe*, as in *It'll **maybe** rain tomorrow* or *He'll **maybe** come later.*

- *shall* also does not occur, while *shan't* is seen as a very 'English' usage. Instead, *will* is used, for example in *Will I open the window?*

- *need* is used in a 'passive' sense without the particle *to* – *The car needs washed, The cat needs out,* as well as in its 'active' sense with *to* – *I'm needing to wash the car.* The verb *need* is best described here as a main verb with modal meaning, rather than as an auxiliary verb.

Here are some examples from literature of the nonstandard use of two modal verbs in one VP. Firstly, Highland Scots dialect, from Robert Louis Stevenson's *Catriona* (1893), set in the 1750s:

> 'But I will be honest too,' she added, with a kind of suddenness, 'and I'll never **can** forgive that girl.'

Secondly, Southern American usage, from Flannery O'Connor's *Wise Blood* (1952):

> I **might could** make it 50 dollar.

Double modals have also been recorded in present-day Edinburgh speech, but they are said to be infrequent. Some examples are:

> He'll **no can** come this week

> I **might could** have done that when I was younger

with one 'triple modal', for StE *It's possible you'll be able to do that.*

> You'll **might could** do that

8.6   Semi-auxiliary and catenative verbs

8.6.1   Semi-auxiliaries

This category of verb has already been mentioned in sections 8.2 (*be to*), 8.3 (*have to*) and 8.6. The label **semi-auxiliary** refers to the fact that these constructions function something like auxiliary verbs – modals, *have*, *be* and *do* – but not completely so. One way they differ from modals is in being able to combine with each other, or with other auxiliaries, in a long chain:

> It **seemed to be going to prove to** have been the wrong decision.

The set of semi-auxiliaries consists of the auxiliaries *be* and *have* followed by *to*, or by another word and to, and is illustrated in the following activity.

Activity 8.11

(i) Discuss the meaning which the semi-auxiliary verbs contribute to the VPs in the following sentences.

(ii) Identify the tense as present or past.

be to	**I'm to do** the washing-up, am I?
be about to	Jane **was about to leave**, when the phone unexpectedly rang.
be going to	Well, **are** you **going to finish** your dinner or not?
be bound to	The fire**'s bound to go out** if you don't make it up regularly.
be certain to	And when the post comes, **will** you please **be certain to look** for that letter I'm expecting.
be liable to	The baby **is liable to wake up** as soon as its light.
be supposed to	What **am I supposed to do** about it, then?
be sure to	When you leave the house, **be sure to lock** the back door.
have to	It's twelve o'clock. I **have to go** now.
or	
have got to	It's twelve o'clock. I**'ve got to go** now.
had better	You**'d better lie down** if you're feeling poorly.

In this (incomplete) set of semi-auxiliaries, the verbs *be* and *have* behave just like ordinary auxiliaries themselves – that is, they can function as operator-verbs, as in *Is Sarah **certain to** come?* or *Have I got to go to bed now?*

8.6.2 Catenatives

Another set of verbs resembles semi-auxiliaries, but instead of *be* or *have* a lexical verb is followed by one or more infinitives linked by *to*. These verbs, which can be followed by other verbs in a kind of 'chain', using *to* as a link, are called *catenative verbs* (the word is derived from the Latin *catena*, which means *a chain*). Their meaning as catenatives differs from their meaning when used as single verbs.

Activity 8.12

(i) Discuss the meanings of the catenative verbs.

(ii) Identify the tense as present or past.

(iii) Write other sentences in which the main verb of each catenative construction is used as a single lexical verb, and compare the meanings. Are they similar and related, or quite different? For example:

The car **appeared to swerve** erratically. *(catenative)*
The car **appeared** round the corner. *(single verb)*

(iv) What is different about the verb *keep* in a catenative construction?

appear	Bill **appeared to enjoy** the concert.
come	Mary **came to enjoy** learning German once she'd been on holiday to Bavaria.
get	I **got to know** her well during our time together on the committee.
happen	Charles **happens to know** a friend of mine whom I've not seen for many years.
keep	Bill **kept interrupting** the conversation until we all told him to shut up.
prove	That mistake **will prove to have been** very costly.
seem	These batteries never **seem to last** for more than a few weeks.
tend	Jane **tends to prefer** tea without sugar, but it's better to ask her.
turn out	That outing **turned out to have cost** me over twenty pounds!

8.6.3 Auxiliary or catenative verb?

A test to show that a verb is a catenative and not an auxiliary is to change the **declarative** (statement) form into the **interrogative** (question) form. Catenatives, like lexical verbs, require *do* as an operator,

Charles **happens to know** this friend of mine.   (*declarative*)

*****Happens** Charles **to know** this friend of mine?

Does Charles **happen to know** this friend of mine?   (*interrogative*)

8.7 Predicators in phase in VP structure

In a sentence like:

She **tried to gain** support for the demo.

the verb *tried* + *to* is not a catenative like those described in section 8.6., You cannot say **Support *tried to be gained*, and so both *tried* and *gain* must be separate lexical verbs functioning as predicators.

This is an area of English grammar in which there are several competing analyses among contemporary linguists. Some describe *to gain*, together with the rest of the clause, as a **complement** of *tried*. But in an introductory textbook like this it would probably be more confusing than helpful to discuss the alternatives in any detail.

So the analysis that seems to be the most straightforward at this beginning stage has been chosen, and these VP structures are called **predicators in phase,** the term already introduced in section 6.5.1.2(e). The word *phase* is used in the sense of a *series* – two or more lexical verbs following each other, sometimes linked by the word *to*, when the second verb is an infinitive – *She wanted to come* – or else without a linking word, when the second verb is an *-ing* participle – *The baby started **crying***.

This allows us to analyse a clause as having two predicators, but only when they are in this special phase relationship. Notice that the auxiliaries, semi-auxiliaries and catenatives which are followed by *to* are similarly constructed and are related forms of predicators in phase which have acquired special meanings. The structure of clauses with predicators in phase is therefore analysed as:

> S   P   P   O
> She tried to gain support for the demo.

> S   P   P   A
> The baby started crying in the middle of the night.

8.8 Aspect

The traditional grammatical term **aspect** is used to refer to the length of time an action or state has gone on, and in English this is done by using the auxiliary verbs *be* and *have* to represent two different kinds of aspect.

8.8.1 *Progressive aspect*

If the auxiliary verb *be* is followed by the *-ing* participle of the next verb, its meaning is to represent a temporary action that is *progressing*, or *continuous*, at a particular time. You can use progressive aspect in relation to a future event:

(i)   Carol will **be coming** round later.

or to the present:

(ii)   **Aren't** you **enjoying** your rice pudding?

or to the past:

(iii)   As he **was going** downstairs, the door-bell rang.

(iv)   I **was eating** my dinner when the phone rang.

Notice that you cannot use progressive aspect with a verb that refers to a **state**, called a **stative verb**:

(v)   *I **am disliking** tea with sugar.

(vi)   *Darling, I **am loving** you.

Disliking and *loving* are states of mind or attitude that do not normally vary from hour to hour or day to day, unlike verbs like *go* and *eat* in (iii) and (iv), which are called **dynamic verbs**. Many verbs can be used in both stative and dynamic senses, with very little difference of meaning in some cases between the simple past and the progressive past:

(vii)   I **learn** Russian at school.

(viii)   **I'm learning** Russian at school.

Activity 8.13

In the following sentences the VPs are not marked for progressive aspect. For each sentence:

(i) Rewrite it using progressive aspect if the sentence allows. (It may be helpful to put it in a context, and write additional sentences, before or after.)

(ii) If the sentence does not allow progressive aspect, discuss the reasons why not.

(iii) If the sentence does allow progressive aspect, explore the differences of meaning between the version with progressive and without (or non-progressive).

Remember that the first verb in a finite VP is marked for tense. Keep the same tense in sentences (a)–(j).

(a) We approached the house on foot.
(b) Someone will enquire about your problem.
(c) I can hear someone at the door.
(d) He never forgets his sister's birthday.
(e) The full moon shone brightly on the fields.
(f) Home-made wines improve if you keep them for several months.
(g) My back aches.
(h) The cups are on the dresser.
(i) I hope that you will help me.
(j) I hoped that you would help me.

8.8.2   Perfect aspect

If the auxiliary verb *have* is followed by an *-en/-ed* participle in a VP, its meaning is to do with the length of time, or duration, up to the present, of an event, or else with the effects of an action which are still operating. Like many features of English grammar, the details of the uses and meanings of perfect aspect are somewhat complex, and are more fully described in reference grammars.

Activity 8.14

In the following sentences the VPs are marked for perfect aspect.

(i) Rewrite them omitting aspect, making any other grammatical changes in the sentence that seem necessary to make good sense, but keeping the same tense. Discuss any difficulties that may arise in doing this.

(ii) Rewrite them changing the tense from present to past, or vice-versa.

(iii) Discuss the differences of meaning between the different versions of the sentences.

(a)   We have lived in this house for seven years.
(b)   We had lived in that house until we moved to London.
(c)   She has always been keen on cycling.
(d)   You have finished that little job quickly, haven't you?
(e)   Let's have dinner now that everyone has finally arrived.
(f)   I'll be down as soon as I've done my hair.
(g)   They washed up after we had left.
(h)   Val said that she had intended to bring the book.
(i)   I would have prepared the spare bedroom if I had known that you hadn't booked a hotel room.
(j)   Every time we've gone on holiday to Scotland, the weather has been perfect.

8.8.3   *Tense and aspect*

All the examples in this chapter so far have been of finite, tensed VPs, in which the first verb is marked for either present or past tense. Remember that, strictly speaking, even in a VP which refers to future time, like *I shall see you next week*, we describe the modal auxiliary *shall* as being marked for present tense, even though we may informally refer to the VP as being in the 'future tense'.

All the sentences in Activity 8.14 combine tense with perfect aspect, and so we refer to the VP as either **present perfect** or **past perfect.** Similarly, a finite VP marked for progressive aspect will be either **present progressive** or **past progressive.** We also very commonly combine both aspects in one VP, as in:

(a)   What **have** you **been doing** since last week?
(b)   Paul **has been watching** television all the afternoon.
(c)   I didn't know she **had been inquiring** for me.

Sentences (a) and (b) are **present perfect progressive,** and (c) is **past perfect progressive**.

In addition, it is perfectly normal to combine a modal with either or both aspects:

(d)   Fiona **ought to have saved** enough money by now.
(e)   You **should be getting** ready to go out soon.
(f)   I **might have been digging** the garden, but for the rain.

8.9   Word order in VPs

The order of the auxiliary verbs in finite active VPs was described in section 6.6.2:

$$VP\ =\ tense + (modal) + (have + \text{-}en/\text{-}ed) + (be + \text{-}ing) + main\ verb$$
$$Tense\ =\ \text{present }or$$
$$\text{past}$$

The bracketed items are optional, and need not be chosen to make a grammatical finite VP. Tense and a main lexical verb are obligatory components, and tense is marked by inflecting the first verb.

If **perfect aspect** is chosen, (*have* + *-en/-ed*) means that *have* requires the following verb to be in its *-en/-ed* participle form, e.g. *have* **gone**, *has* **seen**, *have* **decided**, *has* **been** *seeing*.

If **progressive aspect** is chosen, (*be* + *-ing*) means that the following verb must be in its *-ing* participle form, e.g. *were* **talking**, *was* **running**, *has been* **fighting**.

Activity 8.15

Identify the function of the verbs in the VPs of the following sentences.

Mark them **m** (*modal*), **h** (*have*), **be, do, s-aux** (*semi-auxiliary*), **cat** (*catenative*) or **v** (*lexical verb*).

For example:

```
    m        h     be   v              h    cat         v
I would not have been writing this if I had happened to meet you last week.

    be   s-aux  v                    m     h    v
I was having to hold my tongue or I would have upset him.

    v         v
I prefer to wear a hat in cold weather.
```

(a) **Has** your Uncle **been telling** you the news?
(b) I **have had to come** down early on purpose.
(c) I **was beginning to feel** so very tired.
(d) You **were** hardly **anticipating** that fate.
(e) I **am not going to talk** about my own affairs.
(f) I **have been looking** forward to talking about it.
(g) What **can** they **want** more?
(h) **Can** we **ask** who **has left** the money?
(i) And we **shall** all **be able to share** in it evenly and equally.
(j) We **should like to know** just at what we **are to rejoice**.
(k) But why **should** they **feel** like that?
(l) Well, who **will do** it?
(m) I am afraid that people **will come to think** I am better off than I am.
(n) That **would have been** quite a natural interpretation.
(o) Or perhaps they **would like** to guess?
(p) Someone **may happen to put** the question.
(q) So no one **need feel** sensitive for my sake.
(r) I **begin to understand** it.

(sentences adapted from I. Compton-Burnett, *A Family and a Fortune*)

8.10 Voice

A second function of *be* as an auxiliary occurs when it is followed by the *-en/-ed* participle of another verb, not the *-ing* participle, to mark the **passive voice**. The passive form of a VP is related to its active form. The active voice is thought of as more basic, and is unmarked. The marked passive form is said to derive from the active by means of a **transformation**. For example, here are two actual news items from different broadcasts in 1978 describing the same event:

(a) *S*   *P*
Black Nationalists in the Rhodesian transitional government   have

      Od
rejected the latest Anglo-American proposals for majority rule elections.

(b) *S*   *P*
The British and American proposals for Rhodesia   have been bluntly

     Ca
rejected   by two of the black leaders in the transitional government.

The same information was given, but in two different forms. The VP *have rejected* is in the unmarked active voice, and *have been rejected* is in the marked passive voice. So (a) is an **active clause**, and (b) a **passive clause**. The transformation of (a) into (b) can be simply described by using reduced forms of the clauses. It is the structure of the clauses that is changed, not the meaning:

(a) *S*   *P*   *O*
Black Nationalists   have rejected   the proposals

(b) *S*   *P*   *Ca*
The proposals   have been rejected   by Black Nationalists

1. The grammatical object of (a), *the proposals*, becomes the grammatical subject of (b).
2. The grammatical subject of (a), *Black Nationalists*, becomes the complement in a PrepP and follows the preposition *by*.
     The PrepP then functions as an adverbial complement (Ca) of the verb.
3. The auxiliary verb *be* is introduced into the VP, and the main verb takes its *-en/-ed* participle form.

The verb must be transitive and be followed by a grammatical object for passive voice to be used, because the object becomes the subject of the passive clause. But it is possible to omit the adverbial complement in the passive clause:

(c) The proposals have been rejected.

This means that if you do not know the **actor** (who did it), or the **agent** (who caused it) of the process represented by the VP of the predicator, or if you wish to avoid saying who or what it was, you can do so by using a passive clause. Many passives occur in texts without the PrepP with *by* (called the **agentive phrase**).
   For example, in these sentences from George Orwell's *Animal Farm*, ch. 3:

The mystery of where the milk went to **was** soon **cleared up**. It **was mixed** every day into the pigs' mash.

the VPs *was ... cleared* up and *was mixed* are passives. There is no obvious actor or agent who did the clearing up, and we can infer from the story that it was the pigs who mixed the milk into their mash, so active clauses would be inappropriate. The chapter ends with two more passive constructions in the last sentence:

> So **it was agreed** without further argument that the milk and the windfall apples (and also the main crop of apples when they ripened) **should be reserved** for the pigs alone.

The form of the passive construction, *be + -en/-ed* participle, is similar to that of *be + adjective*, for example, *I was happy*, in which the verb *was* links the subject *I* to the intensive complement *happy*. If the complement is an adjective which is, or looks like, the *-en/-ed* participle of a verb, then the difference between a passive and *be + adjective* construction may be fuzzy. For example, *I was pleased* may simply be equivalent to saying *I was happy*, but could be the passive form of *Something pleased me*. This again illustrates how grammatical categories overlap.

Activity 8.16

(i)   Write the following active clauses in the passive voice, where this is possible.

(ii) If there is no passive counterpart, say why.

(a)   Blows from Boxer's hoofs broke the heads of three of the men.
(b)   A cow's horn gored another in the belly.
(c)   Jessie and Bluebell nearly tore off the trousers of another.
(d)   The cowardly enemy was running for dear life.
(e)   The animals chased them right down to the bottom of the field.
(f)   They were weary and bleeding.
(g)   The explosion had partially destroyed the foundations of the windmill.
(h)   The animals heard the solemn booming of a gun.
(i)   Boxer had lost a shoe and split his hoof.
(j)   We have driven the enemy off the sacred soil of Animal Farm.
                         (adapted from George Orwell, *Animal Farm*, ch. 8)

Activity 8.17

Write the following passive clauses in the active voice. Supply a subject if necessary.

(a)   The animals slain in the battle were given a solemn funeral.
(b)   Two whole days were given over to celebrations.
(c)   A special gift of an apple was bestowed on every animal by Napoleon.
(d)   The case of whisky had been overlooked by the animals at the time when the house was first occupied.
(e)   Straw was laid down outside the doors of the farmhouse.
(f)   Comrade Napoleon had pronounced a solemn decree: the drinking of alcohol was to be punished by death.

(g) Napoleon gave orders that the small paddock was to be ploughed up.
(h) Once again all rations were reduced by the pigs.
(i) Later, a schoolroom would be built in the farmhouse garden.
(j) For the time being, the young pigs were given their instruction by Napoleon himself in the farmhouse kitchen.

Activity 8.18

Passives are quite common in academic and scientific prose.

(i) Identify the passive VPs in the following extract.

(ii) Rewrite the extract using only active VPs (except for the quoted example *the war was started by Hitler*), and suggest why they are less suitable than passives in this context.

The original presentation of transformational syntax was made with reference to English, and English has so far received the most attention. Formally marked passive sentences of the type *the war was started by Hitler* are given a different treatment from that which they would receive in immediate constitutent analysis. In immediate constituency the sentence just cited may be simply regarded as the result of successive expansions of a basic sentence structure. Transformationally the sentence is said to have been produced by a specific transformation, applied to an underlying kernel sentence Hitler started the war.

(R. H. Robins, *General Linguistics*, 1964)

8.10.1 Using the passive

In an active clause (one with its verb in the active voice) like:

S	*O*	
Napoleon bestowed	**a special gift of an apple** on every animal.	
actor & theme	affected	

the subject is *Napoleon*, the actor who performed the action of *bestowing*, and also the **focus of information**, coming first in the clause as its **theme**, while the grammatical object is the affected item, what was bestowed, *the apple*.

If we transform the clause by using the passive voice:

S		*Ca*
A special gift of an apple was bestowed on every animal		*by Napoleon.*
affected & theme		actor

the 'semantic roles' of actor and affected remain the same – Napoleon still gives the apple – but the focus on the grammatical subject as theme has shifted to the affected item. (Theme is described in more detail in sections 12.2.1 and 12.2.3.)

The other principal use of the passive has already been stated in this section – to give you a grammatical way of not naming a person if you don't know the actor or agent of an action (who did it or caused it), or it doesn't matter, or you want to avoid naming them.

8.10.2 *Voice and aspect together*

The passive auxiliary *be* (*be-pass*) can be used to form the passive in the same VP with a combination of modal, semi-auxiliary, progressive *be* (*be-prog*) or perfect *have*.

                m   **h**   **be-pass**   **v**   **v**
The appliance **shall** **have** **been** **purchased** and **used** solely within the EEC countries.

                m   **be-pass**   **v**
The appliance **should** **be** **returned** with this guarantee on

be-pass   **v**
being **found** defective.
(*being found* is a nonfinite VP – section 8.11)

It is in fact grammatically possible to say something like:

          m   **h**   **s-aux**   **be-prog** **be-pass** **v**
The house **may** **have** **been** about to **be** **being** **built**.

but VPs as complex as that are very rare.

8.11 Nonfinite VPs

The infinitive and the two participles of verbs have already been described as **nonfinite**, that is, they are not marked for present or past tense. A VP marked for present or past tense is therefore a **finite VP**.

Practically all the VPs quoted in this chapter have also been finite VPs, because the first verbs, either main or operator-verbs, were marked for present or past tense. A finite VP of two or more verbs consists of an operator-verb marked for tense, followed by one or more nonfinite verbs, including the main lexical verb. Lexical verbs are only marked for present or past tense themselves when they are single-verb VPs.

If a VP contains no finite operator-verb or main verb, but only nonfinite verbs, then it is called a **nonfinite VP.** Therefore, finite VPs function as predicators in finite clauses, and nonfinite VPs in nonfinite clauses.

The nonfinite VP *being found* in the clause quoted at the end of section 8.10.2, *on **being found** defective*, consists of the nonfinite *-ing* participle *being* and the *-en/-ed* participle *found*. It is therefore passive. The same verbs can be used in a VP such as *was **being found***, in which *was* is an operator-verb in the past tense, and so marks the VP as finite.

Nonfinite VPs function in subordinate clauses of various kinds in the structure of clauses (see chapter 11), and also as post-modifiers in NP structure. A participle used as a NP pre-modifier is usually identified as an adjective (section 3.4.4)

Activity 8.19

The verbs and VPs in the following extracts from Katherine Mansfield's *Bank Holiday* (1922) are printed in bold type.

(i)   Say whether they are finite or nonfinite verbs, or participial adjectives.

(ii)   Discuss the function of the nonfinite verbs or VPs.

A stout man with a pink face **wears** dingy white flannel trousers, a blue coat with a pink handkerchief **showing**, and a straw hat much too small for him, **perched** at the back of his head

A little chap in white canvas shoes, his face **hidden** under a felt hat like a **broken** wing, **breathes** into a flute; and a tall thin fellow, with **bursting** over-ripe button boots, **draws** ribbons – long, **twisted**, **streaming** ribbons – of tune out of a fiddle.

A crowd **collects**, **eating** oranges and bananas, **tearing** off the skins, **dividing**, **sharing**.

The young ones **are larking**, **pushing** each other on and off the pavement, **dodging**, **nudging**; the old ones **are talking**: 'So I **said** to 'im, if you **wants** the doctor to yourself, **fetch** 'im, **says** I.'

It is a **flying** day, half sun, half wind.

9. Clauses

Recapitulation

Clauses were introduced in chapter 2 as the grammatical structures which language provides for encoding our experience of the world and communicating this experience to other people. The *clause* is the linguistic 'frame' through which we express an underlying *proposition*.

9.1 Transitivity

The word *proposition* is used in studying language to refer to the meaning underlying a clause, in which one or more **participants** do something or are affected by something. What they do, or what is done to them, is called the **process**. This process could be an **action**, like *standing, moving, getting up, throwing, striking*, and so is called an **actional process**, or it could be one of a number of processes which are not actional, and classed as **mental processes**. These include *talking* (a **verbal process**), *seeing* (a **perceptive process**), or *thinking* (a **cognitive process**) and so on. Processes take place typically in **circumstances** of time and place and manner.

We may also wish to describe **attributes** which **relate** people and things to their qualities or roles – *That meal was first-class, Robert seems unhappy, Mary became manager*. The processes here, represented by the verbs *was, seems, became*, are neither actional nor mental, but **relational**, because they relate the participants to their attributes or roles.

9.1.1 Transactive and non-transactive processes

If we wanted to express a proposition relating two participants, the **actor** (*old man*) and an **affected** thing (*his bag*), with a process (*carry*) ongoing in the past (+ *past progressive*), in the circumstances of a particular place – (*along the road*), a simple clause would be *An old man was carrying his bag along the road*. The process of *carrying* has two participants, an actor who carries and an affected thing or person that is carried, and is called a **transactive process.**

If we wanted to express a proposition that related a single participant (*old man*) – the *process* – (*sit*) – which has taken place – (+*past*) – in the circumstances of a particular place – (*by the road*), the simplest clause would be *An old man sat by the road*. The old man is again the actor, but affecting nothing or nobody except himself, so the process of *sitting* is called **non-transactive** – nothing is *transacted*, or passed across from one participant to another.

9.1.2   Transitive and intransitive clauses

In a simple statement like *An old man was carrying his bag along the road* the participant actor who performs the process is expressed as the NP functioning as the **subject** (**S**) of the clause, and comes first, *An old man...* The process *carry + past progressive* is expressed in the **predicator** (**P**). The function of predicator is always performed by a verb or VP, and follows the subject – *The old man was carrying...* The affected item, *his bag*, is expressed as the NP functioning as the **object complement**, or simply **object** (**O**), of the clause, and usually follows the verb, *The old man was carrying his bag...* The circumstances of place are expressed by the **adverbial** (**A**), in this clause the PrepP *along the road*. A verb or VP with a subject and object, expressing a transactive process, is called **transitive**:

Transitive clause

S	P	O	A
The old man	was carrying	his bag	along the road

The verb *sat* in the clause *The old man sat by the road* represents a non-transactive process and does not take an object NP, and is called **intransitive**:

Intransitive clause

S	P	A
The old man	sat	by the road

9.2   Mood

9.2.1   Declarative mood – 'I'm telling you this.'

A clause like this which makes a statement (*declaring* something) is said to be in the **declarative mood**:

S	P	A
An old man	sat	by the road.

Mood in grammar expresses the function or purpose of an utterance, that is, what use we are making of speech or writing in relation to the person we are addressing – telling them something, asking them something, or requesting them to do something. This is called an **interpersonal** function. We recognise mood by the order of the subject and the predicator in the clause. A clause in declarative mood has its subject first, and predicator following, SP. If a sentence is complex and contains subordinate clauses (see chapter 11), its mood is determined by the main clause.

9.2.2 Interrogative mood – 'I'm asking you this'

The main function of interrogative mood is to question, to seek information. In *yes/no* interrogatives (section 8.4.1.2), the subject does not come first, but follows the operator-verb.

> *op-v S   P   A*
> Did the old man   sit by the road?

> *op-v = P   S   A*
> Was   the old man   by the road?

Here are some other examples of **yes/no interrogatives** in *Animal Farm*. In (i) and (ii), the main verb *be* also functions as operator-verb:

> *P   S*
> Is it because this land of ours is so poor?

> *P   S*
> Is it not crystal clear that all the evils of this life of ours spring from the tyranny of human beings?

> *op-v S   P*
> Will there be sugar after the Rebellion?

> *op-v S P*
> Did we not give him 'Animal Hero, First Class', immediately afterwards?

and secondly, **wh-interrogatives**. In *wh*-interrogatives (section 8.4.1.1) the *wh*-word comes first.

> *wh-S P   A*
> **Who** sat by the road?

> *wh-O op-v S   P   voc*
> **What** does that mean, Mollie?

>   *wh-O   op-v S P   A*
> And you hens, **how** many eggs   have you laid this year?

> *wh-A A   op-v S P   A*
> **Why** then do   we continue in this miserable fashion

>   *wh-A   P   S*
> And you, Clover, **where** are   those four foals you bore?

The only time a *wh*-word does not comes first in its clause is when it is part of a PrepP which forms a *wh*-phrase, when the preposition precedes the *wh*-word. For example:

In which town do you live?

For whose benefit was it done?

Although interrogatives are a principal grammatical means of asking questions, it is not essential to use the interrogative form. The clause:

A	*S*	*P*	*O*	*voc*
Surely	you	remember	that,	comrades?

is in declarative mood (SP order), but is a question. In writing, this is shown by the question mark, and in speech by distinctive intonation.

9.2.3 *Imperative mood* – 'I want you to do this'

Giving orders or making requests may be expressed in the imperative mood, in which the subject *you* is usually omitted, and the predicator comes first:

P	*A*
Sit	by the road!

The order can be made less peremptory in various ways, still using the imperative mood, for example:

P	*A*	*S*
Do sit	by the road,	old man.

but if expressed as a request rather than an order, then the interrogative mood may be used:

op-v	*S*	*P*	*A*
Would	you	sit	by the road, please?

Sometimes the person addressed is named. This is referred to as the *vocative* (voc).

P	*voc*
Fix your eyes on that,	comrades!

voc	*P*
Boxer!	Get out quickly!

Certain texts with special functions, like cookery books and instruction manuals, are likely to contain lots of clauses in imperative mood. For example:

Mix flour, suet, salt, pepper and chopped meat. **Add** the grated onion. **Moisten** with gravy. **Place** on a greased baking-tin. **Bake** in a fairly hot oven till brown and crisp. **Serve** with thick brown gravy and vegetables.

(*Cookery recipe*)

Check that the voltage on the rating plate corresponds to that in your home. **Connect** the appliance to the mains and **ensure** that it is working properly before storing food.

(*Manual for installing a refrigerator*)

Remember that the terms *declarative*, *interrogative* and *imperative* refer to the grammatical category called **mood**, and are marked in the structure of a clause and the order of S and P, not in the function of the clause in communication. You can ask questions without using interrogative mood, and give directives without using imperative mood.

The category of mood can apply only to main clauses, not to subordinate clauses.

Activity 9.1

Say whether the bracketed clauses in the following texts are declarative, interrogative, or imperative in grammatical mood.

(a) ['What are they doing?'] Alice whispered to the Gryphon.
(b) ['They're putting down their names,'] the Gryphon whispered in reply.
(c) ['Herald, read the accusation!'] said the King.
(d) ['Consider your verdict,'] the King said to the jury.
(e) ['Of course twinkling begins with a T!'] said the King sharply. ['Do you take me for a dunce?'] [Go on!']
(f) ['Are they in the prisoner's handwriting?'] asked another of the jurymen.
(g) ['It doesn't prove anything of the sort!'] said Alice. ['Why, you don't even know what they're about!']
(h) ['Read them!'] said the King.
(i) The White Rabbit put on his spectacles. ['Where shall I begin, please your Majesty?'] he asked.
(j) ['Begin at the beginning,'] the King said, very gravely, 'and [go on till you come to the end:] [then stop.']

(from *Alice in Wonderland*, chs XI and XII)

9.3   Kernel clauses

We can call a clause like *The old man was carrying his bag* or *The old man sat by the road* a **kernel clause**. The structure of a kernel clause is represented as SP(C)(A) – the subject S and predicator P are grammatically essential. The addition of complement(s) (C) and adverbial(s) (A) depends upon the kind of verb in the predicator and the meaning expressed.

The word *kernel* is used as a metaphor to suggest something that is central or basic, and the structure of other types of clause can then be described in terms of their differences from kernel clauses. Clauses which are **derived** from basic kernel clauses are called **derivations**, or **transformations**, because a kernel clause may be transformed into another kind of clause. A kernel clause is:

(a) finite,
(b) declarative,
(c) in the active voice,
(d) with phrases as constituents,
(e) without any recursive or embedded structures, and
(f) consisting of a subject and a predicator, with possibly one or more complements (depending upon the meaning, and the type of verb), and one or more adverbials (optional to the grammar), in the order S P (C) (A).

9.4 Subject and complements in kernel clauses

The argument discussed in chapter 2 and in section 9.1 relates the grammar (or syntax) of clauses to our ability to make meaning – to interpret our experience of the outside world, or our thoughts and feelings – in terms of participants, related to actional and mental processes, or attributes and relational processes, within circumstances of time, place and manner. This was represented in section 2.14 as:

meaning:	actor	process	affected/attribute	circumstance
grammar:	subject (S)	predicator (P)	complement (C)	adverbial (A)
			= object (O), or	
			= intensive complement (Ci), or	
			= adverbial complement (Ca)	

The function of **predicator**, which encodes the process event or state, is always performed by a VP, which we may think of as the 'head' of a clause, because the other constituents of a clause are largely determined by the kind of verb we use in the predicator. As a process can have one, two or more participants involved in it, so the predicator VP will have one, two or more dependent grammatical constituents in the clause. A single participant is the **subject** of a clause. Any other participants are represented by **complements**, which follow the predicator – SPC.

9.4.1 Subject

The subject of a kernel clause is a NP, which may represent either the **actor** or the **affected** person or thing, in relation to the process. Sometimes the process is a kind of action which happens to a person rather than one deliberately performed, as in *Helen slipped on the ice*. Helen did the slipping, but is equally affected by the act of slipping over. Remember that actor and affected are not precise terms, but indicate very generally the **semantic role** played by the participant in relation to the process. The subject comes first in a kernel clause. The number (singular or plural) and person (1st, 2nd or 3rd) of the subject may affect the form of the verb in the predicator, because the verb is said to **agree** with the subject. In practice, this only affects the *-s* form of the verb, in StE and most of the dialects. The only exception is the verb *be*, which has more forms than all other verbs (section 3.3.4.1).

> I **feel** rather tired today.   *base form*
>
> She **feels** rather tired today.   *-s form*

Activity 9.2

(i)   Identify the subjects of the following kernel clauses.

(ii) Say whether the process is actional, mental or relational.

(iii) If the process is actional or mental, discuss whether you think the subject of each clause is an *actor*, performing the process, or is *affected* by it, or perhaps both, or neither.

(This cannot apply to the subjects of clauses containing relational processes, discussed later in section 9.6.1.1.)

(a) Hidesato was returning home from a journey.
(b) His road led him past a mountain to a lake.
(c) A bridge spanned the lake.
(d) An enormous dragon lay across the road in front of the lake.
(e) Hidesato was a very brave man.
(f) He clambered right over the dragon.
(g) He heard a voice behind him.
(h) Hidesato turned round.
(i) He saw a majestic-looking man.
(j) The man was wearing a dragon-crown.

> (adapted from 'My Lord Bag of Rice',
> in *Folk and Fairy Tales*, Ruth Manning-Saunders, 1978)

9.4.2   Complements (I) – object (O)

Section 9.1.2 introduced the transitive clause in which the predicator VP is followed by a grammatical object. You cannot normally omit an object without making the clause ungrammatical or changing the meaning:

> *S*   *P*   *O*
> The tailor   found   little work.

> *The tailor found. (*ungrammatical*)

> *S*   *P*   *O*   *A*
> He   stood   his yardstick   in the corner.

> *S*   *P*   *A*
> He   stood   in the corner. (*grammatical, but different meaning*)

But although the semantic (meaning) relationship of *actor–action–affected* is a very common one, the sequence *subject–predicator–object* (*SPO*) does not always have this meaning. For example, in the clauses:

(i) They took the dog to the vet.
(ii) They took a walk into the country.

the dog in (i) is the grammatical object of *took*, and also the affected thing in relation to *they*, the actors. But in (ii), it is difficult to argue that *a walk* is an affected thing, though it is quite clearly the grammatical object of *took*. The phrase *take a walk* is a **lexical unit,** that is, it functions just like a word in having a meaning similar to, if not quite the same as, the verb *walk* in *They **walked** into the country* (see section 4.1, in which complex prepositions like *on top of* are described as lexical units, because they function like single prepositions).

The subject *His road* in sentence (b) in Activity 9.2 is not an actor, 'doing' something to Hidesato, nor is *A bridge* in (c) 'affecting' the lake.

Activity 9.3

(i) Identify the grammatical objects (O) in the following kernel clauses.

(ii) Discuss which objects, if any, you think refer to *affected* persons or things in their meaning.

(a) Hidesato showed no fear.
(b) The monstrous centipede was destroying the countryside.
(c) The hero was carrying his bow and arrows.
(d) He fitted an arrow to his bow.
(e) The arrow struck the centipede in the middle of its flat forehead.
(f) Hidesato heard the Dragon King's sigh of thankfulness.
(g) The Dragon King gave many gifts to Hidesato.
(h) The magic bag of rice filled itself again.
(i) Hidesato presented the magic bells to the temple.
(j) He changed his name to My Lord Bag of Rice.

(Ibid)

9.4.3 *Complements (2) – intensive (Ci)*

The predicator of a clause, a VP, is its 'head' phrase, so even if there is no definable process, a clause must have a VP filling the predicator slot. The commonest verb of this kind is *be*. As a main verb in a clause it acts as a link between the subject and something we want to say about the subject. It may link a subject with an **attribute** of the subject, e.g. [*happy* (+*past*), *Mole*] represents a proposition which becomes *Mole was happy* in a clause.

Or the verb *be* may point to a definition or a description, e.g. the proposition [*wonderful* (+*present*), *day*] might be spoken as *The day is wonderful*, or *This is a wonderful day*. Similarly, we might say *Here is the place for lunch* or *There's something in the water*, in which case the subjects of the clauses, *this*, *here*, *there* are not really participants at all, but fill the subject slots so that we can make a general statement about what we see. You cannot say *Is raining or use the construction **Is someone at the door* to make a statement. You have to have a 'dummy' subject like *it*, or *there*, and say *It's raining* and *There's someone at the door*.

Verbs like *seem* and *become* also function like *be* as relational verbs, linking the subject of a clause and its **complement** (C). This kind of complement which refers back to the subject is called an **intensive complement** (Ci). Some examples of SPCi structures are:

S   *P*   *Ci*
The Sri Krishna Eating House   **was**   the meanest and shabbiest restaurant in Bombay

S   *P*   *Ci*
The ceiling   **was**   thick with cobwebs that trapped the soot.

S   *P*   *A*   *Ci*
It   **was**   certainly   the cheapest restaurant anyone could possibly find.

S   *P*   *Ci*
There   **was**   nothing to scour the pots with.

A   *S*   *P*   *Ci*
                                          S   *P*   *Ci*
Along the Alibagh-Rewas highway there **were** cafes that **were** pleasanter.

S   *P*   *Ci*   *A*
The floor and the wooden tables   **were**   all black,   too.

S   *P*   *Ci*
The usual customers   **were**   beggars and coolies.

S   *P*   *Ci*   *A*
Hari **became** so tired and weak and anxious   that first night . . .

S   *P*   *Ci*
The whole city   **seemed**   exhausted.

S   *A*   *P*   *Ci*
No one   ever   **seemed**   ready to talk.
                   (adapted from Anita Desai, *The Village by the Sea*, 1982, ch. 8)

Activity 9.4

(i)   Identify the intensive complement (Ci) in the following kernel clauses.

(ii)   List the relational verbs and discuss their meaning.

(a) I am the Dragon King of this lake.
(b) Hidesato remained calm.
(c) The centipede's eyes were two huge balls of fire.
(d) Its back resembled a chain of lighted lanterns.
(e) Its voice sounded like thunder.
(f) Hidesato was being very brave.
(g) The centipede became more and more furious with him.
(h) The brave man felt resolute.
(i) The hideous centipede fell dead at the man's feet.
(j) Hidesato proved a hero.

(from 'My Lord Bag of Rice')

9.5   Kernel clauses in a simple text

The texts used in chapter 2 taken from infant reading primers seemed artificially simple, because our use of English in speech and writing seldom consists of a series of kernel clauses, one after the other. We normally use quite complex combinations of phrase and clause in making up our sentences.

But some English texts are clearly more simple than others in their syntax, and therefore likely to contain kernel clause structures. The following paragraph is adapted from the opening of a short story called 'Old Man at the Bridge':

An old man sat by the road. There was a bridge across the river and people were crossing it. The carts staggered up the bank with soldiers helping push against the wheels. The trucks headed out of it all and the peasants plodded along in the dust. But the old man sat there. He was tired.

(adapted from Ernest Hemingway,
The Short Happy Life of Francis Macomber, 1963)

Here is a step-by-step analysis of the structure of the constituent clauses of this text.

9.5.1   *Identifying the clauses*

Each clause should contain a VP as predicator. It is useful to use conventional signs as shorthand in an analysis, so square brackets [ ] are used to mark the beginning and end of each clause. The VPs are in bold type:

[An old man **sat** by the road] [There **was** a bridge across the river] and [people **were crossing** it] [The carts **staggered** up the bank] with [soldiers **helping push** against the wheels] [The trucks **headed** out of it all] and [the peasants **plodded** along in the dust] But [the old man **sat** there] [He **was** tired]

9.5.2   *Identifying clause constituents*

Next identify the constituent phrases of each clause, to be marked by round brackets ( ):

[(An old man) (sat) (by the road)]
[(There) (was) (a bridge) (across the river)]
and
[(people) (were crossing) (it)]
[(The carts) (staggered) (up the bank)]
with
[(soldiers) (helping push) (against the wheels)]
[(The trucks) (headed) (out of it all)]
and
(the peasants) (plodded) (along) (in the dust)]
But
[(the old man) (sat) (there)]
[(He) (was) (tired)]

9.5.3   Labelling constituent form

The round bracketed phrases can then be labelled according to their form as NP, VP, PrepP, AdjP, AdvP or PossP (see chapter 6). Even if they consist of one word, they are labelled as phrases, because phrases are the **immediate constituents** of clauses, and a phrase consists of one or more words. Conjunctions (*and, but, with*) are marked *cj*.

NP   *VP* *PrepP*
[(An old man) (sat) (by the road)]

NP   *VP*   *NP*   *PrepP*   *cj*
[(There) (was) (a bridge) (across the river)] *and*

NP   *VP*   *NP*
[(people) (were crossing) (it)]

NP   *VP*   *PrepP*   *cj*
[(The carts) (staggered) (up the bank)] with

NP   *VP*   *PrepP*
[(soldiers) (helping push) (against the wheels)]

NP   *VP*   *PrepP*   *cj*
[(The trucks) (headed) (out of it all)] and

NP   *VP*   *AdvP* *PrepP*   *cj*
[(the peasants) (plodded) (along) (in the dust)] But

NP   *VP* *AdvP*
[(the old man) (sat) (there)]

NP *VP* *AdjP*
[(He) (was) (tired)]

The form of the constituents is only one way of identifying them, so the next step is to assign the function S, P, O/Ci or A to the clause constituents. But there is a third kind of complement that must be described before the analysis is continued.

9.5.4   Complements (3) – adverbial (Ca)

Many adverbials that represent the circumstances of time, place and manner in which something happens are often additional information which can be left out without affecting the grammaticality of a clause. But it has been briefly pointed out in section 2.11 that certain adverbials appear to be essential to the grammar of the clause. If the clauses of the adapted text are rewritten without their adverbials, it reads:

> An old man sat. There was a bridge and people were crossing it. The carts staggered with soldiers helping push. The trucks headed and the peasants plodded. But the old man sat. He was tired.

which is not satisfactory. Not only is descriptive detail lost, but most of the clauses are not fully grammatical. The line between grammatical and ungrammatical is not necessarily a clear one, and speakers of English will disagree in particular cases. Do you agree that the text must include most of the adverbials just omitted, in order to be fully grammatical, or perhaps to provide essential information without which the sentence is decidedly odd? Here is a suggested version with essential adverbials included:

> An old man sat **by the road**. There was a bridge **across the river** and people were crossing it. The carts staggered **up the bank** with soldiers helping push **against the wheels**. The trucks headed **out of it all** and the peasants plodded **along**. But the man sat **there**. He was tired.

In fact, only the PrepP *in the dust* has been omitted in this version, but you might disagree and argue that *by the road*, *across the river* or *there* could be omitted too. Hemingway's style is one in which language is pared down to its essentials, as he wrote of it himself:

> If I started to write elaborately, or like someone introducing or presenting something, I found that I could cut that scroll-work or ornament out and throw it away and start with the first true simple declarative sentence I had written.
>
> (Ernest Hemingway, *A Moveable Feast*, 1964, ch. 2)

Some of the adverbials in the paragraph from 'Old Man at the Bridge', are *grammatically* essential. You will see therefore that the first hypothesis about adverbials – that they are optional additions to a clause – needs to be modified.

We need to distinguish between two kinds of adverbial, one that is closely related to the predicator like the grammatical complements (Ci) and (O), and which can be labelled **adverbial complement** (Ca), and another that is more loosely attached, and not a complement, called a **peripheral adverbial** (A). (The adjective *peripheral* is derived from the noun *periphery*, and means *on the outside of*, or *marginal*.) A peripheral adverbial is not grammatically dependent upon the predicator, but more loosely related and generally moveable.

An adverbial following the verb *be* with no other complements in the clause must be a complement:

S	P	Ca
Mole & Rat	were	in the water
the boat	was	outside his hole

because the clauses **Mole & Rat were* and **The boat was* are grammatically incomplete.

9.5.4.1   ADVERBIAL COMPLEMENT OR PERIPHERAL ADVERBIAL?

A test for adverbial complements is (i) to omit the adverbial and see if the clause is still grammatical, and (ii) to try moving the adverbial to another position. If you cannot omit it, it is probably an adverbial complement. If you can move it, it probably is not. But be prepared for disagreement with others over this.

We can try out the test on the clause *I'll put the dinner in the oven at five o'clock*, and ask whether the PrepPs *in the oven* and at *five o'clock* are adverbial complements or peripheral adverbials.

	S	P	O	?A	?A
(i)	I'll	put	the dinner	in the oven	at five o'clock.

Try moving *at five o'clock* to the front of the clause:

	?A	S	P	O	?A
(ii)	At five o'clock	I	'll put	the dinner	in the oven.

or omitting it:

	S	P	O	?A
(iii)	I	'll put	the dinner	in the oven.

Then move the PrepP *in the oven*:

	?A	S	P	O	?A
(iv)	*In the oven	I	'll put	the dinner	at five o'clock.

or omit it:

	S	P	O	?A
(v)	*I	'll put	the dinner	at five o'clock.

or reverse the order of the two PrepPs:

	S	P	O	?A	?A
(vi)	*I	'll put	the dinner	at five o'clock	in the oven

or omit both of them,

	S	P	O
(vii)	*I	'll put	the dinner.

Clauses (iv), (v), (vi) and (vii) are ungrammatical, because *in the oven* cannot be omitted, or moved from its slot in the clause immediately following the predicator. It is therefore an adverbial complement. The verb *put* belongs to a set of verbs which are incomplete without an adverbial complement and an object. The label (Ca) is used to distinguish adverbial complements from other adverbials which are peripheral in clause structure (A):

S	P	O	Ca	A
I	'll put	the dinner	in the oven	at five o'clock.

Activity 9.5

Distinguish between adverbial complements and peripheral adverbials in the following sentences. If the distinction is not clear, discuss why this may be so.

(a) She placed the cloth in the drawer after dinner.
(b) Father is in the kitchen.
(c) I did the washing-up in the sink after supper.
(d) Pat ironed her dress in the kitchen on the ironing board.
(e) She hung the dress in the wardrobe after that.
(f) My married brother lives in London.
(g) Harry laid the cutlery on the dining-room table as a surprise for his mother.
(h) We pushed the chair across the room against the wall.

[NB: In many reference grammars, the traditional term *complement* (or *subject complement*) refers only to what has here been called *intensive complement*, so you must be careful to 'translate' when using other grammar books. In linguistics, *complement* has a much wider general meaning than in traditional grammar, and is used not only for the complements of the VP predicator, as above, but for the NP complement of a preposition in a PrepP (section 6.1.3), and sometimes for the post-modifiers of NPs.]

9.5.5 *Adverbial complements and the predicator*

In the following SPOCa clause:

S	P	O	Ca
I	congratulated	Jane	on her success.

the PrepP *on her success* may be analysed as an adverbial complement because the preposition *on* is determined grammatically by the verb *congratulate*. But in the clause:

S	P	O	Ca
I	put	the dinner	in the oven.

the preposition *in* depends upon the 'context of situation' – where I was putting the dinner – and the verb *put* can be followed by other prepositions of place:

> I put the dinner **on** the table.
> I put the plates **through** the hatch.
> I put my pyjamas **under** the pillow.
> I put my watch **by** my bedside.

and so on. But the PrepP expressing the reason for congratulation after the verb *congratulate* must begin with *on*. On the other hand, the clause *I congratulated him* is quite grammatical without the PrepP *on his success* – a typical conflict between two criteria which help to define an adverbial complement.

Activity 9.6

(i) Fill in the blank spaces with an appropriate preposition for the verb of each clause. Give alternatives if you think there may be some.

(ii) Say whether the adverbial complement can be omitted without making the clause ungrammatical, or changing the meaning significantly.

(a) The minister accused the newspaper . . . libel.
(b) He compared the new report . . . the old one.
(c) Billy told his mother . . . his trip abroad.
(d) She provided them . . . a packed lunch.
(e) This coat will protect you . . . the rain.
(f) I envy him . . . his success.
(g) Tom reminded Jill . . . the time.
(h) The magistrates sentenced them . . . a large fine.
(i) They were convicted . . . disorderly conduct.
(j) The doctor confined her patient . . . bed.

9.5.6 *Phrasal and prepositional verbs*

There are two related kinds of verb which are invariably followed by an adverbial complement.

9.5.6.1 PHRASAL VERBS
For example, in these simple sentences:

> *S   P   Ca A*
> The aircraft **took off** punctually

> *S   P   Ca O*
> My Gran **brought up seven children.**

> *S   P   O   Ca*
> My Gran **brought** seven children *up*.

the adverbs *off* and *up* cannot be left out. They are called adverb **particles**, and function like complements to the verb. The verbs *take off* and *bring up* are **lexical units** (section 9.4.2) and are called **phrasal verbs**. Sometimes they can be replaced by a single verb:

> My Gran **raised** seven children.

A phrasal verb without its adverb particle functioning as adverbial complement is different in meaning, less specific, or it sounds 'wrong' in some way. For example:

phrasal verb with adverb particle			verb without adverb particle	
S	*P*	*Ca*	*S*	*P*
a head	came	out	?a head	came
Mole	sat	down	?Mole	sat
Rat	carried	on	*Rat	carried
The others	made	off	*The others	made
Mole	gave	up	*Mole	gave
Badger	turned	round	?Badger	turned
Badger	set	out	*Badger	set

9.5.6.2 PREPOSITIONAL VERBS

There is another set of verbs which are like phrasal verbs but which are followed by a PrepP instead of an adverb particle. For example:

Rat **got into** a little blue and white boat

Mole **looked at** everything

They are called **prepositional verbs.** The problem is to decide if *get into* and *look at* are complete lexical units, and so together make up the predicator, in which case they are followed by an object:

S	*P*	*Od*
Rat	**got into**	a little blue and white boat
Mole	**looked at**	everything

One argument in favour of this is that both VPs can be substituted by a single verb with a similar meaning,

S	*P*	*Od*
Rat	**entered**	a little blue and white boat
Mole	**saw**	everything

Another test for a prepositional verb as a lexical unit is to try to put the clause into the passive voice. If this produces an acceptable sentence, then the prepositional verb is a lexical unit. But the result is debatable:

?A little blue boat **was got into** by Rat.

?Everything **was looked at** by Mole

Alternatively, we could analyse the PrepPs as adverbial complements,

S	*P*	*Ca*
Rat	**got**	**into** a little blue and white boat
Mole	**looked**	**at** everything

In the following sentences:

> S P   Ca   A
> I 've gone off coffee completely   (*but not* *I've gone coffee off completely)
>
> S   P   O Ca   A
> The taste put me off coffee completely.

the prepositional verbs are *go off* and *put off*, and *coffee* in the PrepP functions very much like an object, so that some linguists would call it a **prepositional object.**

9.5.6.3 PHRASAL-PREPOSITIONAL VERBS

Both kinds of (Ca), the adverb particle and the PrepP, can be combined in a **phrasal-prepositional verb**, so that it is useful to label the adverb particle as (pt). For example:

> S   P   pt Ca
> The race got off to a good start.
>
> P   O   pt Ca
> Don't fob me off with any more rubbish.

There are hundreds of combinations of phrasal, prepositional and phrasal-prepositional verbs. They are especially common in spoken, informal English, and are also often **idioms** – that is, you cannot add the meanings of the separate words together to find the meaning of the combination (for example, *put + up + with = tolerate*, and *go + in + for = use* or *practise*). But the adverb particles and PrepPs in these constructions function grammatically as complements in the clause, even though they are semantically part of the verb.

Activity 9.7

(i)   Identify the predicators of the following clauses as phrasal, prepositional or phrasal-prepositional verbs.

(ii)   Try to find a single-word verb for each clause. Is this always possible?

(iii) Can you spot any other differences between the clauses in their structure?

(a)   Building workers walked out during the morning.
(b)   Can you run that bit of tape through again?
(c)   Dont take your resentment out on me!
(d)   He went off driving altogether.
(e)   I got through the written papers with some coaching.
(f)   I'll knock his block off.
(g)   John put in a brief appearance.
(h)   Many people take in lodgers.

(i)   She is facing up to her responsibilities magnificently.
(j)   Students are sitting in at the university.
(k)   The boys had loaded on too much sand and the wheelbarrow was brimming over.
(l)   The family came up against fresh problems.
(m) The shops put up the prices.
(n)   The travel agent messed our booking up completely.
(o)   They decked themselves out in their best clothes.
(p)   Thise fine weather will bring the crops along very nicely.
(q)   We can play back the recorded programmes.
(r)   You have brought your children up well!

(from A. P. Cowie and R. Mackin,
Oxford Dictionary of Current Idiomatic English,
vol. 1: *Verbs with Prepositions and Particles*, 1975)

9.6   Labelling constituent function

Now to return to the text being discussed in section 9.5. Function can be clearly shown in the form of a 'slot and filler' chart, in which four columns suffice for these simple kernel-type clauses. Here is a possible analysis of the text. The conjunctions are omitted.

	Subject	*Predicator*	*Complement*	*Adverbial*
1	An old man	sat	by the road (Ca)	
2	There	was	a bridge (= delayed S)	across the river
3	people	were crossing	it (O)	
4	The carts	staggered	up the bank (Ca)	
5	soldiers	helping push	against the wheels (Ca)	
6	The trucks	headed	out of it all (Ca)	
7	the peasants	plodded	along (Ca)	in the dust
8	the old man	sat	there (Ca)	
9	He	was	tired (Ci)	

The distinction between an adverbial complement (Ca) and peripheral adverbial (A) is not always clear. For example, the adverbial *across the river* in clause 2 *There was a bridge across the river* might be analysed in three ways:

- As a qualifier of the noun head *bridge* (compare *The bridge across the river was crowded*):

$$S= \quad P \quad =S$$
$$\quad\quad d\ h \quad\quad q$$
There was a bridge across the river

- As a peripheral adverbial, and therefore moveable (*Across the river there was a bridge*):

$$S= \quad P \quad =S \quad A$$
There was a bridge across the river

- As an adverbial complement (A bridge was across the river),

$$S= \quad P \quad =S \quad Ca$$
There was a bridge across the river

There is analysed as a **dummy subject** (S =) and *a bridge* as a **delayed subject** (= S) (section 9.6.2.1 following).

Grammatical categories are sometimes difficult to distinguish clearly, and it can be interesting to discuss alternatives.

Activity 9.8

Discuss the analysis of the adverbial complements and peripheral adverbials in the table printed above.

9.6.1 Types of process in the text

9.6.1.1 RELATIONAL CLAUSES

Clauses (2) and (9) are **relational**, both having the linking verb *be* as predicator In (9), *tired*, a one-word AdjP, is an intensive complement, the attribute of the subject *he*. Clause (2) is described in section 9.6.2.1.

9.6.1.2 ACTIONAL PROCESS CLAUSES

All the other clauses have predicators which stand for **actional processes**: *sat* (2), *were crossing, staggered, helping push, headed, plodded*.

(a) Transitive clauses

Only one clause, (3), is transitive (section 9.1.2), having an object as complement, the pronoun *it* in *people were crossing it*. You could transform the clause into its passive equivalent *it was being crossed*. Transitive clauses must have at least two participants. Most of them (though not all) can take the passive transformation (see section 8.10 on active and passive voice).

(b) Intransitive clauses

The other actional clauses are intransitive and have no object complements, and refer to actions involving one participant only, the grammatical subject.

Even though you can infer from the meaning of (5) that the soldiers would be pushing something (the wheels), the clause contains, not an object, but an adverbial complement, the PrepP *against the wheels*. It is therefore still grammatically intransitive, like the others. You could make it transitive by rewriting it as *soldiers helping push the wheels*, in which *the wheels* is a NP object.

S	P	P	O
soldiers	helping	push	the wheels

9.6.1.3 MENTAL PROCESS CLAUSES

In this short text there are no mental process clauses (see section 2.7 for a short description of types of mental process), but examples from the same story include:

I **was watching** the bridge	*perceptive process*
I **was wondering** how long it would be . . .	*cognitive process*
What animals were they? I **asked**.	*verbal process*
It was my job to **find out** . . .	*behavioural process*

9.6.2 Some transformations – derived clauses

Three of the clauses are, however, not kernel clauses.

9.6.2.1 A SPECIAL KIND OF RELATIONAL – EXISTENTIAL *THERE*

In (2), the subject is *there*, a word which is usually an adverb head of an AdvP. Notice that in clause (8) the word *there* functions as adverbial. But in (2) it has the special function of filling the subject slot.

Say clauses (2) and (8) aloud, and note the difference in your pronunciation of *there* in each spoken clause. In (2) it is unstressed and so reduced in pronunciation. Now say the clauses:

There was a bridge across the river **there**.

There was an old man sitting **there**.

and again check the difference in pronunciation for the two different functions of *there*. Compare the clause:

One time **there** used to be a field **there**.

from *Eveline 2* in section 3.2.

There is used as a **dummy subject,** followed by a suitable form of the verb *be* – *there is, there are, there were* and so on – while *a bridge* is grammatically a complement. It is the **focus of information** as the topic of the clause, and is a kind of **delayed subject.** In English, new information is generally placed at the end of a clause, and in speech is marked by tonic stress. Because we cannot say:

*Was a bridge across the river.

the subject 'slot' has to be filled with something. So this clause, *There was a bridge across the river*, is not a kernel clause, but a transformation of a kernel clause.

Use of the word *there* as subject of a clause is extremely common, and is used to point to the *existence* of something. It is therefore called **existential there**.

Dialect forms
Colloquial forms of existential *there* are recorded. For example:

There's gone a farmer from there... (*Staffs*)

in which the reordering of *There's a farmer gone from there* focuses on the predicator *gone*.

9.6.2.2 PREDICATORS IN PHASE
Clause (5) is also of interest for two other reasons. Firstly it contains two **predicators in phase,** a structure which has already been discussed in section 8.7. It is therefore analysed as:

S	P	P	Ca
Soldiers	helping	push	against the wheels

The form *helping to push* is an alternative you may prefer, but the analysis remains the same, and this clause is therefore not a kernel clause, because it has two predicators. It is possible to derive two clauses from the underlying units of meaning. For example:

[Soldiers were helping]. [Soldiers were pushing against the wheels].

or

[Soldiers were helping [by pushing against the wheels]].

The meaning remains the same, but the grammatical forms are different.

9.6.2.3 NONFINITE CLAUSES
Secondly, clause (5) could not normally stand alone as a sentence:

*Soldiers helping push against the wheels.

This is because in the VP *helping push* neither verb is marked for present or past tense. *Helping* is the *-ing* participle, and *push* is the infinitive, so both are nonfinite, and the clause is therefore called nonfinite also. All nonfinite clauses are subordinate within other clauses or phrases. For this reason also, the clause is not a kernel clause.

In the text, this clause is introduced by the preposition *with*, functioning here as a conjunction:

with soldiers helping push against the wheels

and so we call it a *prepositional clause* (PrepCl). This structure is described in more detail in sections 10.2.1.3 and 11.1.1. Prepositional clauses are always nonfinite.

9.7 The original text

The extract from 'Old Man at the Bridge' was simplified in order to make it easier to illustrate these basic features of kernel clauses. The original is printed below, with the omitted parts in bold type.

Activity 9.9

(i) Check the structure of the clauses against the simplified version.

(ii) Make a fresh analysis of the phrase constituents of the clauses in the extract as NPs, VPs, AdjPs, AdvPs, PrepPs or PossPs, using bracketing.

(iii) Say in what ways the original text is different from the simplified version in vocabulary and grammar, and discuss your response to the two versions.

An old man **with steel-rimmed spectacles and very dusty clothes** sat by the side of the road. There was a **pontoon** bridge across the river and **carts, trucks, and men, women and children** were crossing it. The **mule-drawn** carts staggered up the **steep** bank from the bridge with soldiers helping push against **the spokes of** the wheels. The trucks **ground up and away** heading out of it all and the peasants plodded along in the **ankle-deep** dust. But the old man sat there **without moving**. He was **too** tired **to go any further**.

9.8 More clause structure constituents

The constituents of kernel clause structure so far described are:

1 Subject
2 Predicator
3 Complement [= object, intensive or adverbial complement]
4 Adverbial [peripheral]

in the following combinations or patterns, in each of which one or more peripheral adverbials (A) can always be optionally added at the end of a kernel clause:

1	S P	or	S P A	intransitive
2	S P O	or	S P O A	transitive
3	S P Ci	or	S P Ci A	intransitive
4	S P Ca	or	S P Ca A	intransitive
5	S P O Ca	or	S P O Ca A	transitive

Examples

1a	Children were playing.	(S P)
1b	Children were playing in the street.	(S P A)
2a	People were crossing the bridge.	(S P O)

2b	People were crossing the bridge in haste.		(S P O A)
3a	The old man was tired.		(S P Ci)
3b	The old man was tired after his walk.		(S P Ci A)
4a	The peasants plodded along.		(S P Ca)
4b	The peasants plodded along in the dust.		(S P Ca A)
5a	The old man put his bundle on the ground.		(S P O Ca)
5b	The old man put his bundle on the ground wearily.		(S P O Ca A)
or			
5c	He mistook me for my brother.		(S P O Ca)
5d	He mistook me for my brother yesterday.		(S P O Ca A)

Activity 9.10

The following extract from another Hemingway short story is set out clause by clause.

(i) Identify the constituent phrases and label their function in clause structure as S, P, O, Ci, Ca or A.

(ii) Say whether there are any non-kernel clauses, that is, not declarative, or not in the active voice, or with consituents not in the order SP(C)(A), etc.

1		[It was a hot afternoon in Wyoming]:
2		[the mountains were a long way away]
3	and	[you could see snow on their tops],
4	but	[they made no shadow],
5	and	[in the valley the grain-fields were yellow],
6		[the road was dusty
7	with	[cars passing]]
8	and	[all the small wooden houses at the edge of the town were baking in the sun].
9		[There was a tree over Fontan's back porch]
10	and	[I sat there at a table]
11	and	[Madame Fontan brought up cold beer from the cellar].
12		[A motor car turned off the main road]
13	and	[Ø came up the side road],
14	and	[Ø stopped beside the house].
15		[Two men got out]
16	and	[Ø came in through the gate].
17		[I put the bottles under the table].
18		[Madame Fontan stood up]

(adapted from 'Wine of Wyoming',
The Short Happy Life of Francis Macomber)

(The symbol Ø stands for a grammatical constituent that has been deleted, but which can be understood from the context. This is a feature of the coordination of clauses, and is described in chapter 13.)

9.8.1 *Direct and indirect objects*

A kernel clause which contains a subject and an object is a transitive clause, with
the relation of subject to object often representing that of *actor* to *affected*, in a
very general sense. In the clause:

> *S*　　　*P*　*O*
> The teacher gives lots of encouragement.

the NP *lots of encouragement* is the object of the verb *gives*. *Encouragement* is an
abstract thing that cannot itself be literally affected by *giving*, so we can call it the
goal of the process of giving. It is in a similar grammatical relationship to *the
teacher* as the NP *the pupils* in:

> *S*　　　*P*　　　*O*
> The teacher encourages her pupils.

Both active clauses can be transformed into passive clauses:

> Lots of encouragement is given by the teacher.

> Her pupils are encouraged by the teacher.

In the following clause, another participant is included, represented by the
PrepP *to her pupils*:

> *S*　　　*P*　*O*　　　　　　*Ca*
> The teacher gives lots of encouragement **to her pupils.**

which has an alternative version:

> *S*　　　　*P*　*?*　　　*O*
> The teacher gives *her pupils* lots of encouragement.

But *her pupils* is a NP, and so is not an adverbial complement like the PrepP *to her
pupils*, though it has a similar meaning in this context. Compare the following
pairs of clauses:

> *S*　*P*　*O*　　　　　　*Ca*
> John made a nice cup of tea *for Alice*

> *S*　*P*　*?*　*O*
> John made *Alice* a nice cup of tea.

> *S*　*P*　　*O*　　　　　*Ca*　　　*A*
> Sue bought a new sweater *for John on his birthday*.

> *S*　*P*　*?*　*O*　　　　　　*A*
> Sue bought *John* a new sweater on his birthday.

These clauses can be further changed, by the substitution of pronouns:

> *S*　*P*　*?*　*O*
> She gives *them* lots of encouragement

S P ? O
He made *her* a nice cup of tea.

S P ? O   A
She bought *him* a new sweater on his birthday.

The clause constituents labelled with a question mark have more or less the same meaning as the PrepP adverbials from which they derive, but they differ in grammatical function, which is more like the objects which they precede. They are therefore analysed as **objects**.

To distinguish the two types of object, we call NPs which can be derived from the PrepPs with *to* or *for* **indirect object complements**, or **indirect objects** for short (Oi). They represent the person who receives something – the **recipient** (*her pupils*, corresponding to the adverbial PrepP *to her pupils*) – or who benefits from something done – the **beneficiary** (*Alice/John* corresponding to *for Alice/for John*).

The other objects are called **direct object complements**, or **direct objects** (Od) when they are in contrast with an indirect object.

S   P   Oi   Od
The teacher gives her pupils lots of encouragement.
                  recipient

S   P   Oi   Od
John made Alice a nice cup of tea.
              beneficiary

S   P   Oi   Od
Sue bought John a new sweater.
              beneficiary

Notice that clauses with both direct and indirect objects have two passive transformations,

active
S   P   Oi   Od
The teacher gives her pupils lots of encouragement.
actor   *recipient goal*

passive (i)
S   P   Oi   Ca
Lots of encouragement is given her pupils by the teacher.
goal   *recipient actor*

passive (ii)
S   P   Od   Ca
Her pupils are given lots of encouragement by the teacher.
recipient   *goal*   *actor*

in which both objects can function as subject of the passive clause. The semantic roles of actor (who gave it), goal (what was given) and recipient (to whom it was given) remain unchanged. It is the grammatical focus of information that is changed in each clause with a different constituent as theme.

Activity 9.11

(i) Identify all the PrepPs in the following sentences.

(ii) Rewrite the sentences containing PrepPs which can be transformed into indirect objects.

(iii) List the VPs which are followed by both direct and indirect objects.

(a) They sent postcards to all their friends in Scotland.
(b) She teaches the piano to several children for the fun of it.
(c) I offered several alternative dates for the job to the builder.
(d) He paid the bill for the meal to the cashier.
(e) We showed the letter to our friends for their information.
(f) You owe several pounds to the butcher for last month's meat.
(g) They gave presents to all their grandchildren.
(h) Let me bake a cake for you.

Transitive verbs which take both a direct and indirect object as complements are called **ditransitive** (*di*- means *two*), and those which take only a direct object are called **monotransitive** (*mono*- means *one*). This structure adds a sixth basic pattern to the list of types of kernel clause so far discussed:

> 6   S P Oi Od   or   S P Oi Od A   ditransitive

Examples
> 6a   He told me a good story   (S P Oi Od)
> 6b   He told me a good story last night   (S P Oi Od A)

9.8.1.1 VARIATION IN THE ORDER OF DIRECT AND INDIRECT OBJECT PRONOUNS

The order of the clause constituents in these sentences is S P Oi Od:

S	P	Oi	Od
The teacher	gives	*her pupils*	lots of encouragement.
The teacher	gives	*them*	lots of encouragement.
The teacher	gives	*them*	it.

in which the indirect object precedes the direct object. But the order Od–Oi is used by many speakers in the third clause in which both direct and indirect objects are pronouns, and it is not clear whether this is a standard or nonstandard form:

S	P	Oi	Od
The teacher	gives	it	them.
The teacher	gives	it	her pupils.

9.8.2   *Intensive complements referring to the object*

The intensive complements described in section 9.4.3 referred back to the subject of the clause, but in each of the following clauses there is an intensive complement which describes an attribute of the object:

      S   P   O   Ci   A
(i)   They elected Mary **president** by a big majority.

     op-v S   P   O   Ci
(ii) Do   you like your coffee **black**?

In the first sentence, the clause:

(iii) Mary became president

can be understood as part of the meaning, and in the second:

(iv) Your coffee is black.

In these two clauses (iii) and (iv), the noun *president* and adjective *black* are intensive complements of the subject NPs *Mary* and *your coffee*. The intensive relationship remains the same in (i) and (ii) when the NPs are objects.

Activity 9.12

(i)   Identify the object and intensive complements in the following kernel clauses.

(ii) Write another sentence for each example, using the object as subject, with the same intensive complement.

(a)   We shall have to keep the baby quiet in church.
(b)   The committee appointed him chairman yesterday.
(c)   I think her an unlikely candidate for the job.
(d)   Harry is going to paint his house white.
(e)   Helen prefers the window open at night.
(f)   I consider James justified in his complaint.
(g)   We thought the teacher rather absent-minded.
(h)   The teacher called the boy a fool.
(i)   Jimmy found his bike damaged after school.
(j)   The returning officer declared the MP elected.

This is another kernel clause pattern to add to the others:

    7 S P O Ci   or   S P O Ci A   transitive

Examples

      7a I like my tea sweet.   (S P O Ci)
      7b I like my tea sweet in the morning.   (S P O Ci A)

9.9 Summary of kernel clause patterns

The different kinds of complement after the predicator account for the varieties of kernel clause. Subject and predicator are common to all of them, but it is the verb of the predicator which determines the number and type of complements. Here is the list:

1	S P	no complement	*intransitive*
2	S P Od	direct object	*transitive*
3	S P Ci	intensive complement referring back to the subject	*intransitive*
4	S P Ca	adverbial complement	*intransitive*
5	S P Od Ca	direct object and adverbial complement	*transitive*
or	S P Ca Od		
6	S P Oi Od	indirect object and direct object	*transitive*
7	S P Od Ci	direct object and intensive complement referring to the object transitive	*transitive*

to each of which one or more peripheral adverbials (A) may be optionally added.

Examples

1	S P A	Otter laughed loudly
2	S P Od A	Mole took the oars in haste
3	S P Ci A	It was quiet in the morning
4	S P Ca A	Mole got into the boat after Ratty
5	S P Od Ca A	Rat got the food basket out with care
or	S P Ca Od A	Rat got out the food basket with care
6	S P Oi Od A	Rat gave Mole a sandwich on the bank
7	S P Od Ci A	Toad made Rat cross frequently

Activity 9.13

Check that you can confidently identify the constituents of the following kernel clauses as S, P, Ci, Ca, Od, Oi or A by labelling the words and phrases. For example:

```
S      P            A
Mole  didn't speak  for a long time
```

1	SP	You can't row
2	SPA	Mole didn't speak for a long time
3	SPOd	Badger saw Otter and Mole
4	SPOd	Mole and Rat had a wonderful lunch
5	SPOd	Mole breathed the fresh spring air
6	SPOd	Mole didn't ask any more questions
7	SAPOd	Badger always does that

207

8	SP(A)Od	Mole had never seen a boat *(A) in brackets splits the predicator VP*
9	SPOdA	I won't do it again
10	SPOdA	Mole watched the river for a long time
11	SPCi	This is a wonderful day
12	SPCi	Toad's such a nice person
13	SPACi	I'm *really* very sorry
14	SPCiA	What's a little water to a Water Rat?
15	SPCa	Badger lives there
16	SPCa	It was too late
17	SPCa	Mole got into the boat
18	SPCaA	We don't go there often
19	SPOdCa	Rat helped Mole out of the boat
20	SPOdCi	The bright sunshine made Mole very happy
21		Badger walked two steps forward
22		Here's the place for our lunch
23		I can't *really* see
24		I was very silly
25		Mole and Rat sat on the bank in the sunshine
26		Mole walked for a long time
27		Mole was very hungry
28		Otter saw the food basket
29		Rat climbed into his hole
30		Rat got out the food basket
31		Rat rowed home
32		Rat rowed the boat down a little stream away from the big river
33		Rat sent Toad a letter the next day
34		The boat was outside his hole
35		The hand pushed him to the bank
36		There's something in the water

Activity 9.14

Bracket the predicators in phase in the following clauses. For example:

SPP   Mole ‖learned‖ to ⌈row⌉‖

SPP	Mole learned to swim
SPP	Mole tried to row
SPPCa	Mole went to stay at Rat's house
SAPPCa	Mole just liked being outside
SPPOd/SP	Mole enjoyed watching them work
SPOi/SP	I can teach you to swim
ASPP	Suddenly Mole wanted to stop

9.10 Analysis of a text

The following text is another example of Ernest Hemingway's writing which contains a high proportion of kernel clauses, though seldom written as one-clause, or simple sentences. The way clauses are linked together and embedded in others is the subject of chapter 11.

1 In the morning it was bright, and they were sprinkling the streets of the town, and we all had breakfast in a cafe. 2 Bayonne is a nice town. 3 It is like a very clean Spanish town and it is on a big river. 4 Already, so early in the morning, it was very hot on the bridge across the river. 5 We walked out on the bridge and then took a walk through the town.

6 I was not at all sure Mike's rods would come from Scotland in time, so we hunted a tackle store and finally bought a rod for Bill upstairs over a dry-goods store. 7 The man who sold the tackle was out, and we had to wait for him to come back. 8 Finally he came in, and we bought a pretty good rod cheap, and two landing-nets.

9 We went out into the street again and took a look at the cathedral. 10 Cohn made some remark about it being a very good example of something or other, I forget what. 11 It seemed like a nice cathedral, nice and dim, like Spanish churches. 12 Then we went up past the old fort and out to the local Syndicat d'Initiative office, where the bus was supposed to start from. 13 There they told us the bus service did not start until July 1st. 14 We found out at the tourist office what we ought to pay for a motor-car to Pamplona and hired one at a big garage just around the corner from the Municipal Theatre for four hundred francs. 15 The car was to pick us up at the hotel in forty minutes, and we stopped at the cafe on the square where we had eaten breakfast, and had a beer. 16 It was hot, but the town had a cool, fresh, early-morning smell and it was pleasant sitting in the cafe. 17 A breeze started to blow, and you could feel that the air came from the sea. 18 There were pigeons out in the square, and the houses were a yellow, sun-baked colour, and I did not want to leave the cafe. 19 But we had to go to the hotel to get our bags packed and pay the bill. 20 We paid for the beers, we matched and I think Cohn paid, and went up to the hotel. 21 It was only sixteen francs apiece for Bill and me, with ten percent added for the service, and we had the bags sent down and waited for Robert Cohn. 22 While we were waiting I saw a cockroach on the parquet floor that must have been at least three inches long. 23 I pointed him out to Bill and then put my shoe on him. 24 We agreed he must have just come in from the garden. 25 It was really an awfully clean hotel.

(Ernest Hemingway, *Fiesta*, ch. X)

9.10.1 *Division into constituent clauses*

The clauses are written out below and numbered, with coordinating conjunctions (coj) and subordinating conjunctions (scj), which link them together, placed in columns on the left. The kernel clauses in the text are printed in bold type, and the structure of those that occur in the first eight sentences is analysed:

	ccj	scj	*clause*	*kernel?*
1a			In the morning it was bright,	
1b	and		**S** **P** **O** **they** **were sprinkling** **the streets of the town**	√
1c	and		**S** **P** **O** **A** **we all** **had** **breakfast** **in a cafe.**	√
2			**S** **P** **Ci** **Bayonne** **is** **a nice town.**	√
3a			**S** **P** **Ca** **It** **is** **like a very clean Spanish town**	√
3b	and		**S** **P** **Ca** **it** **is** **on a big river.**	√
4			Already, so early in the morning, it was very hot on the bridge across the river.	
5a			**S** **P** **pt** **A** **We** **walked** **out** **on the bridge**	√
5b	and		then Ø took a walk through the town.	
6a			I was not at all sure x	
6b		x =	**S** **P** **A** **A** **Mike's rods** **would come** **from Scotland** **in time**	√
6c		so	**S** **P** **O** **we** **hunted** **a tackle store**	√
6d	and		Ø finally bought a rod for Bill upstairs over a dry-goods store	
7a			The man who sold the tackle was out	
7b	and		we had to wait for him to come back	
8a			Finally he came in	
8b	and		**S** **P** **O** **Ci** **we** **bought** **a pretty good rod** **cheap**	√
8c	and		Ø Ø two landing-nets.	
9a			**We went out into the street again**	√
9b	and		**Ø took a look at the cathedral.**	√
10a			Cohn made some remark about x	
10b	x =		it being a very good example of something or other	

10c			**I forget what.**	√
11			It seemed like a nice cathedral, nice and dim, like Spanish churches.	
12a			Then we went up past the old fort and out to the local Syndicat d'Initiative office,	
12b			where the bus was supposed to start from.	
13a			There they told us x	
13b	x =		**the bus service did not start until July 1st.**	√
14a			We found out at the tourist office y	
14b	y =		what we ought to pay for a motor-car to Pamplona	
14c	**and**		**Ø hired one at a big garage just around the corner from the Municipal Theatre for four hundred francs.**	√
15a			**The car was to pick us up at the hotel in forty minutes**	√
15b	**and**		**we stopped at the cafe on the square**	√
15c			where we had eaten breakfast	
15d	**and**		**Ø had a beer.**	
16a			**It was hot,**	√
16b	**but**		**the town had a cool, fresh, early-morning smell**	√
16c	and		it was pleasant sitting in the cafe.	
17a			A breeze started to blow,	
17b	and		you could feel that x	
17c	**x =**		**the air came from the sea.**	√
18a			There were pigeons out in the square,	
18b	**and**		**the houses were a yellow, sun-baked colour,**	√
18c	and		I did not want to leave the cafe.	
19a	**But**		**we had to go to the hotel**	√
19b			to get our bags packed	
19c	and		Ø pay the bill.	
20a			**We paid for the beers**	√
20b			**we matched**	√
20c	and		I think x	

20d	x =		Cohn paid,	√
20e	and		Ø went up to the hotel.	√
21a			It was only sixteen francs apiece for Bill and me,	√
21b		with	ten percent added for the service,	
21c	and		we had the bags sent down	
21d	and		Ø waited for Robert Cohn.	√
22a		While	we were waiting	√
22b			I saw a cockroach on the parquet floor	√
22c			that must have been at least three inches long.	
23a			I pointed him out to Bill	√
23b	and		then Ø put my shoe on him.	
24a			We agreed x	
24b	x =		he must have just come in from the garden.	
25			It was really an awfully clean hotel.	

Complete Activity 9.15 before reading the commentary which follows it.

Activity 9.15

(i) Identify the constituents of the kernel clauses (in bold type) which have not been analysed, beginning with clause 9a. Label the constituents as S (subject), P (predicator), C (complement), or A (adverbial).

(ii) Classify the complements as object (O), intensive (Ci) or adverbial (Ca).

(iii) Identify the clause pattern, 1 – 7, to which each conforms.

(iv) Find examples in the non-kernel clauses of,
   (a) Existential *there*.
   (b) Predicators in phase.
   (c) Nonfinite clauses.
   (Section 9.6.2 on derived clauses)

A kernel clause may have more than one adverbial at (A).

Commentary on Activity 9.15

Check-list of kernel clause types in the text
The non-kernel clauses are described in the following chapter 10.

The basic kernel clause patterns to be found in the text are (omitting the peripheral adverbials):

1 S P (intransitive)

6b   Mike's rods / would come
20b we / matched
20d Cohn / paid
22a we / were waiting

2 S P O (monotransitive))

1b   they / were sprinkling / the streets of the town
1c   we all / had / breakfast
6c   we / hunted / a tackle store
10c I / forget / what
14c (we) / hired / one
15d (we) / had / a beer
16b the town / had / a cool fresh early-morning smell
22b I / saw / a cockroach

3 S P Ci

2   Bayonne / is / a nice town
16a It / was / hot
18b the houses / were / a yellow sun-baked colour
21a It / was / only sixteen france apiece

4 S P Ca

3a   It / is / like a very clean Spanish town
3b   it / is / on a big river
5a   We / walked / out
9a   wc / went / out
13b the bus service / did not start / until July 1st
15b We / stopped / at the cafe on the square
17c the air / came / from the sea
19a we / had to go / to the hotel
20a We / paid / for the beers
20e (we) / went / up
21d (we) / waited / for Robert Cohn

5 S PO Ca

9b   (we) / took / a look / at the cathedral
15a The car /was to pick / us / up
23a I / pointed / him / out (to Bill)

6 S P Oi Od

The only example of this pattern is not in fact a kernel clause, because the direct object is an embedded clause:

12   (There) they / told / us / [the bus service did not start until July 1st]

7 S P O Ci

8b   we / bought / a pretty good rod / cheap

Activity 9.16 _____

(i)   Identify the clauses in the following text, which is the continuation of the one just discussed.

(ii)   Identify and analyse the structure of the kernel clauses, using the procedures demonstrated in this chapter.

(iii) Describe the features of the other clauses which make them non-kernel clauses (that is, complex or derived clauses).

(iv) Select parts of the complete text to revise your ability to analyse the structure of the constituent phrases of the clauses.

26 Cohn came down, finally, and we all went out to the car. 27 It was a big, closed car, with a driver in a white duster with blue collar and cuffs, and we had him put the back of the car down. 28 He piled in the bags and we started off up the street and out of the town. 29 We passed some lovely gardens and had a good look back at the town, and then we were out in the country, green and rolling, and the road climbing all the time. 30 We passed lots of Basques with oxen, or cattle, hauling carts along the road, and nice farmhouses, low roofs, and all white-plastered. 31 In the Basque country the land all looks very rich and green and the houses and villages look well-off and clean. 32 Every village had a pelota court and on some of them kids were playing in the hot sun. 33 There were signs on the walls of the churches saying it was forbidden to play pelota against them, and the houses in the villages had red-tiled roofs, and then the road turned off and commenced to climb and we were going way up close along a hillside, with a valley below and hills stretched off back toward the sea. 34 You couldn't see the sea. 35 It was too far away. 36 You could see only hills and more hills, and you knew where the sea was.

10. Complexity in clause constituents

10.1 Complex and derived clauses

The text from Hemingway's *Fiesta*, described in section 9.10, contained a number of kernel clauses, but the other non-kernel clauses remain to be discussed. They either contain complex phrases as constituents, or else differ from a kernel clause in one or more of its basic features:

kernel clause	*non-kernel clause*
(a) finite (tensed),	(a) non-finite, and/or
(b) declarative mood,	(b) interrogative or imperative and/or
(c) in the active voice, and	(c) in the passive voice, and/or
(d) in the order SP(C)(A)	(d) not in SP(C)(A) order

and so they are said to be **derived** from kernel clauses. Some of them will be referred to in this chapter, but there is a more complete commentary in Chapters 11 and 12.

This chapter describes the kind of complexity produced in a clause *within* the clause constituents. A clause may be finite, declarative, active and in SPCA order, but it may also have complex NPs, VPs, PrepPs, AdjPs or AdvPs.

10. 2 Complexity within phrases

10.2.1 *Subordination within NPs and PrepPs*

10.2.1.1. PHRASES EMBEDDED IN NP AND PREPP STRUCTURE
We have already looked at the possibilities of complex structure in NPs and PrepPs in chapter 7, with examples, mainly from newspaper headlines, of NPs with pre- and post-modifiers. The embedding of one NP or PrepP in another,

making the embedded phrase subordinate to the other, has been described as a **recursive** process, because it can recur in a series, as in the NP headline:

DENIAL OF RUMOUR OF REJECTION OF REAGAN'S
COMPROMISE PROPOSAL FOR AID TO NICARAGUAN REBELS

which is a complex NP. Its head word *denial* is post-modified by five PrepPs, four of which are themselves post-modified by the following PrepP. The relationship of the PrepPs to the head word is one of **subordination**. Each one is embedded in the other.

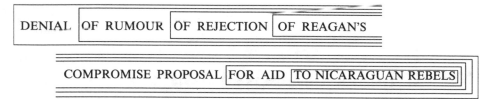

NPs may also have complex pre-modifiers, as in this clause headline:

		S	*P*	*O*

((FREEDOM OF INFORMATION) GROUP)   HAILS   ((HISTORIC

AND DEVASTATING) DEFEAT)

The head word *group* of the NP subject *Freedom of information group*, is pre-modified by the NP *freedom of information*.

```
m                                    h
h              q
         p      h
FREEDOM  OF  INFORMATION   GROUP
```

Headlines are not, of course, the only variety of English to use such structures. The following examples (a)–(e), like many of the texts in this chapter, are taken from George Orwell's novel *Animal Farm*.

Activity 10.1

Analyse the structure, in terms of p, m, h and q, of the complex NPs and PrepPs in italics in the following sentences. Use either labelled bracketing, or tree diagrams.

(a) On Sunday mornings Squealer, holding down *a long strip of paper* with his trotter, would read out to them lists of figures proving that *the production of every class of foodstuff* had increased by 200 per cent.

(b) Then it was discovered that *the greater part of the potato crop* had been frosted in the clamps.

(c) Napoleon decreed that there should be *a full investigation into Snowball's activities*.

(d) The three hens who had been *the ringleaders in the attempted rebellion over the eggs* now came forward.

(e) Now that *the small field beyond the orchard* had been set aside for barley, it was rumoured that *a corner of the large pasture* was to be fenced off and turned into *a grazing-ground for superannuated animals*.

10.2.1.2 NONFINITE CLAUSES EMBEDDED IN NP AND PrepP STRUCTURE

As we saw in chapter 7, nonfinite clauses can function as post-modifiers of NPs and PrepPs, just like other NPs and PrepPs. All three kinds of nonfinite verb can be used – infinitive, *-ing* (present) participle and *-en* /*-ed* (past) participle. Such clauses are embedded within the structure of a phrase. Some examples follow from *Animal Farm*:

```
      S          P     O
                 d     h        q = Nonf Cl
(a)  The animals saw  (no  reason  [to disbelieve Squealer]).
```

```
      S        P         Ca    A        O
                                         h      q
                                                p      h
(b)  Squealer  would read  out   to them  (lists  (of   figures
```

q = *Nonf Cl*
[proving that the production of every class of foodstuff had increased])).

```
                          S                                      P
                          d      h      q = Nonf Cl
(c)  A few days later, when (the   terror  [caused by the executions])  had died
     down ...
```

In (b) and (c) especially, the NonfCls resemble **restrictive relative clauses** in their function (section 10.2.1.4).

Activity 10.2

Identify the nonfinite clauses which are post-modifiers of the head noun in a NP or PrepP in the following sentences.

(a) The general feeling on the farm was well expressed in a poem entitled 'Comrade Napoleon'.
(b) There were many more mouths to feed now.
(c) The poem was surmounted by a portrait of Napoleon executed by Squealer in white paint.
(d) Frederick had wanted to pay for the timber with something called a cheque.
(e) Frederick intended to bring against them twenty men all armed with guns.
(f) In spite of the efforts of Napoleon and Boxer to rally them, the animals were soon driven back.
(g) The sight of their dead comrades stretched upon the grass moved some of them to tears.

Activity 10.3

Mark the post-modifying PrepPs and nonfinite clauses in the structure of the following sentence from *Small World* by David Lodge (1984).

'There's something I must ask you, Fulvia,' said Morris Zapp, as he sipped Scotch on the rocks poured from a crystal decanter brought on a silver tray by a black-uniformed, white-aproned maid to the first floor drawing-room of the magnificent eighteenth century house just off the Villa Napoleone...

10.2.1.3 NONFINITE CLAUSE COMPLEMENTS IN PREPPS – PREPOSITIONAL CLAUSES

Sometimes nonfinite clauses do not directly post-modify a NP, but are embedded in the structure of a PrepP which is itself a post-modifier in a NP. The structure *preposition + clause* was briefly introduced in section 9.6.2.3, and was called **prepositional clause** (PrepCl) (see also section 11.1.1.). In this example from the *Fiesta* text:

$$
\begin{array}{llll}
 & \text{d} & \text{h} & \text{q} \\
\text{10 \quad Cohn made} & \text{some} & \text{remark} & \text{(about} \quad \text{[it being a very good example of} \\
 & & & \hspace{5cm}\text{something or other])} \\
 & & & \quad \text{p} \qquad \text{?} \\
 & & & \quad = PrepCl
\end{array}
$$

the NonfCl *it being a very good example of something or other* functions as the complement of the preposition *about*, just like a NP. Compare the NP complement *the cathedral* in the PrepP *about the cathedral* in:

$$
\begin{array}{llll}
 & \text{d} & \text{h} & \text{q} = PrepP \\
\text{Cohn made} & \text{some} & \text{remark} & \text{(about} \quad \text{the cathedral)} \\
 & & & \quad p \hspace{1.2cm} NP
\end{array}
$$

We can therefore call *it being a very good example of something or other* a **noun clause (NCl)** in this kind of structure. The PrepCl is a post-modifer of the NP *some remark*.

$$
\begin{array}{llll}
 & \text{d} & \text{h} & \text{q} \\
\text{10 \quad Cohn made} & \text{some} & \text{remark} & \text{(about [it being a very good example of} \\
 & & & \hspace{5cm}\text{something or other])} \\
 & & & \quad \text{p} + \boxed{\textit{Noun Clause (NCl)}} = PrepCl
\end{array}
$$

Here are two examples from Orwell's *Animal Farm*:

$$
\begin{array}{llll}
 & \text{m} & \text{h} & \text{q} = PrepCl \\
\text{Clearly there was} & \text{good} & \text{reason} & \text{(for [killing the traitors]).} \\
 & & & \quad \text{p} \quad NCl
\end{array}
$$

$$
\begin{array}{llll}
 & \text{p} & \text{h} & \text{q} = PrepCl \\
\text{They saw that they were} & \text{in} & \text{danger} & \text{(of [being surrounded]).} \\
 & & & \quad \text{p} \quad NCl
\end{array}
$$

218

Activity 10.4

Identify the prepositional clauses in the following sentences from *Animal Farm*, and describe their function.

(a) Boxer saw ahead of him the heavy labour of rebuilding the windmill from the foundations.
(b) Boxer's hoof was a long time in healing.
(c) Squealer had every appearance of being seriously ill.
(d) Squealer had no difficulty in proving that the animals were not short of food.
(e) A young pig named Pinkeye was given the task of tasting all Napoleon's food before he ate it.

10.2.1.4 RESTRICTIVE RELATIVE CLAUSES

Clauses embedded as post-modifiers in NPs were introduced in section 7.2.7, and called **relative clauses** (RelCl) (in traditional grammar they were called **adjective clauses**). They begin with:

- *who, which* or *that* as subject, or
- *who, whom, which* or *that* as object, or
- another *wh-* word like *when* or *where*, which function as adverbials, or
- a PrepP with the relative pronoun *whom* or *which* as head word, such as *by whom, with which, after which*.

(a) Relative pronoun as subject
In the sentence:

> Clearly there was good reason for killing the traitors who had leagued themselves with Snowball.

the relative pronoun *who* is the subject in the RelCl that qualifies the NP *the traitors*:

	RelCl		
	S	*P*	*O*	*Ca*
(the traitors	[**who**	had leagued	themselves	with Snowball]

In the sentence:

> This is the finest cart **that was ever built**, without any exception.

the clause *that was ever built* describes, or defines, the head noun *cart* in the NP *the finest cart of its sort*. Information about carts is **restricted** to the one being talked about. It is called specifically a **restrictive relative clause** because it restricts its reference to that one particular cart. In writing we do not separate off the restrictive RelCl by commas, and in speech we do not speak it with a separate tone-unit. We can diagram the sentence as,

d	m	h	q = *RelCl*		
			S	*P*	*A*	*P*

This is (the finest cart [**that** was ever built]), without any exception.

The relative pronoun *that* is the subject of the relative clause, and its **referent** (what it refers to) is the noun *cart*.

In StE and most dialects, the relative pronoun cannot be deleted when it is the subject of its clause. StE speakers cannot say :

*(A gander [Ø had been privy to the plot]) had confessed his guilt to Squealer.

because the RelCl lacks the subject *who* or *that*, so the clause should read:

(A gander [**that** had been privy to the plot]) had confessed his guilt to Squealer.

In some dialects the relative pronoun as subject may be deleted, however (see section 10.2.1.6 following).

Activity 10.5

(i)   Identify the restrictive relative clauses in the following sentences.
(ii) What is the referent of the relative pronoun in each sentence?

(a)   'I can only regret the wasted years that lie behind me, squandered in trivialities.'
(b)   'The whole world before you, and a horizon that's always changing!'
(c)   Little sleeping-bunks – a little table which folded up against a wall...
(d)   With a blast of wind and a whirl of sound that made them jump for the nearest ditch, it was on them!
(e)   The magnificent motor-car flung an enveloping cloud of dust that blinded and enwrapped them utterly, and then dwindled to a speck in the far distance.
(f) 'All those wasted years which lie behind me, I never knew, never even *dreamt*!'
(g)   'With luck we may pick up a train there that'll get us back to River Bank tonight.'

(b) Relative pronoun as object
There are two possible versions of a RelCl in which a relative pronoun is the object:

(i)   Squealer would talk of (the deep love [**that/which** Napoleon bore to all animals everywhere]).
(ii) Squealer would talk of (the deep love [Ø Napoleon bore to all animals everywhere]).

Orwell's text is (ii), in which the relative pronoun *that* or *which* has been deleted. The NP *the deep love* is next to the RelCl, so the pronoun seems superfluous. This is always a possible choice when the pronoun is the object of the verb of the RelCl. In this sentence:

```
        p      h  q
               O   S   P        P   A
```
Toad talked big (about all [**that** he was going to do in the days to come)].

the referent of the relative pronoun *that* is *all* in the PrepP *about all*. The subject of the RelCl is *he*, and *all* is what he was going to do, and so *that* is the object in its clause, but still comes first, as the link between *all* and *do*. The relative pronoun, as the object of its clause, can be deleted:

Toad talked big about all Ø he was going to do in the days to come.

Activity 10.6

(i)   Identify the restrictive RelCls in the following set.

(ii)   In which sentences is the relative pronoun deleted?

(a)   'Now look here. Let's be sensible. You are the very animals I wanted.'
(b)   'You see – everything that you could possibly want.'
(c)   'And dont argue – it's the one thing I can't stand.'
(d)   The smell of the dust they kicked up was rich and satisfying.
(e)   Mole trudged off to the nearest village for milk and eggs and various necessities the Toad had, of course, forgotten to provide.
(f)   Toad remarked what a pleasant easy life it was they were all leading.
(g)   'We can't leave him here in the distracted state that he's in!'
(h)   And he got into a little blue and white boat which was outside his hole.

(c) Relative pronoun as PrepP complement
This usage can be illustrated in the following sentences:

```
    S                                        P   Ci
        RelCl
        A          S   P    Ca
The day  on which   I   go   on holiday  is   my birthday.
                                RelCl
I think you know the woman   to whom I wrote that letter.
```

The second example is formal in style, and in speaking we would probably say:

I think you know the woman **who I wrote that letter to**.

or

I think you know the woman **I wrote that letter to**.

We do not use *that* as the relative pronoun in this construction – **The day on that I go on holiday* ...

(d) Relative adverbial

The *wh*-adverbs, *why, when, where, how*, also function as markers of relative clauses:

> **RelCl**
> **wh-A   S   P   O   A**
> 'The nearest town [where we can get help from] is five miles away,' said Rat.

In the following sentence, the noun *times* is post-modified by the RelCl *when . . . hours*, marked by the *wh*-adverb *when*:

> **h   q**
> **   RelCl**
> **A   S= P   Ca   = S**
> **   NCl**
> There were (times [**when** it   seemed to the animals [that they
>   worked longer hours]])

'This is the house that Jack built'

A series of restrictive RelCls makes up the nursery rhyme beginning with:

> This is the house [**that** Jack built].
> This is the malt [**that** lay in the house [**that** Jack built]].

and adding further RelCls one at a time until the final verse is reached,

> [This is the horse and the hound and the horn [**that** belonged to the farmer sowing his corn [**that** kept the cock that crowed in the morn [**that** waked the priest all shaven and shorn [**that** married the man all tattered and torn [**that** kissed the maiden all forlorn [**that** milked the cow with the crumpled horn [**that** tossed the dog [**that** worried the cat [**that** killed the rat [**that** ate the malt [**that** lay in the house [**that** Jack built]]]]]]]]]]]]]

Because every post-modified NP comes last in its clause, you can go on extending the rhyme without any difficulty of understanding. Each relative pronoun *that* is the subject of its own clause, except the very last in *that Jack built*. But if you reverse the order of the items in the rhyme and try to *embed* each successive RelCl in this way:

> This is Jack [**who** built the house]].
> This is Jack [**who** built the house [**in which** the malt lay]].
> This is Jack [**who** built the house [**in which** the malt [**that** the rat ate] lay]].

you soon find that you cannot process the sentence mentally. The relative pronouns from *that the rat ate* onwards are the objects in their clauses. Each RelCl is embedded inside another one, and the subject is split off from the verb. The next step makes a quite unacceptable sentence, even though it is logically following the same grammatical rule:

> This is Jack [**who** built the house [**in which** the malt [**that** the rat [that the cat killed] ate] lay]].

You find that the resulting sentence ends with a series of verbs:

> This is Jack who built the house in which the malt that the rat that the cat that the dog **worried killed ate lay**.

so that it is unacceptable as a meaningful sentence and becomes nonsense long before the complete rhyme is set out:

> This is Jack who built the house in which the malt that the rat that the cat that the dog that the cow with the crumpled horn that the maiden all forlorn that the man all tattered and torn **kissed milked tossed worried killed ate lay**. etc, etc.

The original nursery rhyme is imitated by Dickens in this extract from *Bleak House*, chapter LXI. Mr Skimpole is speaking (the successive RelCls are bracketed):

> Observe the case, my dear Miss Summerson. Here is a boy received into the house and put to bed, in a state that I strongly object to. The boy being in bed, a man arrives – like the house that Jack built. Here is the man [who demands the boy [who is received into the house and put to bed in a state [that I strongly object to]]]. Here is a bank-note [produced by the man [who demands the boy [who is received into the house and put to bed in a state [that I strongly object to]]]]. Here is the Skimpole [who accepts the bank-note [produced by the man [who demands the boy [who is received into the house and put to bed in a state [that I strongly object to]]]]]. Those are the facts.

10.2.1.5 NON-RESTRICTIVE RELATIVE CLAUSES

A clause with the same structure as a restrictive relative clause may also function in a looser kind of dependent relationship, in which it is not a constituent of the NP, but of the sentence in which it occurs, adding further information. This type of **non-restrictive relative clause** (sometimes called **adding clause**) is described in section 11.2.3.

10.2.1.6 RELATIVE PRONOUNS AND RELCLS IN THE REGIONAL DIALECTS

Just as the use of *them* as a demonstrative pronoun is widespread in regional dialects (perhaps statistically greater than StE use of *those*), so is the use of *what* as a relative pronoun.

The pronoun *what* has several functions, and it is not surprising that they overlap between StE and the dialects. Young children will often confuse *what* and *which*. One common meaning is as an alternative to *that which*, as in:

> So offers he to giue **what** she did crave. (*Shakespeare*, 1592)

> Milton means **what** he says. (*Ruskin*, 1865)

and the *OED* lists a wide variety of related senses. But using *what* as a relative pronoun where StE has *who/which/that* is dialectal. Charles Dickens provides evidence for nineteenth-century dialectal forms in the speech of his characters:

> 'Them's her lights, Miss Abbey, **wot** you see a-blinking yonder.' (*Our Mutual Friend*)

Examples of contemporary use are:

> ...a slice of turnip and all sorts **what** I'd put in.   (*Cleveland*)

> You could communicate with like a typewriter thing **what** does the Morse Code.   (*Stoke on Trent*)

> For anybody **what** hasn't got a boat of their own, it's just hopeless.
> (*North Yorks*)

Other choices of relative pronoun used today include:

> There were a woman there **as** lives nearby in them there old houses.
> (*Leicestershire*)

> My father could hold his own with anyone down the mines at any job, **which it** was a pleasure when I followed to think of a history like that.
> (*Northumberland*)

as well as the omission of the pronoun where it is required in StE when functioning as the subject in its clause:

> In them days it was the Tunbridge Wells Corporation Ø did it.   (*Kent*)

> I knew a chap Ø worked all his life in one job.   (*York*)

Who and *which* are used less frequently than *that* as a relative pronoun in the dialects, and *whom* occurs only in formal StE speech and writing.

Activity 10.7

(i)   Identify the restrictive relative clauses in the following sentences.

(ii)   Which relative pronoun or adverb is used? Is it subject or object or adverbial or is the relative pronoun deleted?

(iii) Is the RelCl construction StE or dialectal?

(StE sentences adapted from *Animal Farm*, ch. 3; dialectal sentences from *English Accents and Dialects*, A. Hughes and P. Trudgill, 1979.)

(a)   No animal was able to use any tool that involved standing on its hind legs.
(b)   It was the biggest harvest the farm had ever seen.
(c)   There were days when the entire work of the farm seemed to rest upon Boxer's mighty shoulders.
(d)   Boxer was always at the spot where the work was hardest.
(e)   Well the one what's my husband, he said, let her lay there, he said.
(f) The quarrelling and jealousy which had been normal features of life in the old days had almost disappeared.
(g)   After breakfast there was a ceremony which was observed every day of the week.

(h) It was always the pigs who put forward the resolutions.

(i) It was resolved to set aside a small paddock as a home of rest for animals who were past work.

(j) They've got a lot of local talent what come up out of the amateur sides.

(k) The distinguishing mark of Man is the *hand*, the instrument with which he does all his mischief.

(l) There was one thing the animals were completely certain about – they did not want Jones back.

10.2.2 *Coordination within NPs and PrepPs*

The headline quoted in section 10.2.1, *Freedom of information group hails historic and devastating defeat*, also illustrates how words can be related by **coordination** to form a **word-complex**, that is, a structure containing words coordinated together (the brackets ⟨ ⟩ are used to indicate coordinated structures):

> m   &   m   h
> ⟨ *historic and* **devastating**⟩ defeat

or as in the text used in section 9.7:

> S   P   O
> ⟨⟨**carts, trucks** *and* ⟨⟨**men, women** *and* **children**⟩⟩⟩⟩ (were crossing) (it)

The NP subject of this clause contains the coordinated nouns *men, women and children*, forming a word-complex which is itself coordinated with the two other nouns, *carts, trucks*, to form a larger word-complex. In the following clause:

> S   P   Ca
> The trucks ground ⟨**up** *and* **away**⟩
>   adv &   adv

the adverbial complement consists of two coordinated adverbs which form a word-complex.

Phrases which are coordinated within the same structure form a **phrase-complex**:

> d   m   h   q
> An old man (with   ⟨⟨steel-rimmed spectacles) and (very dusty clothes)⟩⟩
>   *PrepP NP1*   *NP2*

in which the PrepP post-modifier has two NP complements, *steel-rimmed spectacles* and *very dusty clothes*, coordinated together,

But pre-modifiers can also form simple lists of attributes, without a conjunction, like Rudyard Kipling's,

> d   m   m   m   m   h
> the ⟨great grey-green, greasy Limpopo⟩ River

which is itself part of a more complex NP:

```
d   h    q
         p   d    m    m         m    m         h        q = Nonf Cl
the banks of  the  ⟨great grey-green, greasy Limpopo⟩ River, all set
                                                       about with fever-trees
```

('The Elephant's Child', *Just So Stories*, 1902)

Coordination is therefore used as well as subordination in NPs and PrepPs to produce complex clause subjects, complements and adverbials, made up of word-complexes or phrase-complexes. In coordination each word or phrase is of equal status. A subordinated word or phrase is embedded within another constituent, and is therefore of unequal status.

Here are some examples of clauses containing word-complexes and phrase-complexes in their structure, marked with brackets ⟨ ⟩, from chapter VII of *Animal Farm*:

```
     S                          P
1  [The envious human beings would ⟨rejoice and triumph⟩]
                                   ⟨v       &    v⟩
```

```
    A    S                   A    P    O
2  [Only ⟨Boxer and Clover⟩ never lost heart.]
         ⟨n    &    n⟩
```

```
   S         P     O
3  [Squealer made excellent speeches on
                             ⟨the joy of service and the dignity of labour⟩.]
                             ⟨NP                 &    NP⟩
```

```
   S              P      Ci
4  [The potatoes had become ⟨soft and discoloured⟩.]
                            ⟨adj &    adj⟩
```

```
   A                   S        P   O      P    Ca
5  [For days at a time the animals had nothing to eat but
                                       ⟨chaff and mangels⟩.
                                       ⟨n     &    n⟩
```

```
   A          S        P    O              A         A
6  [Hitherto the animals had had ⟨little or no⟩ contact with Whymper on
                                                         his weekly visits.]
                                 ⟨d   &   d⟩
```

Notice that when using coordination we often economise in our use of language by omitting words that might have been repeated:

1 would rejoice and (*would*) triumph
2 only Boxer and (*only*) Clover
3 on the joy of service and (*on*) the dignity of labour

Would, only and *on* have been deleted, and can be 'understood' from the context. Wherever there is coordination, there is a possibility of deletion if some items in the second coordinated structure are identical to some in the first.

Activity 10.8

(i) Identify and label the phrases containing coordinated words or phrases in the following clauses from *Animal Farm*, ch. VII.

(ii) Say whether any words or phrases have been deleted from the second coordinated structure.

(a) The price of these would pay for enough grain and meal to keep the farm going.
(b) Napoleon acted swiftly and ruthlessly.
(c) He snuffed in every corner, in the barn, in the cowshed, in the hen-houses, in the vegetable garden, and found traces of Snowball everywhere.
(d) We had thought that Snowball's rebellion was caused by his vanity and ambition.
(e) 'Did we not see for ourselves how he attempted to get us defeated and destroyed at the Battle of the Cowshed?'
(f) They were shaken and miserable.
(g) The grass and the bursting hedges were gilded by the level rays of the sun.
(h) 'The enemy both external and internal has been defeated.'
(i) They sang it three times over – very tunefully, but slowly and mournfully, in a way they had never sung it before.

Here are other examples of such structures, taken from Charles Dickens' *Bleak House*, but more complex:

(i) a series of NPs, many of them single nouns, which form the complex complement of the single preposition *with*:

... and at last we got into a real country road again, with 〈**windmills, rickyards, milestones, farmers' waggons, scents of old hay, swinging signs and horse troughs: trees, fields, and hedgerows**〉 (ch. VI)

(ii) a coordinated series of five complex NPs functioning as object in the clause (the NPs are numbered):

Thus interrupted, Miss Jellyby became silent, and walked moodily on at my side; while I admired 〈*1* **the long successions and varieties of streets,** *2* **the quantity of people already going to and fro,** *3* **the number of vehicles passing and repassing,** *4* **the busy preparations in the setting forth of shop windows and the sweeping out of shops, and** *5* **the extraordinary creatures in rags, secretly groping among the swept-out rubbish for pins and other refuse**〉. (ch. V)

Each head word of this phrase-complex of five coordinated NPs is modified and qualified, to form a typically detailed and lively portayal of the street scene:

```
1  d    m    h                          q
   the  long  ⟨successions and varieties⟩  of streets
```

```
2  d    h       q
           p = PrepCl
              S      A      P      A
   the  quantity  of  people [already  going  ⟨to and fro⟩]
```

```
3  d    h       q
           p = PrepCl
              S          P      &    P
   the  number  of  [vehicles  ⟨passing  and  repassing⟩]
```

```
4  d    m    h                q
                        p  d    h            q                    d
                           p    m    h
   the  busy  preparations  in  ⟨the  setting  forth  of  shop  windows  and  the

   h                q
        p  h
   sweeping  out  of  shops⟩  and
```

```
5  d    m         h       q
        p         h       p  h    Nonf Cl
   the  extraordinary  creatures  in  rags [secretly  groping  among  the  swept-out
   rubbish  for  ⟨pins and other refuse⟩]
```

(iii) a NP-complex functioning as subject of the predicator *persuade* in the clause, each NP itself a complex structure with (mainly) post-modification at (q):

S
⟨His remote impressions of the robes and coronets, the stars and garters, that sparkle through the surface-dust of Mr Tulkinghorn's chambers;

his veneration for the mysteries presided over by that best and closest of his customers, whom all the Inns of Court, all Chancery Lane, and all the legal neighbourhood agree to hold in awe;

his remembrance of detective Mr Bucket with his forefinger, and his confidential manner impossible to be evaded or declined⟩;

P   Oi
persuade him [that he is a party to some dangerous secret, [without knowing what it is]].

(ch. XXV)

The three complex NPs repeat similar structures – *his* + noun head + PrepP . . . – and so are said to be in **parallel**:

His remote impressions of . . .
his veneration for . . .
his remembrance of . . .

In describing the style of this passage, we would say it is an example of **parallelism**.

Activity 10.9

Analyse the structure of the three NPs forming the subject of sentence (iii), noting pre- and post-modification, and any further examples of coordinated structures.

10.2.3   Apposition

A third type of complexity is produced by the relationship between two NPs illustrated in this second quotation from Kipling:

He asked ⟨his tall aunt, the Ostrich⟩, why her tail-feathers grew just so

in which the second NP the *Ostrich* identifies or elaborates on the first NP *his tall aunt*, and is said to be in **apposition** to it – a 'side by side' relationship. It does not mean *his tall Aunt <u>and</u> the Ostrich*. Compare:

⟨his tall uncle, the Giraffe⟩
⟨his broad aunt, the Hippopotamus⟩
⟨his hairy uncle, the Baboon⟩

Here is an example of a clause containing **appositive** phrases in its structure, marked with brackets ⟨ ⟩, from chapter VII of *Animal Farm*:

S		P	P	A

⟨A few selected animals, mostly sheep,⟩ were instructed to remark casually
NP^1, in apposition with   *NP*^{2}

A	O = NCl

in his hearing [that rations had been increased.]]

The second NP, *mostly sheep*, defines the *few selected animals* of the first NP.
    Apposition is a marked feature of tabloid journalism when naming participants in news reports, as in:

Screen goddess Raquel Welch...
Rugby club skipper John Beardsley...
Girl soccer thug Jane Jones...
Former Page Three girl of the year Sarah Wright, 22...

Activity 10.10

(i)   Identify and label the phrases containing NPs in apposition, in the following clauses from *Animal Farm*, ch. VII.

(a) He was rumoured to be hiding on one of the neighbouring farms, either Foxwood or Pinchfield.
(b) Two other sheep confessed to having murdered an old ram, an especially devoted follower of Napoleon.
(c) Napoleon was always referred to in formal style as 'our Leader, Comrade Napoleon.'
(d) Minimus, the poet, had composed another song.

Activity 10.11

(i) Analyse the structure of the following single clause sentences (S, P, C and A).

(ii) Analyse the structure of the NPs and PrepPs (m h q) or (p m h q).

(iii) Identify subordinated phrases and clauses (phrases and clauses which are a part of another phrase, not directly a constituent in clause structure).

(iv) Identify any coordinated words or phrases.

(a) The grey warm evening of August had descended upon the city.
(b) Like illumined pearls the lamps shone from the summits of their tall poles upon the living texture below.
(c) He was a sporting vagrant armed with a vast stock of stories, limericks, and riddles.
(d) Corley was the son of an inspector of police.
(e) He had inherited his father's frame and gait.
(f) His head was large, globular, and oily.
(g) Lenehan's gaze was fixed on the large faint moon circled with a double halo.
(h) He watched earnestly the passing of the grey web of twilight across its face.
                                    (from James Joyce, 'Two Gallants', *Dubliners*, 1914)

10.2.4   Complex AdjPs and AdvPs

Both AdjPs and AdvPs can be coordinated to form phrase-complexes, but the possibilities of subordinate relationships are much more restricted. Lists of adjective modifiers can occur without the use of any conjunction (the following examples are from 'Holiday Memories', 1946, from Dylan Thomas, *The Collected Stories*, 1983):

I remember the sea telling lies in a shell held to my ear for a ⟨**whole, harmonious, hollow**⟩ **minute by a** ⟨**small, wet**⟩ girl.

and with conjunctions:

Children all day capered or squealed by the ⟨**glazed** or **bashing**⟩ sea.

In those ⟨**always radiant, rainless, lazily rowdy** and **sky-blue**⟩ summers departed, I remember August Monday from the rising of the sun over the ⟨**stained** and **royal**⟩ town...

The modifiers of the head word *summers* are pre-modified by the adverb *always*, and the adjective *rowdy* is similarly modified by *lazily*. We usually use a conjunction only between the last two of a list of items.

Here is an example of a similar use of adjectives from Dickens's *Dombey and Son*:

> He drew out so ⟨**bright**, and **clear**, and **shining**⟩, that Miss Tox was charmed with him. The more Miss Tox drew him out, the finer he came – like wire. There never was a ⟨**better** or **more promising**⟩ youth – a more ⟨**affectionate**, **steady**, **prudent**, **sober**, **honest**, **meek**, **candid young**⟩ man – than Rob drew out that night.
>
> (ch. XXXVIII)

The following example from *Bleak House* shows coordinated AdjPs consisting of the same adjective, *unfortunate*, with different post-modifiers. The phrase-complex functions as an intensive complement in the clause:

> S P   Ci
> He has been ⟨**unfortunate in his affairs**, and **unfortunate in his pursuits**, and **unfortunate in his family**⟩; but he don't care – he's a child!
>
> (ch. VI)

Adverbs also can be coordinated to form word-complexes:

> I remember a man crying 'Ride 'em, cowboy!' ⟨**time** and **again**⟩.
> They never forgot to run the water ⟨**loud** and **long**⟩.
>
> (Dylan Thomas, 'Holiday Memories')

Activity 10.12

Identify the adjectives and adverbs which form complex structures in these following sentences.

(a) There were foolish, mulish, religious donkeys on the unwilling trot.
(b) Under invisible umbrellas, stout ladies dressed for the male and immoral sea.
(c) I remember the patient, laborious, and enamouring hobby, or profession, of burying relatives in the sand.
(d) I remember the stable-and-straw smell of hot, tossed, tumbled, dug, and trodden sand.
(e) ...the smell of the known and paddled-in sea moving out and away and beyond and further still towards the antipodes.

A note on AdjPs and NonfCls

Just as NPs can be post-modified by nonfinite clauses (section 10. 2.1.2) – for example:

> S   P   Ca
>   p   d h   q
> The hens had entered into a plot [to murder Snowball].
>   *NonfCl*

so can adjectives:

```
S          P    Ci
                h        q
Frederick  was  anxious  [to get hold of the timber].
                adj      NonfCl
```

In this construction, the NonfCl functions as a complement or post-modifier of the adjective *anxious*. But an alternative analysis, preferred in this book, is to include it in the **predicators in phase** construction (see sections 8.7, 9.6.2.2). The phrase *was anxious* is like a complete predicator in meaning. We can substitute a VP:

```
S          P       P
Frederick  wanted  to get hold of the timber.
```

```
S          P         P
Frederick  was urged  to get hold of the timber.
```

Notice how similar in form are the passive VP *was urged* and the v + adj construction *was anxious*.

10.2.5   Complexity in the VP

We found in chapter 8 that a predicator can be constructed as a VP containing any of the following:

- a modal;
- perfect and progressive aspect (with *have* and *be* as auxiliaries);
- passive voice (with *be* again as an auxiliary);
- one or more semi-auxiliaries.

These choices make it possible, therefore (though not very likely in practice), to construct a complex VP like:

```
           m      h     s-aux           be  be-pass  v
The house  might  have  been about to be  being      demolished.
```

Further complexity in the VP may occur when a clause contains two (or more) **predicators in phase**. The following examples occur in the *Fiesta* text used in chapter 9:

```
    wh-    S        P             P      Ca
12b where  the bus  was supposed  to start  from
```

```
    S        P        P
17a A breeze  started  to blow
```

```
    S P           P         Co
18c I  did not want  to leave  the café.
```

In these clauses the subject of the first verb is both the actor and understood subject of the second.

In three other clauses there is an 'intervening NP' which functions like the object of the first verb and the subject of the second:

```
     S    P              O/S P
7b   we   had to wait for him  to come back
```

```
     S    P    O/S      P    Ca
21c  We   had  the bags sent down
```

```
     P      O/S      P
19b  to get our bags packed
```

It is also common for an AdjP to intervene between the two predicators, as in the example in section 10.2.4, *Frederick was **anxious** to get hold of the timber*, and in this second example from *Animal Farm*:

```
     S         P   Ci      P
The animals were alarmed to hear that three hens had confessed.
```

in which *alarmed*, though derived from a verb, is an adjective functioning as an intensive complement. An example using a non-derived adjective can easily be made up:

```
     S    P       Ci          P       Ca
She  seemed very reluctant to agree to our proposals.
```

Activity 10.13

(i)   Analyse the structure of the italicised VPs in the following sentences, and identify:

    (a)   modal auxiliaries (*m*),
    (b)   *have* as auxiliary for perfect aspect (*h*),
    (c)   *be* as auxiliary for progressive aspect (*be*),
    (d)   *be* as auxiliary for passive voice (*be-pass*),
    (e)   semi-auxiliaries (*s-aux*),
    (f)   catenatives (*cat*), and
    (g)   the main lexical verb (*v*).

(ii) Mark any predicators in phase in addition to a main verb as (*P*).

(iii) Identify any non-finite VPs (*Nonf*).

(a)   A few days later, the terror *caused* by the executions *had died* down.
(b)   Some of the animals *remembered* that the Sixth Commandment *had decreed*: 'No animal *shall kill* any other animal'.
(c)   No one *cared to mention* it in the hearing of the pigs or the dogs.
(d)   Clover *had to ask* Benjamin *to read* her the Sixth Commandment.
(e)   It *appeared to run*: 'No animal shall kill any other animal without cause'.
(f) But they *saw* now that the commandment *had not been violated*.
(g)   On Sunday mornings Squealer *would read* out to them long lists of figures.
(h)   It *was announced* that a gun *would be fired* every year on Napoleon's birthday.

(i)   The pigs *liked to invent* for him such titles as Father of All Animals.

(j)   Frederick and his men *seemed to be plotting to attack* Animal Farm.

(k)   Napoleon *was going to enter* into an agreement with Mr Pilkington.

(l)   The animals *clamoured to be allowed to go out and attack* Pinchfield Farm.

adapted from Animal Farm, ch. VIII

Here is an example of a series of thirteen coordinated *-ing* participles, some with complements, from *Bleak House*, ch. VIII, which make up a **verb-complex** (the participles are numbered):

We are always ⟨*1* **appearing**, and *2* **disappearing**, and *3* **swearing**, and *4* **interrogating**, and *5* **filing**, and *6* **cross filing**, and *7* **arguing**, and *8* **sealing**, and *9* **motioning**, and *10* **referring**, and *11* **reporting**, and *12* **revolving** about the Lord Chancellor and all his satellites, and equitably *13* **waltzing** ourselves off to dusty death⟩, about costs.

An alternative is to analyse the sentence as a series of clauses with the same subject, auxiliary verb and adverb deleted: 'We are always appearing, and (*we are always*) disappearing, and (*we are always*) swearing', and so on.

10.3 Summary

The phrases which make up a clause may themselves be complex structures.

A NP, functioning as subject, object or intensive complement in the clause, may be a complex phrase, with modifiers and qualifiers, and/or a phrase-complex of coordinated and/or appositive phrases. Words may form word-complexes within phrases. This applies equally to NPs which form the complements of prepositions in PrepPs.

AdjPs and AdvPs, adjectives and adverbs, are also likely to occur in phrase and word-complexes of coordinated constituents.

VPs may range in complexity from a single verb to a string containing several auxiliary verbs and two or more main verbs in a predicators in phase or catenative relationship.

When is a kernel clause not a kernel clause?

Kernel clause is a handy descriptive term for a simple finite, declarative, active clause in the order SP(C)(A). If our definition also states that it contains no complex structures, then a clause like *Jack and Jill went up the hill* (SPCa) is not kernel, because its subject NP is the word-complex *Jack and Jill* (the words functioning as NPs). On the other hand, none of us would think of it as particularly complex in the everyday sense of the word.

Complexity is, therefore, a gradable, relative term in the description of grammatical structure – that is, we can grade structures through degrees of complexity from 'least complex' to 'most complex'. *Jack and Jill went up the hill* is at the lowest possible level of complexity within a clause – almost, but not quite, a kernel clause.

11. Complex clauses

In chapter 10 we have seen how complex and coordinated words and phrases can expand the constituents of kernel clauses. Another step towards complexity in language use is to embed one clause within another in a relationship of subordinate clause (SCl) to main clause (MCl).

11.1 Subordinate nonfinite clauses

In each of the following two-clause sentences, there is one main clause and another clause which, if separated off, cannot stand on its own as a simple one-clause sentence. This is the simplest kind of **complex sentence**, consisting of one MCl and one subordinate clause. These subordinate clauses are nonfinite, because the verbs in the predicators are either infinitives or participles, unmarked for present or past tense.

1 [They went straight to the station [on **reaching** the town]].
2 [The Rat was sitting on the river bank, [**singing** a little song]].
3 [Here they saw many handsome boats, [**slung** from the crossbeams]].
4 [The Rat danced up and down in the road, [simply **transported** with passion]].
5 [The Rat came strolling along [to **find** him]].
6 [It wouldn't be safe [for him to **be left** to himself]].
7 [It's never the wrong time [to **call** on Toad]].
8 [The Mole was busy [**trying** to quiet the horse]].

This sample of eight clauses illustrates some of the different ways in which we use nonfinite clauses in complex sentences, and each one is described in the following sections.

11.1.1 Nonfinite prepositional clauses

	S	P	Ca	A = PrepCl
1	[They	went	straight to the station	[**on** reaching the town]].

The NonfCl *on reaching the town* is introduced by the preposition *on*, so it is a **prepositional clause** (section 10.2.1.3). The subject of the nonfinite verb *reaching* is that of its MCl, *they*, and is therefore said to be 'understood'. The PrepCl is functioning like an adverbial in the MCl, and can be brought to the front and made the theme of the sentence:

1 [[**On** reaching the town] they went straight to the station]].

The following PrepCl is from the *Fiesta* text:

```
p      NCl = PrepCl
       S          P     A
```
21b [**with** ten percent added for the service]

The next example is from *Animal Farm*:

```
(MCl                          PrepCl
```
[Napoleon took his meals alone, [with two dogs to wait upon him]].

These prepositional clauses function as part of the structure of the clause, and are not embedded within a NP or PrepP.

Because the preposition complements are not phrases but clauses, the prepositions are functioning like subordinating conjunctions. The PrepCl is functioning as an adverbial within the MCl:

```
S            P    O       Ca     A = PrepCl
                                 scj   S        P      Ca
```
[Napoleon took his meals alone, [**with** two dogs to wait upon him]]

Other prepositions/conjunctions may be complemented by a Nonf Cl, for example *for* in:

```
S           P                  A
                               scj  P        O        A
```
[Snowball had been censured [**for** showing cowardice in the battle]].

Notice that this PrepCl has no subject. We know from the context that it is Snowball who showed cowardice. If the subject of a NonfCl is the same as that of the MCl, it is deleted.

Some prepositions, like *with*, cannot be used as subordinating conjunctions for finite clauses, but others can function both as prepositions and as subordinating conjunctions to finite and nonfinite clauses, for example, *after* and *before*. Others again, like *when*, are conjunctions to finite and nonfinite clauses, but cannot be prepositions. The following constructed clauses show what is meant:

Napoleon took his meals **with Squealer.**	(PrepP)
He ate **with no one else looking on.**	(PrepCl)
*He ate **with no one else looked on**.	(finite clause not grammatical)
They rested **after their work.**	(PrepP)
They rested **after working all day.**	(PrepCl)
They rested **after they had worked all day**.	(finite Cl)

*When a journey by train, it's best to reserve a seat.   (*journey* as a noun – PrepP not grammatical)

When journeying by train, it's best to reserve a seat.   (PrepCl)

When you journey by train, reserve a seat if you can.   (finite Cl)

Activity 11.1

(i) Identify the nonfinite PrepCls in these sentences from *Animal Farm*

(ii) Say whether the clause has a marked subject or a deleted subject.

(a) It was rumoured that Frederick had killed a dog by throwing it into a furnace.

(b) In his speeches, Squealer would talk with the tears rolling down his cheeks of Napoleon's wisdom.

(c) By seeming to be friendly with Pilkington Napoleon had forced Frederick to raise his price.

(d) A mighty cry for vengeance went up, and without waiting for further orders they charged forth in a body.

(e) A gander committed suicide by swallowing deadly nightshade berries.

(f) In rebuilding the windmill, they could not this time, as before, make use of the fallen stones.

11.1.2 *Nonfinite* -ing *clauses without prepositions*

NonfCls with the -*ing* participle also function like adverbials without introductory prepositions.

2 [The Rat was sitting on the river bank, [**singing** a little song]].

Examples from *Animal Farm* are:

⟨[**Smiling** beatifically] and [**wearing** both his decorations]⟩, Napoleon reposed on a bed of straw.

The black cockerel acted as a kind of trumpeter, [**letting out** a loud 'cock-a-doodle-doo' . . .

The subjects of the -*ing* clauses are not stated, and therefore must be the same as the subjects of the MCls – *the Rat*, *Napoleon*, and *the black cockerel*.

11.1.2.1 A NOTE ON 'DANGLING PARTICIPLES'

NonfCls and PrepCls with -*ing* articiples can cause problems if the subject of the main clause is not the implicit subject of the participle. For example:

After walking about two miles from Llangollen, a narrow valley opens on the right.

Flying low over the valley, cows were to be seen everywhere.

The intended meanings are clear enough, but a literal interpretation suggests that *a narrow valley was walking*... and that *cows were flying low*.... Writers on good style have described such constructions as using 'unattached' or 'dangling' participles.

11.1.3 *Nonfinite (reduced) relative clauses*

3   [Here they saw many handsome boats, [**slung** from the crossbeams]].

In this sentence the NonfCl with an *-en /-ed* participle can be expanded into a non-restrictive relative clause (section 11.2.3):

3a   [Here they saw many handsome boats, [**which had been slung** from the crossbeams]].

These sentences have similar constructions:

Napoleon himself, [**attended** by his dogs and his cockerel], came down to inspect the completed work.

On Sunday mornings Squealer, [**holding** down a long strip of paper with his trotter], would read out to them long lists of figures.

These NonfCls can also be expanded to form finite non-restrictive RelCls:

Napoleon himself, [**who was attended** by...

On Sunday mornings, Squealer, [**who was holding** down...

However, this expansion into non-restrictive RelCls does not work with the following sentences in section 11.1.2:

(a)   *⟨[**Who was smiling** beatifically] and [**who was wearing** both his decorations]⟩, Napoleon reposed on a bed of straw.
(b)   *The black cockerel acted as a kind of trumpeter, [**who was letting** out a loud 'cock-a-doodle-doo'].

though a simple rearrangement of the constituent clauses can be made to produce grammatical sentences:

(c)   Napoleon, [**who was smiling** beatifically and wearing both his decorations], reposed on a bed of straw.
(d)   The black cockerel, [**who was letting** out a loud 'cock-a-doodle-doo'], acted as a kind of trumpeter.

Activity 11.2

Discuss the reason why sentences (c) and (d) are grammatical, but not (a) and (b).

11.1.4   *Nonfinite* -en /-ed *clauses*

Other nonfinite clauses, adverbial in function, use an *-en/-ed* participle as predicator:

4   [The Rat danced up and down in the road, [simply **transported** with passion]].

[Three hens confessed that, [**inspired by Snowball**], they had entered into a plot to murder Napoleon].

You can test the adverbial function of these NonfCls by moving them to the front of the sentences:

[[Simply **transported** with passion] the Rat danced up and down in the road].

[[**Inspired by Snowball**], three hens confessed that they had entered into a plot to murder Napoleon].

You cannot do this with the reduced RelCls of section 11.1.3.

11.1.5   *Nonfinite* to-*clauses of purpose*

5   [The Rat came strolling along [**to find** him]].

One of the functions of the *to*-infinitive of the verb is to express **purpose**. We can apply the test of substituting *in order to*:

5a   [The Rat came strolling along [**in order to find** him]].

Further examples can be found in *Fiesta*:

	P	O/S	P		P	O

19   We had to go to the hotel ⟨[**to get** our bags packed and Ø pay the bill]⟩.

or from Animal Farm:

The pigeons [who were still sent out [**to spread** tidings of the Rebellion]] were forbidden to set foot anywhere on Foxwood.

Again we can check the expression of purpose by substituting *in order to* for *to*:

We had to go to the hotel **in order to** get our bags packed...

The pigeons who were still sent out **in order to** spread tidings of the Rebellion...

11.1.6   *Nonfinite* for... to *clauses*

Notice that if other people had had to pack their bags in sentence (19) above, the function word *for* would be introduced:

We had to go to the hotel [**for** the others **to** get their bags packed].

The subject of the NonfCl follows *for* and precedes *to*:

Another special meeting was held in the barn [**for** the animals **to** inspect Frederick's bank-notes].

There is a similar *for . . . to* construction in the next sentence, but the NonfCl is here the complement of the adjective *safe* (section 11.1.9 below) and is not a clause expressing purpose:

6   [It wouldn't be (safe [**for** him **to** be left to himself]))].

This sentence is an example of a common construction called **extraposition** – 'placing outside'. A more formal order of the constituents of this sentence would have been:

    S(= NCl)   **P**   **Ci**
6a   [[**For** him **to** be left to himself] wouldn't be safe].

Extraposition is described in more detail in section 12.2.5. The construction *for to* with no intervening NP is no longer Standard English:

    *We had to go to the hotel **for to** get our bags packed . . .

although it was formerly commonly used, and has survived in some present-day dialects.

11.1.7   Historical and dialectal for to

For to marked the infinitive in Middle and Early Modern English. For example:

    He bigan to schake ys axe **for to** smyte anon   (1297)

    The king of Englande wyst nat where **for to** passe the ryuer of Some, the which was large and depe. (1523)

and is still current:

    Father bent over **for to** release the dog and the dog snapped and growled at him.   (*Kent*)

    You can get yourself a packet of Woodbines **for to** get your first smoke.
                                     (*Newcastle*)

The *Survey of English Dialects* records three other dialectal forms for the construction of a verb phrase like StE *came to see*:

    came for to see   came for see   came see

In Northern and Scots dialects of Middle English the form *till*, from Old Norse, was used for *to*, and both *till* and *for till* are used, as well as *for to*. These examples were recently recorded in Belfast:

    They wanted him in the shipyard at that time **for to** go as their timber expert till America **for till** select timber for them. . . . They wanted him **for to** go **for till** select the timber to be sent till Harland and Wolff's.

    There must be something in a drum for all them people **for to** go **for to** hear them drums.

II.I.8   *Nonfinite NP complement clauses*

7   [It's never the wrong time [to call on Toad]].

This looks like an example of extraposition as in sentence 6 above, *It wouldn't be safe for him to be left to himself*, but it would not be acceptable to say:

 * [[to **call** on Toad] is never the wrong time].

The NonfCl is a qualifier of the NP *the wrong time* and is embedded within the NP. We can diagram this by marking the phrase:

7a   [It's never (the wrong time [to call on Toad])].

so the sentence is an extraposed version of:

7b   [(The wrong time [to call on Toad]) is never].

which we would be unlikely to use.

II.I.9   *Nonfinite AdjP complement clauses*

NonfCls with *-ing* participles and *to*-infinitives can also qualify AdjPs:

8   [The Mole was (busy [**trying to quiet the horse**])].

8a   [Mole found it (hard [**to learn to row the boat**])]

Activity II.3 _____

In the following set of sentences, the NonfCls are bracketed. See if you can classify them according to the descriptions in section II.I.

(a) 'Hooray!' he cried, [jumping up [on seeing them]].
(b) 'I can only regret the wasted years that lie behind me, [squandered in trivialities].'
(c) And then you'll have to arrange [for the cart to be fetched and mended and put to rights].
(d) For the moment he was the skipper of the canary-coloured vessel [driven on a shoal by the reckless jockeying of rival mariners].
(e) He'll continue like that for days now, [like an animal walking in a happy dream].
(f) Late in the evening, they drew up on a remote common far from habitations, and turned the horse loose [to graze].
(g) 'Look, Mole, have you got anything [to do this morning]?'
(h) The two animals were resting, [thoroughly exhausted], by the time Toad appeared on the scene, fresh and gay, [remarking what a pleasant easy life it was they were all leading now].
(i) Toad sat straight down in the middle of the dusty road, [his legs stretched out before him],

(j) [Rounding a bend in the river], they came in sight of a handsome, dignified old house of mellowed red brick, [with well-kept lawns reaching down to the water's edge].

11.1.10 Verbless clauses

In the following clause:

[There were fifteen men], [**with half a dozen guns between them**].

the construction *with half a dozen guns between them* has the structure of a PrepP:

```
p     m          h     q
                 p         h
with  half a dozen  guns  between  them
```

It is similar in meaning to *who had half a dozen guns between them*, which is a non-restrictive relative clause (section 11.2.3), so it functions like a clause, even though it has no predicator. Such constructions (not necessarily using *with*), lacking a predicator but functioning like a subordinate clause, are called **verbless clauses**. Another example is:

[To rebuild the windmill, [**with walls as twice as thick**], was a tremendous labour].

in which the verbless clause has the meaning **which had** *walls as twice as thick*. In the following sentence:

He'll continue like that for days now, like an animal walking in a happy dream, **quite useless for all practical purposes**.

the constituent *quite useless for all practical purposes* functions like an AdvCl of manner. It could be moved to the front of the clause and made thematic (another test for adverbials),

Quite useless for all practical purposes, he'll continue like that for days now, like an animal walking in a happy dream.

Here are some more examples:

[Late in the evening, [**tired and happy and miles from home**], they drew up on a remote common far from habitations], [turned the horse loose [to graze]], and [ate their simple supper [sitting on the grass by the side of the cart]].

[They found him in a sort of trance, [**a happy smile on his face**], [his eyes still fixed on the dusty wake of their destroyer]].

Activity 11.4

Identify and discuss the function of any structures which might be called verbless clauses in the following sentences.

(a) Napoleon reposed on a bed of straw, with the money at his side.

(b) The whole of the big pasture, including the windmill, was in the hands of the enemy.

(c) It was nearly nine-o'clock when Squealer, his eyes dull, made his appearance.

(d) Tired out but proud, the animals walked round and round their masterpiece.

(e) Whymper, his face deadly pale, came racing up the path on his bicycle.

Activity II.5

(i) Identify the nonfinite clauses which function without subordinating conjunctions in the following sentences.

(ii) Say whether the subject is present in the clause, or deleted.

(iii) Are they clearly identifiable as either AdvCls or RelCls?

(a) The animals gambolled round and round the windmill, uttering cries of triumph.

(b) Napoleon reposed on a bed of straw, with the money at his side, neatly piled on a china dish from the farmhouse kitchen.

(c) Boxer put out his nose to sniff at the bank-notes.

(d) The four pigeons returned, one of them bearing a scrap of paper from Pilkington.

(e) Terrified, the animals waited.

(f) And when the nine dogs suddenly appeared on the men's flank, baying ferociously, panic overtook them.

(g) Squealer came skipping towards them, whisking his tail and beaming with satisfaction.

(h) At about half past nine Napoleon, wearing an old bowler hat of Mr Jones's, was distinctly seen to emerge from the back door.

(i) At the foot of the end wall of the big barn there lay a ladder broken in pieces. Squealer, temporarily stunned, was sprawling beside it.

Activity II.6

Identify the different kinds of nonfinite clause in the following short paragraph.

It was nearly nine o'clock when Squealer made his appearance, walking slowly and dejectedly, his eyes dull, his tail hanging limply behind him, and with every appearance of being seriously ill.

II.I.II *Nonfinite clauses functioning like NPs*

A nonfinite clause may be used where a NP typically occurs:

```
S                          P    Ci
[To rebuild the windmill] ... was  a tremendous labour.
NCl
```

The NonfCl *To rebuild the windmill* is the subject of the clause, and is therefore called a **noun clause (NCl)** because it functions like a NP. The use of a NonfCl as subject of a clause is rare in informal varieties of English. It has associations of formality, unlike the construction derived from it by extraposition (briefly mentioned in section 11.1.6):

It was a tremendous labour [to rebuild the windmill].

Some linguists would call the following embedded NonfCl a NCl functioning as the object of *asked*:

S	P	Oi	Od = NCl		
			P	Oi	Od

Clover asked Benjamin [to read her the Sixth Commandment].

because the clause *to read her the Sixth Commandment* functions just like the NP *a question* in:

S	P	Oi	Od = NP

Clover asked Benjamin a question.

This is perfectly acceptable as a description, since the NonfCl corresponds in function to a finite **reported clause** (section 12.1.2), but the concept of **predicators in phase** can also be used to describe this kind of construction (section 9.6.2.2).

S	P	O/S	P	Oi	Od

Clover asked Benjamin to read her the Sixth Commandment].

One argument for this is that there are some verbs in similar constructions which cannot normally take NP objects. For example, *cared* and *hoped in*:

S	P	P	O	A

No one cared [to mention it in the hearing of the pigs].

S	P	P	O	A

They hoped [to complete the building very soon].

You cannot say:

*No one cared this information

*They hoped an early completion.

On the other hand, by using the PrepPs *for this information* and *for an early completion* (**prepositional objects**), both these sentences can be made quite grammatical, so the argument is not at all conclusive.

Notice that you cannot substitute *in order to* (section 11.1.5) and make sense – *No one cared in order to mention it* .... Therefore these NonfCls cannot be AdvCls of purpose.

Extracts from Dickens's novels have already been used to illustrate some of the more complex uses of grammatical structure. A favourite feature of his style is the listing of NonfCls. In the following extract, the two clauses beginning *to ramble* and *to see* are coordinated to form a clause-complex which functions as subject of the verb *had been*:

...every day had been so bright and blue, that

 S

⟨[to ramble in the woods], and [to see the light ⟨striking down among the transparent leaves, and sparkling in the beautiful interlacings of the shadows of the trees⟩ ⟨[while the birds poured out their songs], and [the air was drowsy with the hum of insects]⟩]⟩,

P   *Ci*

had been most delightful.

              (*Bleak House*, ch. XVIII)

Notice that the second NonfCl itself contains several subordinated and coordinated clauses.

Activity 11.7

Identify the finite and nonfinite clauses in the preceding text.

The next extract contains three complex NonfCls functioning as subject, and shows another favourite device of Dickens's writing, **parallelism**, in which the structure of three successive sentences is the same. The text is set out to give you some indication of the structure. The passage is a satire on reading about fashionable society in the daily press.

 S

[[To borrow yesterday's paper from the Sol's Arms of an evening], and[read about the brilliant and distinguished meteors[that are shooting across the fashionable sky in every direction]],

P Ci   *A*

is unspeakable consolation to him.

 S

[To know[what member of what brilliant and distinguished circle accomplished the brilliant and distinguished feat of [joining it yesterday]], or [contemplates the no less brilliant and distinguished feat of [leaving it tomorrow]]],

P   *Oi*   *Od*

gives him a thrill of joy.

 S

[To be informed [what the Galaxy gallery of British Beauty is about, and means to be about], and [what Galaxy marriages are on the tapis], and [what Galaxy rumours are in circulation]]

P Ci

is to become acquainted with the most glorious destinies of mankind].

              (*Bleak House*, ch. XX)

Activity 11.8

Discuss in more detail the structure of the three sentences.

11.2   Subordinate finite clauses

11.2.1   *Noun clauses as subject*

Finite NCls can function as subject in a clause as well as the nonfinite NCls discussed in the previous section:

$S = NCl$ *P   Ci   P*
[That Boxer had worked tirelessly] was plain to see.

That functions as a marker of the NCl and is not a constitutent in the grammar of the clause. This construction, as with a nonfinite NCl in subject position, is formal, and more often written or spoken as:

It was plain to see [that Boxer had worked tirelessly].

an example of extraposition (described in section 12.2.5).

The following text illustrates the formal construction, with a succession of subject NCls, each marked by *that*, preceding the predicate of the clause, *will not perhaps surprise you now*. Some of these NCls are themselves complex, and contain subordinate clauses. It is not easy for unskilled readers to hold these four complex subjects in mind while waiting for the predicate of the sentence to appear:

S(NCl)
⟨[That he has abused his trust in many ways],

S(NCl)
[that he has oftener dealt and speculated to advantage for himself, than for the house he represented];

S(NCl)
[that he has led the house on, to prodigious ventures, often resulting in enormous losses];

S(NCl)
[that he has always pampered the vanity and ambition of his employer, when it was his duty to have held them in check, and shown,

                                                                                      P
as it was in his power to do, to what they tended here or there]⟩; will not,

(A)   O   A
perhaps, surprise you now.

(Charles Dickens, *Dombey and Son*, ch. LIII)

II.2.2   *Noun clauses as object*

In the following sentences, NCls are functioning as the direct objects of the verbs of the predicators, like NPs. The verbs *report* something, and the NCls are what is *reported*. The NCl is marked by the conjunction *that*:

> *S*   *P*   *Oi*   *Od* = *NCl*
> [He warned them [**that** after this treacherous deed the worst was to be expected]].

but the conjunction is often deleted:

> *S*   *P*   *Oi*   *Od* = *NCl*
> Squealer told the animals [he had a terrible piece of news to impart]].

In this construction the main clauses, *He warned them* and *Squealer told the animals*, are called **reporting clauses**, and the object NCls **reported clauses**. The traditional term for this is **indirect speech**, because **direct speech** quotes the actual words used, the MCl **quoting**, and the words being **quoted**:

> He warned them, 'After this treacherous deed the worst is to be expected.'
> *Quoting clause*   *Quoted clause*

> Squealer told the animals, 'I have a terrible piece of news to impart.'
> *Quoting clause*   *Quoted clause*

Direct and indirect speech, that is, the quoting-quoted and reporting-reported constructions, are described in more detail in section 12.1

II.2.3   *Non-restrictive relative clauses*

A second type of relative clause other than restrictive was briefly mentioned in section 10.2.1.5. It has the same structure as a restrictive RelCl, and is marked by *who*, *which* or relative adverbs like *where*. It is not a rank-shifted clause, a constituent of the NP it follows, but a clause in the structure of the sentence. It functions like an appositive clause by providing additional information about a NP without 'restricting' or 'defining it', so some linguists have called it an **adding clause**. The following example is from the *Fiesta* text:

> *MCl*
> 12   [Then we went up past the old fort and out to the local Syndicat d'Initiative
>
>   ***non-restrictive RelCl***
> office], [**where** the bus was supposed to start from]

This type of RelCl is called a **non-restrictive relative clause**. It is usually separated from the MCl by commas in writing, and is spoken as a separate tone-unit. But as with other linguistic categories, the difference between the two types of RelCl may not always be clear

Some examples of non-restrictive RelCls are:

(a) The other farm, **which was called Pinchfield,** was smaller and better kept.
(b) Rumours of a wonderful farm, **where the human beings had been turned out and the animals managed their own affairs,** continued to circulate
(c) The geese, **who had been hiding behind the hedge,** rushed out and pecked viciously at the calves of their legs.

in contrast to restrictive RelCls in:

(d) ...then the sheep **who had been killed** was given a solemn funeral.
(e) Bulls **which had been tractable** suddenly turned savage...
(f) There was not an animal on the farm **that did not take vengeance on them after his own fashion**.

In (c), all the geese had been hiding behind the hedge. The RelCl is *additional* information. In (d) only one of the sheep had been killed. The RelCl is *restrictive* or *identifying* information. We infer these differences of meaning from the punctuation which marks the two kinds of RelCl.

The next sentence contains a restrictive RelCl embedded in a non-restrictive RelCl:

> *non-restrictive RelCl*
> Snowball, [**who had studied an old book of Julius Caesar's campaigns**
>
> *restrictive RelCl*
> [**which he had found in the farmhouse**]], was in charge of the defensive operations.

In this sentence:

> [The Mole was busy trying to quiet the horse], [**which** he succeeded in doing after a time].

the referent of *which* is not a specific noun, but the general action of *quieting the horse*. This is a common feature of non-restrictive RelCls.

Activity 11.9

Identify the non-restrictive RelCls in the following sentences.

(a) The Rat, who had been looking up his friends and gossiping, came strolling along to find him.
(b) Toad set them to capture the old grey horse, who, without having been consulted, and to his own extreme annoyance, had been told off by Toad for the dustiest job in this dusty expedition.
(c) The following evening the Mole, who had risen late and taken things very easy all day, was sitting on the bank fishing, when the Rat, who had been looking up his friends and gossiping, came strolling along to find him.
(d) 'It makes me downright sorry to see you fellows, who ought to know better, spending all your energies in that aimless manner'.

(e) During luncheon – which was excellent, of course, as everything at Toad Hall always was – the Toad simply let himself go.

(f) 'That creek leads to his boat-house, where well leave the boat'.

You can examine the validity of the distinction between restrictive and non-restrictive relative clauses in the following activity:

Activity 11.10

(i) Identify the relative clauses in the following sentences. (a) – (i) are from *Animal Farm*; (j) is from *Dombey and Son* and contains six successive RelCls.

(ii) Say whether you think they are restrictive or non-restrictive.

(iii) Does punctuation clearly mark the non-restrictive kind of RelCl?

(iv) If the sentences are read aloud, are there any differences in intonation, stress or pause which distinguish the two kinds of RelCl?

(v) Say whether the RelCls are marked with a relative pronoun functioning as S or O, or a relative adverb functioning as A.

(a) Napoleon was attended by a black cockerel who marched in front of him.

(b) He always ate from the Crown Derby dinner service which had been in the glass cupboard in the drawing-room.

(c) Napoleon had demanded payment in real five-pound notes, which were to be handed over before the timber was removed.

(d) This time the animals did not have the easy victory that they had had in the Battle of the Cowshed.

(e) At this moment the four pigeons, who had been sent out on the day before, returned.

(f) The fear and despair they had felt a moment earlier were drowned in their rage against this vile act.

(g) The dogs of Napoleon's own bodyguard, whom he had instructed to make a detour, suddenly appeared.

(h) They halted in sorrowful silence at the place where the windmill had once stood.

(i) The small paddock beyond the orchard, which it had previously been intended to set aside as a grazing-ground for animals who were past work, was to be ploughed up.

(j) But one morning when she happened to come upon him suddenly from a by-path among some pollard willows which terminated in the little shelving piece of stony ground that lay between his dwelling and the water, where he was bending over a fire he had made to caulk the old boat which was lying bottom upwards, close by, he raised his head at the sound of her footstep, and gave her Good morning.

II.2.4   *Appositive noun clauses*

The relationship between the non-restrictive relative clause and main clause, in which the RelCl adds information about the MCl, is similar to **apposition** (section 10.2.3), illustrated in the following sentences from *Animal Farm*:

(i)   At the same time there were renewed rumours

    AppCl
      S   P   P   O
    that ⟨[Frederick and his men⟩ were plotting to attack Animal Farm].

(ii)   The look-outs came racing in with the news

    AppCl
      S   P (A)   P   A
    that ⟨[Frederick and his followers⟩ had already come through the five-barred gate].

The subordinate finite clauses are marked by *that*, like a reported clause, but they do not follow a reporting verb. They are in **apposition** to a NP, *renewed rumours* in (i), and *news* in (ii), saying what the rumours and the news actually were. Here is another example, from *The Wind in the Willows*:

> This time the two guests took care **that** [Toad should do his fair share of work].

The clause *This time the two guests took care* does not tell us what the guests took care to do. The clause *Toad should do his fair share of work* provides this information, in apposition to the noun care. It identifies the care that had to be taken. Here are some other examples of **appositive clauses (AppCls)**.

> 'I was just going to send a boat down the river for you, Ratty, with strict instructions **that [you were to be fetched up here at once**, [whatever you were doing]]'.

> The two animals were resting, thoroughly exhausted, by the time Ø **[Toad appeared on the scene**, [fresh and gay], [remarking [what a pleasant easy life it was Ø [they were all leading now]]]].

Notice that the conjunction *that* may be deleted.

11.2.4.1   APPOSITIVE CLAUSE OR RELATIVE CLAUSE?

The structure of an appositive clause looks identical to that of a relative clause, and so may be confused with it. One clear difference, however, apart from its meaning, is that the conjunction *that* does not function as part of the grammar of the appositive clause that it marks, as its subject or object, nor can you substitute *who* or *which* for *that*.

(i)   And there were were rumours that Frederick and his men were spreading around.

(ii)   And there were rumours that Frederick and his men were plotting to attack Animal Farm.

That Frederick and his men were spreading around is a RelCl, in which *that* is a pronoun object of the verb *were spreading*. Its referent is *rumours*:

O   S   P

There were rumours [**that** Frederick and his men were spreading around.
          RelCl

Sentence (ii) tells us what the rumours actually were – it identifies them. The word that is a conjunction marking the clause *Frederick and his men were plotting to attack Animal Farm* as a NCl in apposition to *rumours*. It is not part of the grammar of the clause:

S   P   P

There were rumours **that** [Frederick and his men were plotting to attack
                AppCl

O
Animal Farm].

II.2.5 *Finite adverbial clauses*

In chapter 10, we discovered that clauses frequently operate inside phrase structure. Whereas a kernel clause consists of a series of *phrases* as S, P, C or A, real texts are seldom made up of kernel clauses only. As clauses are called *noun clauses* when they function in the place of a NP, it is not surprising that a subordinate clause that takes the place of an adverbial is called an **adverbial clause** (AdvCl). And just as both finite and nonfinite types of clause can be used as NCls, so both kinds can function as AdvCls. NonfCls functioning as adverbials have already been described in section 11.1.

The adverbial in a clause tells us about the circumstances in which the participants and the process are interacting. The most common adverbials indicate the *time* and/or the *place* and/or the *manner* of the action. For example:

> The Mole had been working **hard** (*manner*) **all morning.** (*time*)

> Mole lived **under the ground.** (*place*)

In these two simple (one-clause) sentences the adverbials are *hard*, an adverb, *all morning*, a NP, and *under the ground*, a PrepP.

Adverbials expressed by finite **adverbial clauses** are always marked by a subordinating conjunction (scj). Among the commonest are *after, as, because, before, if, since, though, till/until, unless, when, while*, and so on. There are also a number of complex subordinating conjunctions, like *as if, in case, in order that, as soon as*, and so on.

Adverbial clauses are often given a descriptive semantic label which attempts to define their meaning more clearly. Here is a selection of traditional labels, with the conjunctions which typically relate to them. The list is only a selection of the commoner types and conjunctions. You will find more detailed lists in descriptive reference grammars

clause type	*scj*
time	after, as, before, since when, until, while
place	where, wherever
manner	as, as if, as though
reason	as, because, since
purpose	so that, in order that
result	so that
condition	if, unless, provided that
concession	although, though

If a clause is marked with a subordinating conjunction, it cannot be used as a simple one-clause sentence,

*As they got into the boat.

*Because you know you've *got* to come.

*Since he had fallen into the water.

Here are some examples of AdvCls taken from *The Wind in the Willows*.

Activity 11.11

(i)   Can the AdvCl be moved to a different place in the sentence? If so, are there any restrictions on the order of the other constituents?

(ii) If the AdvCl cannot be moved without producing an unacceptable sentence, discuss the reasons.

(a) '[Please let *me* row],' [Mole said, [**as** they got into the boat]].
(b) '[All the same, it sounds [**as if** it might have been – well, rather fun].'
(c) '[Don't begin talking in that stiff and sniffy sort of way, [**because** you know you've *got* to come]].'
(d) '[[**If** you haven't], why don't we go out in the boat]?'
(e) [Mole laughed for the first time [**since** he had fallen into the water]].
(f) '[You're getting on fairly well, [**though** you splash a good bit still]].'
(g) '[[**Till** this trip is ended] I ought to stick by Toad].'
(h) '[Why didn't you ask me to lunch, Ratty]?' [he cried [**when** he saw the food basket]].

Activity 11.12

Identify the AdvCls in the following sentences.

(a) 'Come with me, dear Ratty, and your amiable friend also, if he will be so very good.'
(b) 'He must be a very nice animal,' observed the Mole, as he got into the boat and took the sculls, while the Rat settled himself comfortably in the stern.

(c) 'Meanwhile the Mole and I will go to an inn and find comfortable rooms where we can stay till the cart's ready, and till your nerves have recovered from the shock.'

(d) 'Nothing at all,' replied the Rat firmly. 'Because there is really nothing to be done.'

(e) 'This is really one of the nicest houses in these parts, though we never admit as much to Toad.'

(f) 'When we get to the town well go to the railway-station...'

(g) The Mole was by the horse's head, talking to him, since the horse had complained that he was being frightfully left out of it...

(h) When they were quite ready, the now triumphant Toad led his companions to the paddock.

Just as adverbs and AdvPs are not generally fixed in their position in a clause, so adverbial clauses may either precede, or follow, or split the main clause in which they are embedded. For example the sentence in *Animal Farm*:

We will build six windmills [**if** we feel like it].

might have been written:

[**If** we feel like it] we will build six windmills.

or

We will, [**if** we feel like it], build six windmills.

The difference of meaning is one of emphasis and focus of information. The clause which comes first is **thematic** (section 12.2.1) and more prominent.

Another type of adverbial clause is used to compare one thing with another,

Throughout that year the animals worked hard**er** [**than** they had worked in the previous year].

There were **more** hardships to be borne [**than** they had ever experienced before].

The adverb *hard* is in its **comparative** form *harder*. Similarly, the noun *hardships* in the NP *more hardships* is modified by the comparative adjective *more*. Both are followed by adverbial **comparative clauses** beginning with *than*.

Another form of comparative clause uses the **correlative conjunctions** *as...as*, rather than *more...than*:

The men opened fire **as** soon [**as** they got within fifty yards].

12. Derived clauses

12.1 Direct and indirect speech

The sentence:

'What is that gun firing for?' said Boxer.

is an example of **direct speech**. It contains a **quoting clause**, *said Boxer*, and a **quoted clause**, *What is that gun firing for*? It might have been written in **indirect speech** as:

Boxer asked [what the gun was firing for].

with a **reporting clause**, *Boxer asked*, and a **reported clause**, *what the gun was firing for*.

12.1.1 Direct speech – quoting and quoted clauses

When we quote the speech of a person or character, their words are not changed. Quotation marks (or *speech marks*, or *inverted commas*) are placed before and after, and the speaker is named, with some indication of how he or she spoke. The clause which introduces the direct speech (quoted) is the quoting clause, and contains at least a subject and predicator, and possibly other clause constituents. The quoting clause may precede the quoted speech:

Rat asked, 'What are you looking at?'
Then at last **Mole said** quietly, 'So this is a river.'

but conventionally it often follows the speech, with the subject either preceding the predicator (SP):

'And what's on the other side of the Wild Wood?' **Mole asked**.
'The river,' **Rat said**.

or equally conventionally, with the order of subject and predicator reversed (PS). Notice also how a variety of verbs other than *said* can be used to describe the activity:

'He must be a very nice animal,' **observed the Mole**.
'He is indeed the best of animals,' **replied Rat**.

12.1.1.1 ADVERBS IN QUOTING CLAUSES

Information about how a character speaks can be conveyed through the use of adverbs:

'Is boating really so nice?' asked Mole **quietly**.

'No, it isn't!' cried the Rat **indignantly**.

'Ratty,' said the Mole **suddenly**...

'Finest house on the whole river,' cried Toad **boisterously**.

'All complete!' said the Toad **triumphantly**.

'I beg your pardon,' said the Rat **slowly**...

'Now, you dear good old Ratty,' said Toad **imploringly**...

'I dont care,' said the Rat **doggedly**.

'Of course I am,' said the Mole **loyally**.

'All the same, it sounds as if it might have been – well, rather fun!' he added **wistfully**.

'Come along in and have some lunch,' he said **diplomatically**.

Other adverbs are used in this way in the chapter of *The Wind in the Willows* from which these quoted-quoting clauses were taken, and include *cheerily, sleepily, pathetically, faintly, sternly, firmly, savagely, grimly, anxiously, sharply*. Other verbs which describe how a character speaks are *whispered, shouted, murmured, demanded*.

12.1.2 Indirect speech – reporting and reported clauses

We change the grammar of quoted speech if we report it indirectly. The sentence:

quoted speech   *quoting clause*
'And what's on the other side of the Wild Wood?' Mole asked.

has a quoted *wh*-question, and becomes in reporting/reported speech:

reporting cl   reported cl
Mole asked what was on the other side of the Wild Wood.

The tense of the verb in the quoted clause is **backshifted** to past, to match that of the quoting clause. Other changes are required in the next sentence, in which the quoted speech is a yes/no question:

quoting cl   quoted speech
Rat asked, 'Would you like to come over here, Mole?'

reporting cl   reported cl
Rat asked   whether Mole would like to come over there.

The reported clause which is derived from the quoted speech functions like a noun clause (NCl) as the object of the reporting verb, embedded within the sentence.

reporting cl
S   P   O = *reported cl*
[Mole asked [what was on the other side of the Wild Wood]].

> **reporting cl**
> **S   P   O = *reported cl***
> [Rat asked [whether Mole would like to come over there]].

A quoted **statement**, for example:

> Mole said, 'Spring has come!'

becomes in reported, indirect speech:

> **S   P   O = NCl**
> [Mole said **that** [spring had come]].

The conjunction that *marks* the NCl object of *said*. This construction with *that* is used after a set of reporting verbs which includes *know, think, hope, find, show* and so on as well as verbs which describe actual speech like *say, shout, whisper*.

> **S   P   Oi   Od**
> '[You 'll find   that [nothing whatever has been forgotten]]'.
> '[I   'll show you that [nothing has changed]].'

The conjuction *that* may be deleted:

> '[You'll find Ø [nothing whatever has been forgotten]].'
> '[I'll show you Ø [nothing has changed]].'

The reporting-reported clause construction is extremely common in narrative, as the next examples from *Animal Farm* show. The conjunction *that* is simply a function word, and is not part of the structure of the clause (unlike *that* when used as a relative pronoun).

> Benjamin said **that** [he refused to meddle in such matters].

> Squealer would read out to them lists of figures proving **that** [the production of every class of foodstuff had increased by 200 per cent].

> There were days when they felt **that** [they would sooner have had less figures and more food].

Notice that it is possible to reverse the order of reporting-reported clauses only when *that* is deleted:

> [He refused to meddle in such matters], Benjamin said.

Using *that* would be ungrammatical:

> *****That** [he refused to meddle in such matters] Benjamin said.

However, if we wanted to use the clause *He refused to meddle in such matters* as a NCl subject of a sentence, then we would have to mark the NCl with *that*. For example:

> **S = NCl   P   O**
> That [he refused to meddle in such matters] surprised no one.

Reporting verbs may also be followed by *wh*-NCls, in which the *wh*-word is part of the grammar of the clause, and cannot be deleted. For example:

S	P	O
'[I	wonder	[**when** he will be coming]]?'
'[I	wonder	[**what** new fad he has taken up now]]?'
[Mole	asked Rat	[**why** Toad was so boastful]].
[Rat	asked	[**where** Toad had hidden it]].
[They	enquired	[**whether** Badger was stirring]].

or

[They	enquired	[**if** Badger was stirring]].

A series of *wh*-reported clauses can be found in *Bleak House*, ch. VI:

...we wondered ⟨[**what** the house would be like], and [**when** we should get there], and [**whether** we should see Mr Jarndyce ⟨[as soon as we arrived] or after a delay⟩, and [**what** he would say to us], and [**what** we should say to him]⟩.

There is another possible variation in the presentation of reported (indirect) speech, in which the reporting clause *splits* the reported clause:

Even in the farmhouse, [**it was said**], Napoleon inhabited separate apartments from the others.

He considered it beneath his dignity, [**he said**], to have dealings with scoundrels of that description.

Activity 12.1

(i) Identify the reported and quoted clauses in the following sentences from *Animal Farm* ch. VIII.

(ii) Make a list of the reporting and quoting verbs.

(a) The animals were alarmed to hear that three hens had entered into a plot to murder Napoleon.

(b) The animals learned that Snowball had never received the order of 'Animal Hero, First Class'.

(c) 'Impossible!' cried Napoleon. 'We have built the walls far too thick for that.'

(d) Squealer was soon able to convince them that their memories had been at fault.

(e) 'The gun is firing to celebrate our victory!' cried Squealer. 'What victory?' said Boxer.

(f) Napoleon announced that the mill would be named Napoleon Mill.

(g) Snowball was living, so it was said, at Foxwood.

(h) Napoleon assured the animals that the stories of an impending attack on Animal Farm were untrue.

(i) They could no longer remember very clearly what conditions had been like before the Rebellion.

(J) But the superior quality of Napoleon's mind, said Squealer, was shown up in the fact that he trusted nobody

The changes that have to be made when reporting rather than quoting what someone has spoken are therefore:

(a) In declarative clauses

- The reported clause is marked by *that*, which may, however, be deleted.
- Tense in reported speech is *backshifted* – present becomes past.
- 1st and 2nd person pronouns are changed to 3rd person, unless the person is present at the utterance.
- Demonstrative pronouns *this/these* become *that/those*.
- References to time and place are modified.

Quoted (direct) speech
'**I have** no wish to take life, not even human life,' repeated Boxer...

Reported (indirect) speech
Boxer repeated **that he had** no wish to take life, not even human life

Quoted (direct) speech
...Clover took her aside.
   'Mollie,' she said. '**I have** something very serious to say to **you. This** morning I **saw you** looking over the hedge that **divides** Animal Farm from Foxwood...'

Reported (indirect) speech
Clover took Mollie aside and said **that she had** something very serious to say to **her. That** morning **she had seen her** looking over the hedge that **divided**...'

Quoted (direct) speech
'Comrades,' Squealer said, '**I trust** that every animal **here appreciates** the sacrifice that Comrade Napoleon **has** made in taking **this** extra labour upon himself.'

Reported (indirect) speech
Squealer said '**Ø he trusted** that every animal **there appreciated** the sacrifice that Comrade Napoleon **had** made in taking **that** extra labour upon himself.'

(b) In interrogative clauses
In addition:

- Changes in word order are necessary.
- A *wh*-word is inserted in the report of a yes/no question.

Quoted (direct) speech (yes/no question)
'And **shall I** still be allowed to wear ribbons in **my** mane?' asked Mollie.

Reported (indirect) speech
Mollie asked **whether she would** still be allowed to wear ribbons in **her** mane.

Quoted (direct) speech (wh-question)
'Who **will** believe that **I did** not **do this** on purpose?' said Boxer.

Reported (indirect) speech
Boxer **asked** who **would** believe that **he had** not **done that** on purpose.

There is a single example in the *Fiesta* text of a reported clause derived from an interrogative:

    wh-O S   P   **Ca**
14b what we ought to pay for a motor-car to Pamplona

in which the object is the *wh*-word *what*, which comes first in the clause and so precedes the subject. This reported clause can be derived from:

    wh-O op-v S P   **Ca**
    What ought we to pay for a motor-car to Pamplona?

in which both the *wh*-word object and the operator-verb *ought* precede the subject. The interrogative clause can itself be derived from an underlying declarative clause:

    S P   **O**   **Ca**
    We ought to pay *something* for a motor-car to Pamplona.

Activity 12.2

Rewrite the following examples of quoted/direct speech into reported/indirect speech, and explain the changes that you make.

(a)   Clover dropped to her knees at his side.
       'Boxer!' she cried, 'how are you?'
(b)   'We must get help at once,' said Clover.
(c)   'Fools!' shouted Benjamin. 'Do you not see what is written on the side of that van?'
(d)   Squealer cried, 'You do not imagine, I hope, that we pigs are doing this in a spirit of selfishness and privilege? Many of us actually dislike milk and apples. I dislike them myself...'
(e)   'You have heard, then comrades,' Squealer said, 'that we now sleep in the beds of the farmhouse? And why not?'

Activity 12.3

The following sentences contain reported clauses which derive from clauses in direct speech.

(i)   Convert the reported clauses into quoted/direct speech.

(ii)   Describe the grammatical and lexical changes that you have to make.

(a)   Old Major asked the animals what the nature of that life of theirs was.
(b)   Napoleon then and there pronounced the death sentence upon Snowball.
(c)   He asked whether that was simply part of the order of nature.
(d)   Napoleon said that they would begin re-building the windmill that very morning.
(e)   They wondered why they continued in that miserable condition.

(f) He demanded of the cows how many thousands of gallons of milk they had given during the last year.
(g) Old Major put to the vote the question whether rats were comrades.
(h) Squealer cried that a most terrible thing had been discovered. Snowball had sold himself to Frederick of Pinchfield Farm, who was even then plotting to attack them and take the farm away from them.

12.2 Change of order of the constituents, SPCA

12.2.1 *Adverbials brought to the front of the clause as theme – ASPC*

In a declarative clause, making a statement implies 'saying something' about a person, object or idea, which is encoded into language as the grammatical subject. What is 'said about it' is in the remainder of the clause – the predicate. In this kind of unmarked clause the grammatical subject is also the **theme**, or what is being first brought to the attention of the listener or reader.

Therefore when another clause constituent is made the theme and brought to the front, special focus is given to it, and because adverbials are less fixed in their position in a clause than other constituents, **thematic adverbials** are very common.

Adverbials are made thematic more frequently than other clause constituents. The examples of marked theme from the *Fiesta* text are all adverbials (numbers from the constituent clause list in section 9.10.1):

1a   **In the morning** it was bright
4   **Already, so early in the morning**, it was very hot on the bridge across the river
5b   **then** Ø took a walk through the town
8a   **Finally** he came in
12a **Then** we went up past the old fort
13a **There** they told us x
23b **then** Ø put my shoe in him
29c **then** we were out in the country
31a **In the Basque country** the land all looks very rich and green
32b **on some of them** kids were playing in the sun
33d **then** the road turned off

Activity 12.4

(i) Say which of the following clauses has an initial thematic adverbial.

(ii) Rewrite those sentences with the subject as theme.

(a) Clearly there was good reason for killing the traitors who had leagued themselves with Snowball.
(b) On Sunday mornings Squealer would read out to them lists of figures.

(c)   Even in the farmhouse Napoleon inhabited separate apartments from the others.
(d)   All orders were now issued through Squealer or one of the other pigs.
(e)   In his speeches, Squealer would talk with the tears rolling down his cheeks.
(f)   Meanwhile, through the agency of Whymper, Napoleon was engaged in complicated negotiations with Frederick and Pilkington.
(g)   But Squealer counselled them to avoid rash actions.
(h)   Nevertheless, feeling against Frederick continued to run high.
(i)   In the teeth of every difficulty, in spite of inexperience, of primitive implements, of bad luck, and of Snowballs treachery, the work had been finished punctually to the very day.
(j)   At the same time he warned them that after this treacherous deed the worst was to be expected.

12.2.2   Other places for adverbials

Some adverbs are more likely to be found next to the words they modify, rather than at the end of a clause, as in these clauses from the *Fiesta* text:

6d   Ø = (We) **finally** bought a rod for Bill upstairs over a dry-goods store.
25   It was **really** an awfully clean hotel.

and in these examples from *Animal Farm*:

> The animals were **soon** driven back.
> A number of them were **already** wounded.
> For the moment **even** Napoleon seemed at a loss.
> If Pilkington and his men would help them, the day might **yet** be won.
> Another man had his trousers **nearly** torn off by Jessie and Bluebell.

12.2.3   Other clause constituents as theme

It is possible to make objects and other complements thematic in just the same way, though examples are less common in written texts. It is much more frequent in spoken English, when stress and intonation assist in emphasising the thematic constituent. The sentence:

S-theme **P**   **O**
They   reduced the rations for the animals, except those of the pigs and
                                                                      the dogs.

has unmarked theme, the subject *they*. In this form:

O-theme   *S*   *P*
The rations for the animals they reduced, except those of the pigs and
                                                                      the dogs.

the object comes first and is therefore the theme. The subject is the second constituent. In a clause with both a direct and indirect object, either can be made theme:

S-theme P   Oi   Od
They   gave horses a pension of five pounds of corn a day.

Oi-theme S   P   Od
Horses   they gave a pension a five pounds of corn a day.

Od   S   P   Oi
A pension of five pounds of corn a day they gave horses.

12.2.4   *Existential* there

In the clause, *Pigeons were out on the square*, the subject *pigeons* is the unmarked theme. But a marked focus on *pigeons* may be made:

18a   **There** were pigeons out in the square

The delayed subject comes after the predicator *be*, and its place is taken by the 'dummy' subject *there* (section 9.6.2.1). The subjects of these two sentences:

Several days were left when they finished the journey.

'**A parcel** has arrived for you, Ratty,' said Mole.

can be made prominent:

There were *several days* left when they finished the journey.

'**There's** *a parcel* arrived for you, Ratty,' said Mole.

The construction has to be used when *be* is the verb in a clause with no complement, expressing the existence of something, which explains the use of the term *existential there*, for example:

There was endless work in the supervision and organization of the farm.

There were fifteen men, with half a dozen guns between them.

We cannot say:

*Endless work in the supervision and organization of the farm was.

*Fifteen men, with half a dozen guns between them, were.

Activity 12.5

Rewrite these sentences, without using existential *there*, and discuss the changes that have to be made to produce acceptable grammatical sentences.

(a) There were times when it seemed that they worked longer hours than they had done in Jones's time.

(b) Three days later there was a terrible hullabaloo.

(c) There was enthusiastic cheering and stamping of feet.

(d) Then there was a deafening roar.

(e) There were songs, speeches, and more firing of the gun.

(f) That night, there came from the farmhouse the sound of loud singing.

(g) One night there was a loud crash in the yard.

(h) Muriel noticed that there was yet another commandment which the animals had remembered wrong.

12.2.5 Clauses derived by extraposition

The clause:

> S   P   Ci
> [Sitting in the cafe] was pleasant

has as its subject the embedded NonfCl *Sitting in the cafe*, and is therefore not a kernel clause. It is more usual to use 'dummy' *it* as the subject of the clause, and to **extrapose** ('place outside') the embedded clause to the end,

> S P   Ci   S
> 16c it was pleasant [sitting in the cafe]

This is another example, like 'existential there,' of a 'delayed subject' coming after the predicator. This seems to be much preferred in English, especially in informal style, because the new information comes nearer to the end of the clause, where we generally put new information. This is called **end-weighting**, or **end-focus**.

The same structure as a clause with extraposition occurs, however, in a sentence which it would be difficult to rewrite in a basic form. For example:

(i) It was felt that the killings which had taken place did not square with this.

makes an awkward sentence when structured as:

(ii) *That the killings which had taken place did not square with this was felt.

It is awkward because the long subject NCl *That the killings...* makes the clause front-weighted, and this tends to be avoided.

The predicator *was felt* is a passive, and it lacks the agentive PrepP *by the animals*, and is therefore **impersonal**. The active form of the sentence would be:

(iii) The animals felt that the killings which had taken place did not square with this.

Sentence (ii), therefore, is less acceptable because it is over-weighted with information at the front, and also lacks essential information. Notice that sentence (i) closely resembles the structure of a reporting-reported clause (section 12.1.2), with *it was felt* as a kind of reporting clause.

Both finite and nonfinite clauses can function as extraposed clauses. The following example is of an extraposed NonfCl:

It had become usual [to give Napoleon the credit].

which is the derived form of:

[To give Napoleon the credit] had become usual.

Lewis Carroll makes comic use of extrapolation in this extract from *Alice in Wonderland*. The Mouse is reading from a history book:

'...''and even Stigand, the patriotic archbishop of Canterbury, found it advisable –'''

'Found *what*?' said the Duck.

'Found *it*,' the Mouse replied rather crossly: 'of course you know what "it" means.'

'I know what "it" means well enough, when *I* find a thing,' said the Duck: 'it's generally a frog or a worm. The question is, what did the archbishop find?'

The Mouse did not notice this question, but hurriedly went on, ' – "found it advisable to go with Edgar Atheling to meet William and offer him the crown.'''

Activity 12.6

(i)   Rewrite the following clauses, which are derived by extraposition, in their basic forms.

(ii) Discuss the resulting clause in terms of its acceptability.

(iii) Which clauses function like sequences of reporting-reported clauses?

(iv) Indicate which extraposed clauses are finite and which are non-finite.

(a) It seemed to the animals that they worked longer hours than they had done in Jones's time.
(b) It was beneath his dignity to have any dealings with scoundrels of that description.
(c) It was also announced that the gun would be fired every year on Napoleon's birthday.
(d) It had been intended to set aside the paddock as a grazing-ground.
(e) It was impossible now to venture out of the shelter of the buildings.
(f) It was given out that Napoleon had arranged to sell the pile of timber to Mr Pilkington.

12.3   Complex and derived clauses in a text

Here is a descriptive analysis of the second part of the *Fiesta* text (see Activity 9.15, section 9.10.1 at the end of chapter 9), against which you can check your own description. Clauses without comment are kernel clauses.

> **S   P   Ca   A**
> 26a Cohn came down, finally

> **ccj S   P   Ca A**
> 26b and we all went out to the car

> **S P   Ci**
> 27a It was a big, closed car,

> **p   NP**
> 27b with a driver in a white duster with blue collar and cuffs
> (27 is a single clause if you accept the complex PrepP *with a driver ... cuffs*
> as a post-modifier of *car*, but 27b may be analysed as a verbless
> prepositional clause, very similar in function to a non-restrictive RelCl
> beginning *which had a driver ...* (section 11.1.1)).

> **ccj S   P   O/S P   O   pt**
> 27c and we had him put the back of the car down
> (derived clause, predicators in phase, with intervening NP *him*)

> **S   P   pt O**
> 28a He piled in the bags
> (adverb particle between P and O)

> **ccj S   P   pt ⟨A   &   A⟩**
> 28b and we started off up the street and out of the town
> (phrase-complex, adverbial PrepPs)

> **S   P   O**
> 29a We passed some lovely gardens

> **ccj S P   O**
> 29b and Ø had a good look back at the town
> (*back* and *at the town* are analysed as post-modifiers of *look*)

---

ccj   *A*   *S*   *P*   *Ca Ca*

29c   and then we were out in the country, green and rolling

    (thematic adverb *then*; coordinated adjectives post-modifying *country*, but non-restrictively, and so possibly another verbless clause; compare *which was green and rolling*)

---

ccj   *S*   *P*   *A*

29d   and the road climbing all the time.

    (nonfinite clause)

S   *P*   *O*

30a   We passed lots of Basques

---

scj   *S*   *P*   *O*   *A*

30b   with oxen, or cattle, hauling carts along the road,

    (*with* functioning as a conjunction, to mark a NonfCl similar in meaning to a non-restrictive RelCl *who had* ... (see 27b))

---

ccj   *S P O*

30c   and Ø Ø nice farmhouses,

    (*we* and *passed* deleted, following coordination)

30d   low roofs, and all white-plastered

    (*with* may be understood, therefore this can be said to function as a clause, like 27b and 30b)

A   *S*   *P*   ⟨*Ci*   & *Ci*⟩

31a   In the Basque country the land all looks very rich and grcen

    (thematic adverbial PrepP; coordinated intensive complement AdjPs)

---

ccj   ⟨*S*   & *S*⟩   *P*   ⟨*Ci* & *Ci*⟩

31b   and the houses and villages look well-of and clean

    (coordinated subject NPs and intensive complement AdjPs)

> **S**   **P**   **O**
> 32a   Every village had a pelota court

> **ccj** **A**   **S** **P**   **A**
> 32b   and on some of them kids were playing in the hot sun.
> (thematic adverbial PrepP)

> **S**   **P**   **S**   **Ca**
> 33a   There were signs on the walls of the churches
> (existential *there* as subject)

> **P**
> 33b   saying x
> (NonfCl, reporting verb)

>   **S** **P**   **[= S]**
>   **P**   **O**   **A**
> 33c   x = it was forbidden [to play pelota against them]
> (reported clause, object of *saying*; extraposition of subject NCl, dummy *it* subject)

> **ccj** **S**   **P**   **O**
> 33d   and the houses in the villages had red-tiled roofs

> **ccj** **A**   **S**   **P**   **pt**
> 33e   and then the road turned off
> (thematic adverb)

> **ccj** **S** **P**   **P**
> 33f   and Ø commenced to climb
> (predicators in phase; *nb* deleted subject following coordination)

> **ccj** **S** **P**   **Ca**   **A**
> 33g   and we were going way up close along a hillside

```
        p    ⟨NP          &   NP⟩
33h   with  a valley below and hills [stretched off back toward the sea].
        (compare 27c and 30b)
```

```
        S    P       O
34    You  couldn't see  the sea
```

```
        S P   Ca
35    It was too far away
```

```
        S    P       A    ⟨O   &   O⟩
36a   You could see only hills and more hills
        (phrase-complex object)
```

```
        ccj  S    P
36b   and  you  knew x
        (reporting clause)
```

```
        wh-Ca S      P
36c   x = where the sea was
        (wh-reported clause, NCl object of knew)
```

The text from Ernest Hemingway's *Fiesta* has produced examples of many of the types of phrase and clause complexity that we find in English. They tend to be used sparingly and singly, however, and this is why his literary style remains relatively simple. In the thirty-six sentences analysed, there is only one subordinating adverbial conjunction, *while*, together with some use of the ambiguous preposition/conjunction *with*, and once, the conjunct *so*. This lack of subordinate adverbial clauses might be thought unusual in a sophisticated writer, and we would need to investigate other novelists' styles to see if Hemingway is unique in this or not.

The text of Orwell's *Animal Farm*, which has been extensively used in this chapter, is relatively uncomplicated in its grammar, but has considerably more variety in its derived forms of clause than Hemingway's.

12.3.1   *Use of the passive voice*

There were no examples of passive clauses in the *Fiesta* text. In active clauses, the subject is the actor, and this frequency of active clauses is one grammatical feature contributing to our response to Hemingway's style. Although George Orwell, writing in one of his essays, advocated the use of the active voice where possible, his practice was not as consistent as his theory, and in *Animal Farm* there are plenty of passives (section 8.10).

12.4   Making information prominent

Another kind of derived clause, which did not appear in the *Fiesta* text, provides a grammatical way of emphasising one constituent of a clause. If we were to speak the following clause, the normal unmarked intonation would place the tonic stress on the first syllable of the word *minutes*:

|The car was to pick us up at the hotel in forty '**min**utes|

because the last constituent in a clause (in this case the PrepP adverbial *in forty minutes*) is generally new information, and therefore the most important part of it in passing on information. If we wished to make a different word or phrase prominent, we could use **contrastive stress** to highlight *car*, *us*, *hotel* or *forty*.

But in writing, the resources of stress and intonation are not available, and so there are grammatical ways of drawing attention to particular items in a clause. Three ways, already described, are:

- to make a word or phrase **thematic**, by placing it at the front of a clause (sections 12.2.1 and 12.2.3), or
- to use *there* as subject and so make the delayed subject more prominent, when using *be* as predicator (section 12.2.4), and
- to use **extraposition** (section 12.2.5).

12.4.1   *Cleft clauses/sentences*

A fourth way of making part of a clause prominent is shown in the following re-arrangements of the clause:

	S	P	O	A
(i)	Toad, Mole and Rat	reached	the high road	in the afternoon

This is a simple one-clause sentence with its clause constituents in the normal unmarked order. We can make either the S, O or A constituents prominent in turn in this way:

(ii)   **It was** Toad, Mole and Rat   **that** reached the high road in the afternoon.

(iii)   **It was** the high road   **that** Toad, Mole and Rat reached in the afternoon.

(iv)   **It was** in the afternoon   **that** Toad, Mole and Rat reached the high road.

The original sentence has been split in two or **cleft**, so the construction is called a **cleft sentence**. The dummy subject *It* is followed by the verb *be*, which links it to the constituent to be made prominent, while the remainder of the sentence follows in a relative clause. Sometimes *that* may be deleted:

It was in the afternoon Ø Toad, Mole and Rat reached the high road.

In these derived clauses, the subject *Toad, Mole and Rat* in (ii), the object the *high road* in (iii), and the time adverbial *in the afternoon* in (iv) follow the subject pronoun *it* and an appropriate form of the verb *be* to form a separate clause. The rest of the clause then follows in its original order, introduced by a relative pronoun, usually *that*, though a *wh*-pronoun or adverb may sometimes be used. Notice, however, that you cannot apply this to the verb in the predicator:

*It was **reached** that Toad, Mole and Rat the high road.

Here are two examples from *Animal Farm*:

(i) But still, *it was* **not for this** *that* Clover and all the other animals had hoped and toiled.

(ii) *It was* **not for this** *that* they had built the windmill and faced the bullets of Jones's guns.

The non-cleft forms of sentences (i) and (ii), in which the adverbial complement is made prominent, are:

(iii) But still, Clover and all the other animals had not hoped and toiled for this.

(iv) They had not built the windmill and faced the bullets of Jones's guns for this.

Two other examples are:

(v) *It was* **nearly nine o'clock** *when* Squealer made his appearance.

(vi) *It was* **a few days later than this** *that* the pigs came upon a case of whisky in the cellars of the farmhouse.

Activity I2.7

(i) Write the basic forms of sentences (v) and (vi).

(ii) Write cleft forms of the following sentences, focusing in turn on different constituents, S, O, Ca and A.

	S	P	O	Ca
(a)	Napoleon	took	his meals	alone.

	S	P	O		A	A	A
(b)	Squealer	executed	a portrait	of Napoleon,	in profile,	in white paint,	on the wall of the big barn.

	A	S	P	Ca
(c)	In the morning	a deep silence	hung	over the farmhouse.

12.4.2 *Pseudo-cleft clauses/sentences*

A fifth method of focusing on a particular constituent of a clause uses another form of cleft sentence, in which an appropriate *wh*-word and the verb *be* are used to split off the item being made prominent.

The prominent item can be spoken or written first in the clause, as in:

(i)   **The car** *was what* was to pick us up at the hotel in forty minutes.
(ii) **We** *were who/whom* the car was to pick up at the hotel in forty minutes *or, preferably,*
(iii) **We** were the ones who/whom . . .
(iv) **At the hotel** *was where* the car was to pick us up in forty minutes.
(v)   **In forty minutes** *was when* the car was to pick us up at the hotel.
(vi) **Pick us up** *was what* the car was *to do* at the hotel in forty minutes.

But a construction in which the *wh*-clause comes first and the prominent item last is used more commonly:

(vii) *What* was to pick us up at the hotel in forty minutes *was* **the car.**
(viii) *Who* the car was to pick up at the hotel in forty minutes *was* **us.**
(ix)   *Where* the car was to pick us up in forty minutes *was* **at the hotel**.
(x)   *When* the car was to pick us up at the hotel *was* **in forty minutes.**
(xi)   *What* the car was *to do* at the hotel in forty minutes *was* **(to) pick us up**

One advantage of this construction is that it enable you to focus on the predicator verb, as in (vi) and (xi), which you cannot do with the ordinary cleft construction. The general verb *do* has to be introduced.

In (vii)–(xi), the phrase made prominent at the end of the clause carries tonic stress in speech, and is an example of new information in **end-focus**. This second type of *cleaving* is referred to as the **pseudo-cleft sentence**.

12.5 Summary

This chapter has outlined a way of describing the structure of complex combinations of clause and phrase. A kernel clause can be expanded by using subordination to become a complex clause – a type of superordinate clause containing a main clause and one or more subordinate clauses, finite or nonfinite. Its constituent phrases can also be extended by coordination and subordination. At the same time, words, phrases and clauses may be coordinated together to form constituents that function just like single words, phrases and clauses. We can call coordinated words, phrases or clauses that function like single constituents word-complexes, phrase-complexes and clause-complexes.

Clauses are combined to form meaningful sequences in written **texts** and spoken **utterances**. This is described in the following chapter, where the concepts of **sentence** and **clause complex** are developed.

12.6 Postscript – ways of diagramming a structural analysis

How you set out an analysis on paper depends upon the purpose of the analysis. The advantage of a diagram over a written description of structure is that a visual picture can make the way a phrase, clause or sentence is structured much clearer. The structure is abstract, and the diagram is a kind of visual metaphor.

There are several different ways of diagramming grammatical structure, but three useful ones will be shown here:

- labelled bracketing;
- linear slot-and filler analysis;
- tree-diagrams.

Each one will be demonstrated using the same *Fiesta* text of chapter 9.

12.6.1 *NP and PrepP structures*

> *NP structure* = (d) (m) h (q)

The brackets indicate optional constituents in a structure, which may or may not be chosen, depending upon meaning. d = determiner; d-Poss = possessive phrase as determiner: m = pre-modifier; h = head noun; q = qualifier = post-modifier.

> *PrepP structure* = p NP

p = preposition; NP = noun phrase.

12.6.1.1 LABELLED BRACKETING

This was demonstrated in chapter 7 on NPs and PrepPs. Use round brackets ( ) to mark phrases, and square brackets [ ] to mark clauses. Words are already marked by spaces. If you wish, you can also label the constituents, using conventional symbols; this is called *labelled bracketing*.

d m h
(a nice town)

d-Poss h
(Mike's rods)

h q
(we all)

p d h q
               = **p d h**
(on the bridge (across the river))

d h q
         = *RelCl*
(the man [who sold the tackle])

12.6.1.2 LINEAR ANALYSIS

A box in each column is a 'slot' which is 'filled' by a particular constituent; the columns are labelled.

	pre-modifier			postmodifier
preposition	determiner	modifier	head	qualifier
p	d	m	h	q
	a	nice	town	
	Mike's (d-Poss)		rods	
			we	all
on	the		bridge	across the river
across	the		river	
	the		man	who sold the tackle (RelCl)

12.6.1.3 TREE DIAGRAMS

These are much clearer to read than bracketing, and show the structure very well, but they are much more trouble to write, and take up a lot of space. The 'tree' is upside down in fact, and the 'branches' become more numerous as you go from the higher to the lower constituents.

For example, in the diagram of *the man who sold the tackle*, the top node is S (*node* is a word from botany meaning *point at which leaves or branches spring from stem*, and is used metaphorically). You read the diagram as, 'the subject (S) of the clause consists of the determiner (d) *the*, head noun (h) *man*, and post-modifying relative clause *who sold the tackle.*

Using a tree-diagram, you can see at a glance that embedded or subordinate constituents are always lower than the constituents they are dependent upon.

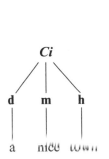

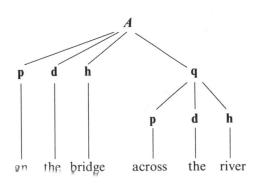

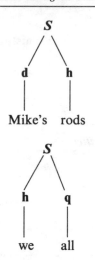

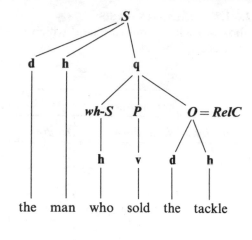

12.6.2   VP structure

VP structure (declarative mood): = (modal)(*have*)(*be*-prog)(*be*-pass)(s-aux)v.

P = predicator; ***modal*** = modal auxiliary verb; ***have*** = perfect aspect, *have* is followed by an *-en/-ed* participle; ***be*-prog** = progressive aspect, *be* is followed by *-ing* participle); ***be*-pass** = passive voice, *be* is followed by an *-en/-ed* participle; **s-aux** = semi-auxiliary **v** = main (lexical) verb.

12.6.2.1   LABELLED BRACKETING

    ***be*-prog v**
    (were   sprinkling)

    modal v
    (would come)

    P   **(A)**   *pt*
    modal *have*   **v**
    (must   have) (just) (come) (in)

    P   **P**
    s-aux   **v**
    (was supposed to start)

    P
    ***be*-prog *be*-pass v**
    (were   being   picked)

    P   **P**
    s-aux v   **v**
    (had to wait) for him (to come) back

12.6.2.2 LINEAR ANALYSIS

modal	*have*	*be*-prog	*be*-pass	s-aux	v
		were			sprinkling
would					come
must	have				(*just*) come (*in*)
			was	supposed to	start
		were	being		picked
				had to	wait (*for him*) to come (*back*)

12.6.2.3 TREE DIAGRAMS

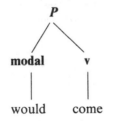

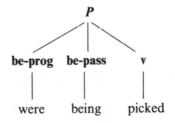

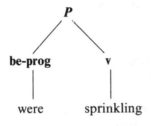

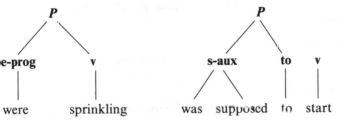

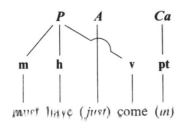

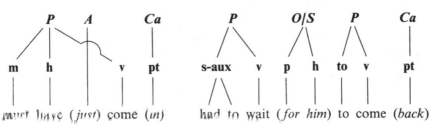

12.6.3 Clause structure

Clause structure (declarative clause) = S P (C) (A)
S = subject; P = predicator; C = complement (O = object complement; Ci = intensive complement; Ca = adverbial complement); A = adverbial.

12.6.3.1 LABELLED BRACKETING

   A   *S* *P*   *Ci*
[(In the morning) (it) (was) (bright)]

  S   *P*   *O*
[(thcy) (were sprinkling) (the streets (of the town))]

  S   *P*   *Ca*
[(The air) (came) (from the sea)]

   S   *P*   *pt*   *A*   *O*
                                              = *NCl (reported)*
[(We) (found) (out) (at the tourist office) [what we ought to pay for a motor-car to Pamplona]]

  wh-O *S*   *P*   *Ca*
[(what) (we) (ought to pay) (for a motor-car (to Pamplona))]]

12.6.3.2 LINEAR ANALYSIS

You can choose to make a chart with the minimum of columns, to show S, P, C and A, with one or two columns on the left for conjunctions and fronted items, e.g. thematic adverbials. As this method requires each clause to be shown on a separate line, you will sometimes have to write out a complex clause on several lines.

If you mark the space for an embedded clause with an asterisk and write this embedded clause on the next line marked also with an asterisk, you can show where the embedding takes place (example below).

cj	theme	S	P	C	A
	In the morning (A)	it	was	bright (Ci)	
and		they	were sprinkling	the streets of the town (O)	
		The air	came	from the sea (Ca)	
		We	found out	*	at the tourist office
	*what (*wh-O*)	we	ought to pay	for a motor-car to Pamplona (Ca)	

You can make a more detailed chart which shows as many of the possible varieties of constituent in a clause as you wish, for example:

| theme/linker | Subject | Predicator | Adv pt | Predicators in phase | | Complements | | Adverbial | Adverbial |
	S	P	pt	NP²/AdjP	P²	Object Co/O	Intensive Ci	Adverbial Ca	Peripheral
In the morning	it	was					bright		
and	they	were sprinkling				the streets of the town			
and	we all	had				breakfast			in a café.
Already, so early in the morning	it	was					very hot		on the bridge across the river.
	We	walked	out						on the bridge
and	Ø	took				a walk			through the town.
	I	was not					at all sure*		from Scotland in time
*Ø	Mike's rods	would come							
o	we	hunted				a tackle store			
and	Ø	bought				a box		for Bill	upstairs over a dry-goods store.
	The man *[who sold the tackle]	was						out,	
	*who	sold				the tackle			
	There	were					pigeons (= S)	out in the square	
and	the houses	were					a yellow, sun-baked colour,		
and	I	did not want			to leave	the café			
But	we	had to go						to the hotel	**
		**to get		our tags	packed				
and		Ø pay				the bill.			
While	we	were waiting							
	I	saw				a cockroach*			
	*that	must have been					at least three inches long		on the parquet floor
	I	pointed (him)	out			him		to Bill	
and then	Ø	put				my shoe		on him.	

12.6.3.3 TREE DIAGRAMS

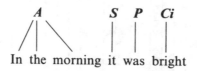

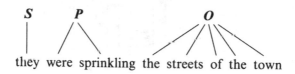

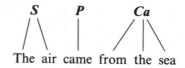

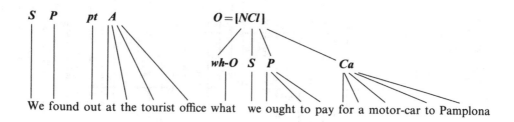

As written sentences consist of clauses and clause-complexes, they can be analysed equally well using all three methods of diagramming. You can make a complete analysis of the structure of a sentence, to include the levels of clause and phrase structure also. For example:

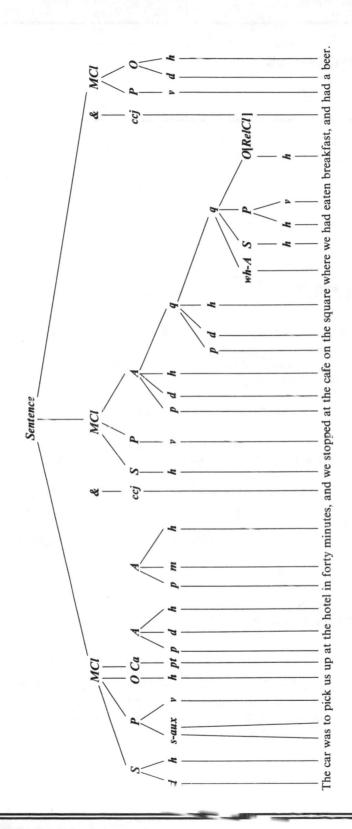

13. Sentences

13.1 Sentence or complex clause?

The rank-scale introduced in chapter 2 stated that a sentence consists of one or more clauses, a clause or one or more phrases, and a phrase of one or more words. But chapters 10 – 12 have shown that this description only works for some sentences, because clauses can be *rank-shifted* and function inside NPs and PrepPs, and also in the place of a phrase as subject, complement or adverbial in clause structure. We have called this the **embedding** of one subordinate constituent in another.

For example, the phrase *the netting* is a NP. If it is post-modified with a PrepP to become *the netting of the pheasant trap*, it is complex, but still a NP – a **complex NP**.

The PrepP *in the long grass* can be post-modified with another PrepP *behind the trap*, to *in the long grass behind the trap*. It is complex, but remains a PrepP – a **complex PrepP**.

Similarly, the NP *the group of abandoned buildings* can be post-modified with a restrictive RelCl as qualifier:

```
d    h    q
          p  m          h        q
(the group (of abandoned  buildings [that lay outside the perimeter of
   Lunghua Camp]))
```

and still be called a NP.

The principle of using the same descriptive label for both the simple and the complex forms of a grammatical phrase was extended in chapter 11 by showing how a simple kernel clause, with phrases as its constituents, may be expanded into a complex clause containing subordinate clauses. In the clause:

```
S           P       Ci        Ca      A
[the distance  seemed  enormous  to Jim  then]
```

the adverbial *then* can be expanded into an adverbial clause:

MCl   *SCl*

S   *P*   *Ci*   *Ca*   *A = Adv Cl*

[the distance seemed enormous to Jim [when he first crept through the barbed wire]]

which is subordinate to the main clause, embedded in it. The main clause and subordinate clause together form one superordinate clause. If this superordinate clause is then printed with a capital letter at the beginning and a full stop at the end, it is called **sentence**, although its form has not changed at all:

The distance seemed enormous to Jim when he first crept through the barbed wire.

so in this case a different word, *sentence*, is used to describe a structure consisting of two clauses, one subordinate to the other, rather than calling the combined structure simply a *complex clause*.

The sentence is adapted from a longer one in J. G. Ballard's novel *The Empire of the Sun* (1984). The original sentence demonstrates a typical complex clause as a printed sentence, in which an Adv Cl is subordinate to a RelCl, which post-modifies the NP *a distance*, which is in apposition to the NP *a few feet*:

MCl

[The first of the traps was only a few feet from the perimeter fence, a distance

RelCl   *AdvCl*

[that had seemed enormous to Jim [when he first crept through the barbed wire]]].

The question then arises, 'Why do we need the term *sentence*?' If a complex NP or PrepP, containing coordinated or subordinated constituents, still remains a NP or PrepP, why call a clause containing subordinate constituents anything other than a *complex clause*? The answer is partly that given to the questioner who asked, 'Why climb Mount Everest?' – 'Because it's there.' The word *sentence* has been used to stand for the highest unit of grammatical structure for centuries, whereas the word *clause*, which has been in the language for just as long, has not been so used.

In fact there are linguists who do not make use of the term *clause* at all, but only *sentence*, and so talk of *kernel sentences* and *embedded sentences*. This has the same logic as using *phrase* to speak of both simple and complex phrases.

However, it has proved very useful to distinguish the basic unit of the grammar as *clause*, and so to see sentences as **stylistic** units of language use, with a special status in writing. We can choose to write in single-clause sentences (as in infant primers), or in highly complex combinations of clauses within a single sentence. There is no limit to the potential length of a sentence – you can always coordinate or subordinate another phrase or clause – and so it proves difficult to define a sentence except in very general terms.

It is in spoken English that the word *sentence* is less useful, and where the term **clause-complex** allows us to distinguish structures typical of speech, which would not usually be acceptable in writing. The term *clause-complex* has been used in this book so far for the labelling of structures which contain two or more clauses related by coordination. These constituent clauses may themselves be complex, in the ways described in chapters 11 and 12. The same term is therefore a useful one for labelling those sentence-like structures in spoken English which consist of a series of clauses, typically linked by *and* or *and then*, and different in style from written English.

Those relationships between words, phrases and clauses, in constructions made up by coordination, apposition and subordination make up part of a writer's **style,** which will be demonstrated from texts of written and spoken English in the next chapter.

13.2 Simple sentences

The traditional classification of different kinds of sentence is:

- **Simple** – a single main clause.
- **Compound** – two or more coordinated clauses.
- **Complex** – a main clause and one or more subordinate clauses.
- **Compound-complex** – two or more coordinated clauses and one or more subordinate clauses.

A **simple sentence** has one clause only. You can write any main clause (MCl) as a simple sentence by starting its first word with a capital letter and ending it with a full stop, question mark or exclamation mark, according to its function as statement, question or exclamation. For example:

> Don't be silly!
> Everything there was quiet.
> Have you got anything to do this morning?
> How cold it is!
> I can teach you to swim.

The grammar of the simple sentence is therefore identical to the grammar of the clause.

13.3 Compound sentences – coordination

If you write two or more clauses coordinated by *and, but* or *or/nor*, then you have a **compound sentence.**

13.3.1 *Coordination with* and

The conjunction *and* is the most commonly used conjunction, as in:

> Mole didn't know about the river **and** he had never seen a boat.

If the subject of the coordinated clauses is the same (whether in noun or pronoun form), it is usual to **delete** the second and later ones. In these two sentences:

Badger turned round and Ø walked away.   (*two clauses*)

Mole just got up, Ø pushed Rat out of the way and Ø took the oars.   (*three clauses*)

you have no difficulty in identifying *Badger* in the first, and *Mole* in the second sentence as the deleted subjects (marked Ø) of their clauses. If we replace the deleted subjects, the style is repetitive:

Badger turned round and he walked away.

Mole just got up, he pushed Rat out of the way and he took the oars.

You can also delete other identical constituents when coordinating two clauses, for example the predicator in.

Ratty carried the hamper **and** Mole Ø the basket.

The fact that you can delete an identical constituent is a test for coordination. You cannot delete an identical item in a subordinate clause:

He was late for breakfast [because he had overslept].

*He was late for breakfast [because Ø had overslept].

13.3.2   *Coordination with* but

The conjunction *but* implies *and yet* and suggests some kind of contrast, as in:

Rat looked for Mole all over the house, **but** he couldn't find him.

Badger walked two steps forward, **but** then he saw Otter and Mole.

The sentences could have been written:

Rat looked for Mole all over the house, **but** Ø couldn't find him.

Badger walked two steps forward, **but** then Ø saw Otter and Mole.

with the subjects of the first clauses, *Rat* and *Badger*, deleted in the second.

13.3.3   *Coordination with* or

The third coordinating conjunction is *or*, which introduces an alternative possibility:

The Toad never answered a word, **or** budged from his seat in the road.

Another way of writing the second sentence, and one which some people would prefer, is:

The Toad never answered a word, **nor** budged from his seat in the road.

because the second clause, like the first, is **negative**, and *nor* is the negative form of *or*. Although *never* in the first clause is also a negative word, the conjunction *nor* more usually follows *neither*, in a **correlative** construction:

> The Toad **neither** answered a word, **nor** budged from his seat in the road.

The pair *neither ... nor* is the negative form of *either ... or*, as in:

> They set off, all talking at once. Each animal **either** trudged by the side of the cart **or** sat on the shaft.

The clauses in a compound sentence have equal status and each of them is a main clause (MCl).

Activity 13.1

Identify (a) the clauses, (b) the coordinating conjunctions and (c) any kinds of deletion in the following compound sentences.

(a) Badger lives there and he's a good friend of mine.
(b) Badger walked two steps forward, but then he saw Otter and Mole.
(c) He's such a nice person, but he isn't really safe in a rowing boat.
(d) Mole had to hurry or he would have been left behind.
(e) Mole sat back and looked at everything.
(f) Mole tried to row, and the next moment – splash!
(g) Otter looked at Rat and they both laughed.
(h) Rat took the oars and started to row.
(i) The eyes moved and the Water Rat's head came out.
(j) Very soon everything was back in the boat and Rat rowed home.
(k) We can take some food and go out on the river for the whole day.
(l) Will you come with me or will you stay at home?

13.4   Complex and compound-complex sentences

The grammar of complex and compound-complex sentences (see the beginning of section 13.2) is identical to that of complex clauses, which has been the subject of chapters 10–12, and so no further comment is necessary here. The 'superordinate clause' consisting of main clause(s) and subordinate clause(s) is called 'sentence' in its written form.

13.5   Compound, complex and compound-complex sentences in texts

The problem for someone teaching or talking about the grammar of English is that the details of the grammar are complex, though the basic principles can be stated comparatively simply. The most recent standard reference grammar was published in 1985 – *A Comprehensive Grammar of the English Language*, by Randolph Quirk, Sidney Greenbaum, Geoffrey Leech and Jan Svartvik. It has 1779 pages. Clearly, a lot of detail has had to be left out of this course book on English grammar.

The combinations of clauses into sentences are many, and are an important guide to **style**. A sentence may contain both coordination and subordination (when it is called a **compound-complex** sentence), and because clauses can be embedded within phrases (e.g. restrictive relative clauses, noun and adjective complements), several times over in a **recursive** structure, some sentences can be very complex.

Most of the examples of sentences discussed in this chapter have been two-clause sentences. They have been modified from the original longer and more complex sentences. To conclude, we ought to examine some extracts from the text we have been using as they were written.

I3.5.I *Bracketing and description*

Sentence structure can be set out in several ways. One is to mark all the clauses with square brackets [ ] (as we have been doing). Coordinated structures within clauses can be marked with caret brackets 〈 〉. The bracketed clauses can then be labelled with their function as MCl, NCl, AdvCl, RelCl, and so on.

Here are some examples of compound, complex and compound-complex sentences. Remember that complexity in a sentence may also be found <u>within</u> any of the clauses at phrase level, together with embedded clauses or coordinated phrases or post-modifiers.

1   Compound – three MCls

The Rat put out a neat little brown paw, gripped Toad firmly by the scruff of the neck, and gave a great hoist and a pull.

MCl 1   [The Rat put out a neat little brown paw],
MCl 2   [Ø gripped Toad firmly by the scruff of the neck], and
MCl 3   [Ø gave 〈a great hoist and a pull〉].

2   Complex – MCl and AdvCl

The water-logged Toad came up slowly but surely over the edge of the hole, till at last he stood safe and sound in the hall.

MCl   [The water-logged Toad came up 〈slowly but surely〉 over the edge of the hole〉,
AdvCl till   [at last he stood 〈safe and sound〉 in the hall]].

3   Complex – MCl and PrepCl

He was streaked with mud and weed, with the water streaming off him.

MCl   [He was streaked with mud and weed,
PrepCl with   [the water streaming off him]].

These three sentences were in fact written as one. The stylistic effect is different:

[The Rat put out a neat little brown paw], [gripped Toad firmly by the scruff of the neck], and [gave a great hoist and a pull]; and [the water-logged Toad came up slowly but surely over the edge of the hole, [till at last he stood safe and sound in the hall, [streaked with mud and weed], and [with the water streaming off him]]]].

4   Compound-complex – three MCls and AppCl

They had a pleasant ramble that day over grassy downs and along narrow by-lanes, and camped, as before, on a common, only this time the two guests took care that Toad should do his fair share of work.

MCl 1		1 [They had a pleasant ramble that day, ⟨over grassy downs and along narrow by-lanes⟩]
MCl 2	*and*	2 [Ø camped as before on a common]
MCl 3	*only*	3 [this time the two guests took care, *that* **AppCl** 4 [Toad should do his fair share of work]]

There are three coordinated MCls, and an AppCl embedded in the NP *care*. Two PrepP adverbials in MCl 1 are coordinated.

Now a rather longer sentence:

5   Compound-complex – with reporting-reported and quoting-quoted clauses

They were strolling along the high road easily, the Mole by the horse's head, talking to him, since the horse had complained that he was being frightfully left out of it, and nobody considered him in the least; the Toad and the Water Rat walking behind the cart talking together – at least Toad was talking, and Rat was saying at intervals, 'Yes, precisely; and what did you say to him?' – and thinking all the time of something very different, when far behind them they heard a faint warning hum, like the drone of a distant bee.

There are fourteen clauses (if you accept *the Mole by the horse's head* as verbless clause),

1		[They were strolling along the high road easily],
2		[the Mole by the horse's head],
3		[talking to him]]],
4	**since**	[the horse had complained]
5	**that**	[he was being frightfully left out of it],
6	**and**	[nobody considered him in the least];
7		[⟨the Toad and the Water Rat⟩ walking behind the cart]
8		[talking together] –
9	⟨**at least**	[Toad was talking],
10	**and**	[Rat was saying at intervals],
11		['Yes, precisely];

12	**and**	[what did you say to him?'] –
13	**and**	[Ø Ø thinking all the time of something very different],
14	**when**	[far behind them they heard a faint warning hum, like the drone of a distant bee].

with the following functions in the sentence:

MCl 1	⎡[1 They were strolling along the high road easily **Vbless Cl** [2 the Mole by the horse's head **NonfCl** [3 talking to him]] ⎤
AdvCl reporting	⎡*since* [4 the horse had complained **NCl rep *that*** [5 he was being frightfully left out of it] **NCl rep *and* Ø** [6 nobody considered him in the least]] ⎤
	⎡**NonfCl** [7 ⟨the Toad and the Water Rat⟩, walking behind the cart **NonfCl** [8 talking together]] ⎤

parenthesis	
MCl 2	[*at least* [9 Toad was talking]]
MCl 3 quoting	[*and* [10 Rat was saying at intervals]]
MCl 4 quoted	[[11 'Yes, precisely]]
MCl 5 quoted	[*and* [12 what did you say to him?']]
MCl 6	⎡*and* [13 Ø Ø thinking all the time of something very different] ⎤
MCl 7	⎡*when* [14 far behind them they heard a faint warning hum like the drone of a distant bee]]]. ⎤

We can build up the complete sentence bit by bit, to show how the clauses fit together into a grammatical pattern.

First, the principal MCls. The conjunction *when* is here functioning as a **coordinator** rather than a subordinator. You cannot reverse the two clauses, as you can if *when* marks an AdvCl. (You may disagree with this analysis.)

We begin with the MCls:

They were strolling along the high road easily, when far behind them they heard a faint warning hum, like the drone of a distant bee.

then add the NonfCl describing Mole:

They were strolling along the high road easily, **the Mole by the horse's head, talking to him,** when far behind them they heard a faint warning hum, like the drone of a distant bee.

then the AdvCl which further explains Mole's actions:

They were strolling along the high road easily, the Mole by the horse's head, talking to him, **since the horse had complained that he was being frightfully left out of it, and nobody considered him in the least**, when far behind them they heard a faint warning hum, like the drone of a distant bee.

or first add the NonfCl describing the Water Rat and Toad:

They were strolling along the high road easily, **the Toad and the Water Rat walking behind the cart talking together,** when far behind them they heard a faint warning hum, like the drone of a distant bee.

Then combine both NonfCls describing Mole, Rat and Toad:

They were strolling along the high road easily, the Mole by the horse's head, talking to him, since the horse had complained that he was being frightfully left out of it, and nobody considered him in the least; the Toad and the Water Rat walking behind the cart talking together, whcn fai behind them they heard a faint warning hum, like the drone of a distant bee.

Add the NonfCl describing Rat's thoughts:

They were strolling along the high road easily, the Mole by the horse's head, talking to him, since the horse had complained that he was being frightfully left out of it, and nobody considered him in the least; the Toad and the Water Rat walking behind the cart talking together, **and (Rat) thinking all the time of something very different,** when far behind them they heard a faint warning hum, like the drone of a distant bee.

Finally add the parenthetical section describing Rat and Toad's conversation:

They were strolling along the high road easily, the Mole by the horse's head, talking to him, since the horse had complained that he was being frightfully left out of it, and nobody considered him in the least; the Toad and the Water Rat walking behind the cart talking together - **at least Toad was talking, and Rat was saying at intervals, 'Yes, precisely; and what did you say to him?'** – and thinking all the time of something very different – when far behind them they heard a faint warning hum, like the drone of a distant bee.

These examples of sentence description will show that there is an infinite variety of possible combinations of clauses in sentence structure. You can always add another coordinated clause, or subordinate clause, or qualify NPs with RelCls, and so on.

Grammatical structure is one of the most important features of **style**, so this kind of analysis is essential, together with a study of the vocabulary, if you want to begin to find out *how* a writer's style works.

Activity 13.2

(i) Practise the analysis of sentences using the following texts by identifying the function of the clauses in sentence structure.

(ii) Select some of the longer clauses, and identify the clause constituents (S, P, C, A).

(iii) Discuss the differences of structure and vocabulary between the two versions.

Text 1a – simplified version

[Rat was very angry]. [He jumped up and down in the middle of the road]. [He shouted all the bad words [he knew]]. [Surprisingly, Toad did not seem to be angry]. But [he was behaving in a very unusual way]. [He was sitting in the middle of the road] and [he looked very happy]. [He said again and again], ['Poop, poop! Poop, poop]!'

'[What *is* the matter with Toad]?' [Rat asked himself]. '[Why isn't he angry]?' '[Come on, Toad],' [said Rat]. '[Help us with the caravan]. [Let's see [if we can move it]].' But [Toad still didn't move].

Text 1b – original version

[The Rat danced ⟨up and down⟩ in the road, [simply transported with passion]]. '[You villains]!' [he shouted, [shaking both fists]]. '[You scoundrels, you highwaymen, you – you – road-hogs]! – [I'll have the law of you]! [I'll report you]! [I'll take you through all the Courts]!' [His home-sickness had quite slipped away from him], and [for the moment he was the skipper of the canary-coloured vessel [driven on a shoal by the reckless jockeying of rival mariners]], and [he was trying to recollect all the fine and biting things [he used to say to masters of steam-launches [when their wash, [as they drove too near the bank], used to flood his parlour carpet at home]]].

[Toad sat straight down in the middle of the dusty road, [his legs stretched out before him]], and [stared fixedly in the direction of the disappearing motor-car] [He breathed short], [his face wore a placid, satisfied expression,] and [at intervals he faintly murmured] '[Poop-poop]!'

[The Mole was busy [trying to quiet the horse]], [which he succeeded in doing after a time]. [Then he went to look at the cart, [on its side in the ditch]]. [It was indeed a sorry sight]. [Panels and windows smashed], [axles hopelessly bent], [one wheel off], [sardine-tins scattered over the wide world], and [the bird in the bird-cage sobbing pitifully] and [calling to be let out].

[The Rat came to help him], but [their united efforts were not sufficient [to right the cart]]. '[Hi! Toad]!' [they cried]. '[Come and bear a hand, [can't you]]!'

[The Toad never answered a word], or [budged from his seat in the road]; so [they went to see [what was the matter with him]]. [They found him in a sort of trance], [a happy smile on his face], [his eyes still fixed on the dusty wake of their destroyer]]. [At intervals he was still heard to murmur] '[Poop-poop]!'

I3.5.2 *Linear analysis*

Another way of diagramming the structure of clauses and sentences is to set out the clauses line by line. An example follows, which shows the structure of the simplified and original texts from *The Wind in the Willows* that were used in earlier chapters.

Simplified version

ccj/scj	marked theme	S	P	C	A
		[They	had	another good day	outside].
But	[on the second evening	Mole and Rat	made *Toad* help	them].	
		[He	didn't like helping		very much].
	[The next day	they	were walking	along a quiet road].	
		[Mole	was leading	the horse	
while		[Rat and Toad	walked	behind the caravan]].	
		[Toad	was talking	a lot].	
	[Suddenly,				
	in front of them	there	was	a cloud of dust].	
		[It	was coming	towards them	very fast].
		[There	was	a lot of noise,	too].
	['Poop, poop!']				
	[The next minute	the cloud and the noise	were	on top of the animals].	
		[They	couldn't see		in the dust]
and		[they	couldn't think		because of the noise].
		[They	tried to jump	out of the way],	
but		[they	couldn't].		
	[In a minute]	the thing	had passed	them].	
	[Slowly	the dust	went away]		
and		[the three animals]	could see	each other	again].
		[[The poor old horse	was	very frightened],	
and		[Mole	had	great difficulty*	
			[*holding	him]].	
		[The caravan	was	on its side	in the road].
		[The windows and two of the wheels	were	broken].	
	[What a sad sight	it	made]!		

Original version

ccj/scj	market theme	S	P	C	A
		[They	had	a pleasant ramble	that day
					over grassy downs and along narrow by-lanes],
and		[Ø	camped,		
as					before, on a common],
	[only this time	the two guests	took	care*	
that*		[Toad	should do	his fair share of work]].	
	[In consequence,				
when		[the time	came for starting		next morning],
		Toad	was	by no means so rapturous	
				about the simplicity of the primitive life],	
and	[indeed	Ø	attempted to resume	his place in his bunk*,	
	*whence	he	was hauled		by force]].
		[Their way	lay,	...across country	...as before, ...
				by narrow lanes,	
	and	[it*	was not	till the afternoon	
*that		[they	came out	on the high road,	
				their first high road]];	
and	[there	disaster,		[fleet and unforeseen],	
			sprang out	on them] –	
		[disaster		momentous indeed to their expedition],	
but	[simply			overwhelming in its effect	
				on the after-career of Toad].	
		[They	were strolling	along the high road	easily,
		[the Mole		by the horse's head,	
			talking	to him,	
since		[the horse	had complained	*	
*that		[he	was being *frightfully*		
			left out	of it],	
and		[nobody	considered	him	in the least]]];
		[the Toad and the Water Rat	walking	behind the cart]	
		[Ø	talking	together] –	
	[at least	Toad	was talking],		
and		[Rat	was saying		at intervals],
	['Yes, precisely]];				
and	[what did	you	say	to him?' –	
and		[Ø	thinking	...of something very different]	...all the time...
when	[from behind them	they	heard	a faint warning hum,	like the drone of a distant bee]],

Original version – continued

ccj/scj	market theme	S	P	C	A
			[[Glancing	back],	
		they	saw	*	
		*[a small cloud of dust,			
		with a dark centre			
		of energy	advancing	on them	at incredible speed]]
while	[from out the dust	a faint 'Poop-poop!'	wailed		like an uneasy animal in pain]
	[[Hardly		regarding	it],	
		they	turned to resume	their conversation,	
when	[in an instant				
[as		it	seemed]		
		the peaceful scene	was changed],		
and	[with a blast of wind and a whirl of sound*	[*that	made them jump	for the nearest ditch],	
		it	was	on them]]!	
		[The 'poop-poop'	rang	with a brazen shout	in their ears],
		[they	had	a moment's glimpse of an interior of glittering plate-glass and rich morocco]	
and		[the magnificent motor-car,	*	[immense, breath-snatching, passionate],	
with		[its pilot		tense]	
and		[Ø	hugging	his wheel],	
			possessed	all earth and air	for the fraction of a second],
		[*	flung	an enveloping cloud of dust**	
		[**that	blinded]		
and		[Ø	enwrapped	them	utterly]],
and	then	[Ø	dwindled	to a speck	in the far distance,]
		[The old grey horse,			
			[dreaming,	...of his quiet paddock],	
...as		[he	plodded along],...		
	in a new raw situation				
	such as this		*simply* abandoned	himself to his natural emotions].	
			[[Rearing,]		
			[plunging],		

Original version – continued

ccj/scj	market theme	S	P	C	A
			[backing		steadily,
					in spite of all the Mole's efforts at his head, and all the Mole's lively language*
			[*directed	at his better feelings]],	
		he	drove	the cart backwards	towards the deep ditch at the side of the road].
		[It	wavered		an instant] –
	[then	there	was	a heart-rending crash] –	
and		[the canary-coloured cart			
		their pride and their joy,	lay	on its side	in the ditch,
				an irredeemable wreck].	

14. The grammar of texts and speech

This final chapter introduces no new concepts, but aims to demonstrate how our understanding of vocabulary and grammar can be used in our reading of different kinds of speech and writing.

14.1   The sentence in written English

You may have been surprised to read in chapter 13 that a sentence might be understood as a unit of style rather than of grammar. The following text shows how one kind of modern advertising has produced a distinctive tone of voice by breaking the conventions of punctuating sentences and paragraphing texts.

Activity 14.1

(i)   Which features of the punctuation and paragraphing of this advertisement would almost certainly be marked wrong in a school or college essay?

(ii)   Rewrite the advertisement using the normal conventions of punctuation and paragraphing. You may want to change or omit some words, but keep to the original wording as exactly as you can.

(iii) Discuss any problems or alternatives.

(The paragraphs are numbered.)

> **Take advantage of us while you can.**
> **Don't worry. We hope to get a bit back later.**

1   It's a kind of 'you scratch my back...' arrangement. The Government is helping smaller businesses grow more prosperous.

2   Because prosperous businesses help the country grow more wealthy.

3   So, if you run your own business, or are tempted to start one, take all the incentives you can get.

4   And there are plenty. Many more than most people realise.

5   You may well get special tax reliefs, for example.

6   And did you know that you could get a loan up to £75,000 guaranteed by the Government?

7   Or that you can get the services of a technical or production advisor, free, for five days?

8   You can get introductions to new export markets.

9   Or help in finding premises.

10   Or you might get a grant to develop new products.

11   In the last few years 86 special schemes have been introduced to help growing businesses grow bigger.

12   Some of them might make all the difference to you.

13   To find out which, send the coupon and get our new comprehensive guide 'How to make your business grow.'

14   Or dial 100 and ask for Freefone Enterprise.

15   The sooner the better — for all of us.

(Guardian, April 1983)

Commentary

Here is one version of a conventional rewriting:

It's a kind of 'you scratch my back...' arrangement. The Government is helping smaller businesses grow more prosperous, because prosperous businesses help the country grow more wealthy, so if you run your own business or are tempted to start one, take all the incentives you can get.

And there are plenty, many more than most people realise. You may well get special tax reliefs, for example, and did you know that you could get a loan up to £75,000 guaranteed by the Government, or that you can get the services of a technical or production advisor, free, for five days? You can get introductions to new export markets or help in finding premises, or you might get a grant to develop new products.

In the last few years 86 special schemes have been introduced to help growing businesses grow bigger. Some of them might make all the difference to you. To find out which, send the coupon and get our new comprehensive guide 'How to make your business grow', or dial 100 and ask for Freefone Enterprise. The sooner the better – for all of us.

Notice the discrepancy between the fifteen paragraphs and seventeen sentences of the original text and the three paragraphs and eight sentences of the rewritten version. Here is the conventionally punctuated text printed sentence by sentence, with the clause structures marked:

1 [It's a kind of 'you scratch my back...' arrangement.]
   simple sentence
   [MCl]

2 [The Government is helping smaller businesses grow more prosperous [because prosperous businesses help the country grow more wealthy], so [⟨[if you run your own business] or [are tempted to start one]⟩, take all the incentives [you can get]].
   compound-complex sentence
   [MCl [because-AdvCl] so [⟨[if-AdvCl] or [(if)-AdvCl]⟩ MCl[RelCl]]]

3 And [there are plenty, many more [than most people realise].
   complex sentence
   And [MCl than [CompCl]]

4 ⟨[You may well get special tax reliefs, for example], and ⟨[did you know ⟨[that you could get a loan up to £75,000 [guaranteed by the Government]], or [that you can get the services of a technical or production advisor, free, for five days]⟩]⟩?
   compound-complex sentence
   [MCl] and [MCl ⟨that [-NCl] or that [NCl]⟩]

5 [You can get ⟨introductions to new export markets or help in [finding premises]⟩], or [you might get a grant [to develop new products]]⟩.
   compound-complex sentence
   [MCl] or [MCl [NonfCl]]

6 [In the last few years 86 special schemes have been introduced [to help growing businesses grow bigger]].
   complex sentence
   [MCl [NonfCl]]

7 [Some of them might make all the difference to you].
   simple sentence
   [MCl]

8 [To find out which], ⟨⟨[send the coupon] and [get our new comprehensive guide 'How to make your business grow.']⟩, or ⟨[dial 100] and [ask for Freefone Enterprise]⟩⟩.
   compound-complex sentence
   [[NonfCl] ⟨⟨[MCl] and [MCl]. or ⟨[MCl] and [MCl]⟩⟩

9 [The sooner the better – for all of us].
   minor sentence, no predicator
   [verbless Cl] (idiom)

The normal conventions of punctuation and paragraphing are broken throughout the original text, in order to produce a particular effect on the readers of the advertisement.

Activity 14.2

What effect on you as reader do the two versions of the advertisement have?

Commentary

Some of the sentences of the text correspond to the *tone-units of spoken English.* Tone-units are units of **information** in speech, and each one is marked by **stress** and a movement of **pitch** on the accented syllable of a particular word – usually the one in the phrase which contains *new* information. This syllable is called the **tonic syllable.**

The tone-unit will sometimes correspond to the grammatical clause, and sometimes to only part of a clause, or to a single word. Sometimes the tone-unit will include more than one clause. It all depends on what we say and how we say it.

If the advertisement text is written down in a transcription of the way it might be spoken, you will see that the tone-units (marked by ||) each contain one or two words marked with tonic stress (in bold type). Pitch movement is not marked in this transcription, but you should read the text aloud and work out the appropriate intonation and pitch movement to match the meanings. There are, for example, several questions, which are marked by a rising pitch on the tonic syllable and on any syllables which follow it in the tone-unit. Here is a possible reading, with the clause-complexes numbered:

1. |it's a kind of **you** scratch **my** back arrangement|
2. |the Government is helping smaller businesses grow more **prosperous** | because **prosperous** businesses help the country grow more **wealthy**|
3. |**so** | if you run your **own** business|or are tempted to **start** one | take **all** the incentives you can **get**|
4. |and there are **plenty** | many more than most people **realise**|
5. |you may well get special **tax** reliefs for example | and did you know that you could get a loan up to £75,000 **guaranteed** by the **Government** | or that you can get the services of a **technical** or **production** advisor | **free** | for **five** days|
6. |you can get introductions to new **export markets** | or help in finding **premises** | or you **might** get a grant to develop new products|
7. |in the last few **years** | 86 special schemes have been introduced to help growing businesses grow **bigger**|
8. |some of them might make **all** the difference to **you**|
9. |to find out **which** | send the **coupon** | and get our new comprehensive guide | How to make your business **grow** | or dial **100** | and ask for Freefone **Enterprise**|
10. |the sooner the **better** | for **all** of us|

This is only one possible reading of the text as spoken English, but it attempts to match the sense of the advertisement, which is trying to persuade and convince and obtain a response. Notice the partial correspondence between the sentences of the original text and the tone-units of the spoken transcription.

The purpose of the unusual punctuation in the advertisement is therefore to make a reader hear the sound of *spoken* English. Pauses are suggested by commas and dashes within sentences. Capital letters and full stops mark as sentences some constituents which are only part of a clause – minor sentences.

Activity 14.3

(i) Discuss how far the punctuation of the advertisement corresponds to the tone-units in the transcription.

(ii) Contrast the effect on a reader of the two differently punctuated versions

(iii) Read the advertisement aloud and make an alternative transcription, commenting on the effect of using different pitch movement and stress placements.

(iv) Identify the mood of the main clauses as declarative, interrogate or imperative, and relate what you find to the intended persuasive power of the text.

Activity 14.4

Does the following advertisement show similar features to the one just discussed?

A body-coloured spoiler and door mirrors. Sprauncy wheels with low-profile tyres. Racy metallic paint in Flambeau Red or Bahama Blue.

Clearly, from the outside, the new Escort Encore is no middle-of-the-road car.

And from the inside?

Open the central locking doors, settle into the Astral velour seats and adjust the steering column.

Switch on the self-seek radio/cassette and cast an eye over the fascia with its tachometer.

Note, too, the tilt or slide sunroof and thoughtful touches like the height-adjustable driver's seat and seat-back stowage nets on the front seats.

Finally, take comfort from the Escort's roomy interior and exceptionally smooth ride.

Your dealer will be happy to show you the new Encore. A shapely car with, as you can see, a most attractive figure.

(*Daily Mirror*, 6 June 1991, p. 29)

14.2   The clause-complex in spoken English

14.2.1   *The grammar of narrative speech*

The term *clause-complex* has already been introduced as a useful alternative to *sentence* when describing the grammatical structure of speech, in which there can be neither capital letters nor full stops to mark the beginning and end of sentences (section 13.1). Features of pronunciation like stress, pause, pitch change, loudness and length of syllable, all contribute to the punctuation and meaning of speech, but there is no one-to-one relationship between features of speech and written punctuation. The expressive resources of speech are far greater than those of writing.

Spoken English can also be just as complex in its structure as written English, but the complexity is of a different kind. We tend to string our clauses together in ways which would look very odd if written down. This is especially so in telling stories, when clauses tend to follow each other either without any linker, or linked by *and*. The linguistic term for the linking of a series of main clauses, with few or no subordinate clauses, is **parataxis**. The clauses are in a **paratactic** sequence.

14.2.1.1   TELEVISION INTERVIEW

Here is a plain transcript of the words in an extract of narrative speech taken from a TV political interview. The transcription marks pauses (.), but omits features like hesitations and fillers:

> well (.) we made several efforts to restore collective responsibility and indeed you'll remember that on the Thursday afternoon (.) after Cabinet on December 19th I reasserted it once again (.) but somehow because of this other emotional thing (.) it was extremely difficult (.) and then as you know we went into recess and had a very very difficult time (.) and we had to restore collective responsibility on January 9th then (.) not merely as a principle but say look (.) all right (.) we agree the principle (.) but it's how it's applied that matters (.) and because it's very sensitive (.) because Westland is near to making a decision (.) we really must keep out and that unfortunately was when he resigned

You can make sense of this quite easily, without any punctuation, but it would not pass as an acceptable piece of writing. The conjunctions *and* or *but* are regularly used to link the clauses. The paratactic structure can be seen more clearly if we set it out with one clause on each line:

well		we made several efforts to restore collective responsibility
and	**indeed**	you'll remember that on the Thursday afternoon after Cabinet on December 19th I reasserted it once again
but	**somehow**	because of this other emotional thing it was extremely difficult
and	**then**	as you know we went into recess

299

and		Ø had a very very difficult time
and		we had to restore collective responsibility on January 9th then
not		merely as a principle
but		say look all right
		we agree the principle
but		it's how it's applied that matters
and	**because**	it's very sensitive
	because	Westland is near to making a decision we really must keep out
and		that unfortunately was when he resigned

How many *sentences* are there, and where would you put the capitals and full stops if it were unchanged as a piece of writing?

Activity 14.5 _____

(i) Write the transcript in a form which would be acceptable for publication in a magazine or newspaper.

(ii) Describe the differences between the written version and the original, and discuss why you had to make the changes.

In describing spoken English the identification of *sentences* is a problem, though *clauses* are quite easy to separate off. This is why the term *clause-complex* rather than *sentence* is useful to refer to groups of linked clauses in speech that function like sentences in writing.

The same language system and vocabulary of English are used to encode our meanings in speech and writing, but the medium of speech is so different from that of writing that there are differences in the way we use grammar and vocabulary in both media. Speech and writing influence each other. We say that someone 'talks like a book', or 'speaks prose' when they sound as if they were reading from a written text. In informal letters we often try to convey the sound of our voice, using CAPITAL LETTERS or <u>underlining</u> to stress words, adding exclamation marks!!!! and using informal vocabulary and slang, which are associated with spoken rather than written English.

14.2.1.2 FIVE-YEAR-OLD'S NARRATIVE
The following transcription of a five-year-old girl's speech, a fragment of which you have seen in section 2.8, will show some of the typical grammatical features of speech when we are telling a story in conversation. The transcription is set out in tone-units, grouped into clause-complexes (1–12), or spoken 'sentences', according to the girl's use of pitch and pause to indicate the likely boundaries. The narrative is continuous, and shows typical abrupt switches from one topic to another:

1	**if**	I switch my blanket off
		there's got a switch
	and	you switch it up

	and	the light comes on
		an orange light comes on
2	and if	you switch it off the light goes off
3	but if	it broke
		we could take it back
	and	then he'll mend it
4	and if	it's coming near night
		he'll give me a new one
5	when	he came home from work
		he give me a new one
	and	he shoved it up his anorak
6		sometimes he always does that
	if	he's got a load of stuff in his motorbike
	but	one day
	when	he was going for Grandma to go to Uncle Ronnie's
		he went in the car
	and	picked [*unfinished*]
7		he went to work last morning
	and	then **when** he was coming home
		he went for Grandma
8		then he came back to my house
	and	my Mummy said
	when	I was playing out
		she said don't be long
	but	I was long
9		she told me
	and	I cried
	and	I washed my hands
	and	then I gobbled my dinner up
	and	then my Dad came home with blue Grandma
	and	blue Grandad
10	and	then **when** my Daddy and Mummy had got ready
		we watched soccer
	and	then we went to Uncle Ronnie's
11		Jane's got a little blue doll
	but	they're decorating Paul's big bedroom
	and so	Paul has to sleep with Jane
	and	then we hide
	and	sometimes he creeps upstairs
12	but	Alan can walk
		my little brother

Commentary

The most obvious grammatical feature in the sequence of clauses is the constant repetition of *and* or *but* to link one series of clauses to another within a clause-complex. This is not only typical of young children, but of adults also, when narrating their experiences (see the TV interview and the narrative texts in activity 14.6 following). The conjunction is not only a necessary linker in the grammar, but is used for other *discourse* purposes.

For example, if you have to pause, but want to keep your turn in the conversation, a long-held *and* or *and then* will effectively do the job. When *and* begins a clause-complex, it can be regarded as the spoken equivalent of the *full stop + capital letter* combination marking sentence boundaries in writing, but you can see that it is used extensively within clause-complexes, simply to link one clause to another, where in writing we would have to choose whether to use a comma, a full stop or simply not to use a conjunction at all.

The transcription could be turned into a written text by adding punctuation marks, and omitting certain spoken linkers. Any edited version of this kind, of course, ceases to be the child's narrative, but demonstrates some interesting facts about her use of the grammar and vocabulary of English as far as she has learned them.

For example, the following version of the beginning of her narrative is punctuated to produce written sentences. There is a temptation to 'improve' her language, and to turn the non-standard features into StE, but this should be resisted, except for editing out her own self-corrections. Here is a version of the transcription set as activity 2.5 in chapter 2:

> If I switch my blanket off, there's got a switch. You switch it up and an orange light comes on. If you switch it off, the light goes off. But if it broke, we could take it back and then he'll mend it. If it's coming near night, he'll give me a new one.

And so on. Already, choices have been made which alter the sense of flow in the spoken version. Sentences 4 and 5 might just as easily have been written as one compound-complex sentence:

> But if it broke, we could take it back and then he'll mend it, and if it's coming near night he'll give me a new one.

If one version of a sentence will do as well as another, or if, rather, the differences are not grammatical but *stylistic*, then the use of a different identifying term for the highest grammatical unit in spoken English is justified. The word *clause-complex*, already mentioned several times, and implying a more loosely linked series of paratactic clauses, unified in meaning by relevance to the topic, may help to avoid the problem of using the word *sentence* when referring to the structure of speech.

Activity 14.6

(i) Rewrite the rest of the child's narrative as a written text in sentences, omitting only those words which belong to spoken English grammar.

(ii) Comment on the nonstandard features of her grammar and vocabulary, and on anything of interest which shows the narrative to be that of a young child, who is also a dialect speaker.

(iii) Make an analysis of the sentence structure of your version, in terms of main, subordinate, and coordinated clauses.

14.2.1.3 ADULT NARRATIVE

Activity 14.7

The following transcription is of part of a conversation in which a young woman is talking about a past boyfriend. Short breaks in the speech are marked (.).

(i) Write a version of the transcription using normal written punctuation. The text includes normal non-fluency features of speech such as hesitations, fillers and repetitions, which you must edit out.

(ii) Discuss the problems encountered in the activity, and the differences between spoken and written English grammar which the text illustrates.

and (.) I I was sort of on the verge of er (.) breaking up with him and I'd sort of (.) started going out with Aubrey really and er (.) was trying to drop Martin cos he was a complete loony anyway (.) he really was crazy (.) and very boring as well and (.) anyway I mu. I must have been mad to suggest it but (.) Ian needed somewhere to stay and I said why don't you go and (.) and see if Martin will let you stay cos you've met him (.) so this evening at the poetry reading I hadn't spoken to Martin all evening (.) erm I'd spent the whole evening chatting to Neil and (.) and left Ian to chat Martin up and I'd been thoroughly mean to him all evening and I think he th. he'd realized then that it was sort of over and (.) em I think that was about (.) it was almost the last (.) well (.) it was the last time we ever really went out together

(original transcription in J. Svartvik & R. Quirk (eds), *A Corpus of Conversational English*, 1980)

14.2.2 *Speech in fiction*

The following extract from Charles Dickens's *Dombey and Son* (ch. XLIV) shows a novelist using the punctuation of a written text to produce the effect of a fast speaker, Susan Nipper, who 'made use of none but comma pauses; shooting out whatever she had to say in one sentence, and in one breath, if possible'. Elsewhere he refers to Susan as 'destitute of punctuation'. She is talking to Mr Dombey about his daughter Florence (Miss Floy):

'There never was a dearer or a blesseder young lady than is my young lady, sir,' said Susan, 'and I ought to know a great deal better than some for I have seen her in her grief and I have seen her in her joy (there's not been much of it) and I have seen her with her brother and I have seen her in her loneliness and some have never seen her, and I say to some and all – I do!' and here the black-eyed shook her head, and slightly stamped her foot; that she's the blessedest and dearest angel is Miss Floy that ever drew the breath of life, the more that I was torn to pieces sir the more I'd say it though I may not be a Fox's Martyr.'

Activity 14.8

(i) Rewrite this extract in the form of a letter that Susan Nipper might have written.

(ii) Discuss the reasons for the changes you have made to the text.

In contrast, the talk of a character called Joseph Bagnet, an old soldier, in Dickens's *Bleak House* is punctuated quite differently:

(*Mr Bagnet and his children are cooking the dinner as a treat for Mrs Bagnet on her birthday.*)

'At half-after one.' Says Mr Bagnet. 'To the minute. They'll be done. You shall have a dinner, old girl. Fit for a queen. George will look us up. At half-after four. To the moment. How many years, old girl. Has George looked us up. This afternoon?' . . .

'George will never desert. And leave his old comrade. In the lurch. Don't be afraid of it.' . . .

Activity 14.9

(i) Rewrite Mr Bagnet's talk in conventional punctuation.

(ii) Discuss the purpose and effect of Dickens's punctuation.

The use of minor sentences is not confined to the speech of characters to convey the sound of their speech, but sometimes occurs in narrative text to indicate the writer's 'tone of voice':

This reply is cut short by Mr Tulkinghorn's arrival. There is no change in him, of course. Rustily dressed, with his spectacles in his hand, and their very case worn threadbare. In manner, close and dry. In voice, husky and low. In face, watchful behind a blind; habitually not uncensorious and contemptuous perhaps.

(*Bleak House*, ch. XXVII)

Conversely, absence of conventional punctuation can be exploited by writers. The following text is only part of a long sentence which extends for twenty-eight lines, taken from the American novelist William Faulkner's story *The Bear*:

'You're damn right I aint,' the boy said, his voice quiet too, cold with rage which was not at Boon, remembering: Boon snoring in a hard chair in the kitchen so he could watch the clock and wake him and McCaslin and drive them the seventeen miles in to Jefferson to catch the train to Memphis; the wild, never-bridled Texas paint pony which he had persuaded McCaslin to let him buy and which he and Boon had bought at auction for four dollars and seventyfive cents and fetched home wired between two gentle old mares with pieces of barbed wire and which had never even seen shelled corn before and didn't even know what it was...

The text represents what the boy is remembering, and so is a form of **interior monologue**, or **stream of consciousness**, indicated by the flow of memory uninterrupted by stops.

14.3   Grammar and style in texts

The usefulness of a grammatical analysis depends upon the purposes of study, but it forms an important part of the study of style which is called **stylistics**. The remainder of this chapter will demonstrate how the analysis of clause and sentence structure helps us towards a more perceptive appreciation of style.

14.3.1   *Text analysis I* – Portrait of the Artist as a Young Man

James Joyce's *Portrait of the Artist as a Young Man* tells the story of the childhood and young manhood of Stephen Dedalus (based upon Joyce's own life). In this extract, Stephen is a small boy at boarding-school:

> The bell rang for night prayers and he filed out of the study hall after the others and down the staircase and along the corridors to the chapel. The corridors were darkly lit and the chapel was darkly lit. Soon all would be dark and sleeping. There was a cold night air in the chapel and the marbles were the colour the sea is at night. The sea was cold day and night: but it was colder at night. It was cold and dark under the seawall beside his father's house. But the kettle would be on the hob to make punch.
> There was a cold night smell in the chapel. But it was a holy smell. It was not like the smell of the old peasants who knelt at the back of the chapel at Sunday mass. That was a smell of rain and turf and corduroy. But they were very holy peasants. They breathed behind him on his neck and sighed as they prayed. They lived at Clane, a fellow said: there were little cottages there and he had seen a woman standing at the half-door of a cottage with a child in her arms as the cars had come past from Sallins. It would be lovely to sleep for one night in that cottage before the fire of smoking turf, in the dark lit by the fire, in the warm dark, breathing the smell of the peasants, air and rain and turf and corduroy. But O, the road there between the trees was dark! You would be lost in the dark. It made him afraid to think of how it was.

The narrative is told from a small boy's innocent point of view, and is a kind of **interior monologue**. Joyce changes the style of the writing as the book progresses, so that the language of each section matches Stephen's age in his development from infancy to manhood. How does the grammatical structure (as far as we can separate it from the narrative story and the vocabulary) help to create the impression of a small boy's thoughts as he is going to bed at boarding-school?

The text can be rewritten to show its sentence structure more clearly, bracketing the clauses and highlighting the conjunctions:

1 [The bell rang for night prayers] **and** [he filed ⟨out of the study hall after the others **and** down the staircase **and** along the corridors⟩ to the chapel].
2 [The corridors were darkly lit] **and** [the chapel was darkly lit].
3 [Soon all would be dark and sleeping].
4 [There was a cold night air in the chapel] **and** [the marbles were the colour Ø [the sea is at night]].
5 [The sea was cold ⟨day and night\rangle]: **but** [it was colder at night].
6 ⟨[It was ⟨cold and dark⟩ under the seawall beside his father's house].
7 **But** [the kettle would be on the hob [to make punch]]⟩.
8 ⟨[There was a cold night smell in the chapel].
9 **But** [it was a holy smell]⟩.
10 [It was not like the smell of the old peasants [who knelt at the back of the chapel at Sunday mass]].
11 ⟨[That was a smell of ⟨rain **and** turf **and** corduroy⟩].
12 **But** [they were very holy peasants]⟩.
13 [They breathed behind him on his neck] **and** [Ø sighed **as** they prayed].
14 [[They lived at Clane], a fellow said]:[there were little cottages there] **and** [he had seen [a woman standing at the half-door of a cottage with a child in her arms] [**as** the cars had come past from Sallins]].
15 ⟨[It would be lovely [to sleep for one night in that cottage ⟨before the fire of smoking turf, in the dark [lit by the fire], in the warm dark, [breathing the smell of the peasants, ⟨air **and** rain **and** turf **and** corduroy⟩⟩]].
16 **But** O, [the road there between the trees was dark]⟩!
17 [You would be lost in the dark].
18 [It made him afraid [to think [of how it was]]].

The grammatical structure of the sentences is relatively simple. There are few complex sentences in sentences 1–13, the only subordinate clauses being:

Ø the sea is at night (*RelCl*)
to make punch (*NonfCl*)
who knelt at the back of the chapel at Sunday mass (*RelCl*)
as they prayed (*AdvCl*)

and the clauses are either simple sentences, or coordinated with *and* or *but* into short compound sentences. Only sentences 14 and 15 are more complex. We get a strong impression of the boy's feelings as he moves from the hall to the chapel, with special emphasis on *dark* and *cold*. Notice the association of ideas – *cold night air, marbles the colour of the sea – the cold sea – the cold night – the seawall at home – the kettle on the hob at home*. This is in the boy's imagination, one thought leading to another.

The cold night *air* then becomes the cold night *smell* – the holy smell of the chapel – which contrasts in his mind with the smell of the peasants. And so on. The simple grammatical structure underpins the repetitive sequence of sights, smells and memories, in the simple vocabulary of a small boy.

Sentence 14, after its initial reported–reporting clause sequence:

NCl   **MCl**
[[They lived at Clane], a fellow said]:

consists of Stephen's memory of what he had once seen:

MCl   *ccj*   *MCl*   *q = NonfCl*
[there were little cottages there] and [he had seen a woman [standing at the

                       A = AdvCl
half-door of a cottage with a child in her arms [as the cars had come past
from Sallins]]].

immediately followed by his 'stream of consciousness' – the thoughts that pass
through his mind, as a result of what he remembers having seen, turned into
words – using the modal phrase *would be lovely* to express his feelings of longing.

MCl   *NCl = extraposed S*
[It would be lovely [to sleep for one night in that cottage ⟨before the fire of

        NonfCl   *NonfCl*
smoking turf, in the dark [lit by the fire], in the warm dark, [breathing the
smell of the peasants, ⟨air and rain and turf and corduroy⟩⟩]].

The principal grammatical features which contribute to the sense that we are
overhearing the boy's imagined thoughts are the phrase-complex *before the fire of
smoking turf, in the dark lit by the fire* and the word-complex *air and rain and turf
and corduroy*. Both are sequences of sense impressions following the verbs *to sleep*
and *breathing*. The longer sentences 14 and 15 mark the unbroken flow of the
boy's thoughts.

This sentence is followed by:

    MCl   *MCl*
But O, [the road there between the trees was dark]! [You would be lost in the

    MCl   *NCl*   *PrepCl = Ca*
                  S extraposed
dark]. [It made him afraid [to think [of how it was]]].

two shorter sentences expressing his fears before the final summing-up. There are
only two finite subordinate clauses in the whole of this extract, both with *as*, and
so expressing a simple time sequence matching the style of the whole passage.

Activity 14.10

(i) Make a grammatical analysis of the sentence structure of the following short
extracts taken from other parts of the same novel, and of any features of the
clause or phrase structure which are prominent.

(ii) Discuss the contribution played by (a) the grammar (b) the vocabulary and (c) the
story, in informing you what age Stephen probably is in each extract.

1

Once upon a time and a very good time it was there was a moocow coming down along the road and this moocow that was coming down along the road met a nicens little boy named baby tuckoo...

His father told him that story: his father looked at him through a glass: he had a hairy face.

He was baby tuckoo.

2

He was caught in the whirl of a scrimmage and, fearful of the flashing eyes and muddy boots, bent down to look through the legs. The fellows were struggling and groaning and their legs were rubbing and kicking and stamping. He ran after them a little way and then stopped. It was useless to run on. Soon they would be going home for the holidays. After supper in the study hall he would change the number pasted up inside his desk from seventy-seven to seventy-six.

3

When evening had fallen he left the house, and the first touch of the damp dark air and the noise of the door as it closed behind him made ache again his conscience, lulled by prayer and tears. Confess! Confess! It was not enough to lull the conscience with a tear and a prayer. He had to kneel before the minister of the Holy Ghost and tell over his hidden sins truly and repentantly. Before he heard again the footboard of the housedoor trail over the threshold as it opened to let him in, before he saw again the table in the kitchen set for supper he would have knelt and confessed. It was quite simple.

14.3.2   Text analysis 2 – news reporting

In *The ABC of Reading* (1961) the American poet Ezra Pound defines literature as 'news that stays news'. Newspaper reporting is, presumably, news that does NOT stay news, and although of no interest to a literary critic, well worth the attention of students of language.

News reporting is controversial when the interpretation of an incident differs from one newspaper to another. A grammatical and lexical analysis of conflicting reports is helpful in confirming opposing points of view which we can discern from a first reading.

Activity 14.11

(i)   Read the following texts, consisting of the headlines and reports from three newspapers. They are describing an incident that took place in February 1984.

(ii)   Discuss your impressions after one or two readings. Are there any significant differences in the way the event was reported?

Report A

MacGregor scraps pit visit in face of angry demo

COAL BOARD boss Ian MacGregor was forced to abandon a pit visit in Northumberland yesterday when 600 angry miners held him hostage for nearly four hours in a colliery office.

When he eventually emerged from the manager's office he was greeted by eggs and slices of bread being thrown at him by the miners protesting at impending pit closures.

In the ensuing melee the 72 year-old NCB chairman was forced against a fence by the police holding back the demonstrators. The fence collapsed and Mr MacGregor fell to the ground, where he lay dazed.

Police and reporters had to help Mr MacGregor toward a waiting car. Earlier, the tyres of the car that had brought him to the pit were let down by protesting miners.

Report B

NCB chief fit after incident at pit

The chairman of the National Coal Board, Mr Ian MacGregor, said last night that he was fit and well after being knocked to the ground earlier in the day by protesting pitmen.

As he attempted to leave one of Britain's most profitable pits, Ellington colliery, in Northumberland – under siege by pickets for more than 12 hours – he faced 600 demonstrators calling for an end to pit closures.

The men, from one of the country's traditionally moderate coalfields, had been demanding an opportunity to put their case to Mr MacGregor, who arrived at the colliery early in the morning through a side entrance to avoid the demonstrators.

After being trapped for four hours inside the main administrative building, Mr MacGregor, who is 72, was forced to abandon a plan to go underground to inspect working six miles out in the north seam. Police arrived to clear a path so that he could try to reach a car park 20 yards from the building. The tyres of his car had been let down, and another vehicle was provided.

Report C

OUT COLD!

Big Mac felled in demo at pit

COAL BOSS IS FLOORED BY PIT MOB

COAL chief Ian MacGregor, 71, was flattened yesterday by a mob of rampaging miners.

Six hundred pitmen smashed through a police cordon as Mr MacGregor left colliery offices where he had been besieged for three hours.

One protester grabbed him by the throat and sent him crashing through a wooden fence.

Several burly policemen were hurled on top of grey-haired Mr MacGregor as the howling horde poured forward.

14.3.2.1 CHOICES OF VOCABULARY (i) – CLASSIFYING THE ACTORS

When journalists report an item of news, they must name the participants. How they name them will sometimes indicate an attitude towards the participants. How we identify or **classify** actors in a report is called **classification**. It is expressed grammatically through the NPs which function as subjects or objects.

An example from the reports we are studying is the classification of the miners as *demonstrators* in reports A and B, but as *howling horde* in C. *Demonstrators* are acting legally by protesting in public, but the word *horde* has connotations of uncontrolled violence, like *mob*, and *howling* is usually associated with animals like wolves. So report Cs classification of the miners is both emotive and biased against them, whereas a phrase like *protesting miners* is probably interpreted as either neutral or in favour of the miners.

The important point to remember is that we cannot avoid giving away our attitude towards participants when using language to talk about them, especially during events like the 1984–5 dispute between the National Coal Board (as it then was) and the National Union of Miners, in which public opinion was divided and strong emotions involved.

Activity 14.12

Discuss the words and phrases in the following lists, used to classify (a) the miners, (b) Mr MacGregor and (c) the police in the three reports. What attitudes — favourable, unfavourable, neutral — are suggested by the different classifications?

Miners

A	B	C
angry demo	protesters	pit mob
miners	protesting pitmen	a mob of rampaging miners
600 angry miners	pickets	six hundred pitmen
demonstrators	600 demonstrators	one protester
protesting miners	men/one man	howling horde
	demonstrators	

Mr MacGregor

A	B	C
Mr MacGregor (2)	NCB chief	Big Mac
MacGregor	chairman of the National Coal	coal boss
Coal Board boss Ian MacGregor	Board, Mr Ian MacGregor	coal chief Ian MacGregor, 71
72-year-old NCB chairman	Mr MacGregor	Mr MacGregor
	Mr MacGregor, who is 72	grey-haired Mr MacGregor

Police

A	B	C
police (2)	police	a police cordon
		several burly policemen

14.3.2.2 CHOICES OF VOCABULARY (ii) – CLASSIFYING THE PROCESSES (WHO DID WHAT TO WHOM?)

As well as naming actors and affected persons, we must also identify the *processes* which are taking place. In an incident which involves violence, the important processes are likely to be **actional**, in which an actor does something which affects another person. How we classify the processes is as important as how we classify the participants, and may equally well give away our attitude.

Actional processes are primarily represented in the VPs of the predicators of clauses, as in *push* or *carry*, but may also be nouns, like *mêlée*, or typically in participial modifiers like *surging* in the NP *surging mob*. So we need to examine a text carefully in finding the processes which are said to have taken place in an incident, and not simply list the verbs. The *actor–process–affected* relationship may not be always expressed in a *SPO* clause, and we have to 'deconstruct' the grammatical structure to identify the underlying relationships accurately.

Activity 14.13 _____

Examine the following deconstruction of the *actor–process–affected* relationships in the three reports, and comment on any differences of interpretation of the incident which are shown. Notice that sometimes the actor has to be inferred, e.g. *After being trapped* in report B does not state the actors in an agentive phrase, *by X*.

What the *miners* did

A		B	
actional process	*affected person*	*actional process*	*affected person*
force	MacG abandon visit	knock to ground	MacGregor
hold hostage	MacGregor	besiege	colliery
greet	MacGregor	call for	MacG not close pits
throw eggs & bread at	MacGregor	demand to put case to	MacGregor
protest at	MacGregor close pits	trap	MacG inside building
let down	MacGregor's car tyres	force to abandon plan	MacG inspect working
		let down	car tyres

C	
actional process	*affected person*
fell	Big Mac
floor	coal boss
rampage (*mob*)	–
flatten	MacGregor
smash through	police cordon
besiege	MacGregor
grab by throat	MacGregor
send crashing	MacGregor
hurl on top of MacG	burly policemen
howl (*horde*)	–
pour forward	–

What *Mr MacGregor* did

A		B	
actional process	*affected person*	*actional process*	*affected person*
scrap pit visit	–	is fit	
emerge from office	–	says: 'fit and well'	–
close pits (*impending*)	–	attempt to leave	–
fall to ground	–	face	demonstrators
lie dazed	–	arrive early	–
		try to avoid	miners
		abandon plan	–
		try to reach car park	–

C	
actional process	*affected person*
leave colliery offices	–

What the *Police* did

A		B	
actional process	*affected person*	*actional process*	*affected person*
hold back	demonstrators	arrive to clear path	–
force against fence	MacGregor		
help to car	MacGregor		

C	
actional process	*affected person*
–	–

14.3.2.3   CHOICES IN GRAMMATICAL STRUCTURE – THEME AND MEANING

'Deconstructing' a text shows up the actor–process–affected relationships more explicitly, but the text as written is what we read, and choices in the grammatical structure are important in directing our attention to one or another of the participants. An important component of the **textual** layout has been described as **theme** (sections 12.2.1 and 12.2.3) – that constituent of a clause which comes first, and has therefore front-focus.

In report A, Mr MacGregor is the subject and theme of the first two sentences, but he is not the *actor* of the processes because both sentences are in the passive voice.

[MacGregor] scraps pit visit in face of angry demo]   (headline)

[1 [Coal Board boss Ian MacGregor] was forced to abandon a pit visit in Northumberland yesterday [2 when 600 angry miners held him hostage for nearly four hours in a colliery office].

[[1 When [he] eventually emerged from the manager's office] 2 [he] was greeted [3 by eggs and slices of bread being thrown at him [4 by the miners protesting at impending pit closures]]].

Activity 14.14

Discuss the differences of emphasis and meaning between the first two sentences of the report and the following version in the active voice.

[[600 angry miners] held Coal Board boss Ian MacGregor hostage for nearly four hours yesterday in a colliery office] and [Ø forced him to abandon a pit visit in Northumberland].

[[The miners] [protesting at impending pit closures], greeted him [by throwing eggs and slices of bread at him [when he eventually emerged from the manager's office]]]

Commentary

The effect of the differences between the passive and active versions of the report is not something that can be objectively proved, and people's responses will differ. But on the whole, it seems likely that when the *subject* of a sentence is also the *theme*, and so has the primary focus of attention, he will be regarded as the person who is doing something, even though the sentence is in the passive voice and he is the *affected person*. At the same time, the miners' responsibility as actors is diminished, because they are named in the *by*-phrase, not as subject. Of course, end-focus is on them and it takes very little thought to sort out who did what. Nevertheless, the use of the passive does have some effect in partially muddling those who 'do' and those who are 'done to'. The report is not wholly consistent in avoiding making the miners the subject of sentences, however. The AdvCl of the first sentence could have been written:

[2 when he was held hostage for nearly four hours in a colliery office by 600 angry miners].

which would have focused even more sharply on Mr MacGregor than:

[2 when 600 angry miners held him hostage for nearly four hours in a colliery office]

In the third sentence, attention is still focused on him as the grammatical subject, following the selection of the *ensuing melee* as the theme of the sentence:

[1 In the ensuing melee the 72-year-old NCB chairman was forced against a fence by the police [2 holding back the demonstrators]].

although the attribution of responsibility for the incident by this newspaper would have been clearer if an active sentence had been written:

[In the ensuing melee the police [holding back the demonstrators] forced the 72-year-old NCB chairman against a fence]

It is the police who cause Mr MacGregor to fall according to report A , nor are the miners reported as *felling*, *pushing*, *flattening* or *grabbing* him.

[1 The fence collapsed] and [2 Mr MacGregor fell to the ground], [3 where he lay dazed].

Only in the first sentence of the fourth paragraph is Mr MacGregor not the subject:

[[Police and reporters had to help Mr MacGregor toward a waiting car].

and though the miners are the actors in the last sentence, they are not presented as the subject:

[Earlier, the tyres of the car [that had brought him to the pit] were let down by protesting miners].

In this report, and headline, Mr MacGregor is the grammatical subject of six clauses, the miners of two, and the police of two. Compare this with the attribution of responsibility for actional processes in the analysis following activity 14.12.

Activity 14.15 _____

Discuss the choices of grammatical structure in the other reports, with particular attention to choices of subject and theme, and their effect on the attribution of responsibility for the action.

Activity 14.16

(i)   Count the number of sentences, clauses and words in each report.

(ii) Describe the sentences as either simple, compound, complex or compound-complex (section 12. 3).

(iii) Analyse the clause structure of each report, and comment on the relative complexity of the constituent NPs, VPs and PrepPs.

(iv) Comment on the vocabulary of the three texts in terms of formality and informality.

(v)   State your conclusions about the structural and stylistic differences between the three reports.

14.3.3   *Text analysis 3 – Dickens's styles*

There are some writers whose style we hardly notice – their language seems 'transparent' to the meaning – and others whose use of different styles draws our attention as much to how the story is told as to what is being told. Both James Joyce and Charles Dickens belong to the second category, and the grammatical structure of their writing is a most important feature of their styles.

This section contains some examples of the varieties of style used by Charles Dickens. The first text consists almost entirely of a succession of coordinated clauses, with little subordination, grouped into mainly compound sentences. The clauses themselves are without elaboration.

Activity 14.17

(i)   Analyse the structure of each clause, in terms of SPCA.

(ii) Discuss the contribution of clause and sentence structure to the descriptive function of this extract.

1

⟨[Chesney Wold is shut up], [carpets are rolled into great scrolls in corners of comfortless rooms], [bright damask does penance in brown holland], [carving and gilding puts on mortification], and [the Dedlock ancestors retire from the light of day again]⟩. ⟨[Around and around the house the leaves fall ⟨thick – but never fast⟩], for [they come circling down with a dead lightness [that is sombre and slow]]⟩. [⟨[Let the gardener sweep and sweep the turf [as he will]], and [press the leaves into full barrows], and [wheel them off]⟩, still they lie ankle-deep]. ⟨[Howls the shrill wind round Chesney Wold]: [the sharp rain beats], [the windows rattle], and [the chimneys growl]⟩.

(*Bleak House*, ch. XXIX)

Activity 14.18

What is distinctive about the grammatical structure of the following text?

2

[[Whether he be cold and cruel], [whether immovable in [what he has made his duty]], [whether absorbed in love of power], [whether determined to have nothing hidden from him in ground [where he has burrowed among secrets all his life]], [whether he in his heart despises the splendour [of which he is a distant beam]], [whether he is always treasuring up slights and offences in the affability of his gorgeous clients] – [whether he be any of this, or all of this], it may be [that my Lady had better have five thousand pairs of fashionable eyes upon her, in distrustful vigilance, than the two eyes of this rusty lawyer, with his wisp of neckcloth and his dull black breeches [tied with ribbons at the knees]]].

(*Bleak House*, ch. XXIX)

Activity 14.19

(i) Comment on the kinds of clause to be found in the following paragraph, looking particularly at the VPs in the predicators.

(ii) Relate the grammar of the text to its function as part of a description of Mr Dombey's journey by railway, soon after the death of his young son.

3

[Away, with a shriek, and a roar, and a rattle, from the town], [burrowing among the dwellings of men and making the streets hum], [flashing out into the meadows for a moment], [mining through the damp earth], [booming on in darkness and heavy air], [bursting out again into the sunny day so bright and wide]; [away, with a shriek, and a roar, and a rattle, through the fields, through the woods, through the corn, through the hay, through the chalk, through the mould, through the clay, through the rock, among objects close at hand and almost in the grasp], [ever flying from the traveller], and [a deceitful distance ever moving slowly within him]: [like as in the track of the remorseless monster, Death]!

(*Dombey and Son*, ch. XX)

The fourth Dickens text is a typical comic one-sentence paragraph, satirising popular religion.

Activity 14.20

Which features of sentence structure does Dickens exploit to make this paragraph a continuous narrative of one sentence? For example, coordination, subordination with finite clauses, subordination with nonfinite infinitive, *-ing* and *-en/-ed* participle clauses, relative clauses, NP complements, extrapolation and so on.

316

4

[It was not unpleasant [to remember, on the way thither, [that Mrs MacStinger resorted to a great distance every Sunday morning, [to attend the ministry of the Reverend Melchisedech Howler]]], [who, [having been one day discharged from the West India Docks on a false suspicion [(got up expressly against him by the general enemy)] of [screwing gimlets into puncheons], and [applying his lips to the orifice]], had announced the destruction of the world for that day two years, at ten in the morning], and [opened a front parlour for the reception of ladies and gentlemen of the Ranting persuasion], [upon whom, on the first occasion of their assemblage, the admonitions of the Reverend Melchisedech had produced so powerful an effect, [that, in their rapturous performance of a sacred jig, [which closed the service], the whole flock broke through into a kitchen below], and [disabled a mangle [belonging to one of the fold]]].

(*Dombey and Son*, ch. XV)

I4.3.4 *Text analysis 4 – Ulysses*

The following extract from chapter 5 of *Ulysses* (published in 1922) illustrates one of the many styles adopted by James Joyce in the novel, which depicts one day in the life of Mr Leopold Bloom, in Dublin, 1904.

This style contains three **modes** of writing: some of the text is (a) **narrative**, telling us what is happening; some is (b) **interior monologue**, telling us what Bloom is thinking and noticing about the world around him; the rest is (c) **dialogue**, what the characters actually say.

Joyce gives very little visual help to his readers in marking these three different aspects of the story (some authors, for example, use italics for interior monologue). He does not use speech marks for dialogue; instead, he sometimes (but not always) introduces direct speech with a dash at the beginning of a line.

(Mr Bloom is wearing a black suit and tie, because he is going to a friend's funeral later that morning. He is carrying a rolled-up newspaper, and is about to go into a chemist's shop to get a prescription made up for his wife, Molly.)

He walked southward along Westland row. But the recipe is in the other trousers. O, and I forgot the latchkey too. Bore this funeral affair. O well, poor fellow, it's not his fault. When was it I got it made up last? Wait. I changed a sovereign I remember. First of the month it must have been or the second. O he can look it up in the prescriptions book.

The chemist turned back page after page. Sandy shrivelled smell he seems to have. Shrunken skull. And old. Living all the day among herbs, ointments, disinfectants. Smell almost cure you like the dentist's doorbell.

– About a fortnight ago, sir?

– Yes, Mr Bloom said.

Commentary

The text which contains each of the three modes is:

(a) Narrative

> He walked southward along Westland row.
> The chemist turned back page after page.

The verbs of the two simple sentences are in the **past tense,** which is here a clear indicator of narrative mode.

(b) Interior monologue

> But the recipe is in the other trousers. O, and I forgot the latchkey too. Bore this funeral affair. O well, poor fellow, it's not his fault. When was it I got it made up last? Wait. I changed a sovereign I remember. First of the month it must have been or the second. O he can look it up in the prescriptions book.
> Sandy shrivelled smell he seems to have. Shrunken skull. And old. Living all the day among herbs, ointments, disinfectants. Smell almost cure you like the dentist's doorbell.

The analysis of interior monologue is not straightforwardly simple, as the narrative was.

But the recipe is in the other trousers.   The tense changes to present, and the sense immediately tells us this cannot be the narrator, or 'implied author', speaking to us readers. However, if we were reading the novel, we would already know about Mr Bloom's black suit, so the reference to other trousers (his everyday pair) would make sense. We would also know that Mrs Bloom has asked him to get the 'recipe' for her lotion made up at the chemist's, and so on.
  The initial *But* suggests an alternative, 'on the other hand', and must refer to Bloom's thought (unstated) – 'I'll go into the chemist's now. But...'

O, and I forgot the latchkey too.   The *O* and the *and* are typical of informal *spoken* English, as is all the interior monologue.

Bore, this funeral affair.   A formal written version would be, *This funeral affair is a bore*, with the structure SPCi. The complement has been brought to the front as **theme,** and the indefinite article a has been omitted, as in speech. *This funeral affair* is a reference to the funeral that Bloom says to himself as an honest, but private comment.

O well, poor fellow, it's not his fault.   *O well* is again an informal spoken introduction to Bloom's quiet joke.

When was it I got it made up last?   Bloom's mind skips back to the lotion for his wife. The referent of it (usually the nearest NP in the preceding text) cannot be *the funeral* – it does not make sense, and we always try to make sense of what we read or hear. The phrase *made up* can refer to a prescription because they **collocate** together – the two are likely to occur together – so it must be that.

He has forgotten the recipe, so he will have to ask the chemist to look it up, and tries to remember the date of the last prescription.

Wait. I changed a sovereign I remember.   He has a flash of memory and tries to relate the last visit with some other event.

First of the month it must have been or the second.   Another example of marked theme, *First of the month*. The underlying clause is, *It must have been the first of the month or the second*. The omission of *the* also makes it sound more authentically like speech.

O he can look it up in the prescriptions book.   The *O* prefaces the conclusion of this little section of the interior monologue.

Notice that Joyce does not describe Bloom actually going into the shop and asking for the prescription. But as the following narrative sentence refers to the chemist, we infer what has happened.

Sandy shrivelled skull he seems to have.   Another example of marked theme, this time the object is fronted. The alliteration of ⟨s⟩ and ⟨sh⟩ is probably deliberate.

Shrunken skull.   As written, a minor sentence. It lacks a subject and predicator, which we can supply as he seems to have.

And old.   Another minor sentence – an afterthought.

Living all day among herbs, ointments, disinfectants.   A nonfinite clause, which in written English we would expect to be subordinate to a main clause. The breaking up of Bloom's thoughts into short sentences produces the effect of a quick succession of observations to himself.

Smell almost cure you like the dentist's doorbell.   Almost a complete clause, but omitting *the* and *would*.

This consistent representation of unspoken thoughts makes use of grammatical features of deletion and fronting (theme) common in informal spoken English, and the present tense contrasts immediately with the narrative.

(c)   Dialogue

> – About a fortnight ago, sir?
> – Yes, Mr Bloom said.

The dialogue needs little commentary. It is a polite, formal interchange between an old-fashioned tradesman – he addresses Bloom as 'Sir' – and a customer. The quoting clause *Mr Bloom said* marks the speaker in a conventional way. As readers, we infer Bloom's initial inquiry.

Activity 14.21

Read the remainder of the extract which follows, and write an analysis and commentary on it, with special reference to the grammatical features which mark the different modes of writing.

He waited by the counter, inhaling slowly the keen reek of drugs, the dusty dry smell of sponges and loofahs. Lot of time taken up telling your aches and pains.
– Sweet almond oil and tincture of benzoin, Mr Bloom said, and then orangeflower water . . .
It certainly did make her skin so delicate white like wax.
– And white wax also, he said.
Brings out the darkness in her eyes. That orangeflower water is so fresh. Nice smell these soaps have. Pure curd soap.
– Yes, sir, the chemist said. That was two and nine. Have you brought a bottle?
– No, Mr Bloom said. Make it up, please. I'll call later in the day and I'll take one of these soaps. How much are they?
– Fourpence, sir.
Mr Bloom raised a cake to his nostrils. Sweet lemony wax.
– I'll take this one, he said. That makes three and a penny.
– Yes, sir, the chemist said. You can pay all together, sir, when you come back.
– Good, Mr Bloom said.
He strolled out of the shop, the newspaper baton under his armpit, the coolwrappered soap in his left hand.
At his armpit Bantam Lyons' voice and hand said:
– Hello, Bloom, what's the best news? Is that today's? Show us a minute.
Shaved off his moustache again, by Jove! Long cold upper lip. To look younger. He does look balmy. Younger than I am.
Bantam Lyons' yellow blacknailed fingers unrolled the baton. Wants a wash too. Take off the rough dirt. Good morning, have you used Pears' soap?

14.3.5   Text analysis 5 – conversation

It was stated earlier (section 14.2.1) that the structure of spoken English can be as complex as that of written English, but that its complexity is of a different kind.

Activity 14.22 _____

(i)   Analyse the structure of the following narrative, spoken by adults in conversation, with special reference to the coordination, subordination and complexity of clauses.

(ii)   Rewrite the text as if it were dialogue in a novel.

(iii)   Discuss the changes that you have made.

(iv)   What kind of complexity is most prominent in the narrative?

(The original transcription is edited to omit performance features.)

Two married couples, A (wife) and B (husband), C (husband) and D (wife) are discussing holidays and crossing the Channel by ferry. In this extract, D does not speak.

C   I mean how did you find that side of it because (.) you know (.) some
    people say that driving a car across a ferry is the devil of a job (.) I mean
    taking a car across (.) to the continent (.) on a ferry is hell
A   no it isn't at all
B   why
C   I don't know but
B   well I mean (.) we've done it (.) I mean across the Channel (.) is that what
    you mean?
C   yes that's exactly what I mean across the Channel
B   innumerable times (.) there's no trouble with it (.) you just drive the thing
    on (.) you get out of it you take what you want you lock the car up (.) you
    go to (.) if you've got a cabin (.) if it's a night crossing you automatically
    had a cabin but on the cross Channel ones you don't (.) but if it's a day one
    you can have a day cabin if you want to pay for it (.) only a couple of
    pounds and you just
C   well I'll tell you the sort of thing I've heard I mean every summer you see
    stories of tremendous queues at the
B   but they're people who haven't booked (.) mind you last summer there was
    a weekend when the queues were so bad that even people who'd booked
    couldn't get to the boats
A   but certainly in the past we've just rolled up (.) if we go Southampton le
    Havre or Cherbourg then we book (.) and I do wonder what would happen
    if for example (.) there are often people who broke down for example so
    they missed their booking or their child has been ill so they'd stopped
    somewhere and they've missed their booking and those people have to wait
    for a vacancy (.) in the years we've been they've got on usually (.) there
    haven't been masses of people waiting to get on (.) but (.) when (.) the year
    that we did break down we were actually booked back across from
    Boulogne or Calais or somewhere and we just drove up and got on to the
    boat that happened to be there

> (Original transcription from D. Crystal and D. Davy,
> *Advanced Conversational English*, 1975)

14.3.6   *Text analysis 6 – dialectal speech*, Sons and Lovers

Standard English is used for almost all purposes in writing and printing, but written
evidence of spoken dialectal forms may be found in novels and short stories.

Activity 14.23 _____

Use the sorted data below to explain the spelling of words in the following text.

(i)   Distinguish features of pronunciation which are dialectal from those which
      indicate informal speech and 'eye-dialect'.

(ii) Identify and explain any dialectal vocabulary and grammar.

(iii) Compare Walter Morel's speech with Mrs Morel's.

At half past eleven her husband came. His cheeks were very red and very shiny above his black moustache. His head nodded slightly. He was pleased with himself.

'Oh!-Oh!-waitin' for me lass? I've bin 'elpin' Anthony, an' what's think he's gen me? Nowt b'r a lousy hae'f-crown, an' that's ivry penny –'

'He thinks you've made the rest up in beer,' she said shortly.

'An' I 'aven't-that I 'aven't-you b'lieve me, I've 'ad very little this day, I have an' all.' His voice went tender. 'Here, an' I browt thee a bit o' brandysnap, an' a coconut for th' children.' He laid the gingerbread and the cocoanut, a hairy object, on the table. 'Nay, tha niver said thankyer for nowt i' thy life, did ter?'

As a compromise, she picked up the cocoa-nut and shook it, to see if it had any milk.

'Its a good 'un, you may back yer life o' that. I got it fra' Bill Hodgkisson. "Bill," I says, "tha non wants them three nuts does ter? – arena ter for gi'ein' me one for my bit of a lad an' wench?" "I ham, Walter, my lad," 'e says, "ta'e which on 'em ter's a mind." An' so I took one, an' thanked 'im. I didn't like ter shake it afore 'is eyes, but 'e says 'Tha'd better ma'e sure it's a good un, Walt' – an' so, yer see, I knowed it was. – He's a nice chap, is Bill Hodgkisson, 'e's a nice chap!'

'A man will part with anything so long as he's drunk, and you're drunk along with him,' said Mrs Morel.

'Eh tha mucky little 'ussy, who's drunk, I sh'd like ter know?' said Morel. He was extraordinarily pleased with himself, because of his day's helping to wait in the Moon and Stars. He chattered on.

Mrs Morel, very tired, and sick of his babble, went to bed as quickly as possible, while he raked the fire.

(D. H. Lawrence, *Sons and Lovers*, 1913, Cambridge edn 1992)

The following words, phrases and clauses indicate dialectal forms of speech:

waitin' for me lass?
I've bin 'elpin' Anthony
an' what's think he's gen me
nowt b'r a lousy hae'f-crown
an' that's ivry penny
an' I 'aven't
that I 'aven't
you b'lieve me
I've 'ad very little this day I have an' all
here an' I browt thee a bit o' brandy-snap
an' a coconut for th' children
nay tha niver said thankyer for nowt i' thy life did ter
it's a good 'un you may back yer life o' that
I got it fra' Bill Hodgkisson'
'Bill' I says

'tha non wants them three nuts does ter
arena ter for gi'ein' me one
for my bit of a lad an' wench'
'I ham Walter my lad'
'e says
'ta'e which on 'em ter's a mind'
an' so I took one an' thanked 'im
I didn't like ter shake it afore 'is eyes
but 'e says
'Tha'd better ma'e sure it's a good un Walt'
an' so yer see I knowed it was
he's a nice chap is Bill Hodgkisson
'e's a nice chap
eh tha mucky little 'ussy
who's drunk I sh'd like ter know?

14.3.7 *Postscript*

The analysis of these texts shows how important grammatical and lexical choices are in affecting the style of speech and writing. If we can recognise and specify these choices, we can then use this knowledge in the formal study of style, called *stylistics*. We study grammar not just for its own sake (though some of us do enjoy it), but in order to apply what we have learned in an interesting and useful way. We should also become more aware of the choices of vocabulary and grammar that are open to us when we write and talk.

Bibliography

Those books marked with an asterisk* should be suitable for class use, but most textbooks and reference grammars are intended either for university students or foreign learners.

Reference grammars

1. Quirk, R., Greenbaum, S., Leech, G. and Svartvik, J., *A Comprehensive Grammar of the English Language* (Longman, 1985).
2. Quirk, R., Greenbaum, S., Leech, G. and Svartvik, J., *A Grammar of Contemporary English* (Longman, 1972). The smaller, but still comprehensive grammar which preceded (1).
3. van Ek, J. and Robat, N., *The Student's Grammar of English* (Blackwell, 1984).

Introductory Grammars

4. *Crystal, David, *Rediscover Grammar* (Longman, 1988) – 'An easy guide for getting it right'.
5. *Huddlestone, R., *English Grammar: An Outline* (Cambridge University Press, 1988).

Descriptive Grammars

6. *Leech, G., Deuchar, M. and Hoogenraad, R., *English Grammar for Today* (Macmillan, 1982).
7. Halliday, M. A. K., *An Introduction to Functional Grammar* (Edward Arnold, 1985).

8. Huddleston, R., *Introduction to the Grammar of English* (Cambridge University Press, 1984).
9. Young, D. J., *The Structure of English Clauses* (Hutchinson, 1980).

Dialectal grammar

10. Trudgill, Peter, *Dialects* (Routledge, 1994).
11. Hughes, A. and Trudgill, P., *English Accents and Dialects* (Edward Arnold, 1979).
12. Trudgill, Peter, *Accent, Dialect and the School* (Edward Arnold, 1975).
13. Wakelin, M., *English Dialects: an Introduction* (Athlone Press, 1972).

Index of texts quoted and used for exemplification and analysis

General index